LANDLORD & TENANT LAW

by

**Dr Nat Khublall,
BSc (Lond), MSc (Rdg), DSc (Rdg), FRICS,
Fellow of the Royal Institution of Chartered
Surveyors,
of Lincoln's Inn, Barrister.**

Publisher: Dr Nat Khublall

Email: nat1938@ymail.com

© Nat Khublall
Ebook 2016 Amazon KDP

Print on Demand 2016 Createspace

ISBN 9781511715928

All rights reserved. No part of the publication may be reproduced, stored in a retrieval system, or transmitted, in any form or by any means, electronic, mechanical, photocopying, recording or otherwise, without the prior written permission of the publisher.

No responsibility for loss, of whatever nature, occasioned to any person acting or refraining from acting as a result of the material in this publication, can be accepted by the publisher. Professional advice should be sought from an experienced practitioner in landlord and tenant law before acting on any aspect of the contents of this book.

CONTENTS

Title Page	i
Preface	iv
Chapter 1 Introduction to Landlord & Tenant Law	1
Chapter 2 Creation of Leases and Tenancies	11
Chapter 3 Types of Leases and Tenancies	24
Chapter 4 The Formal Lease	34
Chapter 5 Rights and Obligations of the Parties	43
Chapter 6 Rent	61
Chapter 7 Repairs and Repairing Obligations	83
Chapter 8 Fixtures	113
Chapter 9 Assignment and Subletting	128
Chapter 10 Termination of Leases and Tenancies	155
Chapter 11 Residential Tenancies: Rent Act Protection	184
Chapter 12 Other Residential Tenancies	209
Chapter 13 Public Sector Secure Tenancies	243
Chapter 14 Long Residential Leases: Houses	259
Chapter 15 Long Residential Leases: Flats	302
Chapter 16 Commonhold	348
Chapter 17 Business Tenancies	369
Chapter 18 Agricultural Holdings and Farm Business Tenancies	397
Author's other books	412

PREFACE

There has been an apparent and long-felt need by students and property professionals for a concise, yet comprehensive, and easily comprehensible book on the subject of landlord and tenant law. The aim of this book is to meet these requirements.

This book has been designed to cover the various degree and professional examinations which include landlord and tenant law as a subject or part of an examination paper. In particular, students preparing for degree examinations in law and estate management, the legal practice course and the bar vocational course, among others, would find this book helpful either as their course material or for revision. This book would also be of interest to practitioners in this area, such as solicitors, barristers, chartered surveyors and estate managers.

The topics covered are the usual common law matters such as creation of leases and tenancies, the rights and obligations of the parties to a tenancy, and their termination. Most importantly, several chapters are devoted to the relevant statutory provisions in respect of residential, commercial and agricultural tenancies. Statutory developments on collective enfranchisement and extension of leases of flats, commonhold and farm business tenancies are covered as well.

As this book does not cover an exhaustive exposition of the law, reference should be made, as appropriate, to the up-to-date standard works for a more detailed discussion. This new edition contains the amendments relating to the section 21 notice under the Housing Act, 1988, with effect from 1 October, 2015.

The law is stated as in the year 2015. Although a 100% accuracy cannot be guaranteed, the author takes full responsibility for any deficiency but without legal liability. Therefore, every reader is advised to check other sources for corroboration before making any important decision based on the information in this book. Comments on any aspect of this book are welcome.

Dr Nat Khublall
April 2016

dispose of land without ministerial consent. By reason of this prohibition, the type of agreement entered into between Camden and the housing association would have been *ultra vires* if it had been a lease as held by Millet J. Therefore, on a true construction, the agreement was a licence rather than a lease.

Reasons for Distinguishing a Lease from a Licence

There are various reasons why a lease must be distinguished from a licence. These reasons are as follows:

(a) A licence is not protected by the Rent Act, 1977, and the Protection from Eviction Act, 1977, whereas a tenant may be protected if certain conditions are satisfied.

(b) Since a lease, if legal, is a right in *rem*,[9] it will bind a purchaser of the reversion. Even if the lease is only effective as an equitable interest in land, it is registrable under the Land Charges Act, 1972,[10] as an estate contract, and if registered it will bind the purchaser of the reversion. A licence, as a general rule, cannot bind a person taking the land from the licensor (the person who has granted the licence).[11] As an exception, however, if the licensee spends money on the land under an expectation induced or encouraged by the licensor that the licence will not be revoked, then in equity the licensor will be estopped from defeating such expectation.[12] If the licence is enforceable on this basis against persons claiming through the licensor, the position depends on notice as the interest is not registrable.

(c) Since a tenant under a lease has an estate or interest in the land, the lessor commits a trespass if he re-enters without the permission of the tenant. However, if only a licence has been granted, the licensor will only be liable for a breach of contract, according to the terms of the licence, but he will not be a trespasser on the land. This is a

---

[9] In *rem* (Latin, "power about or against 'the thing'") is a legal term describing the power a court may exercise over property.
[10] In the case of unregistered land. In relation to registered land, a notice can be put on the land register, though not in respect of a lease that does not exceed 3 years.
[11] *Glore v Theatrical Properties Ltd* [1936] 3 All ER 483.
[12] *Inwards v Baker* [1965] 2 QB 29.

situation where the licence has been revoked and, if appropriate, the licensor may be liable for damages in accordance with the terms of the licence.

(d) A lease is irrevocable although it may be voidable for breach of covenant if it contains a forfeiture clause. On the other hand, a licence may in general be revoked at any time, even in breach of contract, whereupon the licensee becomes a trespasser.[13] However, if the contract was specifically enforceable, such as where the licence is coupled with an interest in land, the licence may be irrevocable according to its terms.[14]

(e) Provided there is no covenant prohibiting assignment, a tenant may assign his lease, but in general a licence is not assignable.

THE GENERAL LAW

Under the general law what is discussed is basically the common law in relation to a number of topics, set out below, which are basically the law of landlord and tenant.

(a) Creation of leases

(b) The lease in the form of an example of a lease;

(c) Covenants in a lease.

(d) Rent in its different common law concepts.

(e) Repairs and repairing obligations.

(f) Fixtures having regard in particular to what are removable by the tenant.

(g) Assignment, sub-letting and devolution by operation of law. Also, the main provisions of the Landlord and Tenant (Covenants) Act, 1995, are discussed with reference to the position after an assignment.

---

[13] *Wood v Leadbitter* (1845) 13 M & W 838.
[14] *Hurst v Picture Theatres Ltd* [1915] 1 KB 1; *Winter Garden Theatre (London) Ltd v Millennium Productions Ltd* [1948] AC 173.

6

(h) Finally, the various methods of terminating leases and tenancies are discussed.

RIGHTS OF TENANTS TO ACQUIRE THEIR LANDLORDS' INTEREST

These rights are discussed in a few chapters.

(a) **Long Leaseholders of Houses.** These leaseholders are entitled to acquire the lessors' reversionary interests under the Leasehold Reform Act, 1967. Alternatively, they may decide to extend their leases for another 50 years on expiry of the existing leases.[15]

(b) **Long Leaseholders of Flats.** In the case of long leaseholders of flats they were belatedly given similar rights as in (a) to collectively buy out their landlord's interest (known as collective enfranchisement) or to extend their leases individually by another 90 years. These rights are conferred by the Leasehold Reform, Housing and Urban Development Act, 1993.[16]

(c) **Right of First Refusal**. Under Part I of the Landlord and Tenant Act, 1987, leaseholders of flats within a block are entitled to purchase their landlord's interest under what is known as the "right of first refusal". If the landlord decides to sell his interest he is obliged to make an offer first to his tenants.[17]

Commonhold

Commonhold is a new type of ownership of land, and some would argue that it is a new type of land tenure. There is no legal basis for this view. It was introduced by the Commonhold and Leasehold Reform Act, 2002. This system of landholding is intended to supplement the leasehold system with regard to flats held under long leases. The legal basis here is different from the collective enfranchisement of flats outlined above. That system provides for the long leases of flats to continue but the lessees share the freehold

---

[15] Refer to Chapter 14 for more information
[16] Refer to Chapter 15 for a brief discussion.
[17] This right (RFR) is discussed as part of Chapter 15.

ownership of the common parts. However, in the creation of a commonhold, all the pre-existing leases cease to exist, and the commonhold[18] is owned by a commonhold association registered under the Companies Act, 1985. The former lessees of flats share the ownership of the commonhold association which is registered as the freeholder at the Land Registry. A brief discussion is set out in Chapter 16.

Instead of creating a commonhold in relation to existing long residential leases, it can be created by a developer who carries out the development and sells units.[19] In due course the unit-holders will own the commonhold by being the members of the commonhold association.

LEASES AND TENANCIES SUBJECT TO STATUTES

Almost all types of tenancies and leases are subject to some form of control or protection. The three main uses in general in respect of land are residential, commercial and agricultural. Many residential tenancies in both the private and public sectors are subject to some form of protection in favour of tenants. Business tenancies are in respect of land being used for various types of commercial activities and are subject to the provisions in Part II of the Landlord and Tenant Act, 1954. In the case of agricultural land there was a comprehensive system of security of tenure under the Agricultural Holdings Act, 1986. There is no longer security of tenure in respect new tenancies granted since 1 September, 1995. These tenancies are known as farm business tenancies, pursuant to fundamental changes made by the Agriculture Tenancies Act, 1995.

The various types of tenancies and leases, which are subject to some form of statutory control are the following:

(a) Protected and statutory tenancies under the Rent Act, 1977, and there are criminal sanctions for harassment.

(b) Assured tenancies and assured shorthold tenancies (AST) under the Housing Act, 1988, as amended.

---

[18] Registered as a freehold estate of commonhold land in the Land Registry
[19] A unit is a flat and the owner is a unit-holder.

(c) Landlord and tenant relationship in respect of Public Housing. This is covered mainly as secure tenancies under the Housing Act, 1985.

(d) Long residential leases in respect of houses subject to security of tenure, enfranchisement and extension of leases under the Leasehold Reform Act, 1967, and the Local Government and Housing Act, 1989.[20]

(e) Tenants of flats in a block are entitled to a right of first refusal (RFR) to buy their landlord's interest by virtue of the Landlord and Tenant Act, 1987.

(f) Long leaseholders of flats have been conferred with a collective right to acquire the landlord's interest in a building or individually they can extend their leases by 90 years. These rights are pursuant to the Leasehold, Reform, Housing and Urban Development Act, 1993, as amended by the Commonhold and Leasehold Reform Act, 2002.

(g) Unit-holders, i.e., owners of flats, in a commonhold are not subject to the relationship of landlord and tenant.[21] Prior to the creation of the commonhold, the owners of leasehold flats could have acquired their landlord's interest pursuant to the 1987 Act (see (e) above) or the 1993 Act (see (f) above).

(d) Business tenancies subject to Part II of the Landlord and Tenant Act, 1954. This Act covers tenancies for various commercial uses, shops, offices and industrial uses.

(e) Agricultural holdings and farm business tenancies under the Agricultural Holdings Act, 1986, and Agricultural Tenancies Act, 1995, respectively.

A few centuries ago, landlord and tenant relationship was based almost 100% on the common law. Today, as can be seen from the various Acts of Parliament, most of which were enacted in the 20th

---

[20] Which has replaced Part I of the Landlord and Tenant Act, 1954.
[21] Another method of creating a commonhold is by a developer taking the initiative and selling units in the course of the development or after the development has been completed.

century, statutory control in one form or another, applies to almost every type of tenancy and land use in the main sectors: residential, commercial (including industrial) and agricultural.

End

CHAPTER 2

CREATION OF LEASES AND TENANCIES

INTRODUCTION

The law of landlord and tenant embraces both leases and tenancies. There is a technical difference between a lease and a tenancy; the former is a "term of years", i.e., a lease for a defined or ascertainable number of years (even if the term is less than a year), while the latter refers to an interest which is granted for a period, usually for a year or lesser period, which automatically renews itself until determined by notice by one or both parties.

The terms "lessor" and "lessee" under a lease correspond to the terms "landlord" and "tenant" respectively under a tenancy. In spite of these technical differences, however, such terms are used interchangeably, and a lease is sometimes referred to as a tenancy and vice versa. The same applies throughout this book except where the context implies or something is stated to the contrary.

There are certain essential requirements which must be satisfied to create a lease or tenancy. The hallmark essentials are:

(a) exclusive possession;

(b) a term; and

(c) a rent.

As said in *Street v Mountford*[22] if the above are satisfied there will be a tenancy.

CREATION OF LEASES

The parties to a lease must be legally competent persons. There must be two separate persons as a person cannot grant a lease to himself. A lease is a grant of an estate or interest in land, based on a bilateral contract in which the tenant is not only given an estate in the land, but

---
[22] [1985] AC 809, 827 per Lord Templeman.

provides among other matters for the tenant to pay a rent (usually the main consideration) and sometimes to carryout repairs. Where a landowner wishes to confer a proprietary interest which will bind not only him but also an assignee of the reversion, the estate created must conform to the requirements of the law. In the case of the intention to create a leasehold estate, the requirements below must be satisfied.

(a) Exclusive Possession. Where the intention is to create a leasehold estate the right to exclusive possession of the land must be given to the lessee (tenant). A tenant who is given exclusive possession is able to exercise the right of ownership over the land[23] albeit for a temporary period. Before any permission to occupy land can be regarded as a lease, there must be exclusive possession.

In *Bruton v London Quadrant Housing Trust*[24] the House of Lords held that an agreement to grant exclusive possession (applying the indicia of a tenancy set out in *Street v Mountford*) of a flat created a tenancy, even though the landlord housing trust had no freehold or leasehold estate out of which it could grant a legal estate to the tenant, but was only a licensee from the freehold owner. As noted in the case this was the basis on which the tenant agreed to the arrangement.[25]

If X agrees to allow Y to use his land for a particular purpose, that agreement probably does not give Y a lease but only a licence. A licence is merely a permission to occupy land, without which it will be a trespass to be on the land. Again, a lodger in a boarding house does not normally have a lease of his room as control is retained by the landlady; he is commonly a licensee and not a tenant.[26] Also, where the premises are not clearly defined, any agreement purporting to be a lease will necessarily be a licence for lack of definition. But once the premises are clearly defined, the mere imposition of user restrictions which can be made of them will not prevent a lease from being created. Once exclusive possession is granted under a lease, it

---

[23] The land subject to the lease must be described and identified with certainty (*Glasworthy Mining Ltd v Federal Commissioner of Taxation* (1973) 128 CLR 199 at p211) (an Australian case). Because of inadequate or imprecise plans the boundary of the leasehold premises appeared to run through the tenant's bathroom in *Wallington v Townsend* [1939] Ch 588.
[24] [2000] 1 AC 406 (HL).
[25] There is some confusion in respect of this decision. See (2000) 4 L & T R 119 M. Powlowski and Brown.
[26] *Marchant v Charters* [1977] 1 WLR 1181.

will be a trespass to enter on the land without the lessee's permission, and in this respect even the lessor (landlord) is excluded.

Exclusive possession is not a decisive test by itself.[27] Other facts may show that what is in fact created is a licence.[28] In *Street v Mountford*,[29] the House of Lords disapproved of many of the earlier cases and were of the view that exclusive possession will presume the existence of a tenancy unless rebutted with reasons why there should not be a tenancy.

In *Street v Mountford* itself the agreement which was described as a licence was held to be a sham as it was drawn up with the sole intention of avoiding the Rent Act, 1977. Other decisions in this area relating to residential tenancies are *Antoniades v Villers*[30] and *Hadjiloucas v Crean*.[31] In both these cases, the Court of Appeal ruled that separate identical agreements labelled as "licences" entered into by two parties living together and occupying the same accommodation set out the intended relationship between the parties. In other words, these agreements were not a sham as in *Street v Mountford*. In *Antoniades*, the agreement gave the licensor the right to use the rooms "let" in common with the licensees and others. The licensees in the other cases were entitled to occupy the said premises at the same time. In these two cases, the accommodation was large enough to facilitate sharing.

<u>Difference in Construction of Document</u>. The Court of Appeal in *IDC Group Ltd v Clark*[32] held that an agreement for the occupation of business premises, which was made by deed, drawn up professionally, and described as a licence and not an easement, may be significant in the construction of an agreement for business, but not for residential, accommodation. Another relevant case in this regard is *Clear*

---

[27] See *Essex Plan v Broad Minster* [1988] 43 EG 84. In this case an agreement to occupy business premises as a licensee for a year with an option to take a 30-year lease from the commencement of the licence created, on its true construction, no more than a licence, irrespective of whether it conferred exclusive possession.

[28] See *Abbeyfield (Harpenden) Society Ltd v Woods* [1968] 1 WLR 374 as regards exclusive possession of one room in an old people's home; *Barnes v Barrett* [1970] 2 QB 657 in respect of a house-sharing without rent or a fixed term.

[29] [1985] AC 809 (HL).

[30] [1988] 3 WLR 139.

[31] [1988] 1 WLR 1006.

[32] (1992) 65 P & CR 179.

Channel UK Ltd v Manchester City Council [33] in which the court was surprised that a contract of a reputable commercial organisation drafted with legal advice with the intention expressed in the contract that it should not create a tenancy, should then invite the court to conclude that it was a tenancy.

The relationship of the parties is determined by law according to the substance of the transaction and not the label the parties choose to use.

An occupier of residential accommodation for a term at a rent (or payment) is a lodger (not a tenant) if the landlord provides attendance or services that require the landlord or his servants to exercise unrestrained access to and use of the premises.[34] But the fact that the occupier chooses not to avail himself of the attendance or services cannot convert a licence into a tenancy as was the position in *Uratemp Ventures Ltd v Collins*.[35]

(b) Definite Period. A lease can be for any definite period, e.g., 3 days or 3 hours.[36] A definite period with the date of commencement is another requirement which must be satisfied. This requirement must be clearly defined or ascertainable.[37] In general, the commencement date must be fixed or must be capable of ascertainment before the lease takes effect. The maxim *id certum est quod certum reddi potest* (that is certain which can be made certain) applies.

In *Lace v Chantler*[38] in which a lease was granted for the duration of the war, the lease was held to be void for uncertainty as one could not tell when the war would end. However, the requirement as to certainty was relaxed somewhat in *Re Midland Railway Co's Agreement*[39] in which the period was for six months followed by a half-yearly tenancy until the tenancy was determined. This decision was followed in *Ashburn Anstalt v Arnold*.[40] The Court of Appeal

---

[33] [2005] EWCA Civ 1304; [2006] 1 EGLR 27 at 28-29.
[34] *Brillouet v Landless* (1996) 28 HLR 836.
[35] [2000] 1 EGLR 156, 157 (per Peter Gibson LJ).
[36] Per Black J in *Boylon v Mayor of Dublin* [1949] IR 60 at p 73.
[37] The locus classicus is *Lace v Chantler* [1944] KB 368, which was applied in *Prudential Assurance Co Ltd v London Residuary Body* [1992] 2 AC 386.
[38] [1944] KB 368.
[39] [1971] 1 Ch 275.
[40] [1981] Ch 1. The initial lease was for one year after which the tenant might continue in occupation until the owner gave three months notice and the premises were required for redevelopment.

rejected the argument that nothing was mentioned about the tenant's right to determine the tenancy. Since there was clearly an element of uncertainty in these two cases as to whether there was a fixed term lease or a periodic tenancy, both were overruled by the House of Lords in *Prudential Assurance Co Ltd v London Residuary Body*.[41]

In *Prudential Assurance Co Ltd,* a lease relating to a strip of land had been given to the original occupier until the strip was required for road widening. The strip came to be owned by the London Residuary Body, a non-highway body, which sought to terminate the occupation on giving six months' notice to quit. With regard to the issue of whether any lease had been created, the House of Lords held that no fixed term lease had been created. As rent was paid every six months, this gave rise to a yearly tenancy and, therefore, it could be terminated by giving six months' notice to quit. However, the term in the agreement which prevented the landlord from getting back possession unless the strip was required for road widening was inconsistent with the nature of a periodic tenancy and, therefore, was inapplicable. In the light of this decision, *Lace v Chantler* is authority for a fixed term lease.

(c) **Intention of the Parties**. The requirement as to the intention to create an estate in the land and the relationship of landlord and tenant must be satisfied. It is not the expressed intention that matters, but rather the situation created by the parties. The court may be swayed by the purpose of the transaction, and where the label given connotes the grant of a licence, the substance of the transaction may suggest the grant of a tenancy or lease. Thus, a transaction which is described as a licence but is modelled upon the common law form of a lease will in substance be regarded as a lease. In the House of Lords case, *Street v Mountford*,[42] the occupier who allegedly took a room under a licence was held to be a tenant rather than a licensee in the light of the surrounding circumstances. The occupier was expressly given exclusive possession of the room she occupied, and this was very important in deciding whether she had a tenancy or a licence, though it does not necessarily follow that an occupier who is given exclusive possession can never be a licensee.

---

[41] [1992] AC 386.
[42] [1985] 2 WLR 877.

(d) **Reservation of Rent.** Rent is the consideration for the use of the land by the tenant. It was said in *Street v Montford*[43] that a lease was the grant of a term at a rent with exclusive possession. But the Law of Property Act, 1925, states expressly that rent is not necessary[44] as observed by the Court of Appeal in *Ashburn Anstalt v Arnold*[45] in referring to the definition of a "term of years absolute". The definition given is based on the common law. In both *Prudential Assurance Co Ltd v London Residuary Body*[46] and *Canadian Imperial Bank of Commerce v Bello*[47] Scott LJ and Dillon LJ respectively accepted as good law that the reservation of rent is not essential but restricted it to fixed term leases as, in their view, it is difficult to accept a periodic tenancy could be granted without any rent.

Where a written agreement is regarded as a sham and the terms negotiated contemplate exclusive possession, the court is likely to hold that the agreement is a tenancy.[48]

(e) **Statutory Requirement.** In general, all leases must be made by deed[49] and must satisfy section 1(1) of the Law of Property Act, 1925, as to duration, before the lease can be legal.[50]

Writing to Satisfy Section 2 of the 1989 Act

The granting of a lease is usually a two-stage process. Once negotiations have been concluded, an agreement for the lease is entered into. This agreement embodies all the important terms to be incorporated in the lease. There is a requirement that the agreement for the lease or the lease itself must be in writing as required by the

---

[43] [1985] AC 809, per Lord Templeman.
[44] Section 205 of the LPA 1925 defines a lease as a term of years "whether or not at a rent".
[45] [1989] Ch 1.
[46] [1992] AC 386.
[47] Lexis 8 November 1991.
[48] *Demuren v Seal Estates Ltd* (1979) EGD 334; *Street v Mountford* [1985] 2 WLR 877.
[49] Section 52(1) of the Law of property Act, 1925, except if the lease does not exceed 3 years (s 52(2)).
[50] Section 1(1) of the LPA, 1925, refers to two legal estates, one of which under para. (b) is "A term of years absolute." The other under para (a) is "An estate in fee simple absolute in possession".

Law of Property (Miscellaneous Provisions) Act, 1989. The second stage is the formal granting of the lease.

<u>Contracts for leases and Agreements for Leases.</u> The Law of Property (Miscellaneous Provisions) Act, 1989, has made a significant development in the way contracts relating to land are entered into. Any contract to grant a lease after 27 September 1989 must comply with the 1989 Act. Section 2 provides as follows:

> "(1) A contract for the sale or other disposition of an interest in land can only be made in writing and only by incorporating all the terms which the parties have expressly agreed in one document or, where contracts are exchanged, in each.
>
> (2) The terms may be incorporated in a document either by being set out in it or by reference to some other document.
>
> (3) The document incorporating the terms or, where contracts are exchanged, one of the documents incorporating them (but not necessarily the same one) must be signed by or on behalf of each party to the contract.
>
> (4) Where a contract for the sale or other disposition of an interest in land satisfies the conditions of this section by reason only of the rectification of one or more documents in pursuance of an order of a court, the contract shall come into being, or be deemed to have come into being, at such time as may be specified in the order."

Based on the above, it follows that the agreement for a lease must be in writing in one document in which all the terms are set out. But where there is another document as well reference must be made to it. The document incorporating all the terms must be signed by or on behalf of each party. Where documents are exchanged each party is required to sign his copy for exchange. In *Enfield LBC v Arajah*[51] a signature by one of three tenants did not satisfy the requirement under section 2(1) of the 1989 Act. However, this provision does not apply to a lease covered by section 52(2) of the LPA, 1925, i.e., leases not

---
[51] [1995] EGCS 164 CA (Civ div).

exceeding three years.[52] But an oral agreement to grant a lease for more than three years is void.[53]

The earlier provision under section 40(1) of the LPA, 1925, which no longer applies, was simply to require some evidence in writing and, in the absence of that evidence, it was unenforceable. In contrast, section 2(1) of the 1989 Act states that an agreement can only be in writing. Therefore, where there is no writing there is no contract or agreement. This being the position, the basis for invoking the doctrine of part performance has been removed. Lack of writing means there is no contract. An oral agreement is not relevant, though under the old law, a tenancy under equity could have come into existence. However, where there is no writing to satisfy the 1989 Act, anyone who under an oral agreement entered into possession and commenced paying rent, he could be held to have a periodic tenancy rather than a fixed-term tenancy.

Doctrine Under Walsh v Lonsdale

The doctrine in this case is based on a divergence of common law and equity, prior to the passing of the Judicature Act, 1873. A lease which was not made by deed and a contract for a lease both resulted in two entirely different interests according to the common law and the equitable doctrine was invoked. The position at common law was that the tenant was a year to year tenant if he entered into possession and paid rent. However, in equity he was entitled to the execution of a legal lease with all the provisions of the void lease or of the contract entered into.

The point at variance referred to above is that associated with a lease not made by deed and had to be considered in *Walsh v Lonsdale*.[54] The claimant agreed to take a lease of a mill for 7 years. Part of the agreement was that a deed should be executed with a provision, *inter alia*, that the landlord might require one year's rent in advance. No deed was executed, and the tenant was let into possession paying rent quarterly, not in advance, for a year and a half. The landlord then demanded a year's rent in advance and, upon the tenant's refusal, distrained for the amount. This resulted in the tenant bringing an action for damages for the illegal distress and specific

---

[52] Section 2(5) of the Law of Property (Miscellaneous Provisions) Act, 1989.
[53] *Hutchison v B & D F Ltd* [2009] L & TR 12 ChD.
[54] (1882) 21 Ch D 9.

performance of the contract for the lease and an interim injunction to restrain the distress.

The tenant argued that he was given possession and paid rent under a contract which did not operate as a lease and, therefore, was a yearly tenant. Thus, the condition requiring a year's rent in advance was inconsistent with a yearly tenancy, which could be determined by half a year's notice. For this reason the distress was illegal. This argument was rejected. It was decided that the tenant held under a contract for a lease specifically enforceable. As regards both rights and liabilities he would occupy if a formal lease had been executed as a deed. Therefore, if a deed had been executed according to the contract, the defendant would have been entitled to distrain for the rent not paid in advance. The mere fact that the formal lease had not been actually executed could not prejudice his rights.

The doctrine in *Walsh v Lonsdale* is an example of the principle that equity regards as already done what the parties to the transaction have agreed to do. This doctrine has wide application, not confined to a contract or agreement for a lease.

Whether a Contract for a Lease is as Good as a Lease

From the case above, it should not be regarded that an agreement for a lease is always as effective as a lease. In litigation between the parties, only where the circumstances would justify a decree for the execution of a lease by deed, the court would grant it. Because of a few limitations a lease is not always as good as a lease, as can be seen below.

<u>Specific Performance is Discretionary</u>. An agreement for a lease is for the purpose of granting a lease and can exist as an equitable lease before a formal lease is granted. But specific performance cannot be demanded as of right to enforce the agreement as it is an equitable remedy which is granted at the discretion of the court.[55] The person seeking to enforce the agreement must have acted reasonably and ethically in all the circumstances having regard to the maxim: "he who comes to equity must come with clean hands". Where a person

---

[55] *Cornish v Brook Green Laundry Ltd* [1959] 1 QB 394. It was held in *Amec Properties Ltd v Planning Research and Systems Plc* [1992] 1 EGLR 70 that specific performance will not normally be refused even if the prospective tenant is insolvent although not in liquidation.

will be unable to perform the covenants in the lease on account of his insolvency or where he has already committed a breach, specific performance may not be decreed.[56]

Where a Third Party Acquires an Interest. After the agreement for the lease has been entered into, an unscrupulous person could create a right in favour of a third party in respect of the same property. In this regard, an agreement for a lease is void against a *bona fide* purchaser for value of the legal estate without notice. Therefore, to protect oneself against this situation in terms of priority, it is important to follow either (a) or (b) below:

(a) If the subject property is unregistered land, a Class C(iv) land charge, as an estate contract, must be registered[57] so that the equitable lease will bind a purchaser (a term which is wider than a mere purchaser).

(b) In the case of registered land, the equitable lease will be regarded as a minor interest and, as such, a notice should be placed on the land register to bind a subsequent purchaser. Since it is not a legal interest, it will not be regarded as an overriding interest[58] to bind a third party. However, if the equitable lessee is in actual occupation of the land at the time the third party acquires a right in respect of the land, the third party may be bound by the equitable lease. In this regard, para. 2 of Schedule 1 to the Land Registration Act, 2002, states:

> "An interest belonging to a person in actual occupation, so far as relating to land of which he is in actual occupation, except for an interest under a settlement under the Settled Land Act 1925 (c. 18)."

Assignment. As an agreement for a lease is not a legal estate, only the benefits are assignable. In the case of an assignment of a legal estate, both the rights and obligations will pass.

---

[56] *Coatsworth v Johnson* (1886) 55 LJQB 220; *Rouf v Tragus Holdings Ltd* [2009] EWHC 96 (Ch), [2009] All ER (D) 29 (Jan).
[57] Pursuant to the Land Charges Act, 1972, s 2(4).
[58] Formerly under section 70 of the Land Registration Act, 1925. The provision is now under the Land Registration Act, 2002, Sch 1.

<u>No Application of Section 62 of the LPA, 1925</u>. This provision applies only where there is a conveyance[59] of land so as to pass certain rights, such as easements, enjoyed with the land. It does not apply under an agreement for a lease.

<u>No Privity of Estate</u>. In the absence of a legal lease, there can be no privity of estate. Therefore, as such, some of the obligations entered into by the parties to the agreement for the lease may not be enforceable against a third party who has acquired an interest in the property.

FORMAL LEASES

At common law leases could be made orally. However, oral leases were considered to be unsatisfactory in proving that a lease was actually granted.[60] The position after 1925 is that a lease must be made in the proper way, i.e., by deed, since all grants are void for the purpose of conveying or creating a legal estate unless made by deed.[61] But as mentioned earlier this provision does not apply to leases or tenancies or other assurances not required by law to be made in writing.[62]

A lease which does not comply with the definition of a term of years absolute and has not been created in the required form[63] can take effect only as an equitable interest.[64]

When No Need for Formality

By virtue of section 54(2) of the LPA, 1925, no formality is required for a lease which:

(a) takes effect in possession;

---

[59] As defined in section 205 (1)(ii) of the LPA, 1925.
[60] In an attempt to prevent fraud in such and other situations, s1 of the Statute of Frauds, 1677, enacted that writing was necessary to create a lease. The Real Property Act, 1845, s3, provided that "a lease required by law to be in writing made after the first day of October, 1845, shall be void at law unless also made by deed".
[61] Law of Property Act 1925, s 52(1).
[62] *Ibid*, s 54(2).
[63] *R v Tower Hamlets LBC, ex p Von Goetz* [1997] QB 1019.
[64] LPA, 1925, s1(3). See also *Walsh v Lonsdale* (1882) 21 Ch D 9.

(b) is for a term not exceeding three years, whether or not the lessee is given a power to extend the term; and

(c) is at the best rent reasonably obtainable without taking a fine (i.e., a premium).[65]

It should be noted that the term "possession" includes the right to receive the rents and profits (e.g., from subtenants in actual possession). Once the three conditions set out above are complied with a legal estate can be created orally or in writing. In the case of registered land this is an overriding interest,[66] formerly under section 70(1)(g) of the Land Registration Act, 1925, which provision is now under the Land Registration Act, 2002.

By virtue of section 54(2) of the LPA, 1925, a mere oral lease suffices to create a legal term of years, if the three conditions above are satisfied.

Assignment

Once a legal lease has been validly created a deed is required to effect a legal assignment of the lease notwithstanding whether the lease was made by deed. This applies also to an oral lease created by virtue of section 54(2) above.[67]

MAIN REQUIREMENTS RELATING TO AN AGREEMENT FOR A LEASE AND A LEASE

An agreement for a lease not exceeding three years is specifically enforceable in these situations:

---

[65] *Fitzkriston LLP v Panayi* [2008] EWCA Civ 283; [2008] L & TR 26. In this case a one year tenancy at a rent of £4,000 pa by a document not properly executed as a deed took effect at will only because it was not at the best rent reasonably obtainable, ([2009] Conv 54 J. Brown); *Looe Fuels Ltd v Looe Harbour Commissioners* [2008] EWCA Civ 414, [2009] L & TR 3 (judge entitled to find as a fact that a bargain between the parties gave the best rent that could reasonably be obtained).

[66] Under the Land Registration Act, 2002, Sch 1 (formerly under s 70(1)(g) of the LRA, 1925.

[67] *Crago v Julian* [1992] 1 WLR 372; *Camden LBC v Alexandrou* (1997) 74 P & CR D33.

(a) if it is made in writing to satisfy section 2(1) of the Law of Property (Miscellaneous Provisions) Act, 1989;

(b) if it was made on or before 27 September, 1989, and it is evidenced in writing to satisfy section 40(1) of the Law of Property Act, 1925;

(c) in the event it was made orally, there are sufficient acts of part performance on or before 27 September, 1989; and

(d) if made after 27 September, 1989, the requirements under section 2(1) of the 1989 Act are satisfied.

The methods of creating a lease at law are:

(a) by deed to satisfy section 52(1) of the law of Property Act, 1925, which states "All conveyances of land or of any interest therein are void for the purpose of conveying or creating a legal estate unless made by deed";

(b) in writing if it does not exceed three years;

(c) orally where the term does not exceed three years and complies with the conditions in section 54(2) of the LPA, 1925;[68] and

(d) in an appropriate case, if the tenant with the consent of the landowner entered into possession and pays rent regularly, in which case a periodic tenancy will be implied.

End

---

[68] "(2) Nothing in the foregoing provisions of this Part of this Act shall affect the creation by parol of leases taking effect in possession for a term not exceeding three years (whether or not the lessee is given power to extend the term) at the best rent which can be reasonably obtained without taking a fine."

CHAPTER 3

TYPES OF LEASES AND TENANCIES

INTRODUCTION

This chapter deals with the various types of leases and tenancies which can be created. The requirements which must be satisfied to create leases and tenancies and the legal formalities are discussed in Chapter 2. The different categories of leases and tenancies must comply with such requirements and formalities.

The classification of leases and tenancies are discussed under different headings which are:

(a) fixed-term leases, e.g., a lease for 21 years or 99 years;

(b) yearly tenancies (which are periodic tenancies);

(c) other periodic tenancies, e.g., weekly, monthly or quarterly;

(d) a tenancy at will (with the landlord's consent);

(e) a tenancy at sufferance, e.g., where a tenant holds over without consent;

(d) concurrent leases, e.g., where another lease is granted before the end of an existing lease; and

(e) tenancy by estoppel, e.g., based on implications and conduct.[69] A recent case based on estoppel is *Mitchell v Watkinson & Williams*[70] in which it was held that a written tenancy agreement had created a tenancy by estoppel. The Court held that they were not estopped from denying that the tenancy under which the land was held by them had been created by implication, on the terms of a written tenancy agreement, but not by the written tenancy agreement.

---

[69] A tenancy that exists despite the fact that the person who granted it had no legal right to do so. Such a tenancy is binding on the landlord and tenant but not on anyone else. If the landlord subsequently acquires the right to grant the tenancy, it automatically becomes a full legal tenancy.

[70] [2014] EWCA Civ 1472; [2015] L & TR 22.

At common law there is freedom to enter into the various types of leases and tenancies, and naturally they will end in accordance with the contractual provisions or with notice to quit in respect of periodic tenancies. However, by the intervention of statutes, most lessees and tenants are conferred with certain statutory rights either to continue in occupation of the premises or to force the landlord to dispose of his estate or interest to the lessee. This applies particularly to residential properties under various Acts of Parliament, discussed in later chapters (11 to 16).

LEASE FOR A FIXED-TERM

The term "lease" is technically used to mean a leasehold interest in land which will subsist for a fixed term, and will come to an end automatically at the end of that term, e.g., a lease for seven years will end at the end of 7 years, unless the lease provides otherwise.[71] The fixed-term[72] indicates a certain period of certain duration, no matter how long or how short the period for which it is granted. A tenancy, on the other hand, is used to refer to a periodic tenancy, which continues indefinitely until determined by an appropriate notice to quit from either party. For example, a weekly, monthly, quarterly or yearly tenancy can be determined by either party serving an appropriate notice.[73]

Certainty of Term and Commencement Date Specified

A lease must be for a fixed period which is to be agreed before the lease takes effect. The term must be for a definite period. In effect, this means that it must have a certain beginning[74] and a certain ending. However, the parties may agree that the lease shall begin on the occurrence of a certain event.[75]

---

[71] There are various statutory provisions that confer security of tenure on certain types of leases and tenancies discussed in Chapters 11, 12, 13, 14, 17 and 18 in respect of protected residential tenancies, business tenancies and agricultural tenancies.
[72] Can be for any length, 99 years or 999 years are common.
[73] Subject to the statutory right of the tenant to challenge the notice to quit.
[74] *Harvey v Pratt* [1965] 1 WLR 1025.
[75] *Swift v Macbean* [1942] 1 KB 375.

Even though a lease is granted for a fixed period, it is capable of being determined before the period ends naturally. For example, if the lease contains a forfeiture clause in respect of a breach of covenant by the lessee, the lessor can decide to bring it to an end prematurely. Also, the commencement date of the term must be specified.

A lease granted after 1925 at a rent or fine (premium) is void if it is to start more then 21 years from the date of its creation.[76] Also, a contract to grant such a lease is void as well. But it is possible to create a reversionary lease, i.e., to commence at some future date, in which case it must be created by deed[77] and must commence within 21 years from its creation.

At common law, a lease for a fixed period automatically comes to an end when the period expires. No notice is required to determine the lease. There are, however, certain statutory modifications to this common law rule. These exceptions are many and they relate to residential, business and agricultural leases and tenancies discussed in later chapters.

A lease is void if the date of its termination remains uncertain after it has taken effect. It becomes a tenancy at will, though in other respects it shares the characteristics of a periodic tenancy.[78] It was held in *Lace v Chantler*[79] that an agreement to let a house for the duration of the war was void for uncertainty. The House of Lords has reaffirmed this principle in *Prudential Assurance Co Ltd v London Residuary Body*.[80]

Perpetually Renewable Leases

Leases of this type were inconvenient and, therefore, were modified by the LPA, 1922. A lease made after 1925 that is meant to be a perpetually renewable lease will operate as a lease for 2,000 years by virtue of section 145 of the LPA, 1922.

Care should be taken in drafting renewal clauses in a lease. Although a lease is not expressly made perpetually renewable, it

---

[76] Section 149(3) of the LPA, 1925.
[77] *Long v Tower Hamlets LBC* [1998] Ch 197; see also *Wolf v Wolf* [2004] STC 1633 (reversionary lease executed by parents in favour of daughters as part of inheritance tax saving scheme set aside by parents' mistake as to its legal effect).
[78] *Ramnarace v Lutchman* [2001] 1 WLR 1651.
[79] [1944] KB 368.
[80] [1992] 2 AC 386.

could be converted by reason of the language used in the renewal clause into a term that will endure for 2,000 years, save where the lessee chooses to determine it earlier. For the purpose of limiting permissible renewals within reasonable bounds, any agreement to renew a lease for more than 60 years from the end of the lease in question is void.[81]

Leases for Lives or Until Marriage

A lease can be granted for the life of the lessee. Words which indicate that the lease should be valid so long as the tenant paid the agreed rent were construed in *Doe d Warner v Browne*[82] as a lease for life. In *Zimbler v Abrahams*[83] the Court of Appeal arrived at the same conclusion. In this case, a weekly lease was granted for "as long as the tenant lives and pays the rent regularly". In spite of the term being somewhat uncertain, the court held that there was an enforceable agreement to grant a lease for life. Whether or not the words used in the agreement will give rise to a lease or tenancy for life will depend on the construction.

The Law of Property Act, 1925, has modified certain leases. By virtue of this Act, certain leases now take effect as a lease for 90 years, such as a lease at a rent, or in consideration of a fine,[84] as in (a), (b) and (c) below:

(a) for life or lives, e.g., to T for life or during the lives of X and Y; or

(b) for any term of years determinable with a life or lives, e.g., to Z for 9 years or to Z for 99 years, if X shall so long live; or

(c) for any fixed-term of years determinable on the marriage of the lessee, e.g., to T for 20 years until T marries.[85]

---

[81] LPA, 1922, Sch 15, para 7(2).
[82] (1807) 8 East 165.
[83] [1903] 1 KB 577.
[84] The word 'fine' includes 'a premium or foregift and any payment, consideration or benefit in the nature of a fine, premium or foregift': LPA, 1925, s 205(1)(xxiii, *Skipton Building Society v Clayton* (1993) 66 P&CR 223.
[85] Section 149(6) of the LPA, 1925.

The determinable event in the above lease is death or marriage, as the case may be, of the original lessee. After any of these events has occurred, a month's notice in writing to terminate the lease on one of the usual quarter days may be served by either side. As regards a lease for life, a period of 90 years is chosen in the Act as a term to exceed the specified life. However, with increasing life-span, an 18-year old tenant could exceed the period of 90 years specified in the statute if he lives beyond 108 years.

YEARLY TENANCIES

A yearly tenancy is usually referred to as a tenancy from year to year which differs from a lease for a fixed-term in that, unless terminated by notice,[86] it may continue indefinitely. The rule as to certainty of duration does not apply in respect of yearly or other periodic tenancies.[87] The rule in *Lace v Chantler* regarding certainty of duration in a lease of a fixed-term also applies in the case of a periodic tenancy. The term, although originally indeterminate, is determinable by either party.[88]

No formality is required to create a periodic tenancy. Yearly tenancies may be created expressly or may arise by implication from possession of land together with the payment and acceptance of rent which must be measured in terms of a year.[89] A yearly tenancy can also arise after a fixed term by statutory rights conferred on the tenant.

Where a yearly tenancy is implied, the tenant will hold under such of the terms of the expired or informal lease or agreement as are not inconsistent with a yearly tenancy. In other words, those terms which are embodied in an expired term (legal or otherwise) will be read into the yearly tenancy in so far as they are not inconsistent with the yearly tenancy.

Although there may be a yearly tenancy, rent may be paid more than once a year. For example, a yearly rent of £20,000 may be payable in four quarterly payments of £5,000 each.

A yearly tenancy continues from year to year until it is determined by notice. Subject to any contrary agreement, half a year's notice is

---

[86] See *Mellows v Low* [1923] 1 KB 522; *Prudential Assurance Co Ltd London Residuary Body* [1992] AC 386.
[87] *Lace v Chantler* [1944] KB 368.
[88] *Prudential Assurance Co Ltd v London Residuary Board* [1992] AC 386.
[89] See *Richardson v Langridge* (1811) 4 Taunt 128 at p 132.

required to determine a yearly tenancy. The term "half a year" means 182 days or, where the tenancy began on the customary quarter day, two quarters.[90] However, in the case of agricultural holdings and farm business tenancies, at least one year's notice must be given.[91] The notice must expire, in all cases, at the end of a completed year of the tenancy. A yearly tenancy is particularly universal in relation to agricultural land.

OTHER PERIODIC TENANCIES

There are other periodic tenancies. These are mainly weekly, monthly and quarterly tenancies. These periodic tenancies can be created in a similar way to a yearly tenancy, i.e., by express words or by inference such as the payment and acceptance of rent which is measured in terms of a week, month or quarter, as the case may be[92] or from an express provision indicating that the tenancy is to be determinable by a specified period of notice.[93]

In the absence of any contrary agreement, a notice to determine a periodic tenancy must be for the full period and must expire at the end of a completed period.[94] However, under the Rent Act, 1977,[95] at least four weeks notice[96] is required for protected residential tenancies. The period of notice now is generally two months under the Housing Act, 1988.

TENANCY AT WILL

A tenancy at will may be created expressly[97] or by implication, such as whenever a person with the consent of the owner occupies land on

---

[90] The 4 quarter days are Lady Day (25 March), Midsummer Day (24 June), Michaelmas (29 September), and Christmas (25 December).
[91] Agricultural Holdings Act, 1986, s 25(1), and the Agricultural Tenancies Act, 1995. ss 5 – 7 (see Chapter 18).
[92] *Cole v Kelly* [1920] 2 KB 106 at p 132.
[93] *Kemp v Derrett* (1814) 3 Camp 510. This is subject to any different indication as in a yearly tenancy with a special period of notice.
[94] *Lemon v Lardeur* [1946] KB 613.
[95] An Act to consolidate the Rent Act 1968, etc, under which at least 4 weeks' notice to quit is required) .
[96] This was the position under the Rent Act, 1957, s 16. The position now generally is two months' notice as explained in Chapter 12.
[97] *Mansfield and Sons Ltd v Botchin* [1970] 2 QB 612.

terms that either party may give notice to bring the tenancy to an end at any time. It is the lowest estate known to the law.[98] A tenancy at will can arise where a purchaser goes into possession prior to completion, or where a prospective tenant goes into possession during negotiations for a lease.[99] This type of tenancy is not a legal estate as it does not satisfy the requirement under the LPA, 1925. Sometimes it may be difficult to distinguish it from a licence. And the court may opt for the latter interpretation.[100] Also, such a tenancy can come to an end if either party does anything inconsistent with the continuance of the tenancy.

If exclusive possession is granted on payment of rent, a lease is likely to have been created. If rent is paid and accepted by reference to a period, a tenancy at will may be converted into a periodic tenancy. The assessment of rent by reference to a yearly basis will create a yearly tenancy.

In *Javid v Aqil*[101] a prospective tenant was let into possession of premises during the negotiation. Nicholas LJ thought that it would be artificial to impose a periodic tenancy on the parties and said:

"They cannot sensibly be taken to have agreed that he shall have a periodic tenancy, with all the consequences flowing from that, at a time when they are still not agreed about the terms on which the prospective tenant shall have possession...."

A tenant at will is somewhere between a licensee and a tenant. As in the case of a licensee, he has no estate or interest in the land to which his possession can be referred.[102] And without any property right for assignment, nor anything that can bind the landlord's successor. Further, the various statutory rights conferred by statutes on business and residential tenants do not apply.[103] Unlike a licensee, a tenant at

---

[98] Per Parke B in *Doe d Gray v Stanion* (1836) 1 M&W 700 (but since 1926 it is necessarily equitable).
[99] *British Railways Board v Bodywright Ltd* (1971) 220 EG 651; *Ramnarace v Lutchman* [2001] UKPC 25, [2001] 1 WLR 1651.
[100] See *Heslop v Burns* [1974] 3 All ER 406, and *Street v Mountford* [1985] AC 809 at p 824.
[101] [1991] 1 WLR 1007. See also *Cricket Ltd v Shaftesbury plc* [1999] 3 All ER 283.
[102] *Ramnarace v Lutchman* [2001] UKPC 25, [2001] 1 WLR 1651.
[103] LTA, 1954, Part II does not apply to a tenancy at will (*London Baggage Co (Charing Cross) Ltd v Railtract plc (No 2)* [2003] 1 EGLR 141. With regard to

will who has possession of the land can bring an action against third parties to which that possession entitles him.[104]

TENNANCY AT SUFFERANCE

A tenancy at sufferance arises where a tenant, having entered under an agreed tenancy or lease, holds over without the landlord's permission after the end of that tenancy or lease. This type of tenancy is more precarious than a tenancy at will. A tenant at sufferance differs from a trespasser in that the tenant entered the land with the consent of the landlord, and from a tenant at will in that no express consent had been given. A tenant at will in an appropriate case is accorded protection under certain statutes.

Under section 18 of the Distress for Rent Act, 1737, a tenant who holds under a periodic tenancy and gives notice to quit but fails to give up possession in accordance with the notice will be liable to double the rent for the period he remains in possession. In such a case, the tenant is not only a trespasser by reason of his notice but will be treated as such by the landlord.[105] In this case, the tenant is not one of sufferance, but his tenancy is statutorily prolonged at double the rent.

Continuing with the position of a tenant at sufferance, since he is in possession he can maintain an action of trespass against a third party or recover possession of the land against a mere wrongdoer. Further, by being in possession after 12 years he can acquire title by adverse possession against the landlord of unregistered land, so long as he does not pay any rent.

Again, a periodic tenancy may arise from inference or presumption.[106] Where a contractual tenant of a residential property who holds over is covered by the Rent Acts, the landlord may have no choice but to accept rent as the tenant becomes a protected statutory tenant rather than a tenant being holding over after a contractual tenancy.[107]

---

doubts whether the Housing Act, 1985, Part IV applies see *Banjo v Brent LBC* [2005] EWCA Civ 282, [2005] 1 WLR 2520.

[104] Such as trespass (*Heslop v Burns* [1974] 1 WLR 1241) and probably nuisance (*Hunter v Canary Wharf* [1997] AC 655; *Pemberton v Southwark LBC* [2000] 1 WLR 1672 (tolerated trespasser).

[105] *Ballard (Kent) Ltd v Oliver Ashworth (Holdings) Ltd* [2000] Ch 12.

[106] *Dougal v McCarthy* [1893] 1 QB 736; *Lowther v Clifford* [1926] 1 KB 185 affirmed in [1927] 1 KB 130.

[107] *Morrison v Jacobs* [1945] KB 577.

TENANCY BY ESTOPPEL[108]

Once a lease or tenancy is granted, the general rule is that a tenant is estopped from denying his landlord's title, and the landlord from denying the tenant's title.[109] The rule applies even though the landlord's title is defective, e.g., where the landlord has been a squatter for less than 12 years. Both parties and their successors in title will be estopped from denying that the grant was valid to create the lease or tenancy that it purported to create – hence the doctrine "tenancy by estoppel". Therefore, the attributes of a true tenancy arises,[110] and the covenants contained in any lease are enforceable by the parties, and their successors in title are equally estopped.[111] A landlord cannot deny the validity of the tenancy by alleging his own want of title to create it.

In *Industrial Properties (Barton Hill) Ltd v Associated Electrical Industries Ltd*[112] Lord Denning, MR, said that restricting the application of the doctrine to the period of the tenancy was wrong. Note, however, that the doctrine does not apply to an *ultra vires* act of a corporation to prevent the corporation from claiming that it had no power to grant or receive the tenancy.

A tenancy by estoppel may be converted into an ordinary tenancy. This may occur, for instance, where a person who does not hold the fee simple created a tenancy and subsequently acquires the fee simple. The acquisition of the fee simple will "feed the estoppel" and clothe the tenant with a legal estate as well.[113] An estoppel may arise even where the landlord has an equitable interest.[114] The doctrine applies to

---

[108] See *McIllkenny v Chief Constable of the West Midlands* [1980] QB 283 at p 317 (*estoupail* meaning 'a bung or cork by which you stopped something from coming out', per Lord Denning, MR).
[109] A tenancy by estoppel also binds persons who claim through the land and the tenant, such as successors in title.
[110] *Bank of England v Cutler* [1908] 2 KB 208 at p 234 per Farwell LJ; *Bell v General Accident Fire & Life Assurance corpn Ltd* [1998] 1 EGLR 69 (tenant by estoppel of business premises entitled to protection under the Landlord and Tenant Act, 1954.
[111] *Hill v Saunders* (1825) 4 B & C 529 (the tenant acquires the interest based on whatever the landlord holds).
[112] [1977] QB 580.
[113] *Webb v Austin* (1844) Man & G 701 (but now the legal formalities will need to be satisfied in compliance with the LPA, 1925).
[114] *Universal Permanent Building Society v Cooke* [1952] Ch 95 at p 102.

all types of tenancies and to statutory tenancies under the Rent Acts,[115] and even to licences.[116] It operates whether the tenancy is created by deed, in writing or orally.[117] Once the tenant has left the premises, he can dispute the landlord's title and, apparently, in order to avoid liability under any covenant broken during the term.[118]

CONCURRENT LEASES

A concurrent lease is in effect a lease of a reversion and is granted to commence before the termination or other determination of a previous lease of the same property to another person. It entitles the lessee, as assignee of part of the reversion, to receive the rent under the previous lease, which is still current, and to the benefit of the covenants contained in that lease during the continuance of both the previous lease and the new lease (i.e., the concurrent lease).

A lease which is granted now to take effect in the future is a reversionary lease or a lease of the reversion. The second grant is a *pro tanto* disposition of the reversion,[119] and it creates a landlord and tenant relationship between the first and the second lease. There will be rights and liabilities as to rent and other matters capable of running with the tenancy.[120] Such a lease is not affected by the perpetuity rule as the lease is already vested in the named tenant but actual possession is in the future.

As a lease of the reversion is effectively an assignment of the reversion, it must comply with the rules governing assignment of reversions. Therefore, unless made by deed it will not have any effect at law.

End

---

[115] *Stratford v Syrett* [1958] 1 QB 107.
[116] *Terunnansev v Terunnanse* [1968] AC 1086.
[117] *E H Lewis & Son Ltd v Morelli* [1948] 2 All ER 1021.
[118] *Harrison v Wells* [1967] 1 QB 263 (though this inequitable result is questionable).
[119] *Cole v Kelly* [1920] 2 KB 106.
[120] *Horn v Beard* [1912] 3 KB 181.

CHAPTER 4

THE FORMAL LEASE

INTRODUCTION

A lease is a conveyance by way of a demise of land or tenements. In the LPA, 1925, the word "conveyance" includes a lease unless the context requires otherwise, but an agreement for a lease exceeding three years is not an "assurance of property or of an interest therein", and an oral lease is not a "conveyance" as defined by section 205 of the LPA, 1925, as held in *Rye v Rye*.[121]

What Leases Must be by Deed

A lease not exceeding three years may be oral (parol) or in writing.[122] Such a lease:

(a) must be at the best rent reasonably obtainable without taking a fine; and

(b) taking effect in possession.

It may be oral or in writing as the parties may decide, but a lease which is more than three years from its making must be made by deed. Under section 52(1) of the LPA, 1925, leases of land, except such as are not required by law to be made in writing, are void for the purpose of creating a legal estate unless made by deed.

When an intending lessee has agreed to take a lease from an intending lessor, it often occurs that a considerable time is spent in settling the exact form of the lease, but once agreement is reached on all the points the lease is engrossed and signed (no seal is required

---

[121] [1962] AC 496.
[122] The requirements of the Law of Property (Miscellaneous Provisions) Act, 1989. Section 2, must be satisfied: "(1) A contract for the sale or other disposition of an interest in land can only be made in writing and only by incorporating all the terms which the parties have expressly agreed in one document or, where contracts are exchanged, in each."

since 1989)[123] and delivered by both parties and duly stamped. The lease which in form is a deed embodies the contract between the lessor and the lessee. If any dispute arises later the lease will be construed as showing the intention of the parties when they entered into it.

The common practice today is for a lease to be made in two parts: (a) the lease which is executed by the lessor and delivered to the lessee, and (b) the "counterpart" which is executed by the lessee and given to the lessor. The two parts are supposed to be identical, and being formal the words "lessor" and "lessee" are normally used instead of "landlord" and "tenant".

Requisites of a Good Lease. These requisites are:

(1) There must be a lessor who is able to grant a lease.

(2) There must be a lessee who is capable of taking the thing demised.

(3) There must be a thing demised which is demisable.

(4) If the thing demised or the term expressed to be granted but not grantable without a deed, the lease must be created by deed. The lease must contain a sufficient description of the lessor, the lessee, the thing demised, the term granted, the rent and covenants, and all necessary circumstances, such as signing and delivery, among other ingredients as appropriate; all these ingredients must be observed.

(5) The term granted must be adequately defined.

(6) On the part of the lessor there must be expressed an intention to demise and on the part of the lessee there must be an acceptance of the thing demised and of the estate.

---

[123] Under section 1(1) of the 1989 Act any rule of law which (a) restricts the substances on which a deed may be written, (b) requires a seal for the valid execution of an instrument as a deed by an individual, or (c) requires authority by one person to another to deliver an instrument as a deed on his behalf to be given by deed, is abolished.

CONTENTS OF A LEASE

There are usually six parts to a lease by deed as follows:

(1) <u>The Premises.</u> This precedes the habendum (see below) and contains: (i) the date; (ii) the parties; (iii) the consideration (the rent); (iv) the operative words (usually "demise" or "let"); (v) the description of the demised premises (i.e., the parcels); and (vi) the exceptions and reservations in some cases, as may be appropriate. Sometimes a lease may also contain recitals, which are inserted prior to the testatum (i.e., witnessing clause which is included in the premises) and consist of agreed statements of fact.

(2) <u>The Habendum.</u> The habendum fixes the commencement of the lease and the length of the term. In the absence of any commencement date the term operates from the date of delivery of the deed.

An option to renew the term will run with the lease[124] even if it is contained in a separate document but forming part of the same transaction.

(3) <u>The Reddendum.</u> This is the reservation of rent to be paid by the lessee (whose name is mentioned) to the lessor. The reddendum also contains a reference to the date on which the first payment of rent to be made, and a condition that if the lessor re-enters into possession, the lessee must pay a proportionate amount of the rent up to the date of such re-entry.

(4) <u>The Covenants.</u> These are promises entered into by the parties to do or not to do certain things. There may also be covenants which are not expressed in the lease but which are implied by law, either because of omission or because of some expressed clause in the lease or because they are implied by statute.

(5) <u>Exceptions and Reservations.</u> An exception excludes from the grant some component part of the demised property, whilst a reservation reserves for the lessor some right over the lessee. Thus, a

---

[124] LPA 1925, s142.

certain field (corporeal) may be excepted, whereas an incorporeal right, e.g., a right of way (an easement), may be reserved.

(6) The Provisos. These show how the term may be ended, extended or created or qualify some liability on the part of one or the other of the parties.

(7) The Stamping. This was regulated by the Stamp Act 1891, but because of a great deal of avoidance, leases are now subject to SDLT, which is a tax on transactions rather than on documents as was the position under the 1891 Act. This is a complex area and information can be obtained from HMRC and the internet.[125]

Section 62 of the LPA, 1925, provides that under a conveyance certain rights and privileges will pass to the lessee. These are all fixtures, easements and other privileges which will pass provided there is no stipulation to the contrary in the lease.

SPECIMEN OF A LEASE

An example of a short and simple lease is set out below.

THIS LEASE is made on the .... day of................... 2016

BETWEEN John Doe of .... in the county of .... (hereinafter called "the Lessor") of the one part and George Brown of .... in the county of .... (hereinafter referred to as "the lessee") of the other part.

WITNESSETH as follows:

1. In consideration of the Rent and the Lessee's Covenants hereinafter reserved and contained

The Lessor DEMISES unto the lessee

ALL THAT messauge or office building with external parking spaces

---

[125] Also, refer to Chapter 2 of *Taxation of Real Property*, 2014, by Dr Nat Khublall for certain aspects of SDLT. This book is available as an eBook and a print on demand book from Amazon and Createspace respectively.

and a small storage shed attached thereto and forming part thereto known as No 20 Park Crescent .... in the county of .... which premises are coloured pink on the Plan annexed to these presents EXCEPT AND RESERVING AND SUBJECT to the exceptions and reservations set out in the Schedule hereto

TO HOLD the same unto the lessee from the ..... day of .... for the term of ....years

YIELDING AND PAYING yearly the net rent of £............. clear of all deductions by equal quarterly payments to be made on the .... day of .... next.

2. The LESSEE HEREBY COVENANTS with the Lessor as follows:

(a) TO PAY the rent hereby reserved at the times and in the manner hereinbefore mentioned;

(b) TO PAY all taxes, business rates, duties, assessments, impositions and outgoings whatsoever now payable or hereafter during the said term to become payable in respect of the demised premises;

(c) TO KEEP the premises and any additions thereto and the fixtures in good condition and repair;

(d) TO KEEP the demised premises insured against loss or damage by fire or otherwise in any office approved by the Lessor in the sum of £ ...., and upon request to produce the insurance policy and the receipt for the premium paid in respect of the current year;

(e) TO ALLOW the Lessor or anyone on his behalf at all reasonable times during the term hereby granted to enter upon and inspect the demised premises;

(f) NOT TO ASSIGN, sublet or part with possession of the demised premises or any portion thereof without the written consent of the Lessor, such consent not to be unreasonably withheld;

(g) NOT TO CARRY ON or permit to be carried on at any time during the said term in the demised premises or any part thereof any manufacturing business or industrial operation; but to use the demised premises only as an office or similar use.

THE LESSOR HEREBY COVENANTS with the Lessee that the Lessee performing and observing all the covenants herein contained shall peacefully enjoy the demised premises during the said term without any interruption by the Lessor or any other person lawfully claiming through, under or in trust for the Lessor.

PROVIDED THAT if any part of the rent hereby reserved is in arrear for 21 days, whether or not lawfully demanded, or upon the occurrence of a breach of any of the Lessee's covenants herein contained, or if the Lessee shall become bankrupt or enter into a composition with his creditors it shall be lawful for the Lessor to re-enter upon the premises or any part thereof in the name of the whole and thereupon the term hereby granted shall absolutely cease and determine.

IN WITNESS WHEREOF the said parties to these presents have hereunto set their hands the day and year first above written.

Lessor's Signature................................
Witness ....

Lessee's Signature ....
Witness ....

THE PLAN AND SCHEDULE referred to. ....

All leases and agreements for leases are required to be stamped by the Stamp Duty Land Tax introduced on 1 December 2003.[126]. Such transactions are to be stamped in accordance with the prescribed scale The prescribed scale, in respect of *ad valorem* duties are subject to change from time to time.

---

[126] Finance Act 2003, s 42.

Registration and Priority in Relation to Leases Involving Third Parties.

A lease can be legal or equitable. The latter will bind a third party only in certain circumstances.

(a) *Unregistered Land.* Where an equitable lease is created in respect of unregistered land, it will bind a third party, such as a purchaser, only if it was registered as a Class C(iv) land charge as an estate contract.[127] Any failure to register such a lease will not bind any purchaser from the landlord. A purchaser could also include a legal lessee.

(b) *Registered Land.* Leases granted for terms exceeding seven years since 13 October 2003 must be registered by virtue of the Land Registration Act 2002.[128] Where the unexpired term of an existing lease with over seven years is transferred it must be registered as well. Further, a lease of any length is also required to be registered if it is granted more than three months in advance of the date on which the lessee is to take possession.

Kinds of Registered Leasehold Title

Under section 10(1) of the Land Registration Act, 2002, titles to leasehold estates the classes of title with which an applicant may be registered as proprietor are:

(a) absolute title;

(b) good leasehold title;

(c) qualified title; and

(d) possessory title.

Other provisions under section 10 of the Act are relevant in deciding under which of the above classes a leasehold title will be

---

[127] This is under the Land Charges Act 1972, s 2(4).
[128] This 2002 Act has replaced the Land Registration Act 1925.

registered. For example, under section 10(2) a person may be registered with absolute title if the registrar is of the opinion that the person's title to the estate is such as a willing buyer could properly be advised by a competent professional adviser to accept, and the registrar approves the lessor's title to grant the lease.

According to section 10(3) a person may be registered with good leasehold title if the registrar is of the opinion that the person's title to the estate is such as a willing buyer could properly be advised by a competent professional adviser to accept.

The other subsections are as follows:

> "(4) In applying subsection (2) or (3), the registrar may disregard the fact that a person's title appears to him to be open to objection if he is of the opinion that the defect will not cause the holding under the title to be disturbed.
>
> (5) A person may be registered with qualified title if the registrar is of the opinion that the person's title to the estate, or the lessor's title to the reversion, has been established only for a limited period or subject to certain reservations which cannot be disregarded under subsection (4).
>
> (6) A person may be registered with possessory title if the registrar is of the opinion—
>
>> (a) that the person is in actual possession of the land, or in receipt of the rents and profits of the land, by virtue of the estate, and
>>
>> (b) that there is no other class of title with which he may be registered."

Provision is made for the upgrading of inferior titles to absolute or good leasehold titles or of good leasehold to absolute.[129] Likewise, where a leasehold estate has been entered as possessory for at least 12 years, the registrar may upgrade it to good leasehold or absolute on being satisfied that the proprietor is in possession of the land.

---

[129] Section 62 of the Land Registration Act, 2002.

Rectification of a Lease

Rectification of a lease applies where the true intention of the parties as agreed by them is not reflected in the lease. This was the position in *Ahmad v Secret Garden (Cheshire) Ltd.* [130]

The company took a lease of a property which was intended as a residence for the director and that the rest should be converted into a children's nursery. Planning permission was refused, so the company sublet to the director and others. However, the lease prohibited subletting and did not reflect the actual agreement the parties had made. Therefore, the tenant made an application to the court for rectification of the lease. Rectification was ordered. The Court of Appeal dismissed the appeal made by the landlord and in its judgment helpfully restated the principles to be applied to rectification of leases. The party seeking rectification must show that:

(a) the parties had a common continuing intention, whether or not amounting to an agreement, in respect of a particular matter in the instrument to be rectified;

(b) there was an outward expression of accord (quality of evidence);

(c) the intention continued at the time of the execution of the instrument sought to be rectified;

(d) by mistake, the instrument (the lease) did not reflect that common intention;

End

---

[130] [2013] EWCA Civ 1005.

CHAPTER 5

RIGHTS AND DUTIES UNDER A LEASE OR TENANCY

INTRODUCTION

The rights and obligations of the parties under a lease or tenancy are governed by covenants. A covenant is a contract or promise contained in a deed. Covenants in a deed are expressed covenants and, in addition, other covenants necessary to give effect to the intention of the parties may be implied by law. Similar covenants may be implied in leases not made by deed. A term will not be implied if it is inconsistent with an express term. Where there is any doubt the *contra proferentum* rule[131] will apply. Also, some leases may be subject to what is known as the "usual" covenants in addition to certain express covenants and terms.

Essential Terms. The essential terms in a lease are:

(a) the names of the parties;

(b) an adequate description of the demised premises;

(c) the rent, if any,[132] reserved under the lease, or some method of ascertaining the rent; and

(d) the commencement date and the duration of the lease.[133]

POSITION IN THE ABSENCE OF EXPRESS COVENANTS

More covenants, implied and express, are normally given by the lessee.

---

[131] The *contra proferentem* rule states, broadly, that where there is doubt about the meaning of the contract, the words will be construed against the person who put them forward.

[132] The reservation of rent is not essential (see *Ashburn Anstalt v Arnold* [1989] Ch1 in which it was said there can be a lease without a rent).

[133] Certainty of duration is important (see *Lace v Chantler* [1944] KB 368 applied in *Prudential Assurance Co Ltd v Residuary Body* [1992] AC 386.

Position of the Lessor/Landlord. The following implied covenants of the lessor/landlord will apply in so far as there are no express provisions in the lease/tenancy on these matters.

(a) <u>Implied Covenant for Quiet Enjoyment</u>. The object of this covenant is to afford to the lessee quiet enjoyment[134] of the demised premises during the term of the lease. This covenant is implied in every lease that does not expressly deal with the matter.[135] Any act of the landlord, such as intimidation, to force the tenant to leave is a breach.[136] This covenant applies to the lessor's own acts, whether rightful or wrongful, but only to rightful acts of persons claiming under him.[137] The lessor is not liable for the wrongful act of a stranger. Nor is he liable under the covenant for any act committed by a person claiming not under him but under a title paramount to his.[138] This covenant does not require a lessor to repair the premises.

A covenant for quiet enjoyment does not entitle a tenant who takes premises under a defective state to complain. His only right of action would be under statute or the terms of the tenancy.[139] The same applies where the premises had been built originally to an unsatisfactory standard.[140]

A landlord who is liable for repairs must take all reasonable precautions to protect the tenant's enjoyment, rather than all possible precautions.[141]

Where scaffolding was necessary for the landlord to carry out repairs, he was obliged to do under the lease, an injunction was

---

[134] See (1976) 40 Conv (NS) 427; (1977) 40 MLR 651; [1978] Conv 419 (M J Russell).
[135] *Markham v Paget* [1908] 1 Ch 697; but see *Gordon v Selico Co Ltd* [1986] 1 EGLR 71 at p77. Slade J held that no covenants were to be implied "where it was intended ... to provide a comprehensive code in regard to repair and maintenance. Presumably this applies to repairs and maintenance only.
[136] *Branchett v Beaney* [1992] 3 All ER 910.
[137] *Jones v Langton* [1903] 1 KB 253; *Goldmile Properties Ltd v Lechouritis* [2003] 1 EGLR 60 (express covenants).
[138] *Jones v Lavington* [1903] 1 KB 253; see also *Celsteel Ltd v Alton House Holdings Ltd (No 2)* [1987] 1 WLR 291 in which a lessor was not liable for what a predecessor in title had done.
[139] *Baxted v Camden LBC (No 2)* {2001] QB 1.
[140] *Southwark LBC v Tanner* [2001] AC 1.
[141] *Goldmile Properties Ltd v Lechouritis* [2003] 15 EG 143.

refused even though this would cause substantial interference with the tenant's business.[142]

(b) <u>No Derogation from Grant</u>. The law will not allow the lessor by his own act to frustrate the purpose for which the land was known to have been let. For example, if the land was let for the purpose of drying timber, the lessor cannot afterwards erect buildings so as to prevent the free passage of air.[143] The lessor must not seek to take away with one hand what he has given with the other. As Bowen LJ put it: "a grantor having given a thing with one hand is not to take away the means of enjoying it with the other."[144] In the absence of a specific covenant, a tenant cannot complain that the lessor has let adjacent premises to another engaging in the same trade.[145] An interference amounting to a derogation from the grant must be substantial. Thus, the introduction of a parking scheme causing customers to shop elsewhere was held to be insubstantial as to amount to a breach of the covenant. This covenant binds not only the lessor but also persons claiming under him.

(c) <u>Covenant for Title and to Give Possession</u>. This covenant implies that the lessor has a good title to the land and that he will give possession on the date fixed for the purpose of the term. This covenant is really part of the covenant for quiet enjoyment dealt with above, but may be considered as a separate covenant. Its scope is limited to the commencement of the lease or tenancy, and is in no sense a general warranty as to title for the rest of the term.

On the grant of a head lease, statute will imply covenants for title by the landlord to the tenant if the lease is expressed to be granted

---

[142] *Century Projects Ltd v Almacantar (Centre Point) Ltd* [2014] EWHC 394 (Ch).

[143] See *Aldin v Latimer Clark, Muirhead & Co* [1894] 2 Ch 437; *Romulus Trading Co Ltd v Comet Properties Ltd* [1996] 2 EGLR 70 (grant of adjoining premises to competing business held not to be derogation); cf *Chartered Trust plc v Davies* [1997] 2 EGLR 83 (held to be derogation as landlord failed to use his powers to prevent his other tenant from substantially interfering with the manner in which the tenant ran his business of selling puzzles and executive toys in a "niche" shop in Bognor Regis); *Dorrington Belgravia Ltd v McGlashan* [2010] L & TR 3 (landlord not entitled to build a further storey on roof where roof with skylights formed part of demised premises.

[144] *Birmingham, Dudley & District Banking Co v Ross* (1888) 38 ChD 295 at p 313.

[145] *Port v Griffith* [1938] 1 All ER 295.

"with full title guarantee" or "with limited title guarantee".[146] The use of these key words, and therefore whether covenants for title are implied, is a matter for agreement between the parties. Prior to 1 July, 1995, statutory covenants for title which were available to be implied did not apply on the grant of a lease, unless no rent was reserved. Two implied covenants will apply whichever key words are used:

(1) Right to Grant – that the landlord has the right to grant the lease with, if appropriate, the concurrence of any one else joining in it;[147] and
(2) Further Assurance – that the landlord will do all he reasonably can at his own cost to give the person to whom he disposes of the property the title he purports to give.[148]

Freedom from incumbrance could be under the implied covenant for title. It varies in form depending whether the lease is granted with full title guarantee or with a limited title guarantee.

(d) <u>Fit for Human Habitation</u>. The general rule is that the landlord gives no undertaking that the premises are fit for habitation. The landlord is not liable for letting a tumbledown house. Like the concept of *caveat emptor* in relation to a purchaser, the lessee should also be aware of the state of the premises.[149] However, in the case of furnished premises, he will be liable if the premises are unfit for human habitation at the commencement of the tenancy.[150] Apart from this, the lessor gives no implied undertaking that the premises are or will be fit for habitation or for any particular use.[151] Where a building is in multiple occupation (e.g., flats or rooms separately let) but the lessor retains control of the means of access, etc, without the lessees undertaking any liability for repairs for them, it may be implied that the lessor will undertake reasonable care to keep them in repair.[152] This can be contrasted with the decision in *Duke of Westminster v*

---

[146] Section 1 of the Law of Property (Miscellaneous Provisions) Act, 1994.
[147] Section 2(1)(a) of Law of Property (Miscellaneous Provisions) Act, 1994.
[148] Section 2(1)(b), *ibid.*
[149] *Southwark LBC v Tanner* [2001] 1 AC 1
[150] *Smith v Marrable* (1843) 11 M & W 5 (bugs).
[151] *Stokes v Mixconcrete (Holdings) Ltd* (1978) 38 P & CR 488.
[152] *Liverpool City Council v Irwin* [1977] AC 239.

Guild[153] in which the lessor had no liability to repair a drain under adjacent land. Caveat leesse applies.[154]

(e) <u>Repairing Obligations of Common Parts</u>. In the light of the development of the common law, a lessor may now owe a duty of care in tort for negligence in respect of defective premises. A lessor may not be able to rely on the immunity established in *Cavalier v Pope*.[155] In *Rimmer v Liverpool City Council*[156] in which a tenant was injured by reason of a defective glass panel, the Court of Appeal held that a landlord who designs and builds does owe a duty of care to tenants or other persons who are likely to be affected by the design.

The development of the law under (d) and (e) above has been somewhat extensive in the last few decades. In the United States the courts have declared that the law must accommodate changing circumstances.[157] As regards making buildings fit for habitation, reference should be made to a number of statutes which are discussed in Chapter 7 on repairs and repairing obligations.

(f) <u>Other Obligations of the Landlord</u>. Briefly these are houses let at a low rent, house let for a short term, landlord's duty under the Defective Premises Act, 1972, and a local authority's obligation under the Human Rights Act, 1998.

As regards a house let at a low rent, the L&T Act, 1985,[158] provides that a person taking a house at a low rent not exceeding £80 pa in London and £52 pa elsewhere where the contract is made on or after 6 July, 1957, it is implied that the house at the commencement of the tenancy is fit for human habitation, regardless of any stipulation to the contrary. This is an unreal position in this day and age, in view of the escalation of rents. The said 1985 Act, under ss 11-16, imposes

---

[153] [1983] 267 EG 763.
[154] *Southwark LBC v Tanner* [2001] 1 AC 1 at p 12 per Lord Hoffmann.
[155] [1906] AC 428 (HL).
[156] [1985] QB 1; [1984] 1 All ER 930; *Target v Torfean Borough Council* [1992] 3 All ER 27 (where the Court of Appeal held that *Rimmer* was not overruled by *Murphy v Brentwood DC* [1991] AC 398 (HL). In *Liverpool City Council v Rimmer* [1977] AC 239, the House of Lords held that the owner of a building with several flats is liable as landlord to keep in reasonable state of repair the lifts, common staircases and rubbish chutes, and over which tenants of the flats have implied easements – although such a covenant is not expressly provided.
[157] See the US case *Javins v v First National Realty Corp* 428 F 2d 1071 (1970).
[158] Ss 8-10. See Chapter 7.

further obligations on the landlord for a term less than 7 years after 24 October, 1961.[159] A landlord's obligation under the 1972 Act is set out in Chapter 7, while a local authority's position under the 1998 Act is briefly set out in Chapter 13.

Position of the Lessee/Tenant. The implied obligations of the lessee/tenant are as follows:

(a) <u>Covenant to pay Rent</u>. This applies where rent is reserved; if none, the tenant must pay a reasonable rent for use and occupation.[160]

(b) <u>Covenant to Pay Taxes and Other Imposition</u>. The tenant must pay his council tax and other charges (e.g. charge for water), except those for which the lessor/landlord is liable. Council tax is normally the liability of the occupier.

(c) <u>Covenant not to Commit Waste</u>. This covenant will depend on the tenancy agreement. All tenants are liable for voluntary waste, while tenants for fixed terms, including a yearly tenant, are in addition liable for permissive waste. However, the liability of a yearly tenant for permissive waste is limited to keeping the premises wind and water tight. Periodic tenants are required to use the premises in a tenant-like manner, i.e, the tenant is expected to do the little jobs which a reasonable tenant would do.[161]

(d) <u>Covenant to Use Premises in a Tenant-Like Manner</u>. A tenant is required to use the premises in a tenant-like manner[162] and to deliver possession to the landlord on termination of the tenancy in the same state as when let, reasonable wear and tear excepted.[163]

(e) <u>Covenant to Allow Landlord to Inspect</u>. The tenant is required to allow the landlord to view the state of the premises (but not necessarily to repair) where there is a covenant to repair.

---

[159] Discussed in Chapter 7.
[160] *Gibson v Kirk* (1841) 1 QB 850.
[161] *Warren v Keen* [1954] 1 QB 15.
[162] *Ibid.*
[163] *Marsden v Edward Heyes* [1927] 2 KB 1.

(f) <u>Covenant of Weekly Tenant</u>. These tenants are required to allow the landlord to enter for the purpose of executing repairs.

(g) <u>Covenant to Deliver up Possession</u>. At the end of a lease or tenancy the entire premises are required to be delivered up to the lessor/landlord.

"Usual" Covenants

A lease may provide that the "usual" covenants shall apply in the absence of express covenants. Where this applies, the lease will be subject to all those covenants which are "usual" in a lease of the kind under consideration. In such a case, the covenant for quiet enjoyment will be given on the part of the landlord. On the other hand, the tenant will be liable under a number of covenants:[164] to pay rent, to pay rates and taxes (except those for which the landlord is liable), to keep and deliver the premises in good repair, to allow the landlord to view if the landlord is liable for repairs and a right of re-entry. It should be noted that the list of "usual" covenants is neither fixed nor closed and what covenants are "usual" in any particular case is a question of fact, depending on the custom of conveyancers in the locality as to what covenants are "usual".[165]

SOME EXPRESS COVENTS COMMONLY FOUND IN LEASES

The covenants which are commonly expressed in leases[166] are given below.

(a) <u>Covenant for Quiet Enjoyment</u>. A covenant for quiet enjoyment has already been discussed under the landlord's implied covenants.

---

[164] See *Hamshire v Wickens* (1878) 7 Ch D 555.
[165] *Flexman v Corbett* [1930] 1 Ch 672.
[166] With regard to covenants in leases in particular see *Investors Compensation Scheme Ltd v West Bromwich Building Society* [1998] 1 WLR 896; *Holding & Barnes plc v Hill House Hammond Ltd* [2001] EWCA Civ 1334, [2002] 2 P & CR 11.

(b) <u>Covenant to Pay Rent</u>. Unless the lease provides for the payment of rent in advance, rent is payable in arrears.[167] A rent may be made to vary with the circumstances, e.g., as in *Walsh v Lonsdale*,[168] and may be reserved in kind or in services. Rent continues to be payable even if the premises cannot be used for the intended purpose. However, the doctrine of frustration may apply in an appropriate case.[169] An assignee of the tenant is expected to observe the covenant to pay the rent.[170]

A covenant to pay rent should state precisely the dates when rent is to be paid. Rent is due on the first moment of the day fixed for payment, and it is in arrear if it is not paid by midnight.[171]

(c) <u>Covenant Against Assignment and Underletting</u>. Where the lease is silent on the question of assignment or underletting, the tenant is entitled to assign his interest or to sublet without the consent of the landlord.[172] A covenant not to assign or sublet any part of the premises is broken where the tenant assigns or sublets the whole of the premises.[173] However, a covenant not to sublet is not broken by a sublease of part of the premises.[174]

If the lease contains a covenant not to assign or sublet, an assignment or subletting made in breach of the covenant is valid, but the breach may result in forfeiture of the lease (if the lease contains a forfeiture clause) or may entitle the landlord to claim damages. Where the tenant sells a business which is being carried on in the premises and makes the buyer a partner, such a transaction constitutes a parting with possession.

If a covenant absolutely prohibits assignment or underletting, the landlord cannot be compelled to relax the prohibition even if his behaviour is unreasonable. A landlord may demand a fine or premium for relaxing such a prohibition. However, where the landlord's consent is required to assign or sublet, such a consent shall not be

---

[167] *Coomber v Howard* (1845) 1 CB 440.
[168] (1882) 21 Ch D 9.
[169] *National Carriers Ltd v Panalpina* [1981] AC 675.
[170] *Estates Gazette Ltd v Benjamin Restaurants Ltd & Anor* [1994] 1 WLR 1528 (CA).
[171] *Dibble v Bowater* (1853) 2 E & B 564.
[172] *Leith Properties Ltd v Byrne* [1983] QB 433.
[173] *Field v Barkworth* [1986] 1 WLR 137.
[174] *Sweet & Maxwell Ltd v Universal New Services Ltd* [1964] 2 QB 699.

unreasonably refused[175] and in such a case he cannot exact a fine for the consent,[176] unless there is some agreement to the contrary in the lease. Alternatively, the tenant can apply to the court for a declaration that the landlord has unreasonably withheld his consent. A covenant not to assign is not broken by a subletting.

As far as a building lease is concerned, the tenant may assign without consent in the face of a covenant prohibiting assignment, except during the last seven years of the term.[177]

Even though there may be an absolute covenant prohibiting assignment or subletting, it is always open to the landlord to relax the covenant should he feel disposed to do so. Moreover, the landlord would not be debarred from demanding a payment for the permission.

The Landlord and Tenant Act, 1988, imposes duties on a landlord regarding the tenant's application for consent to assign, subletting, charging or parting with possession. It affects only a qualified covenant, and its aim is to prevent undue delay by the landlord in dealing with a consent application. When an application is received, the landlord owes a duty to the tenant within a reasonable time:

(i) to give consent, except where it is not reasonable to do so; and

(ii) to serve on the tenant a written notice of his decision whether or not to give consent stating in addition if consent is given what conditions, if any, are imposed, and if no consent is given the reason for withholding it.

The above Act has changed the law regarding the giving of consent. A landlord who has not given his reason for refusal within a reasonable time cannot thereafter justify his refusal of consent by putting forward any reasons.[178] Certain propositions of law from the authorities have been deduced in the case *International Drilling Fluids Ltd v Louisville Investments (Uxbridge) Ltd.* [179] These are with regard to the question of unreasonableness in withholding consent. The main purpose of the covenant is to protect the landlord's interest. The onus

---

[175] Section 19(1) of the Landlord and Tenant Act 1927.
[176] Section 144 of the LPA 1925.
[177] L & T Act, 1927, s19(1)(b).
[178] *Footwear Corp Ltd v Amplight Properties Ltd* [1999] 1 WLR 551.
[179] [1986] Ch513 at 510-19, approved by HL in *Ashworth Fraser v Gloucester City Council* [2001] UKHL 59, [2001] 1 WLR 2180.

is on the tenant to prove unreasonableness which is a question of fact depending upon all the circumstances.

(d) <u>Covenant to Pay Rates and Taxes</u>. This covenant is to ensure that the tenant is liable for local rates (e.g., business rates) and taxes (e.g. council tax). The incidence of liability for rates and other taxes is determined in the first instance by the statute under which the charge is imposed, i.e., either by the landlord or by the tenant, generally depending on whether the charge has been incurred for the landlord's benefit, as owner, or the tenant's benefit, as occupier. But as between the landlord and the tenant the charge could be shifted by express agreement. To do so the covenant must be clear and unequivocal in respect of all charges imposed at any time.

The occupier is generally liable for the payment of the ordinary local rates (now business rates or council tax) levied by the rating authority or local council, and charges for water, gas and electricity. Another local rate which is levied in certain districts is drainage rate, the purpose of which is to meet the expenses of draining the land, maintaining embankments and the like. Drainage rate consists of two parts:

(i) owner's drainage rate for new works, and improvement of existing works;
(ii) occupier's drainage rate for other expenses and charges.

Drainage rates under both heads are collected from occupiers, who are entitled to recover from the owner of the land any amount paid by them on account of the owner's drainage rate.

Charges for making up roads usually fall upon the landlord but the tenant may agree to pay them.

(e) <u>Covenant to Repair.</u> In long leases the tenant often covenants to carry out all repairs; in short leases the landlord generally accepts liability for external and structural repairs, the tenant being liable only for internal repairs. In the case of residential leases under seven years the landlord is liable for all external and structural repairs, including repairs to the installations.[180] A few cases decided in relation to these

---

[180] The Landlord and Tenant Act, 1985, s 11.

matters are *Liverpool City Council*[181] *v Irwin* and *O'Connor v Old Eton Housing Association*.[182] In the absence of any provision relating to repairs the position of the parties will be governed by the law of waste, except those cases where the landlord is liable under statutes. The subject of repairs is very wide and is dealt with in Chapter 7.

(f) <u>Covenant to Insure</u>. The object of this covenant is for the tenant or the landlord to insure to the full or some specified value, to keep the premises insured, to produce receipts when required to do so, in the event of loss or damage to use the insurance money for rebuilding, and to make any deficiency out of his own funds.

Under the common law a landlord or tenant who insures voluntarily cannot be required to reinstate the property with the capital sum received from the insurance company, but where there is a covenant to insure by the landlord or the tenant and the property is damaged by fire, the other party may, under section 83 of the Fires Prevention (Metropolis) Act, 1774, demand that the insurance monies be spent on reinstatement, and the landlord could require the company to do this before any settlement is made with the tenant.

(g) <u>Covenant for the Landlord to Enter and View</u>. Where the landlord is liable for repairs, the tenant is obliged to permit the landlord or his agent to enter and view the state of repair of the premises.[183] Also, under certain statutes, the landlord has a right to enter and view in certain other cases. Apart from these cases, the landlord has no right to enter and view the premises during the term, unless he has reserved the right.

(h) <u>Covenant Against Change of User</u>. Such a covenant is to prevent the tenant from changing from one use to another, and is considered to be absolute. However, if the covenant is subject to a qualification, i.e., "without the consent or licence of the landlord", the qualified

---

[181] [1977] AC 239 (a landlord obliged to replace cisterns which caused WCs to overflow).
[182] [2002] 2 WLR 1133 (narrow pipework in a building which did not work, on appeal was held not to be disrepair).
[183] *Mint v Good* [1951] 1 KB 517; *McAulay v Bristol City Council* [1991] 2 EGLR 64 (CA).

covenant is now subject to the proviso that no fine or premium shall be payable for the consent.[184]

(i) Covenant to Use the House as a Private Dwelling House Only. This covenant will prevent the house for some purpose other than a dwelling. Even the taking in of paying guests has been held to be a breach of this covenant. It does not apply to a single paying guest who lives as a member of the family.[185]

(j) Covenant not to Alter the Structure or to make Improvements Without Consent. This is to prevent any structural alteration of the premises without consent. It is subject to a proviso under the Landlord and Tenant Act 1927, s19(2), that such consent shall not be unreasonably withheld. Similarly, a covenant regarding the making of improvements is subject to the said section 19(2). The tenant may apply to the High Court or the County Court for a declaration that the landlord has unreasonably withheld his consent.[186]

(k) Covenant to Yield Up at the End of the Term. Such a covenant may appear to be unnecessary since it is clearly implied, for, as soon as the tenant's right to possession ceases, the landlord is entitled to re-enter permanently. However, the purpose of this express covenant is to strengthen the landlord's claim for damages in the event the tenant holds over.

(l) Covenant Governing Options in the Lease. It is open to the parties of a lease to incorporate a covenant giving an option or options to one or both parties for one or more purposes as given below:

> (i) *Option of Renewal.* Quite apart from any statutory rights of continuation of the tenancy on expiration of the term granted the lease itself not uncommonly provides for renewal at the end of the term. The exercise of the option is usually made subject to certain conditions (e.g., upon observance and performance of the covenants in the lease and is not affected by the rule against

---

[184] L & T Act 1927, s19(3).
[185] *Segal Securities v Thoseby* [1963] 1 QB 887.
[186] For the application of section 19(2) see *Iqbal v Thakrar* [2004] EWCA Civ 592, [2004] 3 EGLR 21; *Sergeant vMacepark (Whittlebury) Ltd* [2004] EWHC 1333 (Ch), [2004] 4 All ER 662.

perpetuities as long as it forms part of the lease or is part of the same transaction, but options to renew a lease granted after 1925 for a term exceeding 65 years from the expiry of the current lease is void.

(ii) *Option to Determine the Lease*. A lease may contain an option conferring a right on either party to determine before the expiration of the term or on the occurrence of a specified event. An option is exercisable only by the person in whom the term or reversion is legally vested and only in accordance with the conditions in the option.

(iii) *Option to Purchase the Freehold*. A lease sometimes contain an option given to the tenant that the landlord will sell his reversion at a certain price if the tenant so desires. Such an option is a collateral independent contract which is not within the relationship of landlord and tenant and, therefore, is personal between the parties and does not run with the land or the reversion. However, an assignee of the reversion will be bound if the option is protected by registration of an estate contract under the Land Charges Act, 1972 (regarding unregistered land) or by an entry of a notice under the Land Registration Act 2002, as the case may be. In the case of registered land,[187] an option exercisable by a tenant in occupation constitutes an overriding interest and, therefore, no registration or entry is required. In many cases, the option to purchase is itself capable of being assigned unless prevented by the terms.

An option is not generally exercisable after the term comes to an end and, in any case, not longer than 21 years from the date of the lease, otherwise it would infringe the rule against perpetuities. The terms of the option will usually stipulate the price but, if not, it will be the open market value of the reversion subject to the existing lease.[188]

In *Interspaces Self Storage Ltd v Harding*[189] there was an express covenant for the landlord to perform certain services. The tenant

---

[187] See the Land Registration Act, 2002, Sch 1.
[188] *Grimes*(AP) Ltd v *Grayshott Motor Co* Ltd (*1967*) 201 EG 586 38.
[189] [2014] EWCA Civ 46, [2014] L&TR 16, Moses LJ, CA (Civ Div).

claimed damages on account of a rubble heap which was an eyesore and was off-putting to potential customers. The claim was for a breach of covenant to perform services and that the tenant had suffered damage as a result by the landlord refusing to renew the retained parts and to tidy and landscape any appropriate part of the common parts. The judge was wrong to reject the claim on the basis that he had; he appeared to have decided the case of an argument that was not put before him at the trial. The ambit of the covenant should have been construed at the date the lease was granted. However, construed objectively, they were not broad enough to impose a generalised obligation of a wholly unspecific ambit to maintain the appearance of the estate. Thus, the judge arrived at the correct decision in refusing the claim.

Construction of Covenants in a Lease

All covenants are to be construed according to the intention of the parties when they entered into the lease. A covenant will depend for its meaning in every case upon the precise words used, but, at the same time, subject to protective legislation applicable to particular classes of tenancy.

In a case involving speedway racing, it was held that nuisance was not an inevitable consequence of such a use in those particular circumstances.[190] But in an earlier case involving land for development and use as a go-kart track, the landlord was liable because "they decided to go ahead with full knowledge that noise nuisance was a necessary or ordinary or natural consequence of go-kart racing and practising."[191]

Duties of Local Authority Under Human Rights Act, 1998.

Under section 6 of the HRA, 1998, a public authority is to ensure that it acts in a way which is not incompatible with a Convention right.[192] This right imposes on a local authority landlord to ensure that the condition of a dwelling-house let as social housing is such that the

---

[190] *Coventry v Lawrence (No 2)* [2014] UKSC 46.
[191] *Tetley v Chitty* [1986] 1 All ER 663 QBD.
[192] Section 1 of the 1998 Act contains the rights and freedoms under the European Convention for the Protection of Human Rights and Fundamental Freedoms.

tenant's right to respect and family life is not infringed.[193] Whether the state of the condition of the dwelling will infringe the Convention right will depend on the circumstances of the particular case, having regard to both the needs and resources of the community and of individuals. The 1998 Act does not impose a general and unqualified obligation on public authorities as regards the condition of their housing stock.[194]

REMEDIES AND RIGHTS

The remedies and rights of the landlord and the tenant are set out in Chapter 7. What is given below is only an outline of such remedies and rights

Landlord' Remedies and Rights

There are many remedies which include forfeiture, damages, entering to carry out repairs, specific performance and protocol for terminal dilapidations.

(a) Forfeiture[195] where it is expressly provided for in the lease may be used against the tenant regarding a breach of covenant.

(b) An action for damages during the currency of the lease may be claimed in appropriate circumstances. No claim can be made for damages for disrepair if the landlord intends to redevelop the property.[196] As it is not practical to obtain valuation evidence in most cases, the amount of damages awarded is usually the cost of the repairs.[197]

(c) The landlord can enter the property subject to the lease to carry out repairs, where he is liable to do the repairs, or where the tenant failed to do so under his obligation and recover the cost from the tenant.[198]

---

[193] *Lee v Leeds City Council* [2002] 1 WLR 488 at p 1506.
[194] *Lee v Leeds City Council* [2002] 1 WLR 488.
[195] For residential properties a court order is required.
[196] Section 18(1) of the 1927 Act.
[197] *Latimer v Carney* [2006] 50 EG 86.
[198] *Jervis v Harris* [1996] 1 All ER 303 (CA); [1996] Ch 195. The amount is not restricted by s 18(1) of the 1927 Act which applies only to a claim for damages.

(d) The remedy of specific performance may be granted by the court in appropriate circumstances.[199]

(e) The landlord has the right to prepare a schedule of dilapidations with regard to a claim for damages on account of the tenant's repairing obligations. This is usually at the end of the tenancy.

(f) Where a lease provides for a guarantor to ensure that the tenant complies with his obligations, the landlord may seek redress from the guarantor in the event the tenant defaults. However, if there is any variation in the terms of the lease, such as where the landlord has given the tenant a licence to carryout improvements, the guarantor should be made a party in the granting of the licence. In *Topland Portfolio No.1 Limited v Smiths News Trading Limited*,[200] the respondent guarantor of a commercial lease was released from liability as the terms of the lease were found to have been varied by a subsequent licence to alter, to which the guarantor had not been a party. On a proper construction, the liability of the guarantor had not been preserved either by the terms of the lease itself or the licence. The Court of Appeal rejected the landlord's appeal.

Tenant's Remedies and Rights

For the tenant, the rights and remedies are damages, self-help, interim injunctions, specific performance, appointment of a receiver, and the appointment of a manager.

(a) The tenant will be able to recover damages for his losses resulting from the landlord's failure to repair, either under an express or implied covenant. He cannot recover any damages if he refuses to allow the landlord to carry out the repairs.[201] A claim can be made for various losses suffered by reason of the disrepair.[202]

---

[199] *Rainbow Estates v Tokenhold* [1998] 2 All ER 860.
[200] [2014] EWCA Civ 18.
[201] *Granada Theatres Ltd v Freehold Investment (Leytonstone) Ltd* [1959] Ch 529.
[202] *Calabar v Sticher* [1983] 3 All Er 759; [1984] 1 WLR 287, and *Mira v Aylmer Square Investments Ltd* [1990] 1 EGLR 45 (CA).

(b) On a failure of the landlord to carryout his repairing obligations, the tenant can carry out the necessary repairs and deduct the cost from the future rent.[203]

(c) In exceptional circumstances, the tenant may apply to the court for an interim injunction requiring the landlord to take action to do the repairs before the case is fully argued in court where there is an immediate need for the work to be done.

(d) The discretionary remedy of specific performance may be granted under section 17 of the Landlord and Tenant Act, 1985, where the landlord has breached a repairing covenant relating to a dwelling. This remedy is under the court's equitable jurisdiction.[204]

(e) The need for the appointment of a receiver is where a landlord has failed to manage a building containing many tenants to deal with matters such as non-collection of rents and not carrying out repairs for many years,[205] or in a situation where the landlord cannot be traced. This procedure does not apply over the management of local authority housing.[206]

(f) With regard to a block with two or more flats, a tenant may apply to a leasehold valuation tribunal (LVT) for the appointment of a manager where the landlord persistently fails to maintain the block.[207] Before making the appointment, the tribunal must be satisfied that the landlord is in breach, the breach is likely to continue and that it is just and convenient in all the circumstances to make the order. This provision is applicable to a local authority landlord, a resident landlord or if the tenant is a business tenant.[208]

Tenant's Statutory Right to Vary a Restrictive Covenant

---

[203] *Lee-parker v Izzet.* [1971] 3 All ER 1099; [1971] 1 WLR 1688.
[204] See *Jeune v Queens Cross Properties Ltd* [1974] Ch 97; [1973] 3 All ER 97.
[205] See *Hart v Emelkirk* [1983] 3 All ER 15; [1983]1 WLR 1289.
[206] *Parker v Camden LBC* [1986] Ch 162; [1985] 2 All ER 141 (CA).
[207] Under Part II of the Landlord and Tenant Act, 1987, as amended by the Housing Act, 1996, ss 85 & 86.
[208] See section 21(3) of the landlord and Tenant Act, 1987.

There is a general jurisdiction in the Upper Tribunal (formerly the Lands Tribunal)[209] to vary or discharge restrictive covenants in certain leases relating to the use of the property demised or buildings on it.[210]

End

---

[209] Transfer of Tribunal Functions (Lands Tribunal and Miscellaneous Amendments) Order 2009 (SI 2009/1307).
[210] Section 84 of the LPA, 1925.

CHAPTER 6

RENT UNDER A LEASE OR TENANCY

INTRODUCTION

Rent is the consideration or part of the consideration on the part of the tenant for allowing him to occupy the demised premises and is payable to the landlord or to some other person authorised to collect the rent.[211] But the word "rent" has a far wider meaning. Apart from its contractual connotation, its significance goes far beyond that of an obligation to give consideration. Rent still reflects the historical basis of the nature of landlord and tenant; the relationship is one of tenure, and rent-service (as rent is historically known) is practically the only surviving incident of tenure.

For general purposes "rent" may be defined as "a certain profit issuing yearly out of land and tenements corporeal". At common law, rent was regarded as of three kinds:

(a) Rent-service.

(b) Rent-charge.

(c) Rent-seck.

Rent-service. Under the common law, rent-service was applicable under various types of tenure, including freehold, but in the course of time rent-service disappeared and/or abolished in respect of all other tenures, except for leaseholds. Today, rent-service is normally referred to as rent, and what is reserved in the lease or tenancy must be certain.[212] It does not matter whether the rent is to be increased or decreased on notice being given.[213]

---

[211] Although rent is usually money payment, it may take the form of delivery of chattels or the peformance of personal services (*Duke of Marlborough v Osborn* (1864) 5 B & S 67) and there may be no rent at all (LPA, 1925, s 205(1); *Ashburn Anstalt v Arnold* [1989] Ch 1.
[212] This is an application of the general principle of contract law.
[213] *Greater London Council v Connolly* [1970] 2 QB 100.

Rentcharge.[214] This is a sum of money charged upon land for a certain term or in perpetuity with an express power of distress[215] to secure payment in the event of default. It differs from rent (or rent-service) in that it is not an incident of tenure, and the owner of a rentcharge has no reversion in the land charged. A "rent-charge in possession", granted for a term certain or in perpetuity is a legal interest in the land under the LPA, 1925, s1. However, section 3 of the Rentcharges Act 1977 provides for the extinguishment of rentcharges over a period of 60 years:

> "(1)Subject to this section, every rentcharge shall (if it has not then ceased to have effect) be extinguished at the expiry of the period of 60 years beginning—
>
> (a) with the passing of this Act, or
>
> (b) with the date on which the rentcharge first became payable,
>
> whichever is the later; and accordingly the land on which it was charged or out of which it issued shall, at the expiration of that period, be discharged and freed from the rentcharge."

The Rentcharges Act, 1977, provides that rentcharges (on freehold land that is not under the classification of "an estate rentcharge") created before 22 August 1977 will be extinguished on 22 August 2037.[216] Meanwhile, a rentcharge can be redeemed earlier. There are many ways in which a rentcharge may be extinguished. These are by release under the LPA, 1925, s 70, where the lesser estate is merged into the greater, if no payment is made for 12 years in respect of unregistered land,[217] and as mentioned above under the 1977 Act.

---

[214] This label is to denote that the land for payment is charged with a 'distresse': See *Jenkin R Lewis & Sons Ltd v Kerman* [1971] Ch 477 at p 484.
[215] See later in the Chapter for amendment to the law of distress.
[216] Refer to Website: http://www.communities.gov.uk/housing/ho...
[217] Limitation Act, 1980, s 38(8). In the case of registered land, there is no automatic extinction by virtue of the Land Registration Act, 2002. A formal application has to be made to the land registry after 10 years.

Rent-seck. This is also known as barren rent and is a rent without any right of distress (which remedy is now given to annual charges under section 121 of the LPA, 1925. A rent-seck is similar to a rentcharge in other ways. But rent-seck has long ceased to exist for the inability of the owner to distrain was removed by the Landlord and Tenant Act, 1730.

Fee Farm Rent

This is a rent reserved on a grant in fee simple, i.e., either a rentcharge or rent-seck, depending whether a power of distress is expressly granted. Fee farm rents, in the form of a rentcharge, are in many parts of the country, i.e., England. They are found in conveyances of land in fee simple for building purposes and are known by different names in different areas, such as "perpetual ground rents" in London, "chief rents" in Lancashire, and "rent-charge" in some places.

RESERVATION OF RENT UNDER A LEASE OR TENANCY

It is usual (though not necessary) for a lease to contain a *reddendum*, i.e., the reservation of rent, followed by an express covenant to pay the rent reserved. Where rent is reserved in the *reddendum* it is not strictly necessary to have a separate express covenant in the lease as the *reddendum* itself is regarded as sufficient evidence of the tenant's promise to pay. If the *reddendum* were omitted but the covenant was included, the covenant alone would be sufficient. Any form of words, such as an express covenant or proviso, that shows an intention to create an agreement to pay rent will be construed as a good reservation.

An additional payment, such as a service charge, can constitute rent even though it is not formally reserved in the reddendum of the lease. A statement that it is deemed to be additional charges will suffice.[218]

Rent Review and Types of Rent

Rent review is a clause in the lease for the revision of the rent over

---

[218] *Sinclair Group Investments (Kensington) Ltd v Walsh* (1996) 71 P & CR 47 CA (Civ Div).

time. Many leases today contain a rent review clause.[219] The object of this clause is to enable the rent to be raised at regular intervals to reflect the fair market rental value of the property. The clause usually contains the machinery to be set up for determining the rent on a review date. In practice many of such clauses have not been drafted properly[220] and, therefore, subject to a great deal of litigation.

A rent review clause can state which party can trigger a rent review and requires that party to serve a notice. But if it states that only the landlord has the right to do so, the tenant is precluded from launching such a review even in a situation where it could result in a reduced rent.[221]

There are various kinds of rent as given below.

(a) *Rack Rent*. This is the full annual value of the property, including land and buildings. It is generally reserved when premises are let for occupation.

(b) *Best Rent*. The best rent is the highest rack rent that can reasonably be obtained for the whole term of the lease.

(c) *Head Rent*. This is the rent paid to the freeholder for a long lease where the property is sublet. It is usually less than the rack rent.

(d) *Peppercorn Rent*. This is a mere admittance of rent liability without any actual value, sometimes reserved before buildings are completed on a building lease.

(e) *Dead Rent*. This is rent reserved on a mining lease or other wasting asset and is payable throughout the term whether or not the mine is worked.

---

[219] See generally Aldridge, Leasehold Law, paras 4.045-4.060.; Reynolds & Fetherstonhaugh, *Handbook on Rent Review*; *Hill & Redman's Guide to Rent Review* (2001).
[220] *United Scientific Holdings Ltd v BurnleyBC* [1976] Ch 128 at p 146 per Roskill LJ; *see London Regional Transport v Wimpey Group Services Ltd* [1986] 2 EGLR 41.
[221] *Hemmingway Realty Ltd v Clothworkers Co* [2005] L & TR 21 ChD.

(f) *Royalty*. This is a form of rent payable for a mine, in addition to any dead rent, in proportion to the minerals extracted.

(g) *Ground Rent*. This is a rent which is less than the rack rent on the same property, the difference having been "capitalised" in the form of a premium taken by the landlord on the granting of the lease (usually a long lease). It is usually reserved in long leases and very common in building leases. Also, it may be a rent reserved that reflects the rental value of the land only as opposed to buildings.

When Rent is Due

The period for which and the dates on which rent is payable is usually specified in the *reddendum*. But in the absence of an express stipulation as to the periods, a yearly rent will be implied. Rent calculated on a weekly or monthly basis in a short periodic tenancy may be construed as an agreement to pay rent weekly or monthly as the case may be.

Rent is payable in arrears, unless agreed to be paid in advance and becomes due in the morning of the day fixed for payment, but it is not in arrear until midnight of the day. Where it is desired to take advantage of a condition of re-entry for non-payment of rent and a demand is necessary, such demand should be made before sunset on the day subsequent to the day when the rent is due. Rent due on a bank holiday is not payable until the following day.

Payment. It should be made in cash. Payment by cheque is a conditional payment and, if dishonoured, does not affect the landlord's remedies. In this day and age, the parties can agree for payment to be made by electronic means into the landlord's bank account. Payment of a deposit does not confer a right to the tenant to refrain from paying rent even if the deposit exceeds the rent due, as the deposit is normally for a different purpose (e.g., security).

Deductions. The tenant is entitled to deduct any sums specifically authorised by the lease or any statute as are allowed by their nature.

Apportionment of Rent. This is the proportional division of liability for rent under the lease. If the land which is subject to the lease becomes divided among several individuals, such as where the landlord disposes of part of his reversion to other persons, an apportionment of the rent will become necessary. Apportionment applies in the following circumstances:

(a) if the landlord sells or leases part of the reversion;[222]

(b) if the tenant assigns part of the land;

(c) if the tenant surrenders part of the land which is accepted by the landlord;

(d) if the tenant is evicted from part of the land; and

(e) where part of the land is acquired compulsorily under an Act of Parliament.

Where the tenant assigns part of the land, the landlord may choose to continue to demand full rent or agree to apportion it between the tenant and the assignee in respect of the part. However, the tenant remains liable on the covenant in respect of the whole, but may seek contribution.[223]

Where the landlord disposes or leases part of his reversion or his estate is divided among several persons, the rent is apportioned among them, but the apportionment is binding on the tenant only with his consent or by a court order.

Where the tenant voluntarily gives up to the landlord or is deprived of possession of part of his land, e.g., by surrender, eviction by title paramount or erosion by the sea, the tenant has a right to a reduction of rent in proportion to the value of the land lost. In addition, the tenant has a statutory right to apportion the rent where part of the land has been compulsorily acquired.

Break Clause and Refund of Rent. In *Marks & Spencer plc v BNP Paribas Securities Services Trust Company (Jersey) Ltd & Anor,* [224] the Supreme Court's decision will not be welcomed by the tenant community. If a tenant successfully breaks his lease, the landlord is generally not obliged to refund to the tenant any advance rent paid for

---

[222] LPA 1925, s 140, and LP (Amendment) Act 1926, s 2.
[223] See LPA 1925, s196(4).
[224] [2015] UKSC 72.

the period after the termination date of the lease, except where the lease expressly requires the landlord to make a refund. This decision is important in that it will change the expectations of many tenants, who, prior to the decision, would have considered that, as a matter of fairness, if not of legal entitlement, a landlord would refund advance rent paid for any period beyond the termination date, following the tenant's exercise of a break clause in the lease. From this decision, it is clear that, although the legal principles may be prejudicial to the tenant or may be a gain for the landlord, it is unlikely any such landlord without compassion will be persuaded to make a refund to the tenant.

Effect of Assignment. An express covenant to pay rent by the tenant will bind the tenant throughout the term of the lease because of the doctrine of privity of contract. This applies to leases granted before 1996.[225] However, a covenant to pay rent is a "real" covenant which will run with the land and will, therefore, bind the assignee as well. In practice, the assignee usually pays the rent, and it is only when he is unable to do so that the landlord calls on the original tenant to pay. Where there is no express covenant to pay rent but is implied by law, the liability to pay rent arises by privity of estate and the tenant for the time being will be liable to pay. Therefore, if the tenant assigns, assuming there is no prohibition against assignment, the original tenant has no further liability.

Special Statutory Provisions

Under the LPA 1925, s141, it is unnecessary to provide in a lease to whom the rent is payable as it goes to the landlord for the time being, and he may exercise the appropriate remedies for non-payment.

In the case of an assignment of a lease for value, the assignee impliedly covenants to indemnify the assignor against any default for non-payment of rent.[226]

By reason of the Limitation Act, 1980, no action can be brought after the expiration of six years from the date on which the arrear of

---

[225] See the Landlord and Tenant (Covenants) Act, 1995. For leases created after 1995 the original parties will no longer be liable under privity of contract after an assignment (see Chapter 9 for details).
[226] See LPA 1925, s77.

rent became due.[227] This applies to all debts, but a part payment or written acknowledgement of the debt causes a fresh accrual of the right of action and the six years run from that time. An action to recover land may be brought at any time within twelve years from the date on which the right of action accrued.[228] Where a lease is in writing, there is no time limit within which an action to recover land may be brought. However, if the tenant pays rent (of £1 or more) to a third person who wrongfully claims the reversion and no rent is received by the person rightly entitled, after 12 years from the date of the first receipt of rent by the wrongful person he will have acquired title to the land. The Crown can bring an action for the recovery of land within 30 years.

Suspension of Rent

The general rule is that rent continues to be payable whatever are the intervening circumstances. However, there are two exceptions to this rule:

(a) where the tenant is evicted by the landlord or someone has lawfully claimed the property by title paramount; and

(b) where the parties agree otherwise or possibly under the doctrine of frustration.[229]

RECOVERY OF RENT

If the tenant fails to pay rent the landlord has four methods by which he can enforce payment as follows:

(a) he can commence court proceedings for the stated rent in the lease (if by deed) or he can sue for the rent stated in the contract (if not by deed) or in the agreement for the lease;[230] or

---

[227] Limitation Act 1980, s 19, to recover rent. Section 8 provides for 12 years in respect of specialty contracts.
[228] Limitation Act, 1980, s 15(1). The period of 12 years applies to all proceedings relating to land. Where forfeiture applies, the landlord must take action to pursue his right to forfeit within 12 years. Because of the practice of waiver it is most unlikely the landlord's right to forfeit will be affected by limitation.
[229] See *National Carriers Ltd v Panalpina (Northern) Ltd* ([1981] AC 675).

(b) he can sue for the "use and occupation" of the land by the tenant;

(c) as an alternative to (a) or (b) the landlord prior to 6 April, 2014, could have levied distress in respect of commercial premises;[231] and

(d) in addition to the above remedies, he may have a right of forfeiture of the lease, provided there is a condition for re-entry specified in the lease. This is not a remedy for recovery of the rent but usually results in prompt payment if the rent is less than the yearly value.

Forfeiture will be considered in detail in the chapter on determination of leases. The first three methods are now considered in some detail.

(A) <u>Action for Recovery of Rent</u>. Where there is an express reservation of rent in the lease, it does not matter whether it is in the *reddendum* or in an express covenant. In either case, the landlord will be able to bring an action for the recovery of the arrears of rent. The same applies if there is a contract or an agreement for a lease, i.e., an agreement in writing or oral agreement provided there is an act of part performance. As mentioned earlier, the action must be brought within six years to comply with the Limitation Act 1980, s 15. If rent is in arrears for eight years or so, only rent for the last six years can be recovered, unless the tenant acknowledges the debt for the longer period. Where there is no right of re-entry, the landlord's only remedy is to sue to recover the rent.

The rent due can be claimed without any need to apply the principle of mitigation.[232] Even where there is a right of re-entry, the landlord can choose to keep the lease alive by suing for recovery of rent, unless election to keep the lease alive is wholly unreasonable and that damages would be an adequate remedy.

---

[230] The rent due can be claimed without any reduction based on mitigation (*Reichman v Beveridge* [2006] EWCA Civ 1659, [2007] 1 P & CR 20).
[231] As from the 6th April, 2014, The Tribunals Courts and Enforcement Act 2007 (TCE Act) has abolished Distress for Rent which has been replaced by a new regime of Commercial Rent Arrears Recovery (CRAR) discussed later in this chapter.
[232] *Reichman v Beveridge* [2006] EWCA Civ 1659, [2007] 1 P & CR 20.

(B) <u>Action for Use and Occupation</u>. In the absence of an express statement of rent in the lease or where there is no express lease, the landlord may be able to sue for "use and occupation" of the premises by the tenant, as the existence of a contract to pay rent is implied from the use and occupation of the premises by the tenant. However, the following conditions must be satisfied:

(1) there must be a lease or tenancy;
(2) the tenant must have occupied the premises;
(3) the landlord must have a legal reversion; and
(4) the lease must not be under seal.[233]

Under section 14 of the Distress for Rent Act, 1737, the landlord can recover a reasonable rent. If the lease does not state the length of the term, he may only recover for the period of actual occupation by the tenant.

(C) <u>Distress</u>. The Law Commission has recommended the abolition of common law distress and its replacement with a statutory system for use in respect of rent arrears under commercial leases. From 6 April, 2014, the procedure of distress has been abolished. Therefore, the law on distress no longer applies but as a historical perspective it can be seen in the Appendix to this chapter.

REPLACEMENT OF COMMON LAW DISTRESS WITH CRAR

With effect from 6 April, 2014, the Tribunals Courts and Enforcement Act 2007 (TCEA) has abolished Distress for Rent; it has been replaced by a new regime of Commercial Rent Arrears Recovery (CRAR).

The 2007 Act is intended to revolutionise the enforcement process for the recovery of rent. The aims are for clarity, simplification and uniformity of the law. The new regime provides for certificated enforcement agents who are required to be competent. The Act has introduced a single, staged fee structure to be applied in any enforcement procedure. Following some years of preparation since the enactment in 2007, Part III of the TCEA is now in force with

---

[233] The requirement for a seal in a lease has been relaxed by the Law of Property (Miscellaneous Provisions) Act 1989.

effect from 6 April 2014.[234] Part III of the TCEA provides for the following:

(a) Landlords' common law right to levy on goods has been abolished.

(b) Recovery of sums for insurance and services is prohibited.

(c) Distress without notice is no longer available.

(d) The complicated fee scales & structures for levying distress have been removed.

(e) No provision in the new regime is made for pound breach (disappeared).

(e) The Landlord and Tenant Act, 1904, no longer applies.

Under section 71 of the TCEA, 2007, the Landlord's right to levy on goods is abolished, including the old process of rent distraint.

Restrictions and Exemptions

The remedy under the new regime will not be available in respect of mixed use or residential premises. The former restriction on the exercise of distress on a Sunday is abolished but the remedy under CRAR can only be exercised between 6 am and 9 pm or other business hours for the tenant in question.
Certain types of goods are exempt from CRAR. They include:

(a) tools of the trade up to a value of £1,350; and

(b) items required to satisfy the basic domestic needs of the tenant.

Abolition of Reserved Rent in Respect of Ancillary Services

CRAR can only be used to recover rent. There is no right to recover any other sums. A reserved rent in respect of ancillary services by the

---

[234] The Taking Control of Goods Regulations 2013, SI 2013 No 1894.

landlord is abolished. In the past services were for utilities, rates, insurance legal fees and other charges. Section 85 prevents any attempts to bypass the regulations with other secondary contractual agreements. The rent arrears must be for a minimum period of seven days before recovery under the new regime.

Distress With Notice

The process of distress without notice has now been removed as a remedy of the landlord to recover his rent. Specifically, Schedule 12, Pt 2, para. 7(1) to the Act states "an enforcement agent may not take control of goods unless the debtor has been given notice." Therefore, an enforcement agent must inform the tenant who is in arrear with his rent, giving him 7 clear days' notice before any distress for rent.

If the landlord considers that it is likely the tenant will remove or dispose of goods in order to avoid recovery, the landlord can make an application for a reduced notice period. On the other hand, once notice has been served, the tenant can apply for it to be set aside or for its execution to be delayed.

Although the form of notice is not prescribed, specific information must be included. As such, landlords should be satisfied that all notices are correct before they are served.

Transparency and Clarity on Costs

In this regard, the main aim is to ensure there is a transparency and clarity on costs involved in the process of distress for rent. The structure of costs aligns more closely with the activities carried out by enforcement agents. It is intended as an incentive to encourage more appropriate enforcement behaviour and, in the process, be both clear and fair to debtors.

The abuse of unregulated fees added to actions has been eradicated with the use of trigger points and set amounts as laid down in regulations.

Controlled Goods Agreement

In seizing goods, the regulations set out a detailed procedure for the enforcement agent to follow. The enforcement agent and tenant can enter into a controlled goods agreement, rather than a walking possession agreement. If such an agreement is breached, the enforcement agent must give the tenant two clear days' notice before being able to re-enter the property.

As mentioned above, a walking possession agreement is now called "Controlled Goods Agreement". In this regard, an enforcement agent is required to leave a detailed inventory of the goods taken under his control.

Although "pound breach" has been abolished, the tenant will commit an offence[235] if the tenant interferes with the process of the secured goods. Another offence could relate to intentional interference with controlled goods without lawful excuse.

An enforcement agent may take control of goods "only if they are goods of the tenant".[236] In this regard, landlords have lost the advantage they formerly enjoyed in relation to the wide range of goods that could be taken.[237]

Minimum Period Before Sale

The minimum period before the sale of goods seized is 7 clear days from the date of their removal unless the goods would become unsaleable or their value substantially reduced. Normally the maximum period for taking control of any goods is 12 months, but if necessary an application can be made for extending it for another 12 months.

Use of CRAR Only in Respect of Commercial Premises

The 2007 Act provides clear definitions of commercial premises in relation to what constitutes a lease and where CRAR (under the 2007 Act) can be used. The Act ensures that it can only be used in circumstances where:

(a) the main terms of the lease are clear and in writing; and

(b) the sums payable are clearly defined and identifiable.

---

[235] Under para. 68 of Sch. 12 to the 2007 Act (TCEA).
[236] Under Sch.12 to the 2007 Act.
[237] Under the Law of Distress Amendment Act, 1908.

The law of distress has been used by landlords as a fast, cheap and easy method in forcing tenants to pay rent arrears. In many cases, the process resulted in tenants having to pay enormous fees in addition to the arrears of rent. The old procedure has been viewed by tenants as archaic and heavy-handed. The new procedure following the reforms seeks to redress the imbalance and remove the archaic nature of the old regime.

For the landlord, it appears that the reforms have created additional bureaucracy. The notice requirement in particular clearly reduces the effectiveness of his remedy by providing the tenant with the opportunity to remove goods from the premises and put them out of the landlord's reach.

Use of CRAR in Other Limited Circumstances

In some other limited circumstances CRAR can be used at the end of the lease:

(a) where control of the goods was taken before the lease came to an end; or

(b) if rent was due and payable before the end of the lease and all of the following circumstances are satisfied:

    (i) the lease did not end by forfeiture;
    (ii) not more than 6 months have passed since the lease ended;
    (iii) the rent was due from the person who was the tenant at the end of the lease;
    (iv) that person remains in possession of any part of the demised premises;
    (v) any new lease that is entered into is a lease of commercial premises (even if that lease is not in writing); and
    (vi) the person who was the landlord at the end of the lease remains entitled to the immediate reversion to the lease.

With regard to the application of CRAR, a lease is treated as having ended when the contractual expiry date and any statutory period of continuation under the Landlord and Tenant Act, 1954, has come to an end. CRAR can be used against a holding over tenant, but it has no application against an occupier who is allowed possession on the basis of an implied tenancy at will during ongoing lease negotiations.

Other Points to Note Regarding CRAR

To exercise CRAR there must be a written lease. CRAR cannot apply to:

(a) a licence to occupy premises;

(b) an implied tenancy (including a tenancy at will); and

(c) a tenancy on sufferance (i.e., a tenancy arising when a tenant wrongfully remains in occupation of premises after his lease has expired and his landlord has not confirmed whether it is willing for the tenant to remain in occupation).

Even where an existing commercial lease refers to distress, it will be automatically updated. This means that the lease can often be construed as referring to CRAR, instead of the old remedy of distress. Therefore, the clause should continue to operate largely as originally intended. But some clauses referring to distress may be deemed to be void. Thus, the specific drafting will need to be considered in each case in order to confirm the position.

In order to exercise CRAR a landlord must operate with care. Where the CRAR provisions are found to have been breached, a court can require that:

(a) the goods are returned to the tenant; and

(b) damages are paid to the tenant on account of any loss arising from the breach.

Differences Between Distress and CRAR

Some similarities and differences between distress and CRAR are in the table below.

	Distress	**CRAR**
1	A relationship of landlord & tenant sufficient without need for a written tenancy	A written lease or tenancy is required. Special rules apply in respect of agricultural tenancies
2	Applies to any sum reserved, and there is no minimum sum or days of rent arrears	Applies to annual rent, VAT and other sums charged on it. There is a minimum of 7 days' rent arrears.
3	Applies to mixed-use premises	Limited to commercial premises, not mixed-use premises, unless residential use is in contravention of the lease.
4	Certified bailiff had to be used.	An enforcement agent must be used and the landlord's instruction must be in writing.
5	No requirement to serve any notice.	At least 7 days notice must be served.
6	Except on a Sunday, entry on any day between sunrise and sunset.	Entry may be on any day between 6 am and 9 pm. Also, entry may be outside these hours if in accordance with the tenant's business hours.
7	Seized goods may be sold after 5 days. No method of sale prescribed.	Goods must be sold after 7 days at a public auction or by other means as ordered by a court (excluding Sundays & bank holidays).

End

APPENDIX TO CHAPTER 6.

What is set out below on distress is given as a historical perspective.

Distress was an ancient self-help remedy under the common law but has fallen into disuse. It involved the taking of another person's chattel without legal process as a pledge for performance of a duty. The landlord was entitled to exercise distress unless he contracted not to do so.[238]

Note In the case of certain residential tenancies, subject to statutory protection, the landlord was required to obtain prior leave of the court before he could levy distress.[239]

Scope of Distress (Now Abolished)

1. Rent. Rent could be distrained for by the landlord as the right of distress is incident to every rent-service. However, the conditions below must be satisfied:

(i) There must be an actual demise at a fixed rent.
(ii) The landlord who levies distress must be the immediate reversioner.
(iii) The rent is due and is in arrear.

As mentioned already, the common law right of distress has been abolished by legislation and replaced by a new procedure applicable only to commercial leases.[240]

2. Rentcharge. Distress can be levied for a rentcharge. The power is given by the document creating it or by statute. The power of distress given by the LPA 1925, s121, arises as soon as payment is 21 days in arrears.

---

[238] *Homes (T & E) Ltd v Robinson* [1979] 1 WLR 452 at p 453, per lord Templeman LJ.
[239] See generally Tanney and Travers, *Distress for Rent*, 2000; Book, *Distress for Rent*, 1999.
[240] See generally Tanney and Travers, *Distress for Rent* (2000); Rook, *Distress for Rent* (1999).

3. <u>Rates and Taxes</u>. The non-payment of rates (e.g., business rates) and taxes (e.g., council tax) can be distrained for (this is outside the scope of this book).

Levying Distress

1. <u>Who Could Distrain</u>. Distress could be levied by the landlord himself in which case no certificate was needed or by a certificated bailiff authorised by him. A certificated bailiff was a person who had been issued with a certificate by a county court judge and acting under a warrant of distress from the landlord. The warrant of distress gave the bailiff implied authority to receive rent, and would render the landlord liable for the irregular but not the illegal acts of the bailiff, whose duty was to take enough goods to recover the rent plus cost and his own fees.

2. <u>Time of Distress.</u> Distress could be levied at anytime between dawn and sunset. No distress could be levied on a Sunday or on a bank holiday. There was no need for the landlord to demand rent before distraining, and when the landlord or his agent went to distrain, or any time previously, the tenant could tender the exact amount of rent due, thereby putting an end to the distress. The tenant could also, at any time prior to the impounding of the distress, tender the full amount of rent due and costs incurred up to that time. After such tender, any further proceeding in distress was illegal.

3. <u>Entry for Distress.</u> The landlord or bailiff could gain entry to the premises by any means though not by force, but once he was inside he could break open inner doors. An illegal entry would render the distress void *ab initio* and the distrainor liable as a trespasser to pay the tenant the full value of the goods seized.

4. <u>Where Distress Could be Made</u>. Distress could be made on the land demised or any part of it and also in these circumstances:

- (i) by agreement upon other land of the tenant;
- (ii) upon the tenant's cattle or stock grazing on any common connected with the land demised;
- (iii) pursued and seized any cattle driven off the land to avoid distress; and

(iv) where the goods had been fraudulently or clandestinely removed, the landlord could, under the Distress for Rent Act, 1737, follow and distrain such goods at any time within 30 days, wherever they were.

5. <u>Seizure</u>. As soon as the distrainor seized goods he was required to serve the tenant with a notice of distress in the prescribed form, which should state the rent due, the goods which had been seized, the place of impounding (if off the premises) and the time (not less than 5 complete days after the service of the notice) when the goods would be sold, unless replevied.

6. <u>Rescous (or Rescue)</u>. This occurred where the owner, or other person, by force took away a thing distrained from the person distraining, after the distrainer has taken possession, but before impounding.

7. <u>Impounding</u>. This was the placing of the goods distrained upon in the custody of the law. The goods were generally left on the premises. When this was the case, it was known as "walking possession". With permission the tenant could continue to use the distress.

8. <u>Pound Breach</u>. This was the breaking of the pound, i.e., by removing the things after they had been impounded. The remedies for this were reception of the goods, and an action for treble damages. Any further pound breach was a criminal offence.

(9) <u>Appraisement</u>. This was the valuation of the goods distrained. The goods needed to be appraised before sale only if the tenant demanded it in writing or in the case of growing crop.

(10) <u>Walking Possession.</u> Where the bailiff had made a distress and by arrangement with the tenant did not remain on the premises, but had the right of re-entry, this was known as walking possession. If he was later prevented from entering the premises, he was entitled to re-enter forcibly, unless he had been expelled by force or deliberately excluded by the tenant.[241]

---

[241] *Mcleod v Butterwick* [1998] 1 WLR 1603

Goods Exempt From Distress

The rule was that all cattle, goods or chattels found on the premises could be distrained for rent, even though they did not belong to the tenant. To this general rule there were, however, several exceptions which could be divided into:

(i) those which were privileged; and
(ii) those which were conditionally privileged.

<u>Absolutely Privileged.</u> These were goods which could in no circumstances be removed, and are set out below.

(1) Property of the Crown.
(2) Property of persons who enjoyed diplomatic immunity.
(3) Property already under custody, e.g., goods taken by a sheriff under an execution or attachment.
(4) The goods of a lodger or sub-tenant and others.[242]
(5) Fixtures.
(6) Things in actual use.
(7) Things delivered to a person in the way of his trade.
(8) Things protected by a county court execution under the Law of Distress (Amendment) Act 1888.
(9) Animals *ferae naturae* (i.e., wild animals).
(10) Perishable goods.
(11) Money except in a bag.
(12) Frames, loomes, machines and materials belonging to third parties in the textile trade.[243]
(13) Railway rolling stock belonging to third parties.[244]
(14) Water, gas and electrical appliances belonging to statutory bodies.[245]
(15) Hired agricultural machines and breeding stock (not belonging to the tenant) on agricultural holdings.[246]

---

[242] Law of Distress Amendment Act 1905.
[243] Hosiery Act, 1843.
[244] Railway Rolling Stock Protection Act, 1872.
[245] Water Act, 1945; Gas Act, 1945; Electricity Act, 1947.
[246] Agricultural Holdings Act, 1945.

Conditionally Privileged Goods. These could only be distrained on if there was not enough elsewhere on the premises. They are set out below.

(a) The tools and implements of a tenant's trade or profession. If they were not in actual use and if there were not enough of other goods on the premises of sufficient value they could be distrained.

(b) Beasts of the plough and sheep fell into this category. Under Henry III, statute 4, no man "shall be distrained by his beasts that gain his land, nor by his sheep, while there is another sufficient distress to be found...."

(c) Assisted stock on agricultural holdings were also in this category. By section 9 of the Agricultural Holdings Act, 1945, where livestock belonging to another person had been taken in by the tenant to be fed at a fair price the stock could not be distrained by the landlord unless there was insufficient distress to be found.

Remedies for Wrongful Distress

A distress could be wrongful for one of three reasons:

(a) it could be illegal, e.g., where no rent was due;

(b) where the distress was legal but the proceedings had been conducted in an irregular manner, e.g., where the distrained goods had been sold before 5 or 15 days had been elapsed as appropriate; or

(c) it was excessive, i.e., if more goods were seized than were reasonably sufficient to satisfy the rent due and cost of the distress.

There were three remedies for a wrongful distress. They are set out below.

(a) Action for Damages. Such an action would lie against the wrongdoer, i.e., the bailiff or the landlord if ratified by him if the distress was illegal. The full value of the goods distrained upon plus damages were recoverable, with no deduction for rent, if any, owing. If the distress was excessive, the tenant could obtain damages as of right. He did not have to show that he suffered any special damages. Where the distress was irregular, the tenant could obtain damages on proof of actual loss.

(b) Action for Double Value. This applied where no rent had been in arrear, or the person who levied the distress had no right to receive the rent.

(c) Injunction. The application for an injunction is an equitable remedy and, therefore, discretionary. It lies at the suit of the tenant to prevent an alleged wrongful distress, but the tenant was required to pay the disputed rent into court pending settlement of the dispute.

End

CHAPTER 7

REPAIRS AND REPAIRING OBLIGATIONS

INTRODUCTION

This branch of the law is often referred to as the "law of dilapidations" which covers every aspect of defective conditions in buildings and the obligations of persons holding land under various tenures and any legal points arising therefrom, e.g., the liability towards a person injured because of a state of disrepair. However, for the purpose of this chapter the coverage is limited to discussion of repairing obligations arising by way of landlord and tenant relationships.

Repairing obligations arise under the lease or tenancy (contractual, under statute or under the law of tort). A question that may arise is to what extent a landlord may be liable for injury or damage caused to an occupier of a property on account of the condition. Also, people who are guests of the occupier or mere visitors who are injured by reason of the state of the premises may be able to sue the landlord or the occupier under statute[247] or in tort for damages. Tortious liability can arise at common law based on negligence or nuisance.

The doctrine of "caveat emptor" applies when a property is being bought so that the buyer should be aware of the condition of the property. If the property is not in a good state of repair, it could be expensive to bring it into a reasonable state of repair. Likewise, a prospective tenant should be aware of the condition of the property and his intended obligations under the lease.

SOURCES OF LIABILITY FOR DISREPAIR

Liability for disrepair of a building is generally imposed by law under one or more of the sources set out below.

1. Law of Contract

Liability to repair is the most common obligation under the law of

---

[247] Occupiers Liability Act, 1957.

contract which imposes upon the parties to a contract a legal duty or obligation to comply with the terms of the contract entered into by the parties.[248] As a general rule the rights and duties created by the contract affect only the parties to the contract (under privity of contract),[249] and a person who is not a party to the contract can have no rights or obligations under the contract. However, in the case of a lease those covenants, such as to repair, which touch and concern the land, are enforceable by and against assignees of the tenant and the landlord. In such a case, an assignee of either the tenant or the landlord may sue the other party, i.e., the landlord or the tenant, who may himself be an assignee.

2. Statutes

In the course of the last 90 years or so several statutes have been enacted, putting a great repairing responsibility on landlords of residential and to a lesser extent agricultural tenancies. Some important aspects of these statutes will be discussed in this chapter.

3. Law of Waste

In addition to any contractual obligation (whether implied or expressed) relating to repairs, a tenant or any other occupier may be liable under the doctrine of waste. Waste can be defined as "unlawful damage done or allowed to happen to land and/or buildings by a person, whose possession is temporary, whereby the value of the property to another person (e.g., the landlord) entitled to the immediate reversion or succession is depreciated". Waste is generally divided into two types as set out below:

(a) <u>Voluntary Waste</u>. This is an act of commission, i.e., a positive act, done to land or buildings or both. Examples of voluntary waste are the pulling down of a building, destroying or removal of landlord's fixtures, converting arable land into meadow, cutting timber, or opening a new mine upon the land. Waste is an alteration to the land or buildings, and where the intention is to improve the property no

---

[248] A lease is essentially a contractual agreement.
[249] Subject to changes to the law in the Landlord and Tenant (Covenants) Act, 1995, in respect of leases and tenancies entered into after 1995. These changes are discussed in Chapter 9.

damages are recoverable because the successor or reversioner suffers no loss. In such a case, it is known technically as "ameliorating" waste.

(b) <u>Permissive Waste.</u> This is an act of omission or negligence, i.e., permitting something causing damage to the premises, such as to allow buildings to fall or rot for want of repair. A tenant is not liable for an "Act of God" such as damage caused by something extraordinary, but if a slate is blown off from the roof it would appear that he is liable to remedy the defect so as to prevent rain and wind entering and causing further damage.

(c) <u>Equitable Waste.</u> This type of waste consists of an act of gross or malicious damage or wanton destruction to property by a tenant who is unimpeachable of waste. This is applicable mainly to persons in succession to a property under a trust. The leading case on equitable waste is *Vane v Barnard.* [250]

Remedies for Waste

The remedy at common law is an action for damages. The measure of damages is the depreciation of the claimant's interest by reason of the waste. Also, an injunction in equity may be issued against the defendant from committing further waste and possibly a mandatory injunction to make good the waste committed. Since the Judicature Acts, 1873-75, these remedies are granted by all courts, and being equitable remedies they are discretionary.

Liability of Tenants for Waste

(a) <u>Tenants for Years.</u> Express covenants in their leases will usually govern the extent of their liability, but where there are no express covenants, it is implied that they must use the premises in a proper and tenant-like manner, and deliver them to the landlord in the same condition as when let, fair wear and tear excepted, which is a very narrow exception as will be seen later. Apart from fair wear and tear, they are liable in tort for both permissive and voluntary waste.

---

[250] (1716) 2 Vern 738.

(b) <u>Yearly Tenants</u>. These tenants are liable for voluntary waste, but it is not quite sure whether their obligation for permissive waste goes further than the implied covenant (which it would seem obliges the tenant to keep the premises wind and water tight.[251]

(c) <u>Other Periodic Tenants.</u> A weekly tenant is not liable for fair wear and tear and must keep the premises in a tenant-lime manner.[252] He must do the little repairs that a reasonable person in his position would do and he and his guests must not damage the premises. Other monthly and quarterly tenants would appear to be in a similar position as a weekly tenant.

(d) <u>Tenants at Will and at Sufferance.</u> These tenants are not liable for permissive waste, and if damage is due to an act of voluntary waste the tenancy may come to an end. In any event, they may be sued in respect of the damage done.

Liability Generally

A lease conveys an estate in the land to the tenant and gives him exclusive possession and control of the premises. As such, the tenant has a duty to take care of the landlord's property. Therefore, it is waste for the tenant to damage the property or to allow it to fall into a state of decay. Waste has been discussed above.

In addition to the tenant's obligation to the tort of waste, the tenant has an implied contractual duty to use the premises in a tenant-like manner and to deliver up possession at the end of the lease to the landlord in the same state as when let, fair wear and tear excepted. Where premises are furnished the foregoing would appear to extend to the furniture as well. In *Warren v Keen*[253] Denning LJ (as he then was) made this statement:

> "Apart from express contract, a tenant owes a duty to the landlord to keep the premises in repair. The only duty of the tenant is to keep the premises in a husband-like, or what is the same thing, a tenant-like manner."

---

[251] *Wedd v Porter* [1916] 2 KB 91.
[252] *Warren v Keen* [1954] 1 QB 15; [1953] 3 WLR 702.
[253] [1953] 1 QB 15; [1953] 3 WLR 702.

The term "tenant-like manner" simply means that the tenant must take proper care of the premises; he must do the little jobs about the place which a reasonable tenant would do. In addition, he must not, of course, damage the house wilfully or negligently; and he must see that he and his guests do not damage it, for if they do he must repair it. Apart from these, if the premises fall into disrepair through fair wear and tear or lapse of time or for any reason not caused by the tenant he is not liable to repair.

Agricultural Leases. A tenant of agricultural land has an implied obligation to farm in a husband-like manner according to the custom of the country, i.e., the "approved habits of husbandry" under similar condition to those of the demised premises in the neighbourhood where those premises lie.

EXPRESS OBLIGATIONS

Apart from the tort of waste and implied contractual obligation, including obligations imposed by statutes, neither party can require the other to remedy a particular disrepair during the term. However, either party may choose to do so on a voluntary basis. Be that as it may, it is normal for the parties to express in some detail their repairing obligations in the lease.

Covenant to Repair

In long leases the tenant often covenants to carry out all repairs, but in short leases the landlord generally accepts liability for external and structural repairs.[254] In this situation, the tenant will be liable only for internal repairs. The extent of one's liability, to be included in the lease, is a matter for negotiations, but there can be no contracting out of section 11 of the Landlord and Tenant Act, 1985.

Obligation of the Landlord. The extent of the landlord's obligations to repair depends upon the meaning given to the words used in the covenant and the intention of the parties. The fact that a landlord covenants to repair does not automatically prevent him making

---

[254] In residential leases of less than 7 years, section 11 of the Landlord and Tenant Act,1985, imposes repairing obligations on the landlord. There can be no agreement to the contrary.

alterations.[255] Regard must be had to what the parties contemplated would be permissible.[256]

Where the landlord is liable for repairs, the tenant must first give notice of the want of repair since the tenant is in possession and control of the premises. The landlord will be liable if he delays unduly after notice has been given to him and, as a consequence of the delay, the tenant suffers injury or loss.

The landlord generally reserves the right to enter to carry out repairs whenever he expressly agrees to carry out repairs. However, in the absence of such reservation, the landlord is said to have an implied licence to enter the premises to carry out the repairs.[257]

If the landlord fails to carry out the required repairs within a reasonable time after receiving notice and, as a result, the tenant has to move to alternative premises he may be able to recover the rent paid for the accommodation elsewhere.[258] A landlord under an express covenant to repair owes a common duty of care to both the tenant and the tenant's visitors. However, liability is conditional upon notice of the defect.

No term is implied into a commercial lease for the landlord to repair retained parts of the building.[259]

Obligation of the Tenant. A covenant to repair by the tenant varies considerably both in form and effect. It is usual for the tenant to agree to repair and to keep the demised premises in repair during the term. Also, there is usually a separate covenant to repair defects within a specified time after written notice has been given by the landlord. The covenants may contain exceptions for damages caused by accidental fire, explosion, storm, tempest or other "Act of God", civil commotion or war.

The tenant will be liable for any damage arising from a wilful or negligent act, and also for damage not caused by his wilful act or default, unless he can prove that the damage is due to one of the exceptions, if any. If the only exception is "fair wear and tear" the tenant will be liable for accidents of every kind. He will only be

---

[255] *Hannon v 169 Queensgate Ltd* [2000] 1 EGLR 40.
[256] *Ibid.*
[257] *Saner v Bilton* (1878) 7 Ch D 815).
[258] See *Calabar v Sticher* [1984] 1 WLR 287; [1983] 3 All ER 759.
[259] *Gavin & Anor v One Housing Group Ltd* [2013] EWCA Civ 580.

exempt from damage caused by normal human wear and the normal effect of time and weather.

To a certain extent, especially in respect of residential leases, the parties' repairing obligations will be governed by statutory provisions, e.g., section 11 of the Landlord and Tenant Act, 1985.

Construction of Particular Covenants

These are covenants given on the part of the tenant.

(a) <u>To Put in Repair</u>. A covenant by the tenant to put the premises in repair will oblige him at the commencement of the term to do all repairs necessary to make the premises fit for the purpose for which they are let. However, it is very rare for the tenant to covenant that he will put the premises in repair at the commencement of the lease. This covenant is somewhat imposed on the landlord in the case of residential premises as under section 6 of the Housing Act, 1957. In such a case, the tenant is entitled to repudiate the lease if the landlord does not comply with the implied statutory covenant.

(b) <u>To Keep in Repair</u>. This covenant by the tenant is sometimes coupled with the covenant "to leave in repair", but strictly this is unnecessary since "to keep in repair" requires him to leave in repair (see below). A covenant to keep in repair creates a continuing obligation during the term of the lease. Even if the premises are not in repair at the commencement of the lease, this covenant will oblige him to put the premises into repair and in any case to keep the premises in repair throughout the term of the lease, and also to deliver up the premises in repair at the end of the lease. The use of the expression "to keep in good condition" imposes a more extensive standard than a covenant "to keep in repair" as considered in *Welsh v Greenwich LBC*.[260] In this case, the covenant "to keep in good condition" was construed to require the tenant to remedy condensation dampness.

The court held in *Twinmar Holdings Ltd v Klarius Ltd*[261] that it was well established that when considering a repairing covenant, the starting point for a tenant was to keep the premises in repair, having regard to their age, character and locality; this would make them

---

[260] [2000] 49 EG 118 (CA).
[261] [2013] EWHC 944.

reasonably fit for occupation of the tenant of the class who would be likely to take them.

(c) <u>To Leave the Premises in Repair</u>. This covenant is quite common in addition to (b) notwithstanding the obligation to deliver up in repair is implied in the covenant to keep in repair. The landlord cannot take advantage of this covenant until the lease comes to an end. Sometimes provision is made in the covenant or in another covenant for a survey before the end of the lease to determine the extent of any disrepair and for the surveyor to prepare a schedule of dilapidations, as appropriate (usually in respect of business premises).

The case *Sunlife Europe Properties Ltd v Tiger Aspect Holdings Ltd*[262] provides a useful reminder of the principles to be applied when settling a tenant's liability for dilapidations at the end of a lease. It also challenges previous dilapidation judgments, such as *Joyner v Weeks*,[263] and provides valuable lessons on the longstanding principle on dilapidations.

FAIR WEAR AND TEAR EXCEPTED

A covenant to repair by the tenant is sometimes qualified by the phrase "fair wear and tear excepted", which is a narrow exception. The effect of this exception (which is commonly found in short leases) is to relieve the tenant from liability arising from:

(a) normal and reasonable use by the tenant for the purpose for which the premises were let; and

(b) normal action of time and the elements of the weather as opposed to abnormal or extraordinary events in nature, such as floods, hurricane or earthquake.

The law on this topic was governed by *Taylor v Webb*[264] until it was overruled by *Brown v Davies*[265] in 1958. It was held in *Taylor v Webb* that a tenant would not be liable for consequential damage from the action of the ordinary elements for which the tenant is exempt

---

[262] [2013] EWHC 944.
[263] [1891] 2 QB 31.
[264] [1937] 2 KB 283.
[265] [1958] 1 QB 117.

under the phrase "fair wear and tear excepted". However, this is no longer the law, and the position now is that the tenant is to take care that the premises do not suffer more than the operation of time and nature would effect. He is bound to keep the premises as nearly as possible in the same condition as when it was let. The tenant must act reasonably in the circumstances and, although he is not strictly liable to replace a fallen slate off the roof, he may be bund to replace it to prevent rain getting in thereby causing damage to the premises.[266]

Another House of Lords' case is *Regis Property C Ltd v Dudley*[267] in 1958 which supports *Brown v Davies*. It was held that the tenant was bound to do such necessary repairs to prevent consequential damage flowing originally from wear and tear. In *Terrell v Murray*,[268] where the tenant's covenant to deliver in repair only contained a fair wear and tear exception, it was held that the tenant was not liable for painting the outside woodwork of the house, for repointing brickwork or for repairing parts of the kitchen floor affected by dry rot.

Meaning of Repair

"Repair" means making good damage so as to leave the house, flat or other building as far as possible as though it had not been damaged.[269] A normal covenant to repair in a lease will make the tenant or the landlord, as the case may be, liable "well and sufficiently to repair" the premises. "Repair" connotes the idea of making good damage so as to leave the premises as far as possible as though it had not been damaged.

Repair involves the renewal of subsidiary parts but not the whole where the whole is worn out. A worn out building is not to be made new. Time must be taken into account.

<u>How Far Repair Includes Renewal.</u> The extent at which one's liability to repair includes renewal is a matter of degree. A landlord who covenants to repair is not bound to modernise the premises.[270] But repair work must be done to modern standards so the result may be

---

[266] *Brown v Davies* [1958] 1 QB 117.
[267] [1959] AC 370.
[268] (1901) 17 TLR 570.
[269] *Calthorpe v McOscar* [1924] 1 KB 716 (CA).
[270] *Tiger Aspect Holdings Ltd v Sunlife Europe Properties Ltd* [2013] EWCA Civ 1656.

more satisfactory than the original construction.[271] If the premises are completely destroyed by fire or some other cause, the tenant may be liable to reinstate, unless he is exempt under the lease. From time to time certain parts, however small or large, will have to be renewed. However, if the building has to be rebuilt because of some inherent defect, then it seems that such rebuilding does not come within the meaning of the word "repair" and, therefore, the tenant is not liable.

It was held in *Proudfoot v Hart*[272] that the tenant was liable to replace completely a rotten floor but if the floor could be repaired he was not bound to put down a new floor. In *Lister v Lane and Nesham*,[273] it was held that the tenant was not liable under a repairing covenant to rebuild an inherently defective house. In *Lurcott v Wakeley & Wheeler*,[274] the tenant was liable for the whole cost of replacing the front wall of a house 200 years old, as the wall was merely a subsidiary part of the building. A tenant is not liable under a repairing covenant to carry out improvements.[275] In *Wood & Another v Cooper*,[276] a tenant was held liable to underpin a house under a repairing covenant, but in *Southeby v Grundy*[277] it was held that the tenant was not liable to replace defective foundations. If a structure has not deteriorated from a previous better condition, there is no disrepair that requires to be renewed.[278]

How Far Repair Includes Painting. In the absence of any covenant to paint, a repairing covenant may impose an obligation to paint. In *Monk v Noyes*,[279] it was held that a tenant's covenant to "substantially repair, uphold and maintain" a house required him to paint inside in order to prevent deterioration of the woodwork. However, in *Proudfoot v Hart*,[280] the Court of Appeal held while the tenant was not required to do purely decorative repairs under a covenant to repair, he was nevertheless liable to paint and paper in so far as necessary to

---

[271] *Ravenseft Properties Ltd v Davstone (Holdings) Ltd* [1980] QB 12.
[272] [1890] 25 QBD 42.
[273] [1893] 2 QB 212.
[274] [1911] 1 KB 905.
[275] *Collins v Flynn* [1963] 2 All ER 1068.
[276] (1934) EG November 10.
[277] [1947] 2 All ER 761.
[278] See *Post Office v Acquarius Properties Lltd* [1987] 1 All ER 1055 (CA); *Janet Reger International v Tirlee Ltd* [2006] EWHC 1743 (Ch).
[279] (1824) 1 C & P 265.
[280] [1890] 25 QBD 42.

make the house reasonably attractive for the class of persons likely to take it.

Standard of Repair. The phrase "well and sufficiently to repair" the premises means that the tenant of a short lease is obliged to hand back the premises in such a state as would satisfy a reasonably-minded tenant of the class likely to take the premises. The premises must be in such a state of repair, having regard to the age, character and locality, as would make it reasonably fit for occupation by the above tenant.[281]

The standard of repair may be more than the minimum in the circumstances. In *Gibson v Chesterton Plc*[282] the court ordered a replacement of a lift in circumstances where repairing the existing lift would have been a waste of time since it would have required repeated repairs in the future. Here the work to be done was once and for all. However, where the obligation to repair is on the tenant and repair and renewal are both viable options, the tenant is entitled to minimise his cost by electing which course to take.[283]

When the lease is for a long term and the character of the neighbourhood has altered the standard of repair must be judged by the conditions which prevailed when the lease was granted, and not the requirement of the class of tenants likely to take it at the end of the lease.

Condensation Dampness. This is a very common problem involving many claims by tenants of houses and flats. In *Southwark LBC v McIntosh*[284] it was upheld that there was no disrepair in respect of the presence of dampness, unless the damp arises from the disrepair to the structure or exterior of the dwelling or unless the damp itself has caused damage to the structure or exterior. Thus, damage to the tenant's goods or decorations by condensation dampness will not support a cause of action. This view was supported in *Lee v Leeds City Council*,[285] in which it was ruled that the earlier case, *Quick v Taff Ely BC*,[286] had been correctly decided. Despite the severe

---

[281] *Proudfoot v Hart* [1890] 25 QBD 42.
[282] [2002] EWHC 19.
[283] *Riverside Property Investments v Blackhawk Automative* [2005] 1 EGLR 114.
[284] [2002] 1 EGLR 25.
[285] [2003] 34 HLR 367 (CA).
[286] [1985] 3 WLR 981.

condensation caused by large metal windows resulting in dampness and damage to the tenant' possessions, he had no cause of action and, therefore, no remedy against the landlord as the latter had covenanted to repair only "the structure and exterior" of the flat.[287]

IMPLIED OBLIGATIONS TO REPAIR

The position of the landlord's obligations will be considered first. In respect of residential properties, they are extensive, mainly under statutes.

Common Law Liability on Landlord

Certain obligations to repair are imposed on landlords. This is the case despite the general rule that in the absence of an express obligation, there is no liability to repair.

Position at Commencement of Tenancy of Furnished Premises. The landlord has an implied obligation to ensure that furnished premises are fit for human habitation on commencement of the tenancy.[288] This common law position has been superseded by the Housing Act, 1985, as amended by the Local Government and Housing Act, 1989. These Acts are important as a guide in respect of determining fitness for human habitation.

Common Parts where Premises are let in a Large Building. Common parts in large buildings and blocks of flats housing many tenants are particularly prune to problems relating to upkeep by the landlords who are in control. Tenants have the use of the common parts which are outside of the premises occupied by them. The common parts comprise, but not limited to, entrance lobby, lifts, staircases, corridors and rubbish chutes. The responsibility for their maintenance falls on the landlord, who is reimbursed through the imposition of a service charge on each tenant. There is an implied obligation on the landlord with effect from 16 January, 1989, as to maintenance of the common parts. For tenancies entered into prior to this date, there may be an implied contractual duty of care as was the position in *Liverpool City*

---

[287] Implied by the L & T Act 1985, s11.
[288] Smith v Marrable (1843) 11 M & W (bugs) 242.

Council v Irwin.[289] The case involved a 15-storey block of flats rented out by the council, without a proper tenancy agreement. The tenancy document was referred to as "conditions of tenancy" but it was silent on the council's obligations. The common parts of the block were in a deplorable state: the lifts were out of order because of vandalism, and the stairs were poorly lit and also vandalised. In considering the conditions of the tenancy, the court held that as a matter of necessity a contractual obligation on the part of the landlord had to be implied into the contractual tenancy document. As such, this obligation imposed a duty of care upon council to maintain the common parts.

Such an implied contractual duty of care applies only to the common parts of a building within the control of the landlord. It is implied in circumstances so that no repair will render the contractual tenancy futile. It is not to be regarded as an absolute duty of care, as the landlord is only required to take reasonable care and applies only to the parties of the contract. Where there are defects in respect of the common parts within the control and management of the landlord, there is no need to serve any notice regarding disrepair.

<u>Common Law Obligation Imposed on Tenants</u>. This is in respect of the tenant's obligation to use the premises in a tenant-like manner. This was decided by Lord Denning in *Warren v Keen*:[290]

> "The tenant must take proper care of the place.... He must clean the chimneys, if necessary, and also the windows. He must mend the electric lights when it fuses. He must unstop the sink when blocked by his waste. In short, he must do the little jobs around the place that a reasonable tenant would do. In addition, he must, of course, not damage the house, wilfully or negligently and he must see that his family and guests do not damage it. If they do, he must repair it."

His Lordship went on to say that "If the house falls into disrepair through fair wear and tear or through lapse of time, or for any reason not cause by him, the tenant is not liable to repair it".

<u>Obligation of the Tenant not to Commit Waste</u>. The doctrine of waste and the tenant's obligation are discussed earlier in the chapter.

---

[289] [1977] AC 239.
[290] [1953] 2 All ER 1118 at p 1121; [1954] QB 15 at p 20.

Obligation of the Tenant to Enable the Landlord's Inspection. Normally an express tenancy will provide for the tenant to allow the landlord to inspect the premises to view their state and condition. Where there is no express agreement, it will be implied, but the landlord will have to serve reasonable notice on the tenant.

COVENANTS IMPLIED BY STATUTE

Implied obligations of the landlord in respect of repair to be carried out on the demised premises are based on a number of statutes.

Houses Let at a Low Rent and Houses on a Short Lease

There are two provisions in the Landlord and Tenant Act, 1985, to consider. One is in section 8(1) which is in respect of houses let at a low rent and the other is under section 11 in relation to houses let on a short lease.

Houses on a Low Rent. Where the letting is on a low rent,[291] it is implied under section 8(1)[292] on the part of the landlord:

(a) a condition at the beginning of the tenancy that the premises are fit for human habitation;[293] and

(b) an undertaking that in the course of the tenancy the premises will be kept in all respects fit for human habitation.

As regards fitness for human habitation, regard shall be had to the following matters set out under section 10 of the 1985 Act:

(a) repair;

(b) stability;

---

[291] The maximum rent limit (unchanged since 1957) is £80 pa in London and £52 pa elsewhere. This limit on rent ensures that the section virtually never applies to recently created leases. Section 8 applies to a lease of dwelling house not exceeding three years if the tenant is to put the premises into repair.

[292] Notwithstanding any agreement to the contrary (words used in section 8.1 itself).

[293] The factors to take into account regarding fitness for human habitation are in section 10 of the 1985.

(c) freedom from damp;

(d) internal arrangement;

(e) natural lighting;

(f) ventilation;

(g) water supply;

(h) drainage and sanitary conveniences; and

(i) facilities for preparation and cooking of food and for the disposal of waste water.

The house shall be regarded as unfit for human habitation if it is defective in one or more of the above matters that it is not reasonably suitable for occupation in that condition.

Regardless of any express obligation to the contrary, these terms will be implied. However, where there is a letting for more than three years and there is an agreement placing an obligation on the tenant to keep the premises in habitable condition, section 8 will be excluded. Although "house" is referred to in the section, it includes flats and bed sits, and tenancies include all sub-tenancies, but licences are excluded. In view of the very low rent limit that has been set for the application of the provision and the escalation of market rents in recent years, the section is now largely irrelevant.

<u>Short Leases and Tenancies Under 7 Years</u>. In the majority of periodic tenancies and short leases granted for less than seven years, section 11 of the Landlord and Tenant Act, 1985, will apply regarding the imposition of a repairing obligation on the landlord. The section applies to any lease or tenancy granted after 24 October, 1961.[294] Section 11 does not apply to business premises, agricultural holdings or to tenancies by local authorities and the Crown granted after 3 October, 1980,

Section 11(1) states:

---

[294] First enacted under the Housing Act, 1961. ss 32 & 33.

"(1) in a lease to which this section applies...there is implied a covenant by the lessor-

- (a) to keep in repair the structure and exterior of the dwelling-house (including drains, gutters and external pipes),
- (b) to keep in repair and proper working order the installations in the dwelling house for the supply of gas, water, and electricity and for sanitation including basins, sinks, baths and sanitary conveniences, but not other fixtures and fittings and appliances for making use of gas, water or electricity, and
- (c) to keep in repair and proper working order the installations in the dwelling-house for space heating and heating water."

The parties cannot contract out of section 11 (as indeed section 8) as section 12(1) specifically prevents any agreement contrary to section 11. But under section 12(2) the county court may:

"... by order made with the consent of the parties, authorise the inclusion in a lease, or in an agreement collateral to a lease, of provisions excluding or modifying in relation to the lease, the provisions of section 11 with respect to the repairing obligations of the parties if it appears to the court that it is reasonable to do so, having regard to all the circumstances of the case, including the other terms and conditions of the lease."

The onus of proving that a particular defect is covered by section 11 is on the tenant.[295] It is not sufficient to show that the premises are damp. The tenant must establish that the cause of the damp is due to the landlord's breach of covenant.[296]

As under section 8, the landlord has the right under section 11(6) on giving 24 hours written notice to enter the premises to view their state and condition. His liability to repair arises when a defect has become patent and was made known to him.[297]

Section 11 does not impose any duty on a landlord:

---

[295] *Foster v Day* (1968) 208 EG 495 CA (Civ Div).
[296] *Southwark LBC v McIntosh* [2002] 1 EGLR 25 Ch D.
[297] *O'Brien & Another v Robinson* [*1973*] A.C. 912 (Housing Act 1961 s.32); [1973] AC 912, (1973) 226 EG 297.

(a) to carry out works or repairs for which the lessee is liable by virtue of his duty to use the premises in a tenant-like manner.[298] Therefore, the tenant is liable to perform minor everyday repairs about the house;

(b) to rebuild or reinstate the premises in case of destruction or damage by fire, or tempest or flood or other inevitable accidents;[299] and

(c) to keep in repair or maintain anything which the tenant is entitled to remove from the dwelling-house.[300]

Meaning of Structure and Exterior

In this regard, a body of case law has been developed over the years. Structure was held in *Irvine v Moran*[301] not to include the entire dwelling-house, but only those elements that gave it its essential appearance, stability and shape. It should be noted that the implied covenants only apply to the structure and exterior of the dwelling-house, i.e., a third floor flat and not the whole building. In *Camden Hill Towers v Gardner*[302] the structure and exterior of a flat was held to include:

(a) the outside walls of the flat and the outside of the interior of the party walls;

(b) the outer sides of the horizontal divisions between the flat and those above and below, and the ceilings and walls of the flat; and

(c) the structural framework and beams directly supporting the floors, ceilings and walls of the flat.

The above will count as the "structure and exterior" regardless whether they form part of the demise to the tenant, but other essential parts of the building will not form part of the "structure and exterior" of the flat. For example, if the roof is in disrepair, the tenant will not

---

[298] Section 11(2)(a) of the Landlord and Tenant Act, 1985.
[299] Section 11(2)(b).
[300] Section 11(2)(c).
[301] [1991] 1 EGLR 261.
[302] [1977] QB 823.

be able to compel the landlord to carry out repairs to the roof under section 11, but a tenant on the top floor will be able to do so.[303]

However, in respect of tenancies granted after 15 January, 1989, a new subsection 11(1A)[304] is inserted in section 11 of the 1985 Act to resolve difficulties in earlier cases. But a tenant will only be able to rely on section 11(1A) where the disrepair is such as to affect the lessee's enjoyment of the dwelling-house or any common parts which the lessee is entitled to use.[305]

Windows of a dwelling-house are regarded as part of the exterior[306] and the same applies to elements such as plasterwork.[307] Floor joists which are entirely within a tenant's flat may also be regarded as part of the structure since they are integral to the structure of the whole building.[308]

Meaning of Installations. The obligation to keep installations covered by section 11 above in proper working order may also include the need to remedy design faults that cause problems in their use. In *Liverpool City Council v Irwin*[309] a landlord was obliged to replace cisterns that had caused WCs to overflow. The problem was due to a design fault. As with the structure and exterior, the liability of the landlord in respect of tenancies granted after 15 January, 1989, is extended to include an installation which serves a dwelling-house and either forms any part of the building in which the lessor has an interest or is owned by him and is under his control.

Under section 15 of the Landlord and Tenant Act, 1985, the county court has jurisdiction "to make a declaration that section 11 (repairing obligations) applies, or does not apply, to a lease—

(a) whatever the net annual value of the property in question, and

(b) notwithstanding that no other relief is sought than a declaration."

---

[303] See *Douglas-Scott v Scourgie* [1984] 1 WLR 716 (CA); cf *Rapid Results College Ltd v Angell* [1986] 1 EGLR 53 (CA).
[304] Inserted by section 116(1) of the Housing Act, 1988.
[305] Section 11 (1B) of the 1985 Act.
[306] *Ball & Plummer* (1879) 2 TLR 877 (CA).
[307] *Staves and Staves v Leeds City Council* (1992) 29 EG 119,
[308] *Marlborough Park Services v Rowe* [2006] 2 EGLR 27 (CA).
[309] [1977] AC 239.

An interesting case under section 11 is *Edwards v Kumarasamy*[310] in which the long leaseholder of a flat was held liable to his subtenant under the 1985 Act for disrepair to communal areas outside of his demise by virtue of having a right over those areas. Edwards injured himself on the defective pathway outside the building. Under the subtenancy, section 11 implies an obligation on Kumarasamy "to keep in repair...any part of the building in which the lessor has an estate or interest." The Court of Appeal held that Kumarasamy's right to use the communal path was a legal easement and, therefore, he had an estate or interest. The path was not part of the building but the court said it was part of the exterior of the building, relying on the decision of *Brown v Liverpool Corporation*.[311] As for the argument that no notice was received regarding the defect of the path, the court said that the general rule is that a covenant to repair obliges the landlord to keep in repair at all times. Here the defect was outside the demised premises and, therefore, there was no need to give notice.

Occupiers Liability Act 1957

The 1957 Act imposes liability on people, including tenants, occupying land.[312] Section 2 provides that:

> "(1) An occupier of premises owes the same duty, the 'common duty of care,' to all his visitors, except in so far as he is free to and does extend, restrict, modify his duty to any visitor or visitors by agreement or otherwise.
>
> (2) The common duty of care is a duty to take such care as in all the circumstances of the case is reasonable to see that the visitor will be reasonably safe in using the premises for the purposes for which he is invited or permitted by the occupier to be there.
>
> (3) The circumstances relevant for the present purpose include the degree of care, and of want of care, which would ordinarily be looked for in such a visitor so that (for example) in proper cases -

---

[310] [2015] EWCA Civ 20.
[311] (1983) 13 HLR 1.
[312] See *Drysdale v Hedges* [2012] 3 EGLR 105. The tenant who was the occupier sued the landlord but the claim was dismissed.

(a) an occupier must be prepared for children to be less careful than adults; and

(b) an occupier may expect that a person, in the exercise of his calling, will appreciate and guard against any special risks ordinarily incident to it, so far as the occupier leaves him free to do so."

An occupier of land is usually the person who has control of the premises. Therefore, a tenant with exclusive possession is the person in control, and the landlord is excluded, except where he retains control of any part of the premises, such as common parts of a block of flats.

The term "visitor" covers any person to whom the landlord has granted implied or express consent to enter. A postman is said to be a visitor, and the same applies to guests of the tenant. The tenant and his family members are visitors in respect of the common parts of a building. As mentioned in section 2(3) the occupier is under a greater duty to children than to adult visitors. Section 2(4) goes on to state that any warning notice to visitors will not absolve him from liability "unless in all the circumstances it was enough to enable the visitor to be reasonably safe". Likewise, an occupier will not be absolved from responsibility in respect of an independent contractor, unless he had acted reasonably in choosing the contractor to do the work.

In the case of business premises, the Unfair Contract Terms Act, 1977, demands that any exclusion of liability by the occupier be shown to be reasonable in all the circumstances, and that liability for personal injury or death cannot be excluded. The 1957 Act imposes a broad liability on the occupier, but with regard to getting the landlord to do any repair work it is of limited use. This is because it applies only to those parts of a building for which the landlord has retained control and, secondly, no liability arises until an actual injury takes place.

Defective Premises Act 1972

This Act under section 1 imposes a duty on a person or persons who undertake work in relation to the provision of a dwelling:

(a) to carry out the work in a professional workmanlike manner;

(b) to ensure proper materials are used; and

(c) to ensure in respect of the work that the dwelling will be fit for habitation when completed.

Section 1 applies to all in connection with the construction industry, such as builders, architects, engineers, surveyors, developers and local authorities involved in the provision of housing. However, section 2 of the Act prevents the application of section 1 to dwellings which are covered by an approved scheme of protection such as the NHBC. Another restriction is with regard to the limitation period of six years,[313] which starts to run on completion of the building. Further, it will apply to work carried out after commencement of the Act, i.e., 1 January, 1974.

Section 3 applies to any work carried out prior to any sale or letting. It is concerned with the duty of care in negligence upon any person carrying out works of construction, repair, maintenance or demolition. The duty imposed by the Act is owed to any person who might reasonably be affected by any resultant defect. Tenants, family members and visitors are covered. The duty continues if the property is sold or let. However, if the defect arises on a failure to perform work, section 3 will not provide a remedy.

With regard to landlord and tenant law, section 4 is the most important section. It provides:

> "(1) Where premises are let under a tenancy which puts on the landlord an obligation to the tenant for the maintenance or repair of the premises, the landlord owes to all persons who might reasonably be expected to be affected by defects in the state of the premises a duty to take such care as is reasonable in all the circumstances to see that they are reasonably safe from personal injury or from damage to their property caused by a relevant defect."

The above includes an obligation implied into the contract by the common law or by statute as well in respect of an express contract to repair. By virtue of section 4(4) of the Act, a landlord who has an express or implied right to enter the premises in order to carry out any

---

[313] Limitation Act, 1980, provides various limitation periods, but for a simple contract it is 6 years.

description of maintenance and repair is treated in relation to section 4 as if he were under a repairing obligation.

Where a landlord is under an obligation to repair, section 4 will not increase the obligation.[314] Further, a landlord has no duty to make premises safe in the absence of disrepair, such as to install a safety glass in a front door.[315]

Knowledge of the Defect. Section 4(2) of the act provides:

> "(2) The said duty is owed if the landlord knows (whether as the result of being notified by the tenant or otherwise) or if he ought in all the circumstances to have known of the relevant defect."

From the above subsection the landlord does not have to be aware of the defect but will be liable if he ought to have been aware of it. In *Clarke v Taff Ely BC*[316] a tenant was injured when a floor collapsed. Although no notice was served on the council regarding the state of the floor, the council was under an obligation to repair and had the right to enter and inspect the premises, which were old.[317]

In *Drysdale v Hedge*[318] it was held that the landlord did not owe a duty of care to her tenant who was injured on painted steps of her property. The tenant alleged that the landlord had breached section 2 of the Occupiers Liability Act, 1957, section 4 of the Defective Premises Act, 1972, and/or the tenancy agreement and the common law. The court held that the landlord was not liable under the 1957 Act because the landlord was not the occupier of the steps as they had been demised to Drysdale. As regards section 4 of the 1972 Act, there was no breach of duty as there was no disrepair. In such a case the only duty of the landlord is to take reasonable care not to create an unnecessary risk of injury.

---

[314] *McNerny v Lambeth LBC* (1988) 21 HLR 188 (flat suffered from condensation dampness).
[315] *Alker v Collingwood Housing Association* [2007] EWCA Civ 343; [2007] HLR 29 (CA) (Civ Div).
[316] (1984) 10 HLR 44.
[317] See also *Smith v Bradford Metropolitan council* (1982) 44 P&CR 171 (CA).
[318] [2012] 3 EGLR 105.

Housing Act 2004

This Act contains a new provision for assessing housing standards in respect of dwelling-houses based on an assessment of hazards. Section 1(3) of the 2004 Act summarises the position relating to hazards. Where a local housing authority regards hazards coming within level 1 and level 2 a number of courses may be taken:

(a) improvement notices may be served on persons having control, such as landlords for leased premises but not tenants paying full rents;[319]

(b) where there is an imminent risk of serious harm to occupiers, the authority may carry out emergency remedial action itself and recoup the expenses under sections 40-42;

(c) prohibition and emergency prohibition orders may be served to restrict the use of the premises under sections 20-27 and 43-45; or

(d) most dramatically a demolition order may be made.[320]

HOUSES IN MULTIPLE OCCUPATION (HMO)

The manager of a HMO, i.e., the person who receives the rent or other payments from tenants or licensees in occupation, has certain statutory repairing duties. An HMO, subject to certain exceptions, is one:

(a) which consists of more than one unit of living accommodation which are not self-contained flats, or it is a self-contained flat and, unless it is a converted building, at least one basic item is shared or missing;

---

[319] *White v Barnet LBC* [1990] 2 QB 328.
[320] Under section 300 the authority may purchase such premises and use them for temporary housing. In *Salford City Council v McNally* [1976] AC 379 this use lasted for seven years in spite of the statutory nuisance. This was a paradoxical situation as the nuisance was condoned for seven years.

(b) which is the only or main residence of the occupiers, who put it to no other use and at least one of them pays rent or provides some other consideration.

There is an obligation in respect of the following:

(a) to maintain and repair the building;

(b) to provide means of escape from fire and there must be no obstruction;

(c) to keep water supply and the drainage system in good, clean and working condition;

(d) to keep the common parts in a safe and working condition and reasonably free of obstruction;

(e) keep outbuildings and yard used by more than one household in repair, clean condition and good order;

(f) to maintain boundary walls, fences, railings in good and safe repair; and

(g) to keep living accommodation including windows and other means of ventilation in good repair, with any fixtures, fittings and appliances in good repair and working order.

A failure to comply with the regulations without reasonable excuse is an offence. The maximum fine on summary conviction is up to the level five scale (£5000).[321]

REMEDIES AND RIGHTS

These are considered under those of the landlord and those of the tenant.

---

[321] Housing Act, 2004, s 234(3) - (5).

Landlord' Remedies and Rights

There are many remedies which include forfeiture, damages, entering to carry out repairs, specific performance and protocol for terminal dilapidations.

Forfeiture.[322] Where this right is expressly provided for in the lease, i.e., re-entry on forfeiture, the landlord may be able to forfeit the tenant's lease for breach of the covenant to repair. He is required to serve a notice upon the tenant in accordance with section 146 of the LPA, 1925. In response to such a notice, the tenant can apply to the court for relief. Where the lease is for seven or more years, with more than three years unexpired, the landlord will have to comply with section 1 of the Leasehold Property (Repairs) Act, 1938.

Damages. An action for damages for the breach during the currency of the lease will reflect the amount by which the value of the reversion has been diminished by reason of the tenant's failure to repair. The amount of damages recoverable will depend on the number of years remaining before the end. The longer the period the lower will be the damages. The cost of putting the premises into repair is not taken into account during the currency of the lease. The total amount of damages, subject to the limit in section 18 of the Landlord and Tenant Act, 1927, cannot exceed the amount by which the reversion has been diminished on account of the breach. If the cost of putting the premises in good repair at the end of the lease is higher the landlord will recover the diminution in value of the reversion, and *vice versa*.[323] No claim can be made for damages for disrepair if the landlord intends to redevelop the property.[324] As it is not practical to obtain valuation evidence in most cases, the amount of damages awarded is usually the cost of the repairs.[325]

---

[322] In the case of residential premises, a landlord requires a court order to re-enter.
[323] See *Latimer v Carney* [2006] EWCA Civ 1417, [2007] 1 P & CR 13. The decision in *Ruxley Electronics Ltd v Forsyth* [1996] 1 AC 344 (cost of cure not awarded for breach of building contract where cost unreasonable and client had no intention to rebuild even if damages were awarded) applies here by analogy (but subject to the cap imposed by section 18 of the L & T Act, 1927): *PGF II SA v Royal Sun Alliance Insurance plc* [2010] EWHC 1459 (TCC).
[324] Section 18(1) of the 1927 Act.
[325] *Latimer v Carney* [2006] 50 EG 86.

There is a limit to the award of damages as in *Van Del Footwear Ltd v Ryman Ltd*.[326] What had to be determined in this case was the drop in the value of the reversion. The court was required to ascertain the actual value at the date of re-entry and the value if there was no breach of covenant. In making these valuations, the lease which had ended and any new lease which might have been negotiated were ignored.

A landlord's loss of rent due to delay in re-letting is recoverable, but subject to a statutory cap [327] on the total amount of the damages.[328] The court has confirmed that even where outdated property stands little or no chance of being re-let, following a tenant's departure, it is still possible for the landlord to succeed in a claim for damages for the loss in value to the reversion caused by the breach of the tenant's repairing covenants.[329]

Long Leases. There are special restrictions in obtaining an order for forfeiture or for damages for disrepair in respect of a lease for more than seven years of which more than three years are unexpired.[330] There are strict procedural requirements for the landlord to follow, whether in respect of forfeiture or for damages. A notice under section 146 of the LPA, 1925, has to be served on the tenant informing him of his right under section 1(4) of the 1938 Act. There is a counter-notice procedure for the tenant to follow whereby the landlord cannot proceed further without leave of the court, which will only be granted if the landlord can establish to the normal civil standard of proof[331] one of the five grounds set out in section1(5) of the 1938 Act.

Entering to Carry Out Repairs. The landlord has a right to enter to carry out repairs, where he is liable to do the repairs. It is usual to insert a provision in the lease for the landlord to enter to do repairs for

---

[326] [2009] EWCA Civ 1478.
[327] Landlord and Tenant Act, 1927, s 18.
[328] See *Hammersmith Properties (Welwyn) Ltd v Saint-Gobain Ceramics and Plastic Ltd and another* [2013] EWHC 1161 (TCC)
[329] *Ibid.*
[330] Leasehold Property (Repairs) Act, 1938, s 7(1).
[331] See *Associated British Ports v C H Bailey plc* [1990] 1 All ER 929.

which the tenant has failed to carry out. The landlord can recover the cost of repairs for which the tenant is liable as a debt from him.[332]

Specific Performance. This remedy can be obtained in appropriate circumstances.[333] The tenant must be informed exactly what works are required to be carried out and a workable agreement for supervision of the said works should be in place. Very rarely this remedy can be obtained.

Protocol for Terminal Dilapidations. A Protocol has been prepared by the Law Reform Sub-Committee of the Property Litigation Association. It relates to claims for damages on account of the tenant's repairing obligations. Once it is incorporated into the CPR, it will encourage and facilitate early settlement of dilapidation claims or the management of proceedings if litigation is necessary.

Tenant's Remedies and Rights

For the tenant the rights and remedies are damages, self-help, interim injunctions, specific performance, appointment of a receiver, and appointment of a manager

Damages. The tenant will be able to recover damages[334] for his losses resulting from the landlord's failure to repair, either under an express or implied covenant. In *Uddin v Islington LBC*[335] the appellant local authority was liable in damages for breach of its repairing obligations in respect of a flat that had been damaged by rising damp. The tenant is prevented from claiming damages in respect of any period before the landlord becomes aware of the want of repair. Once the tenant has served a notice on the landlord to carry out the repairs, a reasonable time must be allowed for him to effect the repairs. He cannot recover any damages if he refuses to allow the landlord to carry out the repairs.[336] The amount of damages recoverable will depend upon the

---

[332] *Jervis v Harris* [1996] 1 All ER 303 (CA); [1996] Ch 195. The amount is not restricted by s 18(1) of the 1927 Act which applies only to a claim for damages.
[333] *Rainbow Estates v Tokenhold* [1998] 2 All ER 860.
[334] Damages must be proved and may well be low. See *Wallace v Manchester City Council* (1998) 30 HLR 1111 (the judge can choose to award a proportion of the rent or a global sum (or a mixture).
[335] [2015] EWCA Civ 369; [2015] HLR 28 CA,
[336] *Granada Theatres Ltd v Freehold Investment (Leytonstone) Ltd* [1959] Ch 529.

particular circumstances. In an appropriate case, the tenant may do the repairs himself and claim the cost from the landlord. A claim can be made for various losses suffered by reason of the disrepair.[337] Damages can be awarded for ill-health resulting from lack of repair. In *Brent LBC v Carmel*[338] an amount of £50,000 was awarded for consequential ill health.

Pure economic loss is not recoverable for breach of a landlord's repairing covenant. Such a loss would only be recoverable if a duty of care could be established in tort.[339] This is not normally possible in a landlord and tenant situation.[340]

Self Help. On a failure of the landlord to carryout his repairing obligations, the tenant can carry out the necessary repairs and deduct the cost from the future rent.[341] Before taking this course of action, the tenant must inform the landlord of the want of repair and that the required repairs are within the repairing obligations of the landlord.

Interim Injunctions. In exceptional circumstances, the tenant may apply to the court for an interim injunction requiring the landlord to take action to do the repairs before the case is fully argued in court. Before any interim injunction is ordered, the court should be satisfied of an immediate need for the work to be done.[342] An application to the court should normally be made on notice to the landlord, having regard to the procedure in set out in the CPR, Parts 23 and 25.

Specific Performance. The remedy may be granted under section 17 of the Landlord and Tenant Act, 1985. In this regard, the Act provides that in any proceedings in which a tenant of a dwelling alleges a breach by the landlord of a repairing covenant in respect of the dwelling, the court may order specific performance of the covenant. The order may require the landlord to carry out the required repairs not only in the actual dwelling but also in the common parts of the building as may be appropriate. This is a discretionary remedy, not

---

[337] *Calabar v Sticher* [1983] 3 All Er 759; [1984] 1 WLR 287, and *Mira v Aylmer Square Investments Ltd* [1990] 1 EGLR 45 (CA).
[338] (1995) 30 HLR 203.
[339] *Caparo Industries plc v Dickman* [1990] 2 AC 605 (HL).
[340] *Eaton Square Properties Ltd v Shaw* [2011] EWHC 2115 (QB).
[341] *Lee-parker v Izzet.* [1971] 3 All ER 1099; [1971] 1 WLR 1688.
[342] *Parker v Camden LPC* [1986] Ch 162.

available as of right, and section 17 does not apply in respect of business premises. But in an appropriate case a tenant may obtain an order of specific performance under the court's general equitable jurisdiction.[343] On a failure of the landlord to comply with the order against him, he can be committed to prison for contempt of court. This is an obvious advantage to the tenant in getting the landlord to act without undue delay.

Until recently it was assumed by some people that it was not possible to obtain a decree of specific performance to enforce a repairing covenant in a lease. However, it has been held that such a decree is possible as in *Rainbow Estates Ltd v Tokenhold Ltd*.[344] But it should not be used to circumvent the tenant's protection given by the Leasehold Property (Repairs) Act, 1938.

Appointment of a Receiver. This situation can arise where a landlord has failed to manage a building containing many tenants, such as non-collection of rents and not carrying out repairs for many years,[345] or in a situation where the landlord cannot be traced. In such a case the court may appoint a receiver to carry out the landlord's duties under section 37(1) of the Supreme Court Act, 1981, or section 38 of the County Court Act, 1984, and the County Court Rules, 1981. This procedure does not apply over the management of local authority housing.[346]

In *Gay v Standard Homes & Counties Properties Ltd*[347] a receiver was appointed but was unable to remedy the considerable neglect. Therefore, the court concluded that the appointment of a receiver would not be adequate.

Appointment of a Manager. With regard to a block with two or more flats, a tenant may apply to a leasehold valuation tribunal (LVT) for the appointment of a manager where the landlord persistently fails to maintain the block.[348] The landlord must be informed of the intended application to the LVT, and if he fails to take action to remedy the

---

[343] See *Jeune v Queens Cross Properties Ltd* [1974] Ch 97; [1973] 3 All ER 97.
[344] [1999] Ch 64.
[345] See *Hart v Emelkirk* [1983] 3 All ER 15; [1983] 1 WLR 1289.
[346] *Parker v Camden LBC* [1986] Ch 162; [1985] 2 All ER 141 (CA).
[347] [1994] 1 EGLR 119 Ch D.
[348] Under Part II of the Landlord and Tenant Act, 1987, as amended by the Housing Act, 1996, ss 85 & 86.

disrepair, the tribunal may appoint a manager to take over the running of the block. Before making the appointment, the tribunal must be satisfied:

(a) that the landlord is in breach;

(b) the breach is likely to continue; and

(c) that it is just and convenient in all the circumstances to make the order.

These provisions are applicable to a local authority landlord, a resident landlord or if the tenant is a business tenant.[349]

End

---

[349] Section 21(3) of the Landlord and Tenant Act, 1987.

CHAPTER 8

FIXTURES

INTRODUCTION

The general rule is that whatever is annexed to the land (soil) becomes part of the land This rule is based on the operation of the ancient maxim *"quicquid plantatur solo, solo cedit"*. Any chattel annexed to the land becomes part of the freehold and could not be removed even by the tenant who put it there, except those for trade, ornamental and domestic purposes and also where there is an agreement to the contrary.

Apart from the exceptions, fixtures are articles, or chattels, which have become legally inseparable from the land. This position has been arrived at by case law.

A fixture is something of chattel nature annexed to land. By annexation, the thing ceases to be a chattel in the legal sense and becomes part of the land,[350] which includes buildings and other improvements on the land.

Definition. A definition of a fixture may be given as any article which is:

(a) annexed to land and/or buildings;

(b) for the purpose of permanently improving the land or buildings; and

(c) is of a kind capable of making such permanent improvement.

It is sometimes difficult to decide whether an article has become a fixture. It is usually a question of law for the judge[351] as opposed to a question of fact and, therefore, must be decided by the court in the event of a dispute between the landlord and the tenant. The decision in one case is no sure guide in another; everything turns upon the

---

[350] In *Elitestone Ltd v Morris* [1997] 1 WLR 687, M & B p 98, HL prefers a tripartite classification into chattels, fixtures and objects which are part and parcel of the land; [1998] Conv 418 (H. Conway).
[351] *Reynolds v Ashby & Son* [1904] AC 466.

circumstances and mainly, but not decisively, upon two particular circumstances:

(a) the degree of annexation; and

(b) the object of annexation.[352]

Whether an article has become a fixture is a matter of degree and varies with the circumstances of the case, depending upon the extent to which the three elements of the definition given above are satisfied.

ORIGIN OF THE LAW OF FIXTURES

In its broad sense a "fixture" includes anything of a chattel nature which is attached to land. However, the origin of the "law of fixtures" is the recognition of the courts to allow limited owners, e.g., tenants, to remove articles annexed to the land and, accordingly, the term "fixtures" includes only those items of a chattel nature attached to land concerning which the question of removal might arise.

<u>Distinction Between Buildings and Fixtures.</u> In so far as the relationship of landlord and tenant is concerned, there is a distinction drawn between "buildings" and "fixtures" for there is no question of removing buildings, or any part of the structure, let to him. Buildings of a permanent and substantial character with firm foundations below the surface are not regarded as fixtures.

It was held in *Boswell v The Crucible Steel Co of America*[353] that "a fixture is something which has been affixed to the freehold as accessory to the house. It does not include things which are part of the house itself in the course of its construction."

From the above case it follows that fixtures do not necessarily include a building or anything which may properly be considered as part of the structure of a building. Thus, the tenant is bound to deliver

---

[352] *Holland v Hodgson* (1872) LR7 CP 387 at p 334 per Blackburn J. See *Melluish v BMI (No 3) Ltd* [1996] AC 545 (contractual term that object shall remain a chattel not decisive: "The concept of a fixture remains personal or removable property is a contradiction in terms and impossibility in law"; [1995] Ch 90 at p 115 per Dilllon LJ in CA.

[353] [1924] [1925] 1 K.B 119.

up all buildings and erections in the nature of buildings at the end of the lease, including any buildings, or parts of buildings, constructed by him at his own expense during the lease, whether for domestic or for trade purposes. However the law, as it is, can be contracted out of to take into account any agreement to the contrary.

As far as lightly constructed buildings are concerned, i.e., those erections which are not securely attached, they are usually removable if erected by the tenant. For example, a wooden windmill and a greenhouse resting on a brick foundation, but not attached thereto, have been held to be chattels. If they were erected by the tenant for the purpose of his trade, they are removable as "trade fixtures".

Chattels. The term "chattels" or "goods and chattels" is the legal name for all physical and material things which are excluded from the legal conception of the word "land", such as furnishings in a house, tools to practise one's vocation, and so on.

EXCEPTIONS TO THE GENERAL RULE UNDER THE COMMON LAW

The harshness under the general rule under the common law, i.e., *quicquid plantatur solo, solo cedit*, has been mitigated by the courts which have allowed tenants to remove fixtures in the following two cases:

1. Fixtures annexed by the tenant for the purpose of his trade.[354] However, these are not removable if to do so would necessitate the destruction of the property to which they are attached.

   Trade fixtures include engine, boilers, pipes and transmission gear, vats and coppers, fixed machinery, fittings and partitions in shops and offices, buildings of light construction, hot-houses and green houses erected by a nurseryman or market

---

[354] *Poole's case* (1703) 1 Salk 368. For a comprehensive discussion of tenant's fixtures in the context of steelwork see *Peel Land & Property (Ports No 3) Ltd v T S Sherness Steel Ltd* [2014] EWCA Civ 100.

gardener. Engines for working collieries,[355] and floor fittings and light fittings,[356] among many other items, have been held to come within the description of trade fixtures.

2. Fixtures erected by the tenant for the purpose of domestic convenience or for ornament. The tenant may remove fixtures he has attached for domestic convenience or ornament provided that they can be removed in their entirety or at least without seriously damaging the freehold. Any damage caused by removing fixtures must be remedied by the tenant.

In *Buckland v Butterfield*,[357] where a conservatory had been erected by the tenant, it was held that it did not come within the exception of "ornamental fixtures" as it could be removed only with substantial damage to the house.

<u>Domestic Fixtures</u>. These include fire-places, furnaces and coppers, stoves and grates, iron backs to chimneys, chimney pieces and over mantels, wainscoting and panelling, cornices and picture rails, baths and wash-basins, blinds, curtain rods, radiators, gas or electric light radiators.

In addition to these exceptions, a further exception has been made by statute in the case of agricultural fixtures.

3. Agricultural fixtures removable under section 10 of the Agricultural Hondings Act, 1986.[358] This exception was first enacted under the Landlord and Tenant Act, 1851. In the case of a farm business tenancy created under the Agriculture Tenancies Act, 1995, fixtures can be removed almost at will during the term of the tenancy.

---

[355] *Lawton v Lawton* (1743) 3 Atk 13. Cf *Herbert v British Railways Board* (2000) 4 L&T Rev D13 rails and sleepers removed by tenant railway board from disused railway line held to be landlord's fixtures, not tenant's).
[356] *Young v Dalgetty plc* [1987] ! EGLR 116.
[357] (1820) 2 Brod & B 54.
[358] Formerly under the Agricultural Holdings Act, 1948.

However, the parties to a tenancy may modify by agreement the above three exceptions. Also, the right of removal of fixtures by the tenant may be extended by local custom or trade usage.[359]

FACTORS TO TAKE INTO ACCOUNT

To decide whether a chattel has become a fixture certain important factors, including those embodied in the definition, must be taken into account. These factors are set out below under annexation and the probable effect of severing the fixtures

Annexation

A chattel may become a fixture simply by attaching it to the land. By annexation to the soil a thing may cease to be a chattel and may become part and parcel of the land. The extent of annexation is not decisive.[360] The degree and object of annexation must also be considered as these vary from case to case.

(a) <u>Degree of Annexation</u>. The general rule is that the chattel must be actually attached to the land. An article is *prima facie* a fixture if it is substantially connected to the land or to a building thereon. If the article, e.g., a cistern, merely rests on the land or building by its own weight, it is *prima facie* not a fixture.[361] But a chattel which is attached to the land or building in some substantial manner, e.g., by nails, etc, will, on the face of it, be a fixture, notwithstanding the fact that it may be easily removed, e.g., fireplaces, panelling and a conservatory on a brick foundation.[362]

---

[359] *Wake v Hall* (1883) 8 App Cas 195.
[360] *Chelsea Yacht & Boat Co Ltd v Pope* [2000] 1 WLR 1941. In this case Blackburn J said: "Perhaps the true rule is, that articles not otherwise attached to the land by their true weight than by their own weight are not to be considered as part of the land, unless the circumstances as such are to shew that they were intended to be part of the land, the onus of showing that they were so intended lying on those who assert that they have ceased to be chattels; and that, on the contrary, an article which is affixed to the land even slightly is to be considered as part of the land, unless the circumstances are such as to shew that it was intended all along to continue a chattel, the onus lying on those who contend that it is a chattel."
[361] *Mather Fraser* (1856) 2 K. & J 536.
[362] *Buckland v Butterfield* (1820) 2 Brod & B 54.

It was held in *Hulme v Brigham*[363] that a printing machine weighing several tons was merely secured by its own weight to the floor and, therefore, it was not a fixture because, *inter alia*, it could be removed without losing its identity.

The degree of annexation is not of great importance in itself and, therefore, must be considered in relation to the nature of the article and the object of attaching it.

(b) <u>Object or Purpose of Annexation</u>. The intention of the person attaching the article is of paramount importance. The object of this test is to decide whether the chattel was fixed for its better enjoyment as a chattel or for the better enjoyment of the land. In other words, if the intention of the tenant was that the attachment of the chattel was only temporary for the better enjoyment of the chattel itself, then the article was to make a permanent and substantial improvement to the premises the article is a fixture.

In *Leigh v Taylor*[364] it was held that a valuable tapestry tacked to a framework, which was nailed to a wall, was not a fixture since the tapestry was annexed for the purpose of its better enjoyment as a chattel.

The following have been held to be chattels and, therefore, removable:

(i) a collection of stuffed birds in cages nailed to the walls;[365]

(ii) an electric light bulb;[366] and

(iii) an army hut bolted to the ground.[367]

In *Botham v TSB Bank plc*[368] the Court of Appeal examined household appliances and held that items such as baths, lavatories,

---

[363] [1943] KB 152.
[364] [1902] AC 157.
[365] *Viscount Hill v Bullock* [1897] 2 Ch. 482 204.
[366] *British Economical Lamp Co Ltd v Empire Mile End Ltd* (1913) 29 TLR 386 ; 31 Digest 186, 3205......143
[367] *Billing v Pill* [1954] 1 Q.B. 70.
[368] (1996) 73 P&CR D1; *Chelsea Yacht & Boat Co Ltd v Pope* [2000] 1 WLR 1941(moring of a house boat was not with the purpose of providing a permanent home, but to prevent it being carried by the tide or the weather and to provide services to it).

and bathroom fittings, as well as fitted kitchen units and sinks will usually be fixtures. But carpets, curtains, most light fittings and gas fires whose only connection to the building is by a pipe to the gas supply are not. The same applies to white goods, such as refrigerators, dishwashers and washing machines, where the degree of annexation is slight and no more needed for normal use. In relation to the purpose of the annexation as the key issue, Roch LJ observed:

> "If the items view objectively, is intended to be permanent and to afford a lasting improvement to the building, the thing will have become a fixture. If the attachment is temporary and is no more than is necessary for the item to be used and enjoyed, then it will remain a chattel."

Similarly, where the aim of attaching an item to the land was to improve the land, rather than for the purpose of using or enjoying the item, it will be accepted as a fixture.[369]

On the other hand, the following are not in the absence of agreement, conferring the right of removal, removable by the tenant:

(a) additions and alterations made by the tenant to the structure of the demised premises even though he may have incurred the entire cost and may have no claim to compensation from the landlord;

(b) ornamental fixtures put by the tenant so as to form an essential part of the permanent architectural design of the premises; and

(c) fixtures which are properly regarded as permanent improvements to the demised premises. Examples in this category are a set of tapestries in a dining room design specially to accommodate them.[370]

Note. As already mentioned above, it should be noted that, even though an article may be regarded as a fixture by reason of its annexation, the tenant who installed it, nevertheless, has a right to remove the fixture as there are certain exceptions to the general

---

[369] See *Lee v Taylor* [1902] AC 157 and *Berkley v Poulett* [1977] 1 EGLR 86.
[370] *Hill (Viscount) v Bullock* [*1897*] 2 Ch. 482 204 and *Spyer v Phillipson* [1931] 2 Ch 183.

common law rule. These exceptions are for trade, domestic, ornamental and agricultural fixtures.

Actual Annexation Distinguished from Constructive Annexation

Before leaving the subject of annexation, it may be desirable, as sometimes necessary, to distinguish actual annexation from constructive annexation.

<u>Actual Annexation.</u> This may be direct or indirect. An article is actually attached to the land when it is physically attached to the soil or a building which is attached to the soil. If the article is actually attached to the soil, it is said to be directly attached; on the other hand if it is attached to a building, it is said to be indirectly attached.

<u>Constructive Annexation</u>. Where an article is not physically attached to the soil or building or other erections thereon, but is nevertheless intended to form part of the land, it will be regarded by the law as a fixture. There are many examples, such as a key to a lock, garden seats resting by their own weight on the ground, stones loosely piled one upon the other for the purpose of making a wall, among others. These articles are said to be constructively annexed to the land.

The consequences of Annexation

Whatever is annexed to the land generally goes with the land. But this may be subject to any contrary intention as agreed by the parties. And also there are the exceptions as mentioned above.

Probable Effect of Severing the Fixture

The act of removing a fixture to restore its chattel nature may cause injury to either the article or to the freehold or to both. Any substantial injury either to the freehold or to the article claimed as removable, resulting from severance, is some evidence of the permanent character and, therefore, goes to show that the object and purpose of the annexation was for the benefit of the freehold rather than for the better use and enjoyment of the article by the tenant.

In some cases, e.g., where the tenant has a right to remove the articles, such as trade fixtures, some unavoidable damage may result in the process of removing. Damage of this nature may not prevent severance of the fixtures provided the tenant is prepared to make good the damage or compensate the landlord in lieu of the tenant himself making good the damage. However, if the damage is likely to be very substantial to the freehold, it is probable that the tenant is not entitled to remove the fixture. But in the removal of trade fixtures a greater degree of injury to the freehold, subject to the tenant's obligation to repair, is allowed than in removing domestic fixtures.

The Length of the Tenancy

The length of the tenancy may also be relevant in deciding whether an article is to be removed as a fixture. A tenant whose term is very long is more likely to annex articles for the benefit of or permanent improvement to the property than a tenant whose term, when the articles are annexed, has only a few years to run.

In *Spyer v Phillipson*[371] a tenant, who had been granted a 21-year lease, installed some antique panelling, worth £5,000, with chimney pieces and fire places to match when the lease had about 11 years to run. The total cost was over £20,000 spent on the various alterations. A few years before the end of the lease the tenant had died, and his executors, desiring to surrender the lease, claimed to remove the panelling, chimney-pieces and fireplaces. The landlord objected. The court held that the tenant's executors were entitled to remove the articles in spite of the landlord's claim that these articles have become landlord's fixtures. This decision was confirmed by the Court of Appeal.

In his comments, the High Court Judge said it would be surprising for the tenant to spend a large sum of money on articles and affixed them on the premises upon the understanding that he would only enjoy them for only a few years after which they would be given to a complete stranger. As regards the mode of attachment, the judge was satisfied from the evidence of the expert witnesses that the normal method was employed whether they were to be fixed permanently or merely for a temporary period. Having regard to these factors, the judge was satisfied that the items were affixed by the tenant for the purpose of their better enjoyment and not with the object of

---

[371] [1931] 2 Ch 183.

permanently beautifying the premises of which he had only a few years' tenancy to run.

THE RIGHT TO FIXTURES AS BETWEEN LANDLORD AND TENANT

The general rule is that a chattel always remain the property of the tenant and is removable by him on termination of his tenancy, whereas a fixture is the property of the landlord and the tenant, in general, has no right of removal. This rule is, however, subject to exceptions, as set out earlier. Therefore, fixtures should be classified into landlord's fixtures and tenant's fixtures.

(a) Landlord's Fixtures. These comprise all fixtures let as part of the premises at the beginning of the term and those installed by the tenant during the term and of which the tenant has no right to remove.

(b) Tenant's Fixtures. These comprise all fixtures the tenant is entitled to remove either through agreement or by operation of law. These are fixtures for trade, domestic and ornamental fixtures recognised as exceptions under the common law and agricultural fixtures in respect of a tenancy under the Agricultural Holdings Act, 1986.[372]

Removal of Fixtures

Apart from agricultural fixtures,[373] the general rule is that the tenant may remove tenant's fixtures as defined above at any time during the term of the lease, except where there is an agreement to the contrary.[374] It seems that once the landlord has resumed possession the tenant's rights to fixtures will be lost, unless the term was uncertain, as in the case of a tenancy at will. In this case the tenant will have a reasonable time after termination within which to remove his fixtures. Also, if the lease has a stipulation that the tenant may

---

[372] Formerly under the 1948 Act (first introduced by the Landlord and Tenant Act, 1851).
[373] It seems a farm business tenant can remove fixtures almost at will during the term. Such a tenancy is created under the Agricultural Tenancies Act, 1995.
[374] *Peel Land and Property (Port No 3) v TS Sheerness Steel Ltd* [2014] EWCA Civ 100.

remove his fixtures at the end of the lease, this will be construed as extending the time for a reasonable period after termination.[375]

In the case of agricultural fixtures put up by the tenant, not being a fixture affixed or, as the case may be, a building erected, in pursuance of some obligation on that behalf or instead of some fixture or building belonging to the landlord, as the case may be, shall be removable by the tenant not later than the expiration of two months from the termination of the tenancy.[376] The right is exercisable by the tenant provided he has paid all rents owing or is not in default in respect of other covenants in the lease and he has given notice to the landlord, at least one month before both the exercise of the right and termination of the tenancy, of his intention to remove the fixture or building. The landlord may serve a counter-notice in writing to the tenant before the expiration of the tenant's notice electing to purchase a fixture or building comprised in the notice at a fair value to an incoming tenant of the holding.

The tenant's rights to remove fixtures in time will be extinguished, and the fixtures will then become part of the freehold. If the landlord has consented to the removal of fixtures out of time but subsequently refuses to allow the tenant to remove the fixtures, the tenant's only remedy is for damages.

Where a tenant intends to renew his lease he should be careful to preserve his rights relating to fixtures. This can be done by either physically removing the fixtures and reinstate them on commencement of the new term or to secure an express stipulation in the new lease in order to preserve his rights to fixtures annexed under the previous lease. If the outgoing tenant decides to sell his fixtures to an incoming tenant, the incoming tenant should also be careful to preserve his rights as well. This can be done along the same lines as for the existing tenant.

Compliance with Lease. The terms of the lease may prevent the tenant from removing tenant's fixtures during the period of the tenancy as indeed it was the position in *Peel Land and Property (Port No 3) v TS Sheerness Steel Ltd.*[377] Under the terms of the lease the tenant was required to install a recycling plant until the end of its lease. Although tenants are frequently able to deal with or dispose of

---

[375] *Stanfield v Portsmouth Corporation* (1858) 4 C B (N 5).
[376] Agricultural Holdings Act, 1986, s10(1).
[377] [2014] EWCA Civ 100.

their fixtures as they see fit, the terms of the lease precluded the tenant from doing so in this case.

The decision did turn on the facts and the particular drafting of the lease, as it will do in every case. Nonetheless, it gives a useful illustration as to how a court will approach this subject.

Farm Business Tenant's Right to Remove Fixtures and Buildings

A farm business tenant is subject to the Agricultural Tenancies Act, 1995. An agricultural tenancy created before 1 September, 1995, is subject the Agricultural Holdings Act, 1986. The position regarding the right to remove fixtures are as follows:

(a) the right of a farm business tenant is under section 8(1) of the 1995 Act; and

(b) the right of a tenant, subject to the 1986 Act, falls under section 10 of the 1986 Act.

Under section 8(1) of the 1995 Act the farm business tenant has the right to remove any fixture affixed, whether for the purposes of agriculture or not, to the holding. This section will also apply to fixtures and buildings acquired by the tenant. There are four exceptions discussed in Chapter 18 on agricultural holdings. The right to remove fixtures "may be exercised at any time during the continuance of the tenancy or at any time after the termination of the tenancy when he remains in possession as tenant (whether or not under a new tenancy), and shall remain his property so long as he may remove it by virtue of this subsection."

Right of Agricultural Tenants to Remove Fixtures and Buildings

This right is conferred by section 10 of the Agricultural Holdings Act, 1986, as set out below:

"(1) Subject to the provisions of this section—

(a) any engine, machinery, fencing or other fixture (of whatever description) affixed, whether for the purposes of agriculture or not, to an agricultural holding by the tenant, and

(b) any building erected by him on the holding, shall be removable by the tenant at any time during the continuance of the tenancy or before the expiry of two months from its termination, and shall remain his property so long as he may remove it by virtue of this subsection.

(2) Subsection (1) above shall not apply—

(a) to a fixture affixed or a building erected in pursuance of some obligation,

(b) to a fixture affixed or a building erected instead of some fixture or building belonging to the landlord,

(c) to a building in respect of which the tenant is entitled to compensation under this Act or otherwise, or

(d) to a fixture affixed or a building erected before 1st January 1884.

(3) The right conferred by subsection (1) above shall not be exercisable in relation to a fixture or building unless the tenant—

(a) has paid all rent owing by him and has performed or satisfied all his other obligations to the landlord in respect of the holding, and

(b) has, at least one month before both the exercise of the right and the termination of the tenancy, given to the landlord notice in writing of his intention to remove the fixture or building.

(4) If, before the expiry of the notice mentioned in subsection (3) above, the landlord gives to the tenant a counter-notice in writing electing to purchase a fixture or building comprised in the notice, subsection (1) above shall cease to apply to that fixture or building, but the landlord shall be liable to pay to the tenant the fair value of that fixture or building to an incoming tenant of the holding."

Remedies in Respect of Fixtures

A wrong in respect of fixtures may give rise to either civil or criminal proceedings, or sometimes both. The object of civil proceedings is to obtain a remedy in the form of damages or loss or injury suffered or an injunction to restrain the defendant from committing a wrongful act. Criminal proceedings are brought with the object of punishing the wrongdoer by means of a fine or imprisonment or both. Criminal offences relating to fixtures may come under the Criminal Damage Act, 1971, or the Theft Act, 1968.

Civil Actions. The following civil actions lie according to the circumstances of the case.

(a) Action for Waste. The landlord may bring an action for damages for waste in respect of any fixtures wrongfully removed by the tenant. The measure of damages is limited to the actual diminution to the claimant's reversionary interest in the land. Only where damages would be an inadequate remedy will a mandatory injunction be granted to require the wrongdoer to replace the fixture removed. An injunction to restrain the commission of waste may be obtained.

(b) Action for Breach of Contract. Where a person contracts with another not to remove fixtures, he may be sued for breach of contract for removing them or may be restrained by an injunction for doing so. An action for damages is the usual remedy for breach of contract. The measure of damages in an action for breach of contract is the actual loss suffered by the claimant as a consequence of the defendant's breach of contract.

(c) Action for the Infringement of the Right to Remove Fixtures. This action is available to any person who has a right to remove fixtures against any person who prevents him from exercising that right. A tenant or any other person who has such a right may claim damages for any loss caused by a wrongdoer or an injunction may be granted to restrain the infringement of the right.

(d) Action of Trespass. Trespass is an unlawful act of direct physical interference with property in the possession of another. It is a tort and is actionable *per se*, i.e., without proof of any actual loss caused thereby. The tort of trespass is against the person in possession of the property, when the wrong is committed, and he is the competent person to sue for trespass, even though the property, e.g., landlord's fixtures, belongs to some other person. The tenant in possession is ultimately accountable to the landlord for damages receivable, waste or contract and damage cause by a trespasser if he does not remedy the damage. The measure of damages in an action for trespass to land or goods brought in respect of fixtures is the value of the fixtures as annexed.

(e) <u>Action of Conversion</u>. Conversion is essentially a tort in respect of fixtures whilst being attached to land. But once the fixtures are severed from the land, an action of conversion may be brought against the wrongdoer in respect of the chattels. Conversion is an act of wilful interference with the chattel whereby the claimant is deprived of possession. There are three types of conversion: conversion by taking, conversion by distraining and conversion by disposing. The proper person to sue is the person in possession of the chattel at the time the wrong is committed. This is the tenant. He is accountable to the landlord. However, the landlord may sue in conversion for deprivation of or injury to his reversionary interest. The measure of damages is limited to the value of the thing as a chattel.

End

CHAPTER 9

ASSIGNMENT, SUB-LETTING AND DEVOLUTION BY LAW

INTRODUCTION

During the subsistence of a lease either the landlord or the tenant may wish to dispose of his interest, i.e., the reversion or the unexpired term of the lease, as the case may be, in some way, or there may be a change of ownership of either interest. This could be due to operation of law. A disposition by an act of a party to a lease may fall under one of the following heads:

(a) sub-lease by the tenant;

(b) assignment by either the landlord or the tenant; and

(c) mortgage term created by demise or sub-demise, but only in respect of unregistered land.[378]

A disposition by operation of law may arise as a result of death or bankruptcy of the landlord or the tenant or under a writ of execution. Before discussing the various types of disposition, it is important to understand the meaning of privity of contract and the meaning of privity of estate. Even though a person might have disposed of his entire interest in a property, he may still be liable under the doctrine of privity of contract for a wrong committed by the assignee of his interest. As the law in this area was reformed by the Landlord and Tenant (Covenants) Act, 1995, the position is different under new leases granted after 1995. Once there is an assignment of a lease granted after 1995, privity of contract will no longer apply.

---

[378] A mortgage by demise or sub-demise (in respect of a leasehold estate) is now obsolete as mortgages are normally created by a legal charge in accordance with the LPA, s 85(1). In the case of registered land, the Land Registration Act, 2002, s 23(1)(a) does not permit the creation of a mortgage by demise or sub-demise. A legal charge is also used to create a mortgage, whether freehold or leasehold, in respect of registered land, and under s 27(1) of the 2002 Act is subject to registration to be effective at law.

PRIVITY OF CONTRACT AND PRIVITY OF ESTATE

These two concepts are discussed separately below. But as will be seen later this area has been reformed substantially by the 1995 Act.

Privity of Contract

A lease is essentially a contract and, as such, both the landlord and the tenant may be bound by all the covenants in the lease for the entire period for which the lease is granted. The landlord and the tenant are parties to the same contract. As such, there is "privity of contract" between them as it is called. So long as the lease lasts, the privity of contract continues, and the parties, i.e., the landlord and the tenant, who originally entered into the contract are bound by the contract.[379] This applies even though the original landlord or original tenant, or both, may be replaced by a new landlord and/or a new tenant.

Privity of contract simply means that only the parties to the contract can sue or be sued under the contract. A third party who is not a party to the contract cannot be sued or himself bringing an action under the contract.

Privity of Estate

The landlord and the tenant are also bound to each other under the doctrine of "privity of estate" since each has an interest in the same land. In respect of some matters, the original parties, so long as they have not disposed of their respective interests, may be bound by both privity of estate and privity of contract.[380] Once one of the parties has disposed of his entire interest, the privity of estate which existed between them comes to an end. In such a case, a new privity arises immediately on disposition between the new party, who has acquired the interest of one of the original parties, and the other original party. Privity of estate is based on tenure; it subsists by the relationship of

---

[379] The original lessor is liable to the original lessee and vice versa: *Warnford Investments Ltd v Duckworth* [1979] Ch 127, but will be released if the lessor unconditionally releases the assignee by accord and satisfaction (*Deanplan Ltd v Mahmoud* Ch151; (1993) 143 NLJ 28 (W H Wilkinson); *City of London v Fell* [1993] 3 WLR 1164.
[380] *Bickford v Parson* (1843) 5 CB 920. See also *City of London Corpn v Fell* [1994] 1 AC 458.

the landlord and the tenant, and follows alike both the devolution of the reversion and of the term.[381]

Privity of estate relates to real covenants in a lease. Such covenants touch and concern the land[382] subject to the lease. In relation to this type of covenant, Farwell J in *Rogers v Hosegood*,[383] said:

> "...the covenant must either affect the land as regards mode of occupation, or it must be such as *per se*, and not merely from collateral circumstances, affects the value of the land."

Examples of these covenants are those to pay rent, to repair and not to assign or sub-let. There may be other covenants in the lease which do not touch and concern land. These are said to be personal covenants. Examples of these are to pay an annual sum to a third party, to pay rates and taxes in respect of other land and to keep in repair other houses of the landlord, nothing to do with the subject lease. Personal covenants are collateral independent covenants and, in general, bind only the original parties under privity of contract.

A person who guarantees the performance of the tenant's obligations will continue to be bound in respect of those covenants which touch and concern the land after the tenant has assigned his interest as in *Kumar v Dunning*[384] in which the Court of appeal adopted the statement of Farwell J, above. The decision in *Kumar* was approved by the House of Lords in *Swift Investments v CESG plc*.[385]

Assignee's Covenant to Indemnify the Assignor

Where a lease is assigned, a conveyance for value implies covenants

---

[381] *City of London Corpn v Fell* [1994] 1 AC 458 at p 464 per Lord Templeman.

[382] This expression was replaced by the LPA, 1925, ss 141 & 142, by the phrase "having reference to the subject-matter of the lease" and thereby affords a clue to the meaning of what at first sight appears to be vague. It covers covenants which directly affect the landlord as landlord and the tenant as tenant. It may also include a covenant by a third party, e.g., one who guarantees the tenant's performance of his obligations (see *Kumar v Dunning* [1989] QB 193).

[383] [1900] 2 Ch 388 at p 395.

[384] [1989] QB 193.

[385] [1989] AC 632 (HL). See also *Coronation St Industries Properties Ltd v Ingal Industries plc* [1989] 1 WLR 304 (HL) in which a working test devised by Lord Oliver in *Swift Investments* was applied by the House of Lords.

by the assignee that he and his successors in title will perform covenants connected with the lease and will indemnify the assignor against liability.[386] No special words need to be used to imply these covenants, which are designed to safeguard the assignors, who may remain personally liable under privity of contract, even after they have parted with the land affected.

SUBLEASE OR SUBLETTING BY THE TENANT

A tenant who has not entered into an absolute covenant to the contrary may sublet his land for any term less by at least one day than his unexpired term. Where there is a qualified covenant to the contrary, i.e., a covenant not to sublet without the consent of the landlord, the tenant must first obtain the consent of the landlord.

Sublease for the Whole Unexpired Term

A sublease or subletting for the entire residue of the head lease is tantamount to an assignment, and the head tenant is thereby divested of his entire interest in the land. Therefore, to avoid such a situation, the term of the sublease should be for a term less than the unexpired term of the head lease by at least one day.

Position of Lessee and Sub-lessee

A tenant who subleases to another takes the position of sub-landlord to his own sub-lessee. But his relationship to his own landlord is not affected as both privity of contract and privity of estate remain. The usual practice is for the sub-lease to contain an express covenant by the sub-lessee to observe and perform all the covenants in the head-lease and to indemnify his immediate lessor against all claims by the head lessor/landlord.

Position of Head-lessor and Sub-lessee

The superior (head) lessor/landlord has no relationship to the sub-lessee, as there is neither privity of contract nor privity of estate between them. Nevertheless, the superior landlord has lost none of his

---

[386] LPA 1925, s77, subject to the provisions of the 1995 Act, discussed later.

rights, since he can recover his rent by the new process of CRAR[387] (replacing common law distress) upon the premises, apply for injunctions to restrain the sub-lessee from breaking restrictive covenants in the head lease and, if the head lease so provides, forfeit the head lease for breach of covenant, although done by the sub-lessee. Where the head landlord is proceeding to enforce a right of re-entry against the head lessee, the sub-lessee may apply to the court for relief and, if the court sees fit, he may be assured in possession.[388]

ASSIGNMENT BY EITHER PARTY

An assignment is the transfer or conveyance of some pre-existing term or reversion, right, title, estate or interest. This could be in respect of the lease or the landlord's interest (the reversion). The person who makes the assignment is called the "assignor", and the person who takes the assignment (either the lease or the reversion) is the "assignee".

Covenants in the lease, which touch and concern the land as opposed to collateral covenants, bind the assignees of both parties to a lease. A very old but leading case in this area is *Spencer's* case.[389] In this case it was held that a covenant relating to something to be done on the land was not binding on the assignee but where it related to something already on the demised premises was annexed to the land and would run with it. A covenant relating to something on the demised premises runs with the land. Spencer's case no longer applies to new leases due to an amendment made by the Landlord and Tenant (Covenants) Act 1995.

In pre-1996 leases, the right passed with the reversion under the LPA, 1925, s 141. Since this section no longer applies to new tenancies, a new provision is necessary. This is section 3(7) of the 1995 Act to abolish as far as necessary the rule in *Spencer's case.*[390] Section 3(7) states:

---

[387] The power of a landlord to take goods from a defaulting tenant without first going to court has instead been formalised in statute in a process known as "Commercial Rent Arrears Recovery" ("CRAR") and is only available to landlords of commercial premises. This means that the common-law remedy of distress has been repealed.
[388] LPA, 1925, s146(4).
[389] (1583) 5 Co Rep 10a.
[390] *Ibid.*

"To the extent that there remains in force any rule of law by virtue of which the burden of a covenant whose subject matter is not in existence at the time when it is made does not run with the land affected unless the covenantor covenants on behalf of himself and his assigns, that rule of law is hereby abolished in relation to tenancies."

Covenant Not to Assign

A covenant not to assign which is entered into by a tenant or sub-tenant simply means that he cannot assign his interest to a third party. However, if the covenant is qualified by the words "without the landlord's consent or licence" (or other words which connote the same meaning), it is implied under the Landlord and Tenant Act, 1927, s 19(1), that the landlord's consent or licence shall not be unreasonably withheld. Therefore, if the landlord unreasonably withholds his consent, the tenant may, nevertheless, assign his interest despite the landlord's refusal to give his consent. Since this could be a dangerous course of action for the tenant to take, he is advised to seek a declaration from the court that the landlord's withholding of consent is unreasonable in which case the tenant will be certain as to his right.

A covenant by a tenant not to assign is not broken by a sub-lease provided the tenant retains a reversion of at least one day. This covenant will be breached by a sub-lease by deed for the whole term of the entire residue of the lease as that amounts to an assignment.

Formal Requirements

By the Law of Property (Miscellaneous Provisions) Act, 1989, s 2, a contract to assign a reversion or a lease must be contained in a document embodying all the terms and must be signed by the parties.[391] Section 2 states:

"(1) A contract for the sale or other disposition of an interest in land can only be made in writing and only by incorporating all the terms which the parties have expressly agreed in one document or, where contracts are exchanged, in each.

---

[391] This provision has replaced section 40(1) of the LPA, 1925, regarding a contract for the disposition of an interest in land must be evidenced in writing

(2) The terms may be incorporated in a document either by being set out in it or by reference to some other document.

(3) The document incorporating the terms or, where contracts are exchanged, one of the documents incorporating them (but nor necessarily the same one) must be signed by or on behalf of each party to the contract."

Simply put, a contract to assign an interest in land (reversion or lease) must comply with section 2 above. Such a contract is registrable under the Land Charges Act, 1972, as an estate contract as Class C(iv) charge in respect of unregistered land. If it relates to registered land it can be protected by a notice in the land register.

Any agreement reached must be by a written contract incorporating all the terms thereof and signed by both parties (although the terms themselves may be set out in a separate document referred to in the contract, and if contracts are exchanged it is sufficient if each party signs one of the documents. Once these conditions are fulfilled, an equitable lease can be created, but if not then the agreement between them cannot amount to a contract to convey an interest in land.

An agreement can only be made in writing to satisfy section 2 of the 1989 Act. If there is no such writing, there is no contract. Thus, the basis of the doctrine of part performance is effectively removed, unlike the old law under which an oral contract to convey land can be enforced if there was a sufficient act of part performance. If the agreement fails to satisfy section 2, it is void *ab initio*. Thus, while under the old law an oral agreement could create a tenancy for a term of more than 3 years, this is no longer possible after 27 September 1989. Where a person takes possession under an invalid contract and pays rent regularly the court may hold that there is a periodic tenancy.

Section 2(1) above does not apply to short leases (three years or less) that fall under section 54(2) of the LPA, 1925.

ASSIGNMENT BY LANDLORD OF HIS REVERSION

The landlord may assign his reversion to another, but in doing so the contract to assign must satisfy section 2 of the Law of Property (Miscellaneous Provisions) Act 1989 (set out earlier). But the assignment itself must be by deed to satisfy section 52(1) of the LPA,

1925. The effect of an assignment by the landlord is to transfer all rights and obligations relating to covenants which touch and concern the land (i.e., under privity of estate) to his assignee.

Position of Assignee of Reversion and the Tenant

The assignee of the reversion can sue the tenant for rent and breaches of other real covenants as soon as he gives the tenant notice of the assignment.[392] In *Re King, Robinson v Gray,*[393] the assignee was held to be liable to sue for breaches occurred prior to the assignment. Prior to this case, it was thought that the assignee had no right to sue the tenant for arrears of rent or breaches of covenant before the assignment. In addition, he takes over the landlord's right to sue in contract.[394] Likewise, an assignee of the reversion acquires the burden of the landlord's obligations under the lease under section 142 of the LPA, 1925. The following points should be noted.

(a) The lease must be in due form, i.e., by deed, but note the doctrine under *Walsh v Lonsdale,*[395] whereby an informal lease (agreement for a lease) was specifically enforceable may be treated in a similar manner as a lease by deed for this purpose.

(b) The reversion may have been assigned in whole or in part. Where only part of the reversion is assigned, there may be a severance as regards the estate (e.g., the lessor grants a life interest to A and fee simple in remainder to B) or a severance as regards the land (e.g., one-third of the land is sold to C and the remaining land is sold to D or retained by the lessor). As regards the former case, i.e., severance of the estate, the persons entitled to the parts of the reversion fall into sections 141 and 142 of the LPA, 1925, and *Re King, Robinson v Gray,*[396] so that the benefit and burden of both covenants and conditions pass to them. In the latter case, i.e., severance of the land, the position is now generally governed by the LPA, 1925, s140(1), whereby all conditions and rights of re-entry become severable on severance of the reversion (land).

---

[392] LPA, 1925, s141.
[393] [1963] Ch 459.
[394] *Arlesford Trading Company v Servansingh* [1971] 1 WLR 1080.
[395] [1882] 21 Ch D 9.
[396] [1963] Ch 459.

(c) The assignee alone is now entitled to sue the tenant for breaches of covenant occurred before or after the assignment, in accordance with *Re King*.

ASSIGNMENT OF THE LEASE BY THE TENANT

Where there is no absolute covenant prohibiting assignment, a tenant (excluding a tenant at will or on sufferance) may assign his unexpired term whenever and to whomsoever he pleases. An agreement to assign or an assignment must comply with the requirements of section 2(1) of the Law of Property (Miscellaneous Provisions Act, 1989, and the LPA,1925, s 52(1), as the case may be. The latter provision is about the need for a deed while the former is the need for writing.

Liability of the Original Lessee

It was the position that an original lessee, who has assigned his unexpired term, would remain liable to the lessor throughout the term for all express covenants in the lease, as he is still a party to the original contract (in respect of the lease). However, the Landlord and Tenant (Covenants) Act, 1995, has made a significant amendment to the law relating to privity of contract, which no longer applies to the assignment of a lease granted after 1995.[397] His liability for implied covenants, however, depends on the doctrine of privity of estate. The assignee becomes liable to the lessor for all covenants which affect the landlord as landlord and the assignee as the new tenant. These covenants may be expressed and, where necessary, may be implied. In the circumstances, therefore, the landlord may sue the assignee in respect of those covenants which are covered by privity of estate, or the original tenant by virtue of privity of contract,[398] subject to the 1995 Act changes.

Indemnities by Assignees

Where under privity of contract an original tenant is sued because of a breach of covenant by an assignee, the tenant may:

---

[397] Discussed later in the chapter.
[398] If the lease was granted before 1996.

(a) claim under the indemnity covenant, if expressed, or implied on an assignment for value of the lease under the LPA, 1925, s77; or

(b) claim indemnity from the assignee who held the lease when the breach occurred.[399]

Example

In 1995 X leased land to Y for 42 years; by successive assignments B is now entitled to the lease (originally granted by X to Y). B has now granted a sub-lease to C for 7 years. If C breaches a real covenant in the head lease, which is now held by B, the head-lessor (X) can either sue Y (by virtue of privity of contract) or B (since privity of estate exists between X and B), but he cannot sue C since there is neither privity of contract nor privity of estate between X and C. If X sues Y, Y may recover from B under an implied right of indemnity.[400] Also, if on the assignment to Z (see illustration below) a covenant of indemnity was given by Z, Y may claim indemnity from Z who may in turn claim from A and so on, provided in each case a covenant of indemnity was entered into on the assignment.

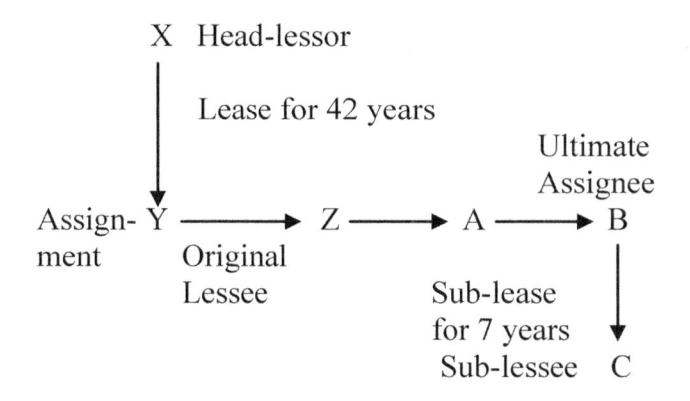

```
        X  Head-lessor
        |
        |  Lease for 42 years
        |                              Ultimate
        v                              Assignee
Assign- Y ────> Z ────> A ────> B
ment    Original                |
        Lessee                  |
                  Sub-lease     |
                  for 7 years   v
                  Sub-lessee    C
```

Note. There is neither privity of contract nor privity of estate between the head-lessor and the sub-lessee. The head lease was granted before the 1995 Act came into force. Therefore, privity of contract applies.

Lessor a Party to the Assignment. Where the lessor is made a party to the assignment, the effect is to confer privity of contract between him

---
[399] *Moule v Garrell* (1872) LR 7 Exch 101.
[400] LPA, 1925, s77.

and the assignee of the tenant. In such a case, there may be a covenant to abrogate the original lessee from being liable for any further obligation under privity of contract relating to the original lease.

Covenants for Title

By virtue of section 76 of the LPA, 1925, certain covenants for title are implied in a conveyance wherein the person conveying is expressed to convey as "beneficial owner". These covenants are set out below:

(a) that the assignor has the power to convey the land (actually his interest in the land);

(b) that the assignee shall have quiet enjoyment (i.e., that he will not be dispossessed by the assignor or any person claiming under him);

(c) that the property is free from incumbrances; and

(d) that the assignor will execute any further assurances necessary to vest the land in the assignee.

The following three covenants are applicable to a term of years (lease) only:

(e) that the lease is valid;

(f) that the rent has been paid; and

(g) that all other covenants have been performed up to the time of the assignment.

Severance of the Term

Severance of the term may occur in two ways:

(i)   where part of the land subject to the lease is assigned to a third party; or

(ii) where the entire land under the lease is assigned to several persons in parts.

An assignee of only a part of the land is liable for a proportionate part of the rent attributable to the whole.[401] However, he is liable for distress for rent due on any part of the land, and he is liable to an action on every covenant running with the land and affecting the part assigned. If an assignee of part of the land suffers distress or pays rent under a threat of distress in respect of the rent due on the whole land, he is entitled to recover on a pro-rata basis from the tenants of the other parts.[402]

MORTGAGE TERM

A legal mortgage of leasehold is similar to a legal mortgage of a fee simple estate since 1 January 1926. Under section 86 of the LPA, 1925, all mortgages of leaseholds were required to be made either:

(a) by a sub-demise (i.e., sub-lease) for a term of years absolute less by one day at least than the term vested in the mortgagor, and subject to a proviso for cesser on redemption; or

(b) by charge by deed expressed to be by way of legal mortgage.

However, by virtue of section 23(1) of the Land Registration Act, 2002, it is no longer possible for a registered proprietor of land to create a mortgage by demise or sub-demise. Thus, the legal charge is the only method of creating a mortgage in respect of registered land. This reform has reflected the reality of the situation as mortgage by demise or sub-demise had become obsolete.

The creation of a mortgage by the two methods (a) and (b) above in respect of unregistered land has not been affected section 23(1) of the 2002 Act and both methods will continue until all land is registered, though there is hardly any mortgage created by demise or sub-demise..

Not only in respect of unregistered land, section 86 of the LPA, 1985, provides where the consent of the lessor to sub-demise by way of mortgage is required, such consent shall not be unreasonably

---

[401] *Curtis v Spitty (1835)* 1 Bing. N.C. 756.
[402] *Witham v Bullock* [1939] 2 KB 81, 86.

withheld. The sub-term granted to the mortgagee is usually less by 10 days or so to provide room for the borrower to create a second and subsequent mortgages.

A lessee who created a mortgagee by sub-demise does not affect the relationship subsisting between him and his landlord. The mortgagee is not himself liable on the covenants in the lease for there is neither privity of contract nor privity of estate between the mortgagee of the term and the landlord. If the mortgagee takes possession (as he is entitled to do) his relation to the landlord is that of sub-lessee.

Section 101 of the LPA, 1925, confers a power of sale to the mortgagee if the mortgage was created by deed and, in the event of its exercise, section 89(1) provides that the conveyance by the mortgagee will operate to convey not only the term of the sub-demise but also the term out of which the sub-demise was created, unless the conveyance provides otherwise.

Where a legal mortgage was created by legal charge expressed to be by way of a legal mortgage no estate in the property is vested in the mortgagee, but nevertheless his powers, protection and remedies are similar to a mortgagee whose mortgage had been made by demise (in the case of freeholds) or by sub-demise (for leaseholds). Where there is an absolute covenant in the lease prohibiting sub-letting or assignment, the only method available to create a mortgage of the lease is by means of a legal charge. It is no longer possible to create a mortgage in respect of registered land by demise or sub-demise.[403]

ASSIGNMENT ON DEATH

On the death of a party to a lease, his rights and obligations relating to the lease devolve in the first instance to his personal representatives whose duties are to collect the assets of the deceased and make payments therefrom to satisfy the debts incurred by the deceased and reasonable funeral expenses and then to vest the residue, if any, in the persons entitled to it either under the will (if one was executed) or under the rules of intestacy. In order to settle the deceased's debts, the personal representatives have power to sell or mortgage any of the deceased's property, including leaseholds.

---

[403] See section 23 of the Land Registration Act, 2002.

Death of the Landlord. Once a reversion is vested in the personal representatives, they take the place of the deceased landlord as regards all rights and obligations under the lease, and may sue the tenant for breaches of covenant committed before the landlord's death. In due course, they will dispose of the reversion in accordance with the will, if any, or under the rules of intestacy (as the case may be) by a simple "assent" in writing.

Death of the Tenant. Once the lease is vested in the deceased tenant's personal representatives, they will take the place of the deceased tenant, but are liable only to the extent of the value of any assets. Vesting of the lease to the persons beneficially entitled is also by a simple 'assent' in writing.

BANKRUPTCY OF LANDLORD OR TENANT

Bankruptcy of Landlord

On the bankruptcy of the landlord, the reversion of the lease together with other assets, if any, vests in his trustee in bankruptcy.[404] Where the reversion is a liability, the trustee may disclaim it under section 54 of the Bankruptcy Act, 1914, as being land burdened with onerous covenants. The effect of the trustee disclaiming the reversion is to vest the reversion in the tenant.

Bankruptcy of the Tenant

Where a tenant of a lease becomes bankrupt, his interest therein vests in his trustee in bankruptcy, provided the lease is not forfeitable on bankruptcy. If the lease is not sold for the benefit of creditors, it will re-vest in the debtor when a discharge order is obtained. The tenant's trustee in bankruptcy, like the landlord's trustee in bankruptcy, is entitled to disclaim a lease with the consent of the court.[405] Any person interested can call upon the trustee to declare whether or not he will disclaim, and such a declaration must be given within 28 days or within such extension of time as the court allows.

A disclaimer has the same effect of surrender of a lease, but in such a case the landlord's consent is not required. A disclaimer will

---

[404] Bankruptcy Act 1914, ss 53 and 167.
[405] Bankruptcy Act, 1914, s54.

extinguish the rights and liabilities between the landlord and the trustee in bankruptcy.

EXECUTION

Execution is a legal process whereby any person, who has obtained a judgment order from a court of competent jurisdiction for payment of a sum of money to him can recover the money, if unpaid, by seizure of property belonging to the person against whom the judgment order was made.

Fieri Facios. Under a writ of *fieri facios* the sheriff may levy the debt on land or goods of the debtor and, therefore, may seize a leasehold interest, including a tenancy from year to year. Any leasehold interest so seized may be sold in satisfaction of a judgment debt.

EFFECT OF THE 1995 ACT REFORM ON COVENANTS

The Landlord and Tenant (Covenants) Act, 1995, was passed to remedy hardships based on assignments of leases granted before 1996 whereby the former tenants continue to be liable for breaches by their assignees. The 1995 Act, which came into force on 1 January, 1996, radically modifies the law and lays down a new code for covenants in leases granted after 1995.[406] The main changes made under section 5 to the then existing law are:

(a) that the contractual liability of original tenants and landlords after they have assigned their interests is terminated; and

(b) that all landlord and tenant covenants, except those expressed to be personal,[407] are enforceable and binding upon successors in title of the original parties.

Therefore, the principle of privity of contract as discussed above no longer applies to new leases. In this regard, sections 78, 79, 141 and 142 of the LPA, 1925 are to be disregarded and they cease to

---

[406] The 1995 Act was based on recommendations of the Law Commission Report of 1988 (amended substantially in the House of Lords' debate

[407] For a personal covenant, see *BHP Petroleum Great Britain Ltd v Chesterfield Properties Ltd* [2002] Ch 194.

have any effect in the new statutory code.[408] But sections 78 and 79 continue to apply in the running of freehold covenants.

The leases to which the Act applies are new leases to be distinguished from other leases and tenancies.[409] A tenancy includes a sub-tenancy and an agreement for a tenancy, but excludes a mortgage term. An agreement must comply with the writing requirement (formalities) of the Law of Property (Miscellaneous Provisions) Act, 1989. The covenants are both those of the landlord and the tenant that relate to the demised premises. Also, it is irrelevant whether or not the covenant has reference to the subject-matter of the tenancy or whether implied or imposed by law.[410]

Prevention of Contracting Out of the Act

The anti-avoidance provisions in section 25(1) of the 1995 Act are widely drafted to make void any agreement to the extent that:

"(a) it would have effect to exclude, modify or otherwise frustrate the operation of any provision of this Act, or

(b) it provides for -

   (i) the termination or surrender of the tenancy, or
   (ii) the imposition on the tenant of any penalty, disability or liability, in the event of the operation of any provision of this Act."

These provisions, nevertheless, allow the parties the freedom to define the scope of their obligations. The landlord is able to define his liability as being limited to the period during which he holds the reversion. In *London Diocesan Fund v Phithwa*[411] the House of Lords held that the following covenant did not frustrate the operation of the Act and was, therefore, effective:

---

[408] Section 30(4) LT(C) A, 1995.
[409] Section 1(1) of the 1995 Act.
[410] Section 2(1) & (2), as amended by SI 1996/2325, art 5, Sch 2, excludes covenants under the Housing Act, 1985, ss 35, 155; Sch 6A, para 1; Housing Association Act, 1985, Sch 2, paras 1, 3; Housing Act, 1996, ss 11, 13; *First Penthouse Ltd v Channel Hotels (UK) Ltd* [2204] 1 EGLR 16 (obligations to grant a sub-lease and pay commission held not to be tenant covenants).
[411] [2005] 1 WLR 3956.

"The landlord covenants with the tenant as follows (but not, in the case of Avonridge Property Co Ltd only, so as to be liable after the landlord has disposed of its interest in the property) ...".

It was observed that there is nothing in the Act to suggest it was intended to exclude the parties' ability to limit liability under the covenants from the beginning in whatever way they may agree. Thus, any agreed limitation as in the covenant above does not impinge upon the operation of the statutory provision. However, it is always possible for a party to release the other from a covenant[412] outside the statutory provisions at the time of the assignment (or sale). Notwithstanding the anti-avoidance provisions in the Act, it has been held by the House of Lords in *London Diocesan Fund and others v Avonridge Property Company Limited* [413] that a lease may provide for the automatic release of the landlord's covenants when it sells its interest in the property.

In *UK Leasing Brighton & Ors v Topland Neptune Ltd & Ors,*[414] a lease had been assigned in breach of covenant, but there was a re-assignment of the lease back to the original tenant, together with the guarantor of the original tenant's obligations giving a fresh guarantee. The court granted a declaration to the effect that there was no contravention of section 25 of the 1995 Act as having the effect of frustrating the operation of the Act.

Transmission of Benefit and Burden

The 1995 Act provides for the automatic running of all landlord and tenant covenants, unless covenants are expressed to be personal to any person. To facilitate this, section 3(1) provides:

"The benefit and burden of all landlord and tenant covenants of a tenancy-

(a) shall be annexed to the whole, and to each and every part, of the premises demised by the tenancy and of the reversion in them, and

---

[412] Section 26(1)(a) of the 1995 Act.
[413] [2005] UKHL 70.
[414] [2015] EWHC 53 (Ch); [2015] 2 P & CR 2.

(b) shall in accordance with this section pass on an assignment of the whole or any part of those premises or of the reversion of them."

Sub-tenants and Assignees

The running of the covenants is still limited in relation to assignments. However, in the case of sub-tenancies, section 3(5) of the 1995 Act expressly preserves the equitable doctrine regarding any landlord and tenant covenant restrictive of the user of land:

"... shall, as well as being capable of enforcement against an assignee, be capable of being enforced against any other person who is the owner or occupier of any demised premises[415] to which the covenant relates, even though there is no express provision in the tenancy to that effect".

In the light of this provision, any restrictive covenant in the head-lease will bind the sub-tenant automatically. By reason of this provision, the case *Caerns Motor Services Ltd v Texaco Ltd*[416] decided in 1994 would be decided differently today. A sub-tenant in a new tenancy is unable to enforce any covenant in the head lease against the landlord. Section 78 of the LPA, 1925, is inapplicable to new tenancies and the effect of the section is not replicated in the 1995 Act.[417] However, a sub-tenant may be able to enforce covenants in a lease against the landlord where the Contracts (Rights of Third Parties) Act, 1999, applies.

---

[415] In *Oceanic Village Ltd v United Attractions Ltd* [2000] Ch 234 "any demised premises" taken to be only premises demised by the lease in question and not to all premises demised by the landlord, if only to have conformity with section 3(2) & (3) where "any demised premises" can only refer to the premises comprised in the relevant lease.
[416] [1994] 1 WLR 1249.
[417] Section 30(4) and s 15. As regards transmission of rights in respect of re-entry refer to section 4. A landlord's right of re-entry is not a landlord's covenant. For pre-1996 leases, the right passed with the reversion under s141 of the LPA, 1925. As this section is inapplicable to new tenancies a specific provision is necessary. Section 3(7) abolishes as far as possible the rule in *Spencer's Case* (1583) 5 Co Rep 16a. Section 3(7) of the 1995 Act states: "To the extent that there remains in force any rule of law by virtue of which the burden of a covenant whose subject matter is not in existence at the time when it is made does not run with the land affected unless the covenantor covenants on behalf of himself and his assigns, that rule of law is hereby abolished in relation to tenancies."

The 1999 Act allows a third party, such as a sub-tenant in relation to the head lease, to enforce a term in the contract if it was the contracting parties express or implied intention that he should, so long as was expressly identified in the contract by name as a member of a class or by description, even if he was not yet in existence when the contract was entered into.[418]

Enforcement of Covenants by Other Persons

There is special provision in section 15 of the 1995 Act for mortgagees of both the reversion and the tenancy. If the mortgagee is in possession of the reversion or of the premises, the benefit and burden in respect of the landlord and tenant covenants will run. The same applies where a landlord grants a further lease of his reversionary interest in the premises.

Release of Tenant's Covenants on Assignment

By virtue of section 5 of the 1995 Act, a tenant who has assigned his tenancy is automatically released in respect of his covenants with effect from the date of the assignment. Correspondingly, he ceases to be entitled to the benefit of the landlord's covenants. Under section 24(2), to the same extent a guarantor is similarly released. Any release is in respect of future liability for a breach of covenant, rather than retrospectively. Therefore, a tenant remains liable for any breach of covenant prior to the assignment.[419]

AUTHORISED GUARANTEE AGREEMENT (AGA)

In view of the changes made by the Landlord and Tenant (Covenants) Act, 1995, a tenant who assigns a lease is usually required to enter into an authorised guarantee agreement (AGA). This is usually for all leases entered into since 1 January 1996 (unless the lease was dated after this date but entered into pursuant to an agreement for a lease dated before 1 January 1996).

An authorised guarantee agreement (AGA) is an agreement by a tenant who has assigned his tenancy to, say, X, and guarantees to the landlord the performance of the tenant's covenants, i.e., if X fails to

---

[418] Section 1 of the Contracts (Rights of Third Parties) Act, 1999.
[419] Section 24(4) of the 1995 Act.

perform them, he (the tenant) will perform them, but only before any subsequent assignment of the tenancy by X to, say, Y.[420] It is possible that the landlord may be able to enter into another AGA with X when he assigns the tenancy to Y.

Any other form of guarantee/agreement is prohibited, particularly those which "exclude, modify or otherwise frustrate the operation of any provision of the Act" (section 25(1)).[421]

Compliance with Conditions

Section 16(2) of the 1995 Act provides that for an AGA to be effective these conditions must be complied with:

(a) under the AGA the tenant guarantees the performance of the relevant covenant to any extent by the assignee;

(b) the AGA is entered into according to the circumstances as in subsection (3); and

(c) the provisions of the AGA confirm with subsections (4) and (5).

Under section 16(5) the tenant's liability may be as principal debtor or as guarantor, in which case the rules of law in respect of guarantees apply.[422]

Subsection (3) in (b) above defines the circumstances as follows:

(a) by virtue of a covenant against assignment (whether absolute or qualified) the assignment cannot be effected without the landlord's consent under the tenancy or some other person;

(b) any such covenant is subject to a lawfully imposed[423] condition that the tenant is to enter into an agreement guaranteeing the performance of the covenant by the assignee; and

---

[420] Section 16(4) of the 1995 Act.
[421] *K/S Victoria Street v House of Fraser* (Stores Management) Limited and others: [2011] EWCA C1V 904. See also *Good Harvest Partnership LLP v Centaur Services* Ltd [2010].
[422] Section 16(8).
[423] See *Wallis Fashion Group Ltd v CGU Life Assurance Ltd* [2000] 2 EGLR 49.

(c) the agreement is entered into by the tenant in pursuance of that condition.

The contents of an AGA are restricted. As to the possibility of the court giving a declaratory relief in a situation where a poorly drafted agreement could be void refer to *Pavilion Property Trustee Ltd v Permira Advisers LLP.*[424] An existing guarantor of an outgoing tenant cannot be validly required to guarantee the liability of the assignee. His obligations cease when the lease is assigned.

In the case of a new tenancy[425] the obligation of the tenant's surety in whatever form it is drawn cannot last longer than that of the tenant[426] who will generally be released on an assignment. However, this is not the case when a lease is disclaimed by reason of the landlord's insolvency.[427] For a detailed attempt to over turn this based on a contractual provision that the guarantor's liability should cease when the tenant's liability ended, refer to *RVB Investments Ltd v Bibby.*[428]

Consent and Reasonableness

Whether a landlord, when giving consent to an assignment, may lawfully make it conditional on the tenant entering into an AGA, depends on the type of tenancy. Residential new tenancies are defined as being "a lease by which a building or part of a building is let wholly or mainly as a single private residence".[429] Tenancies so defined continue to be subject to section 19 of the Landlord and Tenant Act, 1927, which implies into a covenant by a tenant not to assign without the landlord's consent a proviso that the landlord's consent shall not be unreasonably withheld. There is nothing in the 1995 Act to suggest that it is always reasonable for the landlord of a

---

[424] [2014] EWHC 145 (Ch).
[425] Subject to section 1(3) of the Landlord and Tenant (Covenants) Act, 1995.
[426] See section 24(2) of the 1995 Act.
[427] *Scottish Widows Plc v Tripipatkul* [2004] 1 P&CR 19 Ch D.
[428] [2013] EWHC 65 (Ch).
[429] Section 19(1E)(a) of the Landlord and Tenant Act, 1927: "In subsections (1A) and (1D) of this section—
(a) 'qualifying lease' means any lease which is a new tenancy for the purposes of section 1 of the Landlord and Tenant (Covenants) Act 1995 other than a residential lease, namely a lease by which a building or part of a building is let wholly or mainly as a single private residence".

residential new tenancy to make consent to an assignment conditional on the tenant entering into an AGA.

The onus is on the landlord to prove that his refusal to consent is reasonable within section 1(6) of the Landlord and Tenant Act, 1988. Where the covenant not to assign is absolute, the landlord has an absolute discretion whether or not to give his consent. Therefore, in this situation it will always be lawful for the landlord to make the consent conditional on the tenant entering into an AGA.

The position is different where the tenancy is non-residential. In this regard, section 22 of the 1995 Act adds a new section 19(1A) to the 1927 Act, by providing that a landlord may specify in advance his conditions on which consent may be granted. A condition requiring a tenant to enter into an AGA falls within the amended section 19 and, therefore, will be "lawfully imposed".

Protection to former Tenants

Restrictions are imposed by sections 17-20 of the 1995 Act on the liability of a former tenant or his guarantor for a fixed charge:

(a) in respect of post-assignment variations; and

(b) for his right to the grant of an overriding lease.

Assignments Excluded

There are two cases of assignment under section 11 of the 1995 Act which are excluded, i.e., the tenant is not released from liability. One is where the tenant assigns his tenancy in breach of his covenant not to assign. The other is in respect of an assignment by operation of law, such as:

(a) on death of the tenant when the tenancy will be vested in his personal representatives;

(b) on the death of a joint tenant of a legal estate, the interest will be vested in the other joint tenant;

(c) on bankruptcy of the tenant the interest will vest in his trustee in bankruptcy; and

(d) on the registration of a squatter as the new proprietor of the registered estate.

The effect of an exclusion of an assignment, as above, is to defer the release to the next assignment, if relevant.[430]

Landlord's Covenants on Assignment

What is required to be considered here is the release of the landlord from his covenant and the release of any former landlord.

Release of Landlord from his Covenant. Contrasting with the position of the tenant, the landlord is not automatically released from his covenants on the assignment of his reversion. Unlike tenants, landlords do not have the luxury of an automatic release as highlighted in the recent case of *Reeves and Downing v Singh Sandhu.*[431] The reason for this is because the tenant would not be in a position to vet the prospective assignee of the landlord. The position is that the assignee must apply by notice to the tenant for release.[432] Section 8 provides for release only in respect of "landlord covenants", i.e., any covenant which is capable of binding the person from time to time entitled to the reversion. However, this does not apply to a personal covenant.[433] Any application for release must be done before the assignment or within four weeks from the date of the assignment.

In *BHP Great Britain Petroleum Ltd v Chesterfield Properties Ltd*,[434] a landlord assigned the reversion in the premises. He may apply to be released from the landlord's covenants of the tenancy by serving a notice on the tenant under section 8 of the 1995 Act. However, an obligation that is personal to the original landlord is not a landlord covenant. In this case, the original landlord agreed to refurbish a building. There was a personal obligation in the agreement to remedy defective works. The agreement also provided that

---

[430] Section 11(5) of the 1995 Act.
[431] Ch D 13 January 2015.
[432] Under section 6 of the 1995 Act by serving a notice in accordance with section 8. Section 27; SI 1995/2964, Sch, Forms 3-6.
[433] *BHP Petroleum Great Britain Ltd v Chesterfield Properties Ltd* [2002] Ch 194.
[434] [2001] EWCA Civ 179 (HL refused leave to appeal: [2002] 1 WLR 1449).

following completion of the works a lease would be granted, which was what occurred. Because the obligation to do the works was a personal one, the original landlord could not escape liability by serving a section 8 notice when it assigned the reversion.

If the tenant intends to object he must do so within strict time limits. If he gives is consent or he fails to object, the landlord is released. To object the tenant must serve a counter-notice within four months of the service of the notice on him for the release. On receipt of a counter-notice, the landlord may apply to the county court requesting a declaration that it is reasonable for the covenant to be released. Once a release is given, the landlord ceases to be bound by the covenant and will not be entitled to any benefit under it. The same rules apply in respect of the assignment of a part of the reversion. The release of the covenant will apply only to that part.

Release of Former Landlord. A landlord who fails to apply for release within the time limit, or fails in his application to get a release, under section 7 is entitled to apply again when the reversion is next assigned.

Joint Liability

A case may arise where two or more persons may be liable jointly under a covenant. Pursuant to section 13(1) of the 1995 Act, they are jointly and severally liable under the covenant. In this situation, the Civil Liability (Contribution) Act, 1978, is relevant for the purposes of contribution by the joint covenantors.

AGA May Not Let Off the Tenant During the First Assignment

In *Shaw v Doleman* [435] the tenant did not appreciate the true meaning of the AGA. The Court of Appeal confirmed the view taken by some writers as to the effect of the disclaimer of an assigned lease on the obligations of a guarantor. The case highlights that wording common in AGA may not mean quite what the tenant thinks it means. An AGA may only be used to require a tenant to guarantee the next tenant's breach of covenant. The original tenant will be released only on a further assignment.

---

[435] [2009] EWCA Civ 279.

Landlord Serving Section 17 Notice on Former Tenant for Rent Review

With regard to recovery of rent arrears, the landlord now is required to serve a section 17 notice on a former tenant only if the assignee has failed to pay an ascertained sum as held in *Scottish & Newcastle plc v Raguz*.[436] The additional back rent upon determination of the rent review does not become "due" until the actual amount has been ascertained.

Guarantors are not Liable for the Liabilities of Assignees on Assignment

In *K/S Victoria Street v House of Fraser*,[437] the Court explained and clarified the effect of sections 24 and 25 of the Act, and said it was clear that guarantors are not liable for the liabilities of assignees on assignment. Although the court concluded that a tenant's guarantor could not provide a guarantee of an assignee's liability, the guarantor could act as a guarantor for the tenant's obligations under an AGA, thereby resolving the issue left open by the Court in *Good Harvest*.[438] From these cases it seems that the way has been paved for guarantors to provide sub-guarantees under AGA's when tenants are required to provide them when assigning. This being the case, a prudent landlord will ensure a satisfactory provision is made for such an event in its lease. The court in *K/S Victoria* provided a helpful conclusion as to the current position and indicated the following effect of the Act on existing guarantors:

"(i) an existing or contracting guarantor of a tenant cannot validly be required to commit himself in advance to guarantee the liability of a future assignee,

(ii) subject to (iii) and (iv), a guarantor of an assignor cannot validly guarantee the liability of the assignor's assignee,

---

[436] [2008] UKHL 65.
[437] [2012] 2 WLR 470 (CA).
[438] *Good Harvest Partnership Llp v Centaur Services* Ltd [2010] EWHC 330; [2010] EWHC 330 (Ch), [2010] NPC 22, [2010] 14 EG 114.

(iii) such a guarantor can validly do so by being party to an AGA which otherwise complies with section 16, and

(iv) such a guarantor can in any event validly guarantee the liability of an assignee on a further assignment."

In the light of the above, anyone who is being requested to enter into an agreement regarding a guarantee or to act as a guarantor of an AGA, it is prudent to seek specialist legal advice from a competent law firm.

Section 3 of the 1995 Act Does not Apply to Options and Conditional Agreements

In the recent case, *Ridgewood Properties Group Ltd & Ors v Valero Energy Ltd*[439] it was held that section 3 of the Landlord and Tenant (Covenants) Act, 1995, does not apply to options which were not exercised and to conditional agreements. The Act was intended to apply only to the running of covenants in landlord and tenant relationships. The facts in this case were that transfers of property had not provided for the seller's positive covenants, concerning the grant of leases conditional on the obtaining of planning permission or on the exercise of an option, to be enforceable against the buyer.

The covenants were not annexed to the property under section 3 of the 1995 Act as the Act did not apply to options in respect of a lease that had not been exercised, or to conditional agreements to grant a lease.

Repeat Guarantees on Assignment

Repeat guarantees are a common feature of many leases to protect landlords on assignment to companies within the same group. The validity of repeat guarantee clauses was considered in two recent Court of Appeal cases in *Tindall Cobham 1 Ltd v Adda Hotels*.[440] Here the tenants assigned their leases to subsidiary companies in the same group without asking for licences to assign. A clause in the lease required that the tenants obtain express written permission from the landlord but such permission was not sought. The Court of Appeal

---
[439] [2013] 6 EG 105, [2013] 3 WLR 327, [2013] 1 CH 525, [2013] L &TR 20.
[440] [2015] 1 P&CR 5.

held that the assignments were void by virtue of falling foul of section 25 of the Landlord and Tenant (Covenants) Act 1995 and, therefore, the tenants remained liable under their leases. The Court of Appeal considered how section 25 of the Act should be applied to a covenant to ensure its operation remained true to the commercial intentions of the parties. This can be a particularly tricky area of law to get right and falling foul may mean the new guarantee is found to be invalid.

In another case, *Schroder Exempt Property Unit Trust Ltd v Birmingham City Council*,[441] the court dealt with who was liable for business rates after a lease had been disclaimed. As the landlord was entitled to possession of the property, he was liable for business rates but he can recover the amount due from the guarantor. And the landlord, if they wished to minimise their liability for non-domestic rates, can seek to obtain an order requiring the guarantor to accept a new lease.

End

---

[441] [2014] EWCA 2207, [2014] PLSCS 209.

CHAPTER 10

TERMINATION OF LEASES AND TENANCIES

INTRODUCTION

A lease may provide for its own termination, without fault by either party, by providing that either party may serve a notice to quit on the other party. Also, the parties may agree during the currency of the lease to terminate it, and in addition circumstances may arise, which are not provided for in the lease, but which may have the effect of terminating the lease. An example is frustration which is discussed as a ground for termination. .

A lease or tenancy may be terminated in the following ways:

1. By effluxion of time (e.g., a 7-year lease may end after it has run its course).
2. By the exercise of an express power in the lease or tenancy.
3. Surrender of the unexpired term by the tenant.
4. Merger of the two parties' interests.
5. Forfeiture by the landlord for breach of covenant.
6. Enlargement of long leases under section 153 of the LPA, 1925.
7. Notice to quit.
8. Disclaimer.
9. Doctrine of Frustration
10. By becoming a satisfied term.
11. Enfranchisement in Respect of Long Residential Leases.
12. Repudiatory breach and determination.

1. EFFLUXION OF TIME (i.e., by expiry of the term)

At common law, the rule is that a lease or tenancy for a fixed term or certain period will automatically come to an end when the fixed term or certain period has run its course.[442] For example, a lease for a term of 21 years will automatically come to an end after 21 years. No

---

[442] Or where there is a condition in the lease that provides for its automatic determination (*Graves v Graves* [2007] EWCA Civ 660, [2008] HLR 10 – a condition that the lease would end if there was no housing benefit..

notice from either party is necessary to determine the lease. This rule applies only to fixed term tenancies; it is not applicable to periodic tenancies, which are automatically renewed at the end of each period. Also, there are many statutory exceptions under which various tenancies will continue under some form of security of tenure. The statutory exceptions are in these categories:

(a) private residential lettings,[443] subject to the Rent Act, 1977, and are discussed in Chapter 11;

(b) long residential leases,[444] dealt with in Chapter 14;

(c) business tenancies for terms over 6 months,[445] and are discussed in Chapter 17;

(d) leases of agricultural holdings granted for two years or more after 1920,[446] discussed in Chapter 18; and

(e) secure tenancies in the public sector dealt with in Chapter 13.

The main object in those exceptions is to confer security of tenure on tenants. A notice to quit in each case is required, and in each case the tenant may challenge the notice in accordance with the provisions in the respective statutes. Where no notice is served on either side, the tenancy is automatically continued. In the case of the exception under (b), the tenant may have a right to enfranchise the "freehold" interest, i.e., to acquire it. This is under the Leasehold Reform Act, 1967, in respect of houses. There are also certain rights given to leaseholders of flats.[447]

---

[443] These go back to 1915, though now all the provisions are in the Rent Act, 1977, and the Housing Act, 1988, as amended by the Housing Act, 1996.

[444] L & T Act, 1954, ss 1-5, replaced by the Local Government & Housing Act 1989 and other Acts.

[445] L & T Act, 1954, ss 23, 25 & 43.

[446] Now the Agricultural Holdings Act,1986 (formerly the 1948 Act s53) in respect of tenancies created before 1 September, 1995. Such tenancies are now deemed yearly tenancies requiring a notice to quit. All new tenancies created since 1 September, 1995, are now under the Agricultural Tenancies Act, 1995, and are termed farm business tenancies, which have only minimal security of tenure.

[447] Refer to Chapters 14 and 15 in respect of houses and flats respectively.

2. EXERCISE OF EXPRESS POWER IN THE LEASE

The parties to a lease or tenancy may agree to incorporate a power in the lease exercisable by one or both parties to determine the lease or tenancy before the end of the term, i.e., its natural determination. For example, a lease granted by X, the landlord, to Y, the tenant, for a term of 42 years may be made determinable by either party, or both, at the end of, say, 14 or 28 years from the commencement of the term, by the appropriate party giving six months' notice to the other party.

Option in a Clause to Determine a Lease

There can be conditions precedent to the exercise of an option. If applicable, the conditions must be strictly complied with for the exercise to be valid.[448] To avoid expensive litigation, and the possible loss of a valuable right to break, close attention should be given to all the requirements of the clause, including the formal requirements, and follow them precisely. For example a failure to follow a prescribed form of words could render a notice invalid. But in the absence of an express obligation stating that non-compliance would invalidate the notice, the law may look to the effect of the non-compliance in order to decide on the validity of the notice.

3. SURRENDER OF THE UNEXPIRED TERM BY THE TENANT

Surrender is the yielding up of the term to the person who is entitled to the immediate estate in reversion. A surrender may be made expressly or by operation of law, according to the circumstances of the case.

If a tenant surrenders his lease to the immediate landlord, who accepts the surrender, the lease merges in the landlord's reversion and the lease is thereby extinguished. A surrender is ineffective without the landlord's consent given at the time of the surrender.[449] An agreement to surrender is enforceable even after the tenant company

---

[448] See *Friends Life Ltd v Siemens Hearing Instruments* [2014] EWCA Civ 382.
[449] *Barrett v Morgan* [2000] 2 AC 264 at p 272 Lord Millett listing four major differences between surrender and termination by notice to quit.

has entered into administration.[450] The two types of surrender (referred to in the above paragraph) are explained below.

(a) **Express**. If the lease is for a term exceeding three years, the surrender must be by deed, as such a surrender is a conveyance and, therefore, must comply with section 52(1) of the LPA, 1925. A lease which may be made without a deed may be surrendered without a deed, such as a lease not exceeding three years. No particular words are necessary, but in any case a surrender must operate immediately and cannot, it would seem, be expressed to operate in the future.[451] A purported future surrender may, however, amount to an enforceable contract and therefore valid, subject to satisfying the requirement as to writing in section 2 of the Law of Property (Miscellaneous Provisions) Act, 1989.

(b) **Implied Surrender by Operation of Law.** In this case the surrender is implied from the unequivocal conduct of both parties[452] which is inconsistent with the continuance of the existing tenancy. Since such a surrender is implied by operation of law, the legal requirement of intention is not essential but the element of consensus must be present in the transaction which brings about the surrender. In this case no writing or deed is necessary,[453] and it will operate where the tenant accepts a new lease from the landlord before the expiry of the previous lease.[454] There are two other cases. One is where the tenant delivers up possession, which is accepted by the landlord, and the other is where the landlord grants a new lease to a third party with the tenant's consent that his own term shall cease. However, mere abandonment of the premises by the tenant is not itself a surrender.

Section 52(2)(c) of the LPA, 1925, provides that no formality is required to effect a valid implied surrender: "surrenders by operation of law, including surrenders which may, by law, be effected without writing". There is no need for a deed of surrender or writing to satisfy the 1989 Act.[455]

---

[450] *Bristol Alliance Nominee No 1 Ltd v Bennett* [2013] EWCA Civ 1626.
[451] *Murrell v. Milward* (1838) 3 M. & W. 328, 150 E.R. 1170.
[452] See *John Laing Construction Ltd v Amber Pass Ltd* [2004] 2 EGLR 128.
[453] LPA, 1925, s 52(2)(c).
[454] An agreement to increase the rent is not sufficient to conclude that a new tenancy arises: *Jenkin R Lewis & Son Ltd v Kerman* [1970] 3 All ER 414.
[455] Section 2(1) of the Law of Property (Miscellaneous Provisions) Act, 1989.

The effect of a surrender is to transfer all the tenant's rights in the land to his landlord, but subject to sub-leases, if any, which may have been created by the tenant.[456] Where on the surrender of a lease the tenant does not accept a new lease, sub-tenants' interests, if any, are preserved by section 139 of the LPA, 1925, and the landlord is put in the position of assignee of the lease. On the other hand, where a new lease is granted to the tenant, sub-leases will be protected from being extinguished by virtue of section 150 of the LPA, 1925.

Surrender is based on the doctrine of estoppel[457] which operates at the termination of a tenancy much as at the creation of one.

A surrender for consideration is regarded as a land transaction and, as such, it attracts SDLT, regardless of any document.[458]

4. MERGER OF THE LANDLORD'S AND THE TENANT'S INTERESTS

Merger is similar to surrender as discussed above. But in a merger the tenant retains his lease and acquires the immediate reversion expectant on it, or a third party acquires both interests, i.e., the lease and the reversion. In a merger, the lesser estate, i.e., the lease, is merged with the greater estate,[459] i.e., the reversion, and is thereby extinguished, as the lease and reversion cannot be vested in the same person.[460] The conditions to satisfy in a merger are:

(a) the lease and the reversion must be both legal or equitable;

(b) there must be no intervening interests, e.g., there can be no merger if a sub-lessee secures the freehold interest;

(c) the reversion and the lease must both be held in the same right, e.g., if a person in whom a term of years is vested as personal

---

[456] A sub-lessee on a surrender of the head-lease will become a direct lessee of the head landlord (*Mellors v Watkins* [1874] LR 9 QB 400; *David v Sabin* [1893] 1 Ch 523).
[457] *McDougalls Catering foods Ltd v BSE Trading Ltd* [1997] 2 EGLR 65.
[458] Finance Act, 2003, Sch. 17A, para. 16.
[459] They become united in one person in the same right: *Allen v Roachdale BC* [2000] Ch 221.
[460] Once the two interests are merged, the term of years is immediately destroyed and is said to be drowned in the greater estate (Blackstone, vol ii, p 177).

representative purchases the reversion thereof for his own benefit there can be no merger; and

(d) there will be no merger contrary to the expressed or presumed intention of the parties.[461] Where the lessee has the right to enfranchise, his lease will come to an end on the exercise of that right. This will result in a merger.[462]

Where a reversion of a sub-lease comes to an end by either surrender or merger in the reversion on the head-lessee, the latter reversion is deemed to be the reversion on the sub-lease in order to preserve the rights and obligations under the sub-lease.[463]

5. FORFEITURE BY LANDLORD FOR BREACH OF COVENANT OR CONDITION

A lease may be terminated by forfeiture where the landlord is successful in a right of re-entry for breach of a covenant or condition in the lease.

Breach of a Condition in a Lease. There is a distinction between a covenant and a condition in a lease. Re-entry by forfeiture in relation to a breach of a covenant applies only if the right to do so is expressly reserved in the lease. At common law an undertaking by the tenant framed as a condition, if breached, will entitle the landlord to terminate the lease. Thus, under such a condition the lease is conditional upon the tenant fulfilling his obligations. Many leases usually contain in clear and unmistakable words an express clause in which the landlord reserves the right of re-entry if certain covenants are broken. In such a case upon re-entry, the lease is forfeited.[464] Such a condition will entitle the landlord to get rid of an impecunious tenant who is a persistent defaulter in paying rent.

---

[461] LPA, 1925, s 185.
[462] Enfranchisement of houses under long residential leases is discussed in Chapter 14 and in respect of flats see Chapter 15.
[463] LPA, 1925, s 139.
[464] See *Richard Clarke & Co Ltd v Widnall* (1976) 33 P & CR 339. Here a clause in the lease entitled the landlord to serve a notice to terminate the lease on a failure of the tenant to pay rent, and it was construed as a proviso for re-entry. Cf *Clays Lane Housing Cooperative Ltd v Patrick* (1984) 49 P & CR 72: to be a forfeiture clause it must bring the lease to an end earlier than the actual termination date.

Breach of Covenants. Where a covenant is breached, the landlord' remedy is an action for damages and has no automatic right to terminate the lease by re-entry, unless there is an expressed proviso for re-entry contained in the lease and applicable to the covenant which has been breached. On the other hand, as mentioned above, where a condition in the lease is breached, the right of re-entry can be exercised.

Re-entry and forfeiture can arise in different situations as set out below.

Sexual Offences Act 1956. Forfeiture may result where the tenant permitted a house to be used as a brothel as expressly provided for by this Act.

Denial of Title. It is a rule of law that a tenant who denies his landlord's title is automatically made liable to forfeit his lease. However, a merely oral denial of title will not result in forfeiture in the case of a tenancy for years, but may do so in the case of a periodic tenancy

Re-entry Only if Landlord Chooses. There is no automatic termination of a lease on the breach of a condition or of a covenant coupled with a right of re-entry proviso. The effect of a breach is to confer a right to re-take possession if he chooses. However, it should be noted that the right of re-entry is exercisable only in accordance with strict legal requirements.

The threat of forfeiture by the landlord is to prevent the tenant committing a breach of a covenant or where a breach has already been committed to force the tenant to remedy the breach. However, the law does not favour forfeiture and, therefore, a landlord suing for forfeiture is put to strict proof of his case. Also, in some cases both equity and statute have intervened to prevent forfeiture.

The rules for forfeiture for non-payment of rent are different from the rules for forfeiture other than for non-payment of rent. In the case of forfeiture for non-payment of rent, equity would very commonly relieve a tenant, but as a general rule would not intervene in other cases.[465] Today, there is equitable jurisdiction, as amended by statute, to relieve tenants from forfeiture for non-payment of rent. In other cases relief is granted mainly by statute and in proper cases by equity as well.

Effect of Re-Entry. Usually a legal action must be brought by the landlord to enforce a right of re-entry. However, in some cases the tenant will allow the landlord to re-enter without an action. Where the tenant resists re-entry, the landlord is advised not to use force, as he may be criminally liable under the Forceable Entry Acts, 1381, 1391, 1429, and 1623. Once the landlord re-enters, the tenancy is determined.

Continuation of Tenancy. Notwithstanding a breach of a condition or covenant contained in the lease, the tenancy may continue if the landlord does not elect to exercise his right of re-entry, or if he attempts to enforce it but the tenant successfully claims relief from the court. In such a case, the landlord's only claim is for damages against the tenant for the breach complained of.

Rent Act 1977 (replacing the 1968 Act). In the case of residential premises, the landlord cannot enforce his right of re-entry until he has obtained a court order. The Protection from Eviction Act, 1977, seeks to prevent arbitrary re-entry and forfeiture by unscrupulous landlords.

Forfeiture Relating to Statutorily Protected Tenancies. Where a tenancy is protected by the Rent Act, 1977, the Housing Act, 1985 (Part II), and the Housing Act 1988, the effect of forfeiture will depend on which Act protects the tenancy. Under the 1977 Act, the effect of forfeiture proceedings will convert the tenancy to a statutory tenancy, and the landlord will not be able to obtain possession, unless he can establish one of the statutory grounds for possession (discussed in Chapter 11 on protected residential tenancies). However, if the tenancy is an assured tenancy under the Housing Act, 1988, the position is different, and possession can be obtained under certain statutory grounds. Here the tenant has no right to claim relief from forfeiture.[466] In the case of a secure tenancy under the 1985 Act,

---

[465] *Shiloh Spinners Ltd v v Harding* [1973] AC 691.
[466] *Artesian Residential Investments Ltd v Beck* [2000] QB 541; [2000] 2 WLR 357 (CA).

special rules apply.[467] Peaceable re-entry does not apply in relation to residential tenancies that fall under section 2 of the Protection from Eviction Act, 1977, as a court order is required. Thus, a right of re-entry is not lawful under any forfeiture clause or covenant in such a tenancy. This section also applies where the premises are for mixed residential and business purposes.[468]

As for business tenancies, there is protection under Part II of the L & T Act 1954 but such tenancies can be forfeited.[469]

Waiver of Breach. A right of re-entry will be waived by the landlord's subsequent act which acknowledges the tenancy as existing, such as the demand for, or receipt of, rent which accrued after the breach.[470] There are two requirements for waiver:

(a) the landlord is aware of the breach on the part of the tenant entitling the landlord to forfeit the lease; and

(b) the landlord has done an act to recognise the continuation of the lease.[471]

Acceptance of rent[472] after the breach of a continuing covenant, such as to keep the premises in repair, waives the forfeiture only up to the date of payment of rent. The re-entry proviso may be enforced if the breach continues later. Thus, where the breach is of a continuing nature, the breach will not be waived by the acceptance of rent. If a tenant's covenant to keep in repair was broken, the acceptance of rent would have no effect upon the tenant's liability so long as the premises are in a state of disrepair.

For payment to operate as a waiver it must be made and received as payment of rent. But in *Seahive Investment Ltd v Osibanja*[473] a payment made and accepted to secure the dismissal of a bankruptcy petition did not have that effect, even though the petition was based on overdue rent.

---

[467] See s 82 of the 1985 Act.
[468] *Patel v Pirabakaran* [2006] 1 WLR 3112; [2006] HLR 39.
[469] Refer to Chapter 17 on Business Tenancies.
[470] *Segal Securities v Thoseby* [1963] 1 QB 887.
[471] *Matthews v Smallwood* [1910] 1 CH 777.
[472] *Thomas v ken Thomas Ltd* [2006] EWCA Civ 1504.
[473] [2008] 47 EG 112 (CS) CA (Civ Div).

A covenant to prevent assignment can be breached only once, and such a breach will give rise to forfeiture, but if the landlord accepts rent from the new tenant this is tantamount to a waiver of the breach.

Forfeiture for Non-Payment of Rent

At common law a landlord was obliged to make a formal demand for rent before he could take proceedings for forfeiture for non-payment of rent, unless otherwise agreed. To avoid this procedure, which was troublesome, it became usual to incorporate in the lease a proviso for re-entry, whether or not a legal demand for rent has been made. Where there is such a proviso and the tenant is unwilling to give up possession after a breach of which he is aware, the landlord is entitled to bring a simple action for recovery of land.

Formal Demand. In the absence of a proviso exempting the landlord from making a formal demand, the landlord or his authorised agent must demand the exact rent due on the day it falls due at a convenient time before sunset so as to give the landlord enough time to count the money.

Exemption From Formal Demand Under the Common Law Procedure Act 1852. In addition to a proviso in the lease exempting the landlord from making a formal demand for rent, the Common Law Procedure Act, 1852, also dispenses with a formal demand in any action for forfeiture provided:

(i) half year's rent is in arrears; and
(ii) not enough goods are on the premises available for distress[474] to satisfy the arrears due.

Under section 212 of the said Act, the tenant has a right to stay proceedings for re-entry by paying all arrears of rent and costs at any time before trial.

Relief Against Forfeiture for Non-Payment of Rent. Even though the tenant is culpable and has no defence, he may, however, claim relief against forfeiture, as equity considered that a right of re-entry was

---

[474] The law on distress has been replaced by what is known as CRAR discussed in Chapter 6.

merely a security for payment of rent. Therefore, if the tenant paid the rent due and all expenses incurred by the landlord, equity would restore the tenant in possession, despite the forfeiture of the lease, provided it was just and equitable to grant relief. An application for relief must be made within six months from the date of re-entry by the landlord.

Tenant Remedying Breach. In this regard, a positive covenant which has been breached, such as to repair, is capable of being remedied. A case on the point is *Rugby School v Tannahill*[475] in which a covenant in the lease prevented the tenant from using the premises for immoral purposes. As a tenant had used the premises in breach of the covenant, the landlord decided to forfeit the lease. The relevant notice in this regard was served under section 146(1) of the LPA, 1925, but the tenant was not asked to remedy the breach. The Court of Appeal, whilst agreeing with the trial judge that the breach was incapable of being remedied did not agree with the wider view that negative covenants are incapable of remedy. However, in *Scala House Ltd v Forbes*,[476] the Court of Appeal held that a breach of a negative covenant is a once and for all breach and is incapable of remedy, such as an absolute prohibition against assignment, sub-letting or parting with possession.

If a breach is capable of remedy, the tenant should be required to remedy the breach, e.g. paying overdue rent. Subletting contrary to the terms of the lease is not capable of remedy, and the same applies to using the premises for an unlawful purpose. There is a distinction between immoral use of the premises by the tenant, which is not remediable and such use by a sub-tenant which is remediable if the tenant acts promptly on discovering that use.[477]

Relief to Subtenants. Forfeiture of a head-lease will automatically cause all sub-leases to come to an end for subordinate interests must perish with a superior interest on which they are dependent.[478] But relief against forfeiture may also be granted to a sub-tenant, or mortgagee, in like manner as relief to a head-lessee. A sub-tenant may claim relief under the LPA, 1925, s 146(4). A subtenant may obtain

---

[475] [1934] 1 KB 87.
[476] [1974] 1 QB 575.
[477] *Patel v K & J Restaurants Ltd* [2010] EWCA Civ 1211.
[478] *Bendall v McWhirter* [1952] 2 QB 466, per Romer LJ.

relief under the inherent jurisdiction of the court by applying for relief which the lessee could have made.[479] Before relief is granted to a person he must have a legal interest in the land.

Proviso for Re-Entry. This clause in a lease is to dispense with the need to make a formal demand in relation to the breach. The courts will normally construe it *contra proferentum* and apply it in favour of the tenant where there is any ambiguity. Such a proviso can be drafted to include circumstances such as the bankruptcy of the tenant will entitle the landlord to possession.[480]

Forfeiture for Breach of Other Covenants

The landlord's right of re-entry for breach of covenants or conditions, other than for non-payment of rent, is subject to the procedure set out in section 146(1) of the LPA, 1925. The tenant is entitled under sub-section (2) to claim relief against forfeiture. In accordance with the Act, the landlord is obliged to serve a notice in the statutory form.

Relief against forfeiture may be sought only before re-entry. The procedure of serving a preliminary notice before re-entry gives the tenant an opportunity to apply for relief if he so wishes. This can be compared with relief against re-entry for non-payment of rent when relief may be sought not later than six months of re-entry by the landlord. The parties to a lease cannot contract out of the Act so as to prevent the tenant from claiming relief.[481] Neither can the object of sub-section (12) be defeated by unscrupulous use of words in the lease. Section 146 of the LPA, 1925, does not apply in some cases as will be seen later.

Service of Notice Under Section 146(1). Before the landlord decides to enforce forfeiture, either by re-entry or action in the court, the conditions under (a) and (b) below must be satisfied.

(a) The landlord must have served a written notice on the tenant:

    (i) specifying the breach complained of;
    (ii) require it to be remedied, if possible; and

---

[479] *Bland v Ingrams Estates Ltd* [2001] Ch 767, [2002] All ER Rev 737 (P H Pettit).
[480] *Cadogan Estates Ltd v McMahon* [2001] 1 EGLR 47; [2000] 3 WLR 1555.
[481] LPA, 1925, s 146(12).

(iii) in any case requiring the tenant to make monetary compensation for the breach if the landlord requires such compensation.

(b) The tenant must have failed within a reasonable time to remedy the breach (if it can be remedied) and to pay reasonable compensation to the satisfaction of the landlord.

Terms of the Notice. Particulars of the breach must be given in the notice so that the tenant may know what is required of him.[482] Even though monetary compensation may be required, in any case, the landlord may dispense with it.

Mode of Service. Service is by means of a written notice left at the tenant's last known residential or business address or being left for him at the demised premises. Also, if the notice is sent by registered letter or recorded delivery it will be sufficient, provided it is not returned as undelivered.[483]

Where the breach is in respect of a covenant to repair, the landlord must prove that:

(a) the tenant was aware of the service of notice; or

(b) any under-tenant holding under a sub-lease which reserves only a nominal reversion to the lease had knowledge of the service of the notice; or

(c) any person who last paid the rent due under the lease either as an agent for the person in (a) or (b) above or on his own behalf; and

(d) reasonably sufficient time to enable the repairs to be carried out had elapsed since valid service of the notice to any such person.[484]

The Act does not specify what is reasonably sufficient time, but it was held in *Penton v Barnett*[485] that three months is usually considered enough in normal circumstances.

---

[482] *Fletcher v Nokes* [1897] 1 Ch 271; and see *Fox v Jolly* [1916] 1 AC 1.
[483] LPA, 1925, s 196.
[484] L & T Act, 1927, s 18(2).

With regard to a breach by the tenant, the landlord's notice does not have to give full particulars regarding any unauthorised alteration of the premises which is in breach of covenant, and any minor inaccuracy, which will not mislead the tenant, does not invalidate the notice.[486]

<u>No Notice Required</u>. In some exceptional cases, however, no notice by the landlord is required to be served on the tenant. These cases are:

(a) Mining leases which provide for such things as inspection of books, accounts, etc., or of the mine itself, and the relevant covenant or covenants have been breached; and

(b) Certain leases where there has been a breach of a condition against bankruptcy of the tenant or the taking of the lease in execution on a judgment obtained against him.[487]

Relief Against Forfeiture for Breach of Other Covenants

Relief against forfeiture for breach of covenants, other than for non-payment of rent, was first given by the Conveyancing Act, 1881, the relevant provision of which has now been incorporated in the LPA, 1925, s146(2), which is the present law.

Where a landlord is proceeding under section 146(2) to enforce a right of re-entry, the lessee may apply to the court for relief. Relief is given at the discretion of the court, having regard to all the circumstances of the case, and the court may grant relief in appropriate cases upon such terms as to costs, expenses, compensation, etc., as it considers fit.

In *Savva v Houssein*[488] the tenant breached two covenants by displaying advertisement and making alterations to the premises without prior consent of the landlords. The Court of Appeal, while

---

[485] [1888] 1 QB 276 (though here the terms of the lease expressly provided repairs to be done within this time).
[486] *Waycourt Ltd v Viscount Chelsea* [2006] EWCA Civ 500.
[487] LPA, 1925, s146(8), (9), and (10).
[488] [1996] 2 EGLR 65.

leaving in place the former two categories,[489] held that the breaches were capable of remedy.

Under section 146(4), a sub-lessee may apply to the court for an order to vest the demised property in him for the unexpired term of his sub-lease. If relief is granted to the sub-lessee, the court may impose conditions as to costs, payment of rent, compensation, giving security, etc., as appropriate.

Section 146(4) also gives relief against forfeiture for non-payment of rent, whereas section 146(2) does not. Section 146(4) also gives relief to mortgagees of leasehold estates since they are in the position of sub-lessees, even if the mortgage was created by legal charge.[490]

It should be noted that these sub-sections, i.e., (2) and (4), do not confer any right of relief after the landlord has re-entered, even within six months.

Relief Against Notice to Effect Decorative Repairs

A special kind of relief against forfeiture for breach of a covenant relating to internal decoration is given by section 147 of the LPA, 1925. This section provides as follows:

> "(1) After notice is served on a lessee relating to internal decorative repairs to a house or other building, he may apply to the court for relief, and, if, having regard to all the circumstances of the case (including in particular the length of the lessee's term or interest remaining unexpired), the court is satisfied that the notice is reasonable, it may, by order, wholly or partially relieve the lessee from liability for such repairs.
>
> (2) This section does not apply:
>
> > (i) where the liability arises under an express covenant or agreement to put the property in a decorative state of repair and the covenant or agreement has never been performed;
> >
> > (ii) to any matter necessary or proper -
> > (a) for putting or keeping the property in sanitary

---

[489] See *Expert Clothing Service and Sales Ltd v Highgate House Ltd* [1986] Ch 340.

condition, or

(b) for the maintenance or preservation of the structure;

(iii) to any statutory liability to keep a house in all respects reasonably fit for human habitation;

(iv) to any covenant or stipulation to yield up the house or other building in a specified state of repair at the end of the term.

(3) In this section 'lease' includes an under-lease and an agreement for a lease and includes any person liable to effect the repairs.

(4) This section applies whether the notice is served before or after the commencement of this Act, and has effect notwithstanding any stipulation to the contrary."

Relief Under the Leasehold Property (Repairs) Act 1938

This Act further restricts the landlord in the exercise of his rights for breach of a covenant or agreement to repair. The Act applies to all leases of fixed terms, except tenancies of agricultural holdings, let for seven years or more where three years or more of the lease are still to run. Therefore, it has no application to the exercise of the landlord's remedies at the end of the tenancy.

Where a landlord is proceeding either to forfeit or to sue for damages for breach of covenant to repair, he must serve a notice such as required by section 146(1) of the LPA, 1925 (as given above). Within 28 days the tenant may serve a counter-notice on the landlord which means that the landlord cannot proceed further until he gets the leave of the county court. The court may refuse or grant leave and impose such terms and conditions upon the landlord or the tenant, as it may thing fit.

6. ENLARGEMENT OF LONG LEASES

Section 153 of the LPA, 1925,[491] provides for the enlargement of the

---

[491] Section 153, as amended by TLATA, 1996, s 25(1), Sch 3, para 4(16). See (1958) 22 Conv (NS) 101 (T.P.D. Taylor).

unexpired terms of long leases, originally granted for at least 300 years, of which 200 years still to run, into fee simple estates (freeholds), provided:

(a) there must be no rent reserved or the rent must have no money value;[492]

(b) the reversioner must have no trust in his favour; and

(c) the lease must not be liable to be determined by re-entry for breach of any covenant.

For a sub-lease to be capable of enlargement under section 153, it must, in addition, be derived out of a lease which is itself capable of enlargement.

<u>Declaration by Deed</u>. The enlargement of a lease or sub-lease is effected by the tenant or sub-tenant, as the case may be, declaring by deed that the term or sub-term shall be enlarged into a fee simple.

7. NOTICE TO QUIT

A notice to quit by either the landlord or the tenant is necessary in the case of periodic tenancies and also in the case of a fixed term where so provided for in the lease or so provided by statute. Apart from statute, there is no requirement that the notice must be in writing, but it is desirable (as is the usual practice) that the notice is in writing and expressed in clear and definite terms. Where a notice to quit is served, it must comply strictly to any terms of the contractual lease.[493] The validity of a notice to quit depends in particular on three matters.

(a) The correct date for the termination must be stated[494] or a formula from which the correct date can be ascertained can be used. The rigid

---

[492] A lease reserving any form of money payment falls outside the scope of section 153: *Earl Cadogan v Panagopoulos* [2010] L & TR 13 Ch D.
[493] *Dagger v Sheppard* [1946] KB 215 at p 220. Cf *Brown & Root Technology Ltd v Sun Alliance & London Assurance co Ltd* [2001] Ch 733 (break clause personal to original tenant who had assigned the lease but not yet registered the transfer: still exercisable because, on proper construction, right to exercise break clause ceased only after there had been a legal assignment).
[494] *Keepers and Governors of the John Lyon School v Secchi* [1999] 3 EGLR 49,

rule has, however, been relaxed where the date in the notice is one which no reasonable tenant could possibly have supposed was the date correctly intended by the landlord, e.g., where the notice was served in 2014, but by a clerical error 2015 was mentioned. In *Mannai Investment Co Ltd v Eagle Star Life Assurance Co Ltd,*[495] the House of Lords approved this "ordinary commonsense interpretation of what people say". In relation to this case, a tenant served a notice purporting to operate a break clause in a lease by stating 12 January, 1995, instead of 13 January, 1995, as the date for expiry. Nevertheless, the notice was held to be valid.

(b) The notice must be unconditional, meaning it must be expressed in such decisive and unequivocal terms, so that the person to whom it is addressed can entertain no reasonable doubt as to its intended effect.

(c) The notice must relate to the whole of the premises, rather than part only, unless this is permitted by the lease itself or by statute.[496] A landlord of an agricultural holding has such a power if he requires part of the land for certain purposes.[497] As regards a farm business tenancy, a notice to quit part of the farm must be permitted by the lease in writing, and the tenant must be given at least 12 months but less than 24 months notice before the date on which it is to take effect.[498]

As regards tenancies, the parties could agree to a notice of any length, expiring at any time.[499] In the case of agricultural tenancies subject to Agricultural Holdings Act, 1986, created before 1 September, 1995, they are deemed to be yearly tenancies.[500] A farm business tenancy, created on or after 1 September, 1995, is subject the Agricultural Tenancies Act, 1995. The termination of the tenancies under both the 1986 and 1995 Acts are discussed in Chapter 18.

---

[495] [1997] AC 749.
[496] *Re Bebington's Tenancy* [1921] 1 Ch 559, but this decision is out of date in view of section 14(1) & (2) of the LPA, 1925.
[497] Section 31 of the Agricultural Holdings Act, 1986. But this Act does not apply to tenancies beginning on or after 1 September, 1995.
[498] Sections 6 & 7 of the Agricultural Tenancies Act, 1995. This applies only to tenancies for more than 2 years or for year to year. In the latter case, the notice has to be effective at the end of the year of the tenancy.
[499] This is subject to exceptions based on statutes.
[500] For the procedure of serving a notice to quit and length of notice, refer to the Chapter 18 on agricultural holdings.

It should be noted that generally a periodic tenancy cannot be terminated before the end of the first period, and a tenancy for one year and so on from year to year could not be determined before the expiration of two years from its commencement.

Yearly Tenancies

At common law a half year's notice to quit, ending on the anniversary of the date of entry must be given, by either the landlord or the tenant.[501] This does not apply to agricultural tenancies when one year' notice must be given, subject to statutory provisions.[502] If the tenancy began on one of the usual quarter days[503] it is the interval between a quarter day and the next quarter day but one, notwithstanding that, measured by days, such a period may not amount to the required half a year.[504] The period of the notice will be valid even if it is less than half a year in the case of a Lady Day tenancy given on or before Michalemas Day. In this case the notice period will fall short of the 182 days by 5 days. In the event the tenancy began on a day falling between two quarter days, the length of the notice must be at least 182 days.[505]

There are two exceptions relating to the half year notice.

(a) The common law rule may be expressly altered by the parties;[506] any agreement to the contrary must not be repugnant to a yearly tenancy or the concept of such a tenancy.[507]

(b) The half year rule is altered in respect of agricultural holdings. Regardless of any agreement to the contrary, any notice to quit is invalid if it purports to terminate the tenancy before the end of 12 months from the end of the current year of the tenancy.[508] This is a statutory exception.

---

[501] See *Youngmin v Heath* [1974] 1 WLR 135.(personal representative of weekly deceased tenant liable to rent until notice to quit given).
[502] See relevant statutes in Chapter 18 on agricultural tenancies.
[503] Lady Day (25 March); Midsummer Day (24 June); Michaelmas (29 September); and Christmas (25 December).
[504] *Right d Flower v Darby and Bristow* (1786) 1 Term Rep 159.
[505] *Sidebottom v Holland* [1895] 1 QB 378 at p 384.
[506] *Allison v Scargall* [1920] 3 KB 443.
[507] *Prudential Assurance Co Ltd v London Residuary Body* [1992] 2 AC 386.
[508] Section 25(1) of the Agricultural Holdings Act, 1986.

Notice to Expire at End of Current Year. It is important to ensure that a notice to quit a yearly tenancy is such that the termination is at the end of the current year. Thus, a notice given by the landlord must require the tenant to quit the holding exactly on that date, not earlier or later. The end of the current year is midnight of the day prior to the anniversary of the day on which the tenancy commenced. There could be a little relaxation to this strict rule in respect of "end of the current year" to include the anniversary of the day on which the tenancy began.[509]

Other Periodic Tenancies

Weekly tenancies originally required one week's notice for determination. However, premises let as a dwelling are subject to statutory rules. Due to statutory intervention in the case of residential tenancies the period of notice is subject to section 5(1) of the Protection from Eviction Act, 1977. The Act requires a landlord or tenant of residential premises to give at least four weeks' notice before the date on which it is to take effect. This provision overrides any stipulation to the contrary.

Monthly tenancies are determinable by one month's notice, subject to any agreement or special custom to the contrary.

As a general rule, a periodic tenancy may be determined by notice equivalent to the length of the tenancy (i.e., the period of the tenancy) expiring at the end of the period of the tenancy.

Validity of the Notice. A notice to quit is invalid if it is given to expire on the wrong date. A valid notice operates to determine the tenancy, but should the landlord accept rent which became due after determination of the tenancy the effect is to create a new tenancy on the old terms.

The burden of proving validity of the notice is on the person who has served it. The following conditions must be satisfied:

(i)   he must show that the correct day is indicated;
(ii) the notice must be unconditional: and
(iii) it must relate to the whole of the premises.

---

[509] *Sidebottom v Holland* [1895] 1 QB 378.

Service of Notice. The notice may be served on the tenant or left at his place of abode with his wife or servants if its nature is explained. It may be served through the post, but to prove delivery it is advisable that the letter should be registered or sent by recorded delivery.

Statutory Tenancies. A notice served by a landlord to determine a contractual tenancy may operate to convert the contractual tenancy into a statutory tenancy whereby the tenant still has the right to continue in occupation. In such a case, the landlord may only regain possession by obtaining an order from the court, provided he can rely on one or more of the specified grounds.

8. DISCLAIMERS

A tenant who denies his landlord's title in legal proceedings by setting up a title in himself or in a third party operates to determine the tenancy.[510] Such a conduct breaches the implied condition that the tenant shall refrain from any act which will prejudice the position of the landlord.[511] Also, an act of this nature indicates an intention to be no longer bound by the tenancy.[512] This old rule is now somewhat obsolete and must not be confused with disclaimer under statutes or bankruptcy proceedings.

Another type of disclaimer is where the tenant's trustee in bankruptcy disclaims the lease. This applies where the lease is unsaleable or is a liability.[513]

Statute

A right to end a lease by disclaimer sometimes arises by statute. For

---

[510] *Warner v Samson* [1959] 1 QB 297 at p 318 per Hudson LJ and at p 324 per Ormerod LJ.
[511] *W G Clark (Properties) Ltd v Dupre Properties Ltd* [1992] Ch 297.
[512] *Ibid.*
[513] In *Hindcastle Ltd v Barbara Attenborough Association Ltd & Others* [1994] 3 WLR 1100 an original tenant was still liable to the landlord where the disclaimer was by an assignee. This may not be the position now by virtue of the Landlord and Tenant (Covenants) Act, 1995 as the Act has abolished privity of contract in the parties' relationship where there is an assignment in respect of a lease created after 1995.

example, where premises were rendered unfit by war damage, tenants therein were allowed to disclaim their tenancies.[514]

Bankruptcy

The Bankruptcy Act, 1914, gives a trustee in bankruptcy power to disclaim onerous leases belonging to the bankrupt. Disclaimer, if properly made, brings the lease to an end together with the bankrupt's rights and liabilities therein, but does not necessarily affect a third party, e.g., a mortgagee of the lease or sub-lease.

9. DOCTRINE OF FRUSTRATION

A lease can be terminated under the doctrine of frustration so that it can be terminated.[515] An act of frustration is some unforeseen supervening event which has substantially altered the nature of the outstanding rights and obligations of the parties under a contract so that it will be unjust to hold the continuance of the contract.[516] The question of whether the doctrine of frustration could ever apply to a lease itself, as distinct from covenants contained in it, was for some time the subject of conflicting opinions in the House of Lords.[517] In *Matthew v Curling*[518] the tenant had to continue paying his rent notwithstanding that the premises were utterly destroyed by fire. The tenant of premises requisitioned by the Crown acting under statutory powers, where the Crown was the landlord, was held to be liable to pay rent.[519]

The problem has now been resolved in *National Carriers Ltd v Panalpina (Northern) Ltd*,[520] in which the House of Lords, by a majority, held that in principle the doctrine of frustration is capable of

---

[514] L & T (War damage) Acts, 1939 & 1941.
[515] *National Carriers Ltd v Panalpina (Northern) Ltd* [1981] AC 675; (1981) 131 NLJ 189 – H.W Wilkinson.
[516] See *Davis Contractors Ltd v Fareham UDC* [1956] AC 696 at p 729.
[517] See *Cricklewood Property & Investment Trust Ltd v Leighton's Investments Ltd* [1945] AC 221 (HL) (a building lease was not frustrated by war-time legislation prohibiting building).
[518] [1922] 2 AC 180. See also *Redmond v Dainton* [1920] 2 KB 256; *Denman v Brise* [1949] 1 KB 22, [1948] 2 All ER 141.
[519] *Crown Land Commissioners v Page* [1960] 2 QB 274; [1960] 2 All ER 726 (lease not frustrated).
[520] [1981] AC 675; (19810 131 NLJ 189 – H.W Wilkinson.

being applicable to leases, though cases are likely to be rare. In this case, however, the occurring event (i.e., a temporary closure of the adjoining road) was not enough to render the lease frustrated.

10. BY BECOMING A SATISFIED TERM

If a lease is granted as security for the payment of money, the term becomes satisfied when the money is repaid. For example, a mortgage which is created by demise or sub-demise will automatically determine when the mortgage advance is repaid. In such a case, the term granted to create the mortgage becomes satisfied on redemption of the mortgagee. The creation of a mortgage by demise or sub-demise is not normally used today and, in the case of registered land, it is no longer possible as the Land Registration Act, 2002, provides only for its creation by a legal charge.[521]

11. ENFRANCHISEMENT

The Leasehold Reform Act, 1967, confers a right on tenants of long residential leases[522] to acquire the estate in fee simple from the freeholder and any other superior landlord. This Act applies only to houses let originally under a long lease at a low rent, provided the tenant has occupied the house for at least the last two years as his only or main residence.

Long leaseholders holding leases in respect of flats in a building or a large block, in certain circumstances, may also decide to acquire the superior interests. In such a case, the superior interest and any intervening interest will be brought to an end and the freehold will be held by what is known as "the enfranchisement company" on behalf of the former leaseholders.[523]

The effect of a successful enfranchisement is to bring the landlord's and all other superior interests to an end. This effectively brings the relationship of landlord and tenant to an end, involving a special form of merger.[524]

---

[521] See s 27 of the LRA, 2002: legal charge of freehold or leasehold by registered disposition.
[522] The law rent requirement has been removed.
[523] The details are set out in Chapter 15 relating to leasehold enfranchisement.
[524] Further details on enfranchisement are set out in Chapter 14 and 15.

12. REPUDIATORY BREACH AND DETERMINATION

Under the law of contract, a breach of a fundamental term may amount to repudiation of the lease thereby conferring on the other party, at his election, a right to regard the lease as terminated and to sue immediately for damages in respect of any loss sustained.[525] It seems the contractual principle has not yet been accepted for the termination of a lease, though the possibility of terminating a lease under the doctrine of frustration has no doubt opened the door for reconsideration of the issue.[526] Perhaps the case, *Hussain v Mehlman*,[527] may trigger a reversal of principle. Here damages were awarded for repudiatory breach by the landlord who failed to repair the demised premises so as to cause the tenant to move out.

A few cases[528] support repudiatory breach for termination of a lease, though a few years ago the application of repudiatory breach by the tenant was a question for the Court of Appeal in *Reichman v Beveridge*[529] involving claims for future rent which could not be brought. The use of repudiation should not be used as a front to avoid forfeiture rules which are intended to some extent to support tenants.[530]

THE PARTIES RIGHTS ON TERMINATION OF A TENANCY

The parties to a tenancy have a variety of rights on the determination of a tenancy. These rights arise by operation of law, depending on the type of property comprised in the lease, and subject of course to the actual terms and conditions in the lease as agreed by the parties.

---

[525] There are cases in Australia on this point: *Wood Factory Pty Ltd v Kiritos Pty Ltd* (1985) 2 NSWLR 105 at p 115; *Nangus Pty Ltd v Charles Donovan Pty Ltd* [1989] VR 184 at p 188.
[526] See Kevin Gray, *Elements of land Law* Butterworths, 2nd edition, 1993, p 764.
[527] [1992] 2 EGLR 87 at p 89.
[528] *WG Clark (Properties) Ltd v Dupre Properties Ltd* [1992] Ch 297 (disclaimer of lease as repudiation); *Re Park Air Services plc* [1997] 1 WLR 1376; *Abidogun v Frolan Health Care Ltd* [2002] L&TR 275.
[529] [2007] 1 P&CR 358, applying *White & Carter(Councils) Ltd v McGregor* [1962] AC 413.
[530] See *Abidogun v Frolan Health Care Ltd* [2002] L&TR 275 (the said rules apply to repudiatory breach).

Landlord's Rights

The landlord has remedies for recovering damages for breach of covenants by the tenant for waste, to recover possession and for holding over after proper termination of the tenancy.

Remedies for breach of Covenants and Waste

(a) The landlord may sue the tenant for rent accruing prior to the determination of the tenancy (discussed in Chapter 6).

(b) Damages may be awarded in an action for:

- (i) waste (already discussed);
- (ii) mense profits, i.e., damages for failure to give up possession equivalent to the current rental value;
- (iii) breach of covenant (already discussed in earlier chapters); and
- (iv) use and occupation (already discussed).

(c) He is entitled to recover for arrears of rent due prior to the termination of the tenancy[531] within six months of termination, assuming the tenant is still in occupation.

Right to Possession

The landlord may enforce his claim to possession by peaceable re-entry, but he cannot enter forceably as this may constitute a criminal offence.[532] Also, the landlord's right to re-enter may be restricted by statutes, e.g., the Rent Act, 1977, and the Protection from Eviction Act, 1977.

(a) <u>Action for Recovery of Land</u>. Because of the difficulties involved in peaceable re-entry, the usual method to enforce the right to possession is by an action for recovery of land, or (as it is called) an action of ejectment. The action may be combined with all claims for damages.

---

[531] L & T Act, 1709, ss 6 & 7.
[532] Statutes of Forceable Entry of 1381, 1391, 1429, 1588 and 1623.

(b) <u>Recovery of Deserted Premises</u>. These premises may be recovered under section 16 of the Distress for Rent Act, 1737, provided the following conditions are satisfied:

(i) the rent reserved is a rack rent, or three-quarters of the annual value;
(ii) the rent has not been paid for six months; and
(iii) the premises are deserted or uncultivated so that there are not enough goods to satisfy a distress.

Once these conditions are satisfied, the landlord may require two justices to view the premises and affix a notice on a part that can be seen by all that they will return on a specified day (at least 14 days later); and if on the specified day the tenants fails to appear and pay the arrears due the justices may reinstate the landlord in possession of the premises and, therefore, put an end to the lease.

<u>Landlord Not Required to Mitigate his Loss</u>

When a tenant has ceased to occupy the premises, the landlord is not required to mitigate his loss by seeking an alternative tenant.[533]

Remedies for Holding Over
A tenant who holds over in opposition to the landlord's right to possession may incur various statutory penalties as given below:

(a) If the tenant holds over contumaciously after his own notice to quit, he is liable to distress for twice the rent that has accrued under the Distress for Rent Act, 1737.

(b) If he holds over contumaciously after the landlord demands possession by written notice, he is liable to pay twice the annual value for his occupation under the Landlord and Tenant Act, 1730.

(c) If the tenant holds over after his fixed term expires and there is no written notice by the landlord for possession and there is no agreement as to rent, the landlord can claim for use and occupation of the premises under the Distress for Rent Act, 1737.

---

[533] *Reichman v Beveridge* [2007] 08 EG 138.

Recovery of Possession by the Landlord. If a tenancy has been lawfully terminated, the landlord may need to take steps to obtain possession if the tenant does not leave the premises. There are certain statutory rules that govern the rights of certain tenants. These are discussed in later chapters. Once a tenancy has been terminated, it is the usual practice for the landlord to sue the tenant for possession rather than exercising his right of re-entry. The court has a duty to make an order for possession to enforce that right. The following should be noted:

(a) There is a requirement to obtain a court order[534] to recover possession of a dwelling-house.

(b) Criminal offences of unlawful eviction and harassment may be committed relating to enforcement of a right to possession.[535] The Housing Act, 1988, introduced a further offence of harassment against landlords and their agents.

(c) A tenant could obtain damages for unlawful eviction or harassment under section 27 of the Housing Act, 1988. The damages are calculated to reflect the notional gain of the landlord from his wrongful conduct.[536]

(d) The relevance, if any, of the Human Right Act, 1998, against the landlord's right to possession has been advanced by tenants recently. This normally applies to public sector landlords (local authorities). The Supreme Court[537] departed from earlier House of Lords' decisions and concluded, *inter alia*, that the test of proportionality has to be considered and to have the question of dispossession determined

---

[534] Section 3 of the Protection from Eviction Act, 1977, must be complied with. Section 3 is compatible with the ECHR (*R (Coombes) v Secretary of State for the Communities and Local Government* [2010] EWHC 666, [2010] L & TR 29).

[535] See the protection from Eviction Act, 1977, s1(2), and the Criminal Law Act, 1977, s6 (offence of using or threatening violence to enable entry into the premises).

[536] *Sampson v Wilson* [1996] Ch 39. It is to prevent the landlord from benefitting from his "Rachmannite" activities.

[537] See the Supreme court decision in *Hounslow LBC v Powell* [2011] UKSC 8, [2011] 2 WLR 287.

by an independent tribunal in the light of article 8, even if the tenant's right of occupation under domestic law has come to an end.[538]

Tenants' Rights

On termination of a contractual tenancy, the tenant may have the following rights:

(a) <u>Right to Fixtures</u> The tenant's rights to fixtures cover all types of tenancies (already discussed).

(b) <u>Security of Tenure</u>. A statutory tenancy may arise on termination of a contractual tenancy. This is applicable to a tenancy of a dwelling house, business premises or agricultural holdings.[539]

(c) <u>Right to Compensation</u>. In the case of business premises, the tenant may have a right to compensation for improvements carried out by him not as a condition in the lease and for disturbance (this is discussed in Chapter 17). Also, tenants of agricultural holdings and farm business tenants may obtain compensation as well.[540]

Tenants of agricultural holdings may claim compensation for:

(a) improvements;

(b) for improved standard or system of farming; and

(c) for disturbance (discussed in Chapter 18).

<u>Right to Exercise Option.</u> Sometimes a tenant is given an option to renew his lease. Where this is the case, the tenant may exercise the option to take a new lease on termination of his present lease.

---

[538] *McCann v United Kingdom* [2008] 2 EGLR 45, *Kay v UK* [2010] ECHR 37341/06, [2011] L & TR 1 at [73] – [74].
[539] But the Agricultural Tenancies Act, 1995, has modified the security of tenure provisions. See Chapter 18 for details.
[540] See Chapter 18 on agricultural holdings and farm business tenancies.

Right to Enfranchisement. Tenants of long residential leases of houses[541] may have a right to purchase their landlord's and all other superior interests (discussed in Chapter 14). Also, tenants of flats in a block may have the right of collective enfranchisement (discussed in Chapter 15).

Right to Damages for Unlawful Eviction. A tenant may be entitled to damages if he is unlawfully evicted. A relevant case is *Grange v Quinn*.[542]

End

---

[541] Also, tenants of leasehold flats in a block may have the right of collective enfranchisement or to individually extend their leases by 90 years (discussed in Chapter 15).
[542] [2013] EWCA Civ 24.

CHAPTER 11

RENT ACT PROTECTED TENANCIES

INTRODUCTION

There are many chapters that deal with residential leases and tenancies subject to statutory provisions. This chapter deals with tenancies which are concerned with the system of protection conferred by the Rent Act, 1977.[543] Rent Act protection is of less relevance today by reason of the need to encourage owners of residential accommodation to let their properties. Many of the Housing Acts, beginning with one in 1980, were enacted with a view towards this objective. The nature and scope of these Acts, some of which apply to public housing, are considered in subsequent chapters.

In most cases, tenancies relating to residential accommodation created before 15 January 1989 were protected by the Rent Act, 1977.[544] Those which are outside the scope of the 1977 Act are considered later. Most tenancies in the private sector are assured tenancies and assured shorthold tenancies which are discussed in Chapter 12.

Earlier Statutes

Statutory provisions relating to residential tenancies were first enacted in 1915 under the Increase of Rent Mortgage Interest (War Restrictions) Act. This Act was the first of a complex mass of legislation mainly designed to protect tenants of residential properties against their landlords. Restrictions were relaxed to a certain extent after the First World War, but again were re-introduced by the Rent and Mortgage Interest Restrictions Act, 1939. Several Acts were passed between 1920 and 1939; these Acts were amended and

---

[543] While the Rent Act deals with security of tenure and rent control, there is also the Protection from Eviction Act, 1977, which in particular deals with the prevention of harassment of tenants by landlords. Such harassment is a criminal offence.

[544] Such tenancies continue to enjoy protection under this Act. See *Whitehouse v Lee* [2009] EWCA Civ 375 (tenancy granted in 1963 but an order for possession was refused under s 98 of the Rent Act, 1977).

extended principally by the Furnished Houses (Rent Controlled) Act, 1946, and the Rent Act, 1965. The Rent Act, 1968, was passed as a consolidating Act, which has been amended by the Housing Act, 1969, the Housing Act, 1972, the Counter Inflation Act, 1973, and the Rent Act, 1974.

The Rent Act, 1977, has replaced the earlier Rent Acts, notably the 1965 and the 1968 Acts. These Acts brought unto the statute book what are known as "regulated tenancies" and "fair rents". They are still relevant for the purposes of the 1977 Act, which was passed to provide more protection to tenants by way of security in their homes, the regulation of rents and protection from eviction.[545] Security of tenure and rent control are complementary to one another as one cannot work without the other. In order to protect tenants against landlords, it is essential that there must be first protection against eviction without good cause, and protection as to the maximum rent recoverable by the landlord. It is obvious that one without the other is unworkable and, therefore, from the beginning, the relevant statutes conferred both forms of protection on tenants of unfurnished dwellings. It was not until 1946 that there was some effective protection given to furnished accommodation.

Present Acts

The present Acts giving protection are the Rent Act, 1977, and the Protection from Eviction Act,1977, in the private sector, while the Housing Act, 1985, provides for secure tenancies in the public sector, discussed in Chapter 13. Assured tenancies (AT) and assured shorthold tenancies (AST) are under the Housing Act, 1988, as amended by the Housing Act, 1996. Both of these tenancies are in the private sector and while there is security of tenure under the former, there is no such security under the AST, apart from the first six months.

PRIVATE RESIDENTIAL TENANCIES

Any tenancy which is subject to the Rent Act, 1977, is a protected tenancy as the tenants are conferred with security of tenure, which entitles the tenant to remain in possession after his contractual

---

[545] See the Protection from Eviction Act, 1977, which is a very short Act, that imposes a criminal sanction for eviction.

tenancy ends. The tenancy cannot be terminated without an order of the court upon certain limited and specified grounds. Such tenants are said to have regulated tenancies, which are subject to a machinery for determining a "fair rent". This is the maximum rent such a tenant is required to pay. However, such a rent does not mean a "reasonable rent". It is fixed by reference to the market rent, reflecting the current state of the premises,[546] but usually lower than the open market rent. In fixing the rent, it must be assumed that the demand for similar dwellings in the locality is not substantially greater than the supply of such dwellings.[547] This is obviously an artificial situation, as the demand for dwellings far exceed the supply in the highly congested conurbations, such as London and Manchester. It follows that the "fair rent" is subsidised by landlords.

Tenants as Opposed to Licensees

Only tenants generally have rights under the Rent Act, 1977. Licensees and trespassers may have only limited rights, if any. A tenant is given protection if there is no resident landlord who resides in the same accommodation. Thus, where a person is provided with a room in a house in which the owner/landlord and his family live, there will be no protection. That person is likely to be a licensee. To live in the same accommodation with the owner, such as a house or a flat, means there is no protection. But where there is a block of flats, or a large house with self-contained flats, in which the owner lives in one flat and tenants occupy the other flats, they may enjoy the rights conferred by the Act in relation to security of tenure and paying a fair rent, which is determined by a rent officer employed by the local authority. Such a rent is fixed biennially and cannot be altered by the landlord. The landlord cannot evict a protected tenant without a court order based on one or more of the specified grounds laid down in the Act.

To enjoy the protection of the Act, the tenant must be using the property as his only or main residence. Where the landlord can prove otherwise, a tenant will lose protection and can be evicted. Of course, the landlord will need a court order to do so.

---

[546] *Spath Holme Ltd v Greater Manchester & Lancashire Rent Assessment Committee* [1999] QB 92.
[547] Section 70(2) of the Rent Act, 1977. A number of other matters to be disregarded as well under subsection (3).

PROTECTION UNDER THE RENT ACT 1977

By entering into a tenancy which falls within the scope of the Rent Act, 1977, both parties are subject to rights and obligations. The subject-matter must be a dwelling-house which is let as a separate dwelling for the purposes of the Act. The tenancy can be legal or equitable, and it can be granted by the landlord or by a tenant who has granted a sub-tenancy. Both a tenant at will and a tenant at sufferance will fall within the ambit of the Act.[548] As mentioned earlier, only a tenancy, not a licence, can attract the full protection of the Act. Before the greater scope for recovery of possession and the granting of assured shorthold tenancies (AST) became prevalent by virtue of the Housing Act, 1988, many owners were providing licences in respect of residential accommodation. However, many of such licences were in effect tenancies, but only disguised as licences with a view to avoiding the protection accorded by the 1977 Rent Act.[549] The courts were able in general to weed out such a practice.

Whether a dwelling-house falls within the ambit of section 1 of the Rent Act, 1977, is a question of fact. A dwelling is a place where a person carries out the basic activities of living such as sleeping, eating and cooking.[550] Thus, it can be a house, a flat, a single bed-sitting room and in certain circumstances a hotel room,[551] or even a caravan.[552]

With regard to a tenancy within section 1, a quantifiable rent has to be paid. An important aspect of the Act is the mechanism for regulation and control of the rent payable by the tenant. Although the payment of a rent is not essential under the LPA, 1925, under section 1 of the Rent Act, 1977, it is essential, and if it is not payable in the form of money, this aspect of the Act is inoperable.[553]

The words "as a separate dwelling" involves three issues:

---

[548] *Chamberlain v Farr* [1942] 2 All ER 567 (CA).
[549] *Street v Mountford* [1985] AC 809 (HL).
[550] See *Curl v Angelo* [1948] 2 All ER 180 at p 190 per Lord Greene MR.
[551] *Uratemp Ventures v Collins* [2001] 3 WLR 806 (HL).
[552] *Makins v Elson* [1977] 1 WLR 221. Cf *Chelsea Boat and Harbour Ltd v Pope* [2000] 1 WLR 1941 (CA).
[553] *Barnes v Barratt* [1970] 2 QB 657 at p 657E per Sachs LJ.

(a) The word "as" indicates the purpose of the lease that should be considered rather than the actual use that is made of the demised premises.

(b) The use of the word "a" means that the phrase should be given a singular construction.

(c) There is a difficulty of interpreting "separate dwelling".

As regards (a), it does not necessarily mean that a building which is a dwelling-house will always be used as such. It could be used as an office or something else. In relation to (b), although the intention of the Act is to protect the residential occupier and it requires the dwelling-house initially to be let as a separate dwelling, there is nothing to prevent the tenant from immediately sub-letting either part or the whole of the dwelling once the tenancy has commenced. However, one redeeming aspect in favour of the landlord is that on termination of the contractual tenancy no statutory tenancy will arise and the protection accorded by the Act will cease.[554]

With reference to (c) above, the accommodation must be sufficient for the tenant to sleep, cook and eat,[555] but it does not have to be completely self-contained as long as the tenant has exclusive use of the rooms he is occupying. Sharing cooking facilities with his landlord may not cause his accommodation to be outside section 1 of the 1977 Act, but the shared occupation of a kitchen as a living space would do.[556]

EXCLUSIONS FROM THE RENT ACT 1977

The list of exclusions from the 1977 Act, as can be seen below, is very extensive. A tenant of any accommodation in this list will not enjoy the protection of the Act in terms of security of tenure and the rent that can be charged.

---

[554] See *Horford Investments Ltd v Lambert* 1976] Ch 39 in which the Court of Appeal held that the phrase "let as a separate dwelling' should be given a separate a singular construction".
[555] *Wright v Howell* (1947) 92 Sol Jo 26 (CA)
[556] *Uratemp Ventures v Collins* [2001] 3 WLR 806 (HL).

Dwelling-houses with High Rateable Value Under Section 4

A flat or a house with a rateable value of over £1,500 in Greater London or £750 elsewhere cannot be the subject of a protected tenancy. After changing from rateable values (RV) to the community charge and then the council tax in 1993, the then limit of the RV is still relevant.

Tenancies at Low Rents Under Section 5

A tenancy entered into prior to 1 April, 1990, is excluded from protection if the rent reserved is less than two-thirds of the RV on the "appropriate day". This day is 23 March, 1973, except if the property was valued at a later date. As already mentioned, if no rent is payable, there is no protection. Long leaseholders who pay a nominal ground rent to the freeholders are excluded.

Shared Ownership Leases Under Section 5A

These leases do not qualify for protection.[557] Such a lease is granted either by a public body under Part V of the Housing Act, 1985, or a housing association at a premium for a term of 99 years or more. This type of lease was introduced as part of the "right to buy" legislation and enabled a secure tenant to buy out the landlord's interest. The right to a shared ownership lease has been replaced[558] with a new "rent to mortgage" scheme.

Dwelling-houses Let with Other Land Under Section 6

Where the letting is with other land to which it is only an adjunct, it will not be protected. But where the land is not more than two acres of agricultural land the land will be considered to be part of the dwelling-house, and the dwelling will be protected.

Payment for Board and Attendance under Section 7

This applies where there is a bona fide letting at a rent which includes

---

[557] Section 5A of the Rent Act, 1977.
[558] Withdrawn by s 107 of the Leasehold Reform. Housing and Urban Development Act, 1993.

payments in respect of board or attendance. This is provided for in section 7(1) of the 1977 Act. A cup of tea is not board[559] but a continental breakfast in a communal dining room counts as board.[560] An example of attendance would include cleaning the room and providing clean linen.[561]

Lettings to Students Under Section 8

Tenancies granted by specified educational institutions to their students are not protected. These institutions are usually universities and colleges. This exclusion is under section 8(1) of the Act. Certain bodies providing accommodation have been specified for exclusion by the Assured and Protected Tenancies (Letting to Students) Regulations, 1998.[562].

Holiday Lettings Under Section 9.

Where a letting is to confer the right to occupy the dwelling for a holiday, it is not protected. However, where the letting agreement is not truly for a holiday but a sham, there is protection to the tenant.[563]

Agricultural Holdings Under Section 10

Where a dwelling is part of an agricultural holding and is occupied by anyone in control of the holding or the farm, it is not protected. This type of dwelling is subject to the Agricultural Holdings Act, 1986, and, in the case of a farm business tenancy, the Agricultural Tenancies Act, 1995. But where part of a building which falls within section 10 is sub-let as a separate dwelling, the sub-tenant will be protected, both against the tenant and the landlord.

Licensed Premises Under Section 11

A tenancy of a dwelling which is connected to licensed premises for

---

[559] *Wilkes v Godwin* [1923] 2 KB 86 (CA).
[560] *Otter v Norman* [1988] 2 All ER 897 (HL).
[561] *Marchant v Charters* [1977] 3 All ER 918; [1977] 1 WLR 1181 (CA).
[562] SI 1998/1967.
[563] *R v Rent Officer for Camden LBC, ex parte Plant* (1981) 257 EG 731 (tenant studying to be a nurse).

the sale of alcohol is not protected. Since the introduction of the Landlord and Tenant (Licensed Premises) Act, 1990, a tenancy of licensed premises will probably be a business tenancy under Part II of the Landlord and Tenant Act, 1954.

Presence of Resident Landlords Under Section 12

Where there was a resident landlord in the same building as the property which has been let at the commencement of the tenancy, there is no protection. However, where the landlord was in occupation of a self-contained accommodation, as in a large building or block of flats, there will be protection. Section 12 specifies three conditions which must be satisfied for the dwelling to fall within this exclusion. Where there is a resident landlord the potential for social embarrassment could be greater.[564]

Crown as Landlord under Section 13

Where the landlord's interest belongs to the Crown, or a government department, or in trust to Her Majesty for the purpose of a government department, it is excluded from protection. However, the tenancy can be protected if the interest is under the management of the Crown Estate Commissioners under section 13(2).

Interests of a Local Authority and Certain Public Bodies Under Section 14

The types of public authorities are very wide, and include also the Commission for the New Towns, development corporations, the Development Board for Wales, a National Park Authority and an urban development corporation. Where these bodies are the landlord, the dwelling is not protected. However, local authority tenants may well be secure tenants under the Housing Act, 1985.

Interest of Housing Association Under Section 15

There is no protected tenancy if the landlord's interest belongs to a

---

[564] See *Bardrick v Haycock* (1976) 31 P&CR 420 at p 424 per Scarman LJ.

housing corporation, Housing for Wales, a housing trust, which is a charity, a registered social landlord or a cooperative housing association.

Interest of Housing Co-operative Under Section 16

There is no protection where the landlord's interest belongs to a housing co-operative within the meaning of section 27B of the Housing Act, 1985.

Business Tenancies Under Section 24

A business tenancy under Part II of the Landlord and Tenant Act, 1954, cannot be a regulated tenancy under the Rent Act, 1977.

Company Lets Under Section 2(1)(a)

As only an individual is capable of living in a dwelling, a letting to a company is not protected. In this case the letting is between the company and the landlord. But there are circumstances when a company let is subject to the "fair rent" provision.

CONFERMENT OF SECURITY OF TENURE BY THE RENT ACT 1977

Security of tenure consists of a number of rights a tenant may acquire by statutory provisions. For the purposes of the 1977 Act, security of tenure is provided by:

(a) the mechanism of the statutory tenancy which automatically arises after termination of the contractual tenancy if certain pre-conditions are satisfied; and

(b) allowing the landlord to recover possession only under certain statutorily defined grounds.

There is also the right of the tenant's entitlement regarding the payment of a "fair rent" from the date of its registration.

The Statutory Tenancy Arising Automatically

A statutory tenancy arises only after the contractual tenancy is terminated by effluxion of time and confers on the tenant a right to continue in possession of the dwelling under a statutory tenancy. The statutory tenancy cannot be assigned, except in certain statutorily defined situations.[565] The tenancy cannot devolve under a will or intestacy, and on bankruptcy it will not vest in the tenant's trustee in bankruptcy, nor can the tenant sub-let the whole of the premises. Although subject to these restrictions, a statutory tenant can sue in trespass, sub-let part of the premises and, as in an estate in land, a statutory tenancy will bind a successor in respect of the landlord's title.

A statutory tenancy will only arise from a protected tenancy in two situations:

(a) where there was a previous protected tenancy covered by section 1 of the 1977 Act; and

(b) where there is a right to it by succession.

The key requirement in respect of the tenant claiming a statutory tenancy is that he is occupying the premises as a residence. A protected tenancy will last until the end of the contractual relationship between the parties. Termination can be by various means, such as notice to quit, effluxion of time, forfeiture or any other common law methods of termination. After such a termination, the relationship between the landlord and the tenant will continue under section 2(1) of the Act as a statutory tenancy. To satisfy section 2(1), to become a statutory tenancy certain conditions under section 1(2) must be satisfied:

(a) the tenant must have held a contractual tenancy protected by section (1);

(b) the tenancy must have ended;

---

[565] In matrimonial proceedings or with the agreement of the landlord: Rent Act, 1977, Sch 1, Part II, paras 13 & 14; also *Keeves v Dean* [1924] 1 KB 685.

(c) the tenant must have held a protected tenancy of the dwelling-house immediately before the termination of the contractual tenancy; and

(d) the tenant must continue to occupy the dwelling-house as his residence.

Statutory Tenancy Based on Previous Protected Tenancy. There is no need for the contractual tenant to occupy the premises throughout before the end of the contractual tenancy, but he must live in the premises when that tenancy comes to an end. If the whole of the premises were sub-let before the end of the contractual tenancy, the tenant will not become a statutory tenant. However, if only part of the premises was sub-let, he will be a statutory tenant of the part retained as his residence, assuming the part sub-let is considered a separate dwelling.[566] A statutory tenancy depends on the tenant's continued occupation, as it will cease if he no longer occupies the premises. Whether the statutory tenant continues to occupy the premises is a question of fact and the onus is on the tenant to prove that he is in occupation. In the case of a tenant who has a spouse or civil partner, and the tenant is claiming occupation vicariously through his spouse or civil partner the occupation will end on a divorce or if the civil partnership is dissolved.[567]

More than One Home. The residence requirement can be satisfied even if the dwelling-house is just one of the tenant's homes. Under section 1, the occupation is considered at the commencement, while under section 2 what has to be considered is whether the tenant is a statutory tenant after the end of the contractual tenancy. It is possible that section 1 requirement was satisfied, but not section 2 requirement as the tenant may have ceased to occupy the dwelling-house as his residence within the meaning of section 2. However, where a tenant has two homes, say, one outside of London and a flat in London, which he occupies for a few days during the week, he will be regarded as being resident in the flat for the purposes of section 2.[568]

---

[566] See *Berkeley v Papadoyonnis* [1954] 2 QB 149; [1954] 2 All ER 409 (CA).
[567] See *Metropolitan Properties Co v Cronan* (1982) 126 SJ 229; (1982) 262 EG 1077 (CA)
[568] *Bevington v Crawford* (1974) 232 EG 191.

Statutory Tenancy by Succession. When a tenant, who is a protected tenant or a statutory tenant dies, security of tenure may be transmitted to a family member. The family member will acquire, except in a few cases, a statutory tenancy, regardless of whether the deceased tenant was a protected tenant at the time of death or whether his contractual term had already ended and he had become a statutory tenant. Under the Act there cannot be more than two statutory successions in respect of the original tenancy.[569]

In *Northumberland & Durham Property Trust Ltd v Ouaha*[570] the Court of Appeal had to decide whether the appellant, married under a Sharia ceremony, was a "surviving spouse" for the purposes of the Rent Act 1977. There was no civil ceremony and before the death of the Mr Al-Faisal the parties had been divorced but living in the same house. The appeal was dismissed as the appellant was not Mr Al-Faisal's "surviving spouse" within the meaning of that phrase in paragraph 2(1) of Schedule 1 to the Rent Act 1977. Therefore, she did not become a statutory tenant after the death of the secure tenant, and ordered that the Appellant should deliver up possession of the property.

Terms of the Statutory Tenancy. The terms in general will be the same as the previous contractual tenancy.[571] For example, if there was a proviso for re-entry if the tenant became bankrupt, it would be construed in the statutory tenancy that the tenant would not go bankrupt.[572] Any term which is inconsistent with the Rent Act, 1977, will not be read into the statutory tenancy.

CONTROL OF RENT

Rent control has been a significant element in the Acts leading up to the Rent Act, 1977. It is completely absent in the Housing Act, 1988, which adopts a similar system of security of tenure as in the Rent Acts. But there is no system of rent registration under the 1988 Act.

As provided for in the Rent Act, 1977, the level of rent payable under a tenancy can be fixed by a "rent officer", who is a public

---

[569] This area of the law is somewhat wide and complicated, and is beyond the scope of this book.
[570] [2014] EWCA Civ 571.
[571] Section 3(1) of the Rent Act, 1977.
[572] *Cadogan Estates Ltd v McMahon* [2000] 3 WLR 1555 (HL).

official. The rent determined by a rent officer is known as a "fair rent". Such a rent is registered, and it overrides the rent agreed by the parties under the contractual tenancy. A fair rent does not reflect the level of rents based on supply and demand in the market.

Rent Registration

An application by either party to register a fair rent must be made to the rent officer in the prescribed form. Under certain circumstances, they can make a joint application under section 67 of the Rent Act, 1977. Even the local authority has the right to apply under section 68, especially if the tenant is in receipt of housing benefit to ensure that public funds are not being wasted. If either party is dissatisfied with the registered rent, he can make a written objection to a rent assessment committee within 28 days of receiving notice of the registered rent from the rent officer. The committee has the option of either confirming the fair rent as assessed or determine a fair rent itself.

<u>Determining a Fair Rent</u>. Section 70 provides certain guidelines for the rent officer by setting out the factors that he must consider and those which must be disregarded:

"(1) In determining, for the purposes of this Part of this Act, what rent is or would be a fair rent under a regulated tenancy of a dwelling-house, regard shall be had to all the circumstances (other than personal circumstances) and in particular to—

(a) the age, character, locality and state of repair of the dwelling-house,
(b) if any furniture is provided for use under the tenancy, the quantity, quality and condition of the furniture, and
(c) any premium, or sum in the nature of a premium, which has been or may be lawfully required or received on the grant, renewal, continuance or assignment of the tenancy.

(2) For the purposes of the determination it shall be assumed that the number of persons seeking to become tenants of similar dwelling-houses in the locality on the terms (other than those relating to rent) of the regulated tenancy is not substantially greater than the number of

such dwelling-houses in the locality which are available for letting on such terms.

(3) There shall be disregarded—

(a) any disrepair or other defect attributable to a failure by the tenant under the regulated tenancy or any predecessor in title of his to comply with any terms thereof;
(b) any improvement carried out, otherwise than in pursuance of the terms of the tenancy, by the tenant under the regulated tenancy or any predecessor in title of his;

(c) (d) . . .

(e) if any furniture is provided for use under the regulated tenancy, any improvement to the furniture by the tenant under the regulated tenancy or any predecessor in title of his or, as the case may be, any deterioration in the condition of the furniture due to any ill-treatment by the tenant, any person residing or lodging with him, or any sub-tenant of his."

<u>Scarcity Value and Comparison</u>. The rent officer's assessment is based on a consideration of comparable properties in the area. So what is a comparable property? And the Housing Act, 1988, impinges considerably on suitable comparables for the purposes of the Rent Act, 1977. The rents fixed under tenancies subject to the Housing Act will reflect market forces, while those fixed under the Rent Act with the objective of rent control will be artificial rents fixed at a lower level, having regard to the guidelines under section 70 of the Rent Act, 1977. By reason of section 70(2) which renders Rent Act tenancies immune from market forces, most of the rents determined by a rent officer will be significantly below that of properties let at market rents. This is particularly the case because of the exclusion of scarcity value when assessing the rent. The valuation is made on the assumption that the number of similar properties in the area is not significantly less than the number of people seeking accommodation.[573] The provision is aimed at preventing the landlords

---

[573] Economics has been defined by one economist in this way: Economics is the science of wealth. Wealth consists of goods and services which are scarce enough to have a money value. From this definition, scarcity is important in order to attribute a

from benefitting in consequence of the shortage of accommodation in the area. The valuation will reflect the inherent value of the property but not any increase in value attributable to market forces.

Section 70(2) will be relevant where there is a scarcity of accommodation. One of the objectives of the Housing Act, 1988, is to encourage private sector lettings by removing rent control. In this regard, the Housing Act has been largely successful. Therefore, the question that arises is whether a rent officer should reflect the rents on comparable properties let under assured tenancies. The question was answered in the affirmative in *BTE Ltd v Merseyside and Cheshire RAC and Jones.*[574] There was no shortage of accommodation based on evidence as provided by the landlord, and the rent assessment committee accepted the evidence. But the committee said that the new lettings were not suitable comparables to assess a fair rent and relied on similar properties let on regulated rents. This appears to be wrong where there is no scarcity of accommodation.

Other Matters to Exclude in Assessing a Fair Rent. The personal circumstances of the parties are to be ignored in assessing a fair rent. The same applies to any improvement carried out by the tenant, such as the installation of a new kitchen. Section 70(3)(b) specifically excludes improvements, not in pursuance of an obligation.

Maximum Fair Rent. For the first time the Rent Acts (Maximum Fair Rent) Order, 1999,[575] introduced a maximum fair rent limit. This limit is effective after 1 February, 1999. The maximum rent is based on the current rent plus the difference between the current retail price index and the retail price index at the time the rent was last registered, plus 7.5% on the first application after 1 February, 1999, or 5% on any subsequent application. This maximum limit is applicable only where the rent has been registered previously. In 2000 the Court of Appeal held that the 1999 Order was *ultra vires,* but the decision was overruled by the House of Lords.[576]

---

value. Anything freely available, even fresh air to sustain life, has no money value. Therefore, by ignoring scarcity value, the rent will be zero. Hence what rent is fixed by the rent officer is an artificial rent.
[574] [1991] 24 HLR 514.
[575] SI 1999/6.
[576] *R v Secretary of State for the Environment, Transport and the Regions ex p Spath Holme Ltd* [2001] 2 AC 349; [2001] 1 All ER 195 (HL); [2001] 2 WLR 15

The calculation of the maximum rent disregards any variable sum included in the registration.[577] There is no maximum if, because of repairs or improvements to the premises or common parts,[578] done by the landlord or a superior landlord, the new rent exceeds the current rent by at least 15%.

The Effect of Rent Registration

Once a fair rent is registered for any property, it is the maximum recoverable by the landlord. The amount registered will include any sum for services provided by the landlord.[579] It is effective from the date of registration.[580] Prior to the Housing Act, 1980, the fair rent was retrospective to the date of the application. Where the tenant is a protected tenant, i.e., before the termination of the contractual tenancy, and a higher rent was paid under the contract, then the excess over the fair rent registered is not recoverable by the landlord.[581] Any excess rent already paid by the tenant is recoverable under section 57, either by deduction from future payments or by taking proceedings in the county court.

Other Matters

Where no fair rent has been registered, there are still restrictions on what rent the landlord can charge. In the case of a new tenant, the rent will be whatever has been agreed between the parties. If the tenant was previously a regulated tenant who has been granted a new tenancy, the rent will be what was the rent payable previously. If at the end of a contractual tenancy no rent has been registered, the new rent will be the same as at the end of the contractual tenancy under section 45.

---

[577] SI 1999/6 art. 2(5); Rent Act, 1977, s 71(4).
[578] They include the structure and exterior of the building: Rent Acts (Maximum Fair Rents) Order 1999 (SI 1999/6 art. 2(8)(b). Only improvements, etc, effected since any previous application can be considered. See *Toloi v Rent Assessment Committee of the London Rent Assessment Panel* [2013] All ER (D) 83.
[579] Rent Act, 1977, s 71(1).
[580] Rent Act, 1977, s 77 as amended by the Housing Act, 1980, s 61(1).
[581] Rent Act, 1977, s 44(2).

Rent Increase by Agreement. The rent can be increased by agreement between the parties under section 51, and the agreement must be in writing in the specified form.

Premiums. There are restrictions in the landlord charging a premium. This provision is intended to prevent the circumvention of the consequences of rent control by unscrupulous landlords. Therefore, section 119 makes it illegal for any person to demand or receive a premium or loan as a condition of, or in connection with, any grant or renewal or continuance of a protected tenancy.

GROUNDS FOR OBTAINING POSSESSION BY THE LANDLORD

Because a statutory tenancy of residential premises is not a true tenancy but merely a personal right,[582] the rules for bringing it to an end varies from that which applies to an agricultural statutory tenancy.[583] Thus termination by effluxion of time, notice to quit,[584] or any act of the landlord does not apply. The length of the statutory tenancy is indefinite. Hence, a landlord can only lawfully terminate it by proceedings in the court for possession.

If the agreement between the parties are broken by the tenant, e.g., by not paying rent, the landlord may serve a notice to quit on the tenant for the recovery of possession. There are a number of grounds under which the landlord may obtain possession. To recover possession from a protected tenant under the Rent Act, 1977, the landlord must serve notice giving the tenant 28 days of his intention to recover possession. Following the 28 days, an application must be made to the court for an order against the tenant, if he does not leave after expiry of the notice.

The notice to quit must contain the reason why possession is being sought, and the specific ground or grounds must be mentioned in the notice. The landlord is prevented from evicting the tenant by menaces. He could be criminally liable under the Protection from Eviction Act, 1977. Once a notice to quit is served, during the period of the contractual tenancy, the tenancy becomes a statutory tenancy

---

[582] Rent Act, 1977, s 2(1)(a) & (3).
[583] Rent (Agriculture) Act, 1975, s 4(5).
[584] Except by the Rent Act, 1977, s 3(3); Rent (Agriculture) Act, 1976, Sch 5, para. 10.

which will continue until a court order is obtained to bring the tenancy to an end.

Grounds for Possession

The grounds for possession in respect of a Rent Act protected tenancy are based on:

(a) ten mandatory grounds; and

(b) ten discretionary grounds.

Mandatory grounds are grounds under which the court must make an order for possession in favour of the landlord. The court has no discretion if an appropriate ground has been substantiated. On the other hand, the judge has a discretion in deciding whether or not to make an order for possession in respect of the non-mandatory grounds. It is up to the landlord to prove that he is being reasonable. Discretionary grounds reflect the tenant's obligations in the tenancy. Where the grounds are discretionary, it is rare for the landlord to gain possession in the first instance. If an order is made conditions may be imposed. Sometimes, a suspended order may be made.

If a suspended order is made, the tenant will be given a period of time within which to solve the problem so as to remain in possession. Where rent is in arrears, the tenant may be given as much as 28 days to pay or to reach an agreement with the landlord.

The 10 Discretionary Grounds[585]

In relation to the discretionary grounds, the question for the judge is whether it is reasonable to make an order for possession, not whether it is reasonable for the landlord to seek an order. This involves examining not only the consequences for the parties of making the order, but also the consequences of not making it.

The discretionary grounds are set out as cases below, as covered by the Rent Act, 1977:

---

[585] All the grounds in the Rent Act, 1977, in Schedule 15, are referred to as cases, not grounds.

Case One: Breach of Obligation of the Tenancy or Rent Arrears. This is where the tenant has failed to pay his rent or has broken some other condition of the tenancy. This ground covers any other relevant condition in the tenancy, including noise nuisance, unreasonable behaviour and usually racial and sexual behaviour. Where a tenant is insolvent, the landlord has a ground for seeking possession.[586] If a tenant has a counterclaim for breach of the landlord's repairing obligations (under section 11 of the Landlord and Tenant Act, 1985) that can be taken into account.[587]

Case Two: Nuisance, Annoyance, Use for Immoral or Illegal Purposes. This ground applies where the tenant is using the premises for immoral or illegal purposes, such as selling drugs, and using the premises for prostitution. Also relevant are nuisance and annoyance to neighbours.

Case Three: Waste or Neglect. This is concerned with the deterioration of the premises as a direct misuse by the tenant.

Case Four: Furniture. This is in relation to deterioration of the furniture provided for use under the tenancy on account of the ill-treatment by the tenant.

Case Five: Notice to Quit by Tenant. This is applicable where the landlord has arranged to sell or let the property following the tenant's notice to quit.

Case Six: Sub-letting. This is where the tenant has sub-let the premises by creating another tenancy in favour of another person without the consent of the landlord at any time.

Case Seven: Off-licences. This ground has been repealed by the Housing Act, 1980, s 152, Sch 26.

Case Eight: Former Employees. The landlord requires possession for his new employee. This ground applies only to service tenants. The aim is intended to recover possession of the dwelling from the

---

[586] *Cadogan Estates Ltd v McMahon* [2001] 1 AC 378 (HL).
[587] *Televantos v McCulloch* [1991] 1 EGLR 123 CA (Civ Div).

landlord's former employee so that it may be offered to the new employee.

Case Nine: Dwelling Required for Member of Landlord's Family. This ground applies where the dwelling-house is reasonably required for occupation as a residence for the landlord or certain members of his family. In *Clements v Simmonds*[588] it was held that the landlord had no real intention to occupy the house. Therefore, compensation of £60,000 was awarded. This is a case in which the landlord obtained possession by misrepresentation of material facts.

Case Ten: Overcharging Sub-tenant. This ground can be invoked where the tenant is charging a subtenant more rent than the Act permits.

The 10 Mandatory Grounds for Possession

Case Eleven: Returning Owner-occupier. The aim of this ground is to enable an owner-occupier landlord who has let out his house to resume possession if he wishes to move back to the property. This is usually the case where a person has let his house in order to take up an overseas position but retains the option to move back into his house on his return. Before the letting, a notice must have been served on the prospective tenant that possession would be resumed in the future. The landlord must have occupied the house as his residence at some time in the past.

Case Twelve: Retirement Homes. This ground is valid only when a landlord has served notice that the property may be required by the landlord for the personal use as a retirement home. This is broadly similar to ground 11 without the requirement that the property was previously occupied as his residence.

Case Thirteen: Off-season Holiday Lets. In this case the landlord has to substantiate that the letting is for a fixed term of eight months, and that it can be proved that the property was used as a holiday letting for twelve months prior to the present letting. The aim is to enable the

---

[588] [2002] 3 EGLR 32.

landlord to regain possession of the property so that it can be used again for holiday letting.

Case Fourteen: Educational Institutions. Student accommodation is also excluded from the Rent Act protection. If such accommodation is let during a college holiday period for a fixed term not exceeding 12 months, subject to prior notice that possession might be recovered under this ground, the institution may be able to regain possession at the end of such a letting. The accommodation must have been let to students before.

Case Fifteen: Ministers of Religion. This ground is that the property is used normally by a minister of religion and is required for that purpose after a temporary letting to an ordinary tenant.

Case Sixteen: Agricultural Employees. This ground enables a landlord to recover possession of a property so that it can be occupied by an agricultural employee of the landlord.

Case Seventeen: Farmhouses Made Redundant by Amalgamation. Under this ground a dwelling-house was originally occupied by a person responsible for farming land but the dwelling-house has been made redundant under a scheme of amalgamation under the Agriculture Act, 1967. The landlord can recover possession of the property if it is again required for a person employed in agriculture.

Case Eighteen: Farmhouses Made Redundant Without Amalgamation. This ground applies where a dwelling-house was formerly occupied by someone responsible for farming the land where the dwelling is situated. At that time the dwelling was subject to a regulated tenancy and the tenant was served with prior written notice that possession might be recovered under this ground.

Case Nineteen: Protected Shorthold Tenancies. This type of tenancy preceded the assured shorthold tenancy, and was created under the Housing Act, 1980, which permitted a landlord to grant a short fixed-term tenancy of between one and five years without the benefit of security of tenure to the tenant. Such a tenancy was no longer created after 15 January, 1989, unless created pursuant to a contract made before that date. Thus, there are now very few protected shorthold tenancies in existence. Former protected shorthold tenants are granted assured shorthold tenancies.[589]

On termination of a protected shorthold tenancy, the tenant continues to occupy as a statutory tenant. In this case, ground 19 confers on the landlord the right to a possession order, subject to two conditions:

(a) that there has been no further tenancy of the property since the end of the protected shorthold tenancy or, if there was such a grant, it was to a person who prior to the grant was in possession of the property as a protected or statutory tenant; and

(b) the proceedings for possession were commenced after an appropriate notice served by the landlord to the tenant and not later than three months following expiry of the notice.

Case Twenty: Armed Forces Personnel. This is a ground which is similar to grounds 11 and 12 (returning owner-occupier and retirement home respectively). Ground twenty enables a member of the armed forces to purchase a property and to rent it out with the intention to occupy it at some time in the future when recovery of possession is needed, e.g., on discharge or retirement from the armed forces.

Many of the above grounds require certain conditions to be satisfied by the landlord. Information regarding these conditions can be obtained from the statute.[590]

Other Matters:

A few other relevant matters are set out below.

Overcrowding.

This is a ground for possession but it is not listed in Schedule 15 of the 1977 Act. In effect this is a further mandatory ground for

---

[589] Section 34(3) of the Housing Act, 1988.
[590] The Rent Act, 1977, can be downloaded easily. All that is required is to type the name of the Act on a search engine.

possession.[591] A tenant has no security if the occupier is guilty of an offence because the premises are overcrowded.[592] Premises are defined as overcrowded:

1. Where people of different sexes over 10 years (not husband and wife) must sleep in the same room (Housing Act, 1985, s 325).

2. Where the number of people sleeping in the house exceeds the maximum calculated in accordance with section 326 of the 1985 Act as follows:

(1) in computing the number of people, children under age 1 are disregarded and those between 1 and 10 years are counted as half;
(2) rooms of less than 50 sq ft are to be disregarded;
(3) the number of people occupying is the lessor of:

   (a) in a house of
   one room - 2 persons
   two rooms - 3 persons
   three rooms – 5 persons
   four rooms - 7.5 persons
   five and more rooms – 2 persons per room.

   (b) The following number of people per room calculated on floor area of each room:

   At least 50 sq ft but under 70 sq ft – half a person
   At least 70 sq ft but under 90 sq ft – 1 person
   At least 90 sq ft but under 110 sq ft - 1.5 persons
   At least 110 sq ft – 2 persons

There are circumstances where there can be overcrowding but no offence is committed. For example, when children attain the age of one or ten provided the occupier applies to the local authority for alternative accommodation.[593]

---

[591] Refer to section 101 of the Rent Act, 1977.
[592] Rent Act, 1977.
[593] *Henry Smith's Charity Trustees v Bartosiak-Jentys* [1991] 2 EGLR 276 CA (Civ Div)

Sub-tenants

Although a sub-tenant has no right to remain in possession at common law if the head lease is terminated, section 137 of the Rent Act, 1977, provides some sub-tenants with protection against this situation.

No Need to Serve Notices

There are various situations when the landlord is required to serve a notice on the tenant under the statutory code. However, if the court considers it just and equitable to do so, the service of a notice on the tenant in a particular situation may be dispensed with, having regard to all the circumstances, including the hardship as the case may be from the point of view of each party.[594]

Possession Proceedings

Any landlord who wishes to obtain possession of his property subject to the Rent Act protected or statutory tenancy must follow the same procedural rules as in the case of landlords of assured tenants. Due process of law must be complied with.

There are many statutory obligations on landlords to ensure that their rights against residential tenants are exercised exclusively via the courts. They are set out below.

(a) Re-entry Without Due Process. It is unlawful to enforce a right of re-entry or forfeiture of a dwelling or mixed use premises which include a dwelling.[595] A tenant who was not sleeping in the premises on account of a fire but attended almost daily was considered to be in lawful occupation.[596] A sub-tenant enjoys the same protection without a court order for re-entry.[597]

---

[594] See *Fernandes v Parvardin* (1982) 264 EG 49; *Bradshawv Baldwin-Wiseman* (1985) 49 P&CR 382 (CA). On the morning ofr the trial there was no overcrowding (an exceptional circumstance) but overcrowding was established nevertheless.
[595] *Patel v Pirabakaran* [2006] 1 WLR 3112.
[596] *Imperion Investments Corporation v Broadwalk House Residents Ltd* (1994) 71 P & CR 34.
[597] See *Belgravia Property Investments & Development Co Ltd v Webb* [2002] L & TR 29.

(b) <u>Eviction Without Due Process</u>. Landlords are prevented from enforcing a right to recover possession at the end of a tenancy or a licence otherwise than by proceedings in court.[598] In the case of a statutory tenancy, this protection continues even though a court has made an order for possession.[599] This only applies where the premises were let or a licence granted as a dwelling, but not within these classes:[600]

(1) a protected or a long tenancy at a low rent at the end of which a statutory tenancy would arise except where a right to possession arises on the death of a statutory tenant;
(2) an excluded tenancy entered into on or after 19 January 1989 but pursuant to an earlier contract;
(3) a protected occupancy, agricultural tenancy or statutory tenancy, save where a right to possession arises on the death of a statutory tenant;
(4) a farm business tenancy;
(5) a renewable business tenancy; and
(6) a tenancy of an agricultural holding.

End

---

[598] Protection from Eviction Act, 1977, s 3.
[599] *Haniff v Robinson* [1993] QB 419.
[600] Protection from Eviction Act, 1977, ss 3(3), 3A, 8(1).

CHAPTER 12

OTHER PRIVATE SECTOR RESIDENTIAL TENANCIES

INTRODUCTION

This chapter is devoted exclusively to statutory provisions relating to other private sector residential tenancies, excluding those within the Rent Act 1977. This Act is mainly concerned with security of tenure, regulated rent and other related matters.

In order to resolve a landlord and tenant problem, it is important to consider the applicable common law principles and how these principles are modified by statutory provisions. In some cases, the tenancy or lease may not be subject to statutory provisions conferring security of tenure, such as an AST, except for the first six months.

The net effect of the Rent Act, 1977, and its predecessors, is to reduce the supply of rented accommodation in the private sector on account of both security of tenure and the maximum recoverable rent. However, following the introduction of the Housing Act, 1988, dwellings available for rental have been substantially increased than hitherto. The effect is to open the market of private residential accommodation, and this has the consequential effect of increasing the level of "fair rents" though the permitted increase is restricted.[601]

The object behind the 1988 Act is to reduce security of tenure to enable an increase in the supply of accommodation for letting. One of the objectives is to phase out the regulated tenancy and "restricted contract" in respect of resident landlords. The latter was an inferior type of protection under the 1977 Act. The scope of the Rent Act, 1977, has been reduced[602] as no new protected tenancy may be granted after 15 January 1989, but tenancies created before 15 January, 1989, continue to enjoy the protection under the 1977 Act. However, one effect of the 1988 Act is to reduce the succession rights which hitherto existed on the passing away of a protected or statutory

---

[601] Rent Acts (Maximum Fair Rent) Order, 1999 (SI 1999 No 6). Any increase must be by reference to the increase in the UK Retail Prices Index plus 7.5%. A challenge to the Order was rejected in *R v Secretary of State for the Environment, Transport and the Regions. Ex parte Spath Holme Ltd* [2001] 2 AC 349.

[602] Subject to certain narrow exceptions under the Housing Act, 1988, s 34; *Laimond Properties Ltd v Al-Shakarchi* (1998) 30 HLR 1099.

tenant. Developments in October 2016 regarding the section 21 notice and related matters are incorporated in this chapter.

ASSURED TENANCIES

The Housing Act, 1988, provides for the creation of what is known as an "assured tenancy" which is a little different from the "assured shorthold tenancy" (AST). As regards the former, security of tenure remains, though the grounds on which possession can be claimed are strengthened, while the rights concerning succession to the tenancy and rent control are limited.

To dissuade landlords from evicting protected tenants to enjoy the benefit under the new regime given by the 1988 Act, provision has been made for criminal and civil liability for unlawful eviction and protection.[603]

The Housing Act, 1996, provides a further incentive to private landlords to let their dwellings by removing certain restrictive conditions which were necessary to create the less secured shorthold tenancy. The effect of the 1996 Act is that most assured tenancies created after its commencement date are assured shorthold tenancies (ASTs).

Nature of an Assured Tenancy

The Housing Act, 1988, defines a tenancy of a dwelling house which is let as a separate dwelling to be an "assured tenancy" if the following conditions are satisfied:

(a) the tenant or each of the joint tenants (where there is more than one) is an individual; and

(b) the tenant or at least one of them occupies the dwelling-house as his only or principal home; and

---

[603] Protection from Eviction Act, 1977, s 1(3), as amended by the Housing Act, 1988, s 29(1). See also Protection from Harassment Act, 1997, s 1 (general criminal offence of harassment; actionable in damages by the victim: s 3). A relevant case is *Daiichi Pharmaceuticals UK Ltd v Stop Huntingdon Animal Cruelty* [2004] 1 WLR 1503.

(c) the tenancy is not one which cannot be an assured tenancy by virtue of the exclusion set out in Schedule 1[604] or by virtue of section 1(6).[605]

There cannot be an assured tenancy unless it was entered into on or after 15 January, 1988, the commencement date of the Act. The words "dwelling-house is let as a separate dwelling" have been subject to a great deal of litigation and judicial interpretation.

<u>Meaning of "Dwelling-house"</u>. This may be a house or part of a house, including a flat, and even an hotel.[606] However, the premises must be structurally suitable for occupation as a residence and has some degree of permanence.[607] In the case of caravans, they do not come under the scope of the Act, and protection may be accorded by other legislation.[608]

<u>Meaning of "Let"</u>. It refers to the relationship of landlord and tenant, and does not include a contractual licence. A common example of a licence relates to lodgers who do not have exclusive possession because the owner usually provides attendance or services requiring unrestricted access to the premises.[609] However, service tenants enjoy the benefit of the 1988 Act, although the Act enables the employer to recover possession where a such a tenant has left his service.[610]

<u>Meaning of "As"</u>. Regard must be given to the purpose for which a separate dwelling was let. This could be different from what it is actually being used. For example, premises may be let for business

---

[604] Tenancies granted on or after 1 April 1990 cannot be an assured tenancy if the current rent exceeds £25,000 a year. Tenancies granted before this date, before the abolition of domestic rating, are excluded if the property, or any part subject to the tenancy, had a rateable value on 31 March 1990 exceeding £1,500 in greater London or £750 elsewhere.

[605] This provision excludes tenancies granted to homeless persons by private landlords through the arrangement with a local authority.

[606] *Luganda v Service Hotels Ltd* [1969] Ch 209.

[607] *Chelsea Yacht & Boat Co Ltd v Pope* [2000] 1 WLR 1941 (regarding a houseboat.which was not on land and, therefore, not occupied as a dwelling for the purposes of the 1988 Act).

[608] See the Caravan Sites Act, 1968, and the Mobile Homes Act, 1983; *R v Rent Officer of Nottinghamshire Registration Area, ex p Allen* (1985) 52 P & CR 41.

[609] See *Street v Mountford* [1985] AC 809.

[610] Housing Act, 1988, Sch 2, Ground 16.

use, under a covenant, but the tenant may be using the premises as his dwelling. In this situation, no protection is accorded to the tenant under the Act.[611]

Meaning of "A". The house (or part thereof) must be let as a single dwelling. Where there are many separate dwellings in multiple occupation, no protection is accorded.[612] Again, where a house is let to enable the tenant to grant sub-tenancies or licences of rooms to undergraduates, there is no protection under the Act.[613]

Meaning of "Separate". A separate dwelling excludes cases where the tenant shares some living accommodation with the landlord, and it is excluded by the resident landlord exception.[614]

Meaning of "Dwelling". This word has its ordinary meaning of premises being used for cooking, feeding and sleeping.[615] Premises which are let for both business use and residential use, say, in the upper part over a shop, the whole premises will be subject to statutory provisions governing business premises, unless the business part is "de minimis".[616]

Meaning of "Tenant" The word "tenant" in the definition does not include a corporate tenant since security of tenure is not accorded to a corporate tenant, as has been established under the Rent Act, 1977.

Meaning of "Occupation as Only or Principal Home". Like its predecessors, the 1988 Act is intended to protect a tenant in the occupation of his home. Those who sub-let, without occupying themselves will have no protection. The requirement of "only or principal home" of an assured tenancy is stricter than the position under the Rent Act, 1977. Where a tenant has more than one home, protection will only be accorded to his principal home, which is a question of fact. This requirement is the same in respect of public

---

[611] *Wolf v Hogan* [1948] 2 KB 194.
[612] *Horford Investments Ltd v Lambert* [1976] Ch 39.
[613] *St Catherine's College v Dorling* [1980] 1 WLR 66, in which the Court of Appeal held that a letting to enable a number of people the exclusive use of particular rooms was not a letting of the house as a single dwelling.
[614] Housing Act, 1988, s 3, and Sch 1.
[615] *Westminster City Council v Clarke* [1992] 2 AC 268
[616] Housing Act, 1988, Sch 1; *Lewis v Weldcrest Ltd* [1978] 1 WLR 1107.

sector tenants under the Housing Act, 1985. In the case of joint tenancies, only one of the tenants needs to satisfy the requirement and, as in the case of the Rent Act, 1977, occupation by a tenant's spouse or civil partner, in the absence of a joint tenancy, will satisfy the requirement as the only or principal home.[617]

Exceptions Regarding Assured Tenancies Under the 1988 Act

There are many exceptions regarding tenancies which cannot be assured tenancies under the 1988 Act.

<u>Houses Let by Public Bodies</u>. This exception relates to tenancies granted by public bodies, such as local authorities, the Commission for the New Towns and housing action trusts. However, protection under these tenancies are accorded by the code of protection for public sector housing under the Housing Act, 1985. Educational institutions and similar bodies who provide tenancies to their students are conferred with similar exemptions as under both the 1988 and the 1985 Acts.[618]

<u>Letting by a Resident Landlord</u>. Where the landlord was also residing in a building, of which a dwelling forms part, when the tenancy began and in which he has continued to reside, the tenancy will not be an assured tenancy. However, this exception does not apply to tenancies in respect of a purpose-built block of flats. The 1988 Act provides that a landlord, one of two or more joint landlords, must occupy as his only or principal home, but the Act specifies periods of non-residence which may be overlooked. A landlord who has purchased the building is given up to six months to move in and up to two years when a landlord has died during which time the premises are vested in his estate. Where the landlord is not only a resident but shares accommodation with the tenant, the tenancy is excluded from the Protection from Eviction Act, 1977.

---

[617] Family Law Act, 1996, as amended by the Civil Partnership Act, 2004, s 82, Sch
[618] Housing Act 1988, Sch 1, para 8; Housing Act, 1985, Sch 1, para 10. These also apply to Crown lettings, but no exemption is provided for tenancies by the Crown Estate Commissioners or Duchies of Lancaster or Cornwall.

Holiday Lettings. Such lettings are excluded from the Housing Act, 1988, as well under any other system of control.[619] A leading case in this area is *Buchmann v May*,[620] in respect of a three-month letting to an Australian with a temporary visitor's permit. She signed a tenancy which stated "solely for the purpose of the tenant's holiday in the London area". The Court of Appeal said the onus was on the tenant to show that the document was a sham or the result of mistake or misrepresentation and, in addition, said that the court would be astute to detect a sham if evasion was suspected. However, as the tenant could not prove otherwise, she failed.

Tenancies at a Rent Exceeding an Upper Limit Per Annum. Since 1 April, 1990, any tenancy granted where the yearly rent exceeded £25,000 it could not be an assured tenancy, as at this level of rents there was no hardship to tenants to prevent a free market rent. Tenancies granted before the abolition of domestic rating were also excluded if the property (or a part of it) had a rateable value on 31 March, 1990, exceeding £1,500 in Greater London or £750 in other areas. These are known as high rent tenancies. The £25,000, referred to, has been increased to £100,000 with effect from 1 January 2010. At this upper limit, very few properties would be excluded from the scope of the 1988 Act.

Tenancies at a Low Rent. Where no rent is payable under a tenancy or it was created on or after 1 April, 1990, at a rent not exceeding a yearly rent of £1,000 in Greater London or £250 elsewhere, it is excluded.[621] In the case of tenancies created before 1 April, 1990, they are excluded if the current rent is below two-thirds of the rateable value on 31 March, 1990. Under these provisions are excluded long leases, such as for 99 years at a low rent (or ground rent), which were granted in return for substantial premiums to reflect the capital value of the property. The code in the 1988 Act is not suitable for these leases, but other types of protection (for long leaseholders) is given under other legislation as discussed in Chapters 14 and 15.

---

[619] Protection from Eviction Act, 1977, s 3A.
[620] [1978] 2 All ER 993.
[621] Housing Act, 1988, Sch 1, para 3, and para 3A inserted by References to Rating (Housing) Regulations, 1990 (SI 1990, No 434).

Implied Terms in Respect of Assured Tenancies

<u>No Assignment or Under-Letting</u>. This is the most important implied term in respect of an assured tenancy. It prevents the tenant parting with possession in respect of the whole or any part of the property without the landlord's permission. And in this regard, section 19 of the Landlord and Tenant Act, 1927, which implies that such permission "shall not be unreasonably withheld" is excluded. Therefore, a landlord is entitled to refuse consent to an assignment or a sub-letting, even where his refusal is unreasonable. The aim is to enable a landlord to choose the tenant to occupy his property. Also, such a term is not implied in the case of a fixed term assured tenancy, where the general law concerning assignment and sub-letting, including section 19 (as above), applies.

<u>Transfer of Assured Tenancy</u>. The court has the power to order a transfer of an assured tenancy to the other spouse, civil partner or cohabitant on divorce, or making a property adjustment order relating to a civil partnership or on separation of cohabitants.[622]

<u>Implied Term Regarding Repairs</u>. Section 16 of the 1988 Act provides that in any assured tenancy the landlord is entitled under an implied term to carryout repairs, and the tenant is obliged to allow access for such a purpose.

ASSURED SHORTHOLD TENANCY (AST)

The AST is now the common form of residential tenancy which is used in the private sector. A lease term referring to the document as a "short assured tenancy" was held not to be an AST.[623] An AST must be granted for at least six months, and the landlord can bring it to an end by giving two months' notice. However, for periodic ASTs longer than weekly or monthly, the period of the notice must be consistent with the period (three months notice for quarterly and six months for half yearly and yearly ASTs).

---

[622] Family Law Act, 1996, Sch 7, as amended by the Civil Partnership Act, 2004, section 82.
[623] *Redstone Mortgages Plc v Welsh* [2009] 3 EGLR 71 CC (Birmingham).

This type of tenancy is covered by the definition of an assured tenancy, discussed already, and, in addition, must satisfy a few other conditions as required by the Housing Act, 1996, which has amended the 1988 Act. For tenancies created before 28 February, 1996 (the commencement date of the 1996 Act), the relevant conditions to satisfy were:

(a) a fixed-term tenancy for at least six months;

(b) no power was given to the landlord to end the tenancy at any time earlier than six months from the date of its commencement; and

(c) a notice in the prescribed form was served by the prospective landlord on the prospective tenant before the assured tenancy was entered into, stating that the tenancy was to be a shorthold tenancy.[624]

As long as section 1 of the 1988 Act was satisfied, a failure to satisfy these three conditions resulted in the creation of an assured tenancy, not an AST. As mentioned earlier, the AST is popular among landlords as it is much easier to recover possession because of the special mandatory ground applicable only to AST. This is in addition to the grounds applicable to an assured tenancy. Another distinction is that there is a greater degree of rent control in respect of an assured tenancy. Another incentive for landlords to let is that since 28 February 1997 assured tenancies created will be an AST, unless they fall within certain narrow exceptions. What this means is that now the AST is the order of the day, unless special steps are taken to create an assured tenancy. Thus, there is no longer any need to comply with:

(a) any minimum term;

(b) prohibition on landlord's break clauses;

(c) any requirement to serve a prior notice on the prospective tenant;

(d) granting only fixed terms, as periodic tenancies now are included; and

---

[624] *Panayi v Roberts* [1993] 2 EGLR 51.

(e) warning to the tenant as to the nature of the tenancy.

The main protection given to the tenant is that he is protected for at least six months, though the tenancy can be terminated earlier if there is a breach of any important term, such as non-payment of rent.

The exceptions when assured tenancies may be still created are set out below.

(a) <u>Excluded by Notice</u>. This is where a prospective landlord notifies a prospective tenant prior the tenancy being created that the tenancy is not to be an AST or, after a tenancy has been created, the landlord serves a notice on the tenant that it is no longer an AST.

(b) <u>Excluded by Tenancy Provision</u>. Here the tenancy itself contains a provision that it is not an AST.

(c) <u>Successor to Rent Act Provision.</u> This applies when an assured tenancy arises in favour of a successor under section 39 of the 1988 Act on the death of a Rent Act tenant whose tenancy was not an AST. What was formerly protected under the 1977 Act becomes an assured tenancy under the Housing Act, 1988, after a succession.

(d) <u>Tenancies Replacing Non-Shortholds</u>. This situation arises where before the grant of a tenancy, the tenant had an assured tenancy, then the new tenancy is also an assured tenancy, if granted by the same landlord, though there is no need for the premises to be the same. However, the tenant can serve a prescribed form notice before the grant of the replacement tenancy that it is to be an AST.

As an AST can be created informally in respect of periodic tenancies, the tenant can acquire a written statement of the terms of the tenancy under section 20A of the 1988 Act.[625] The landlord on receipt of a written notice regarding a written statement will have to provide any of the following which is not already in writing in the possession of the tenant:

(a) the commencement date of the tenancy, or in the case of a statutory periodic tenancy, the date it arose;

---

[625] Inserted by section 97 of the Housing Act, 1996.

(b) both the rent and the date it is payable;

(c) any term relating to rent review; and

(d) the term in respect of a fixed-term tenancy.

A landlord is obliged to provide the above, and if he fails to do so without a reasonable excuse is liable to a fine. The various matters set out above are not conclusive evidence of what was agreed.

TENANCY DEPOSITS

There are requirements to safeguard the deposit of a tenant who pays a deposit to guarantee the payment of rent and the performance of other obligations. From the deposit the landlord can recoup compensation for any breach of contract by the tenant.[626]

The landlord must deal with the deposit under an authorised scheme. He must either pay it to the scheme administrator for deposit into a designated account or provide a guarantee, which is supported by insurance that he will repay what becomes due to the tenant.

Various sanctions were imposed by legislation in the event the landlord fails to comply with the statutory requirements. They include a penalty of up to three times the deposited amount payable to the tenant and an inability to obtain possession under the section 21 procedure. It seems the penalty is unduly harsh and is clearly in favour of the tenant. These sanctions were criticised or were held to be unworkable by the courts. From 6 April 2012, they have been replaced by amended provisions in the Localism Act, 2011.

The relevant provisions are set out in the Housing Act 2004, Sections 213 to 215, as amended by the Localism Act 2011, sections 1 and 4.

A deposit which is rolled over from a fixed-term AST to statutory periodic AST will require compliance with the 2004 Act. In *Superstrike Ltd v Rodriques*[627] the deposit was taken before April 2007, i.e. before the requirement to register a deposit became operational, and the AST became a statutory periodic tenancy after April 2007. The Court of Appeal decided two issues in this case: (a)

---

[626] *Ng v Ashley King (Developments) Ltd* [2010] EWHC 456 (Ch).
[627] [2013] EWCA Civ 669.

whether the statutory periodic tenancy was a new tenancy and (b) whether or not the deposit had been received by the landlord in January 2008 when the new tenancy was created. The Court ruled that the tenancy was a new tenancy and that the deposit was received in January 2008 (although it was the same deposit given a year earlier and the landlord had argued that he had not physically received a deposit in 2008).

This case also raises another issue with regard to the service of prescribed information. The lack of serving such information could adversely affect the section 21 notice for possession if it had not been served within the said 30-day period. The Court of Appeal did not address this issue, but it follows that as a statutory periodic tenancy is deemed to have been created in circumstances that require the deposit to be registered then the prescribed information ought to be served in accordance with the legislation.

The Court of Appeal *Charalambous v Ng*[628] provisionally accepted the argument that penalty provisions of the new law would not apply to a landlord holding a pre-2007 deposit, but the court left the question open where a penalty was being claimed. The Deregulation Act, 2015, which incorporates sections 214 and 215 in the Housing Act, 2004, confirms the Court of Appeal's decision in this case that the landlord was not liable to pay a penalty but is only required to protect a pre-2007 deposit in order to serve a notice to end the tenancy.

Another Court of Appeal case was with regard to the payment of a penalty. *Ayannuga v Swindells*,[629] involved a landlord who had not provided the relevant prescribed information[630] within 30 days of the receipt of the deposit to the tenant under the Tenancy Deposit Scheme. In consequence, he was ordered to pay the maximum penalty of three times the deposit to the tenant. In this case, the coming into effect of a statutory periodic AST, after the fixed term AST ended, was regarded as a new tenancy and, therefore, the prescribed information had to be provided again. A failure to do so resulted in the penalty against the landlord.

---

[628] [2014] EWCA Civ 1604.
[629] [2012] EWCA Civ 1789.
[630] Under section 213(5) & (6) of the Housing Act 2004 in accordance with the Housing (Tenancy Deposits) (Prescribed Information) Order, 2007 No 797. The landlord is also required to provide any leaflet published by the applicable Tenancy Deposit Protection Scheme.

The Deregulation act 2015 reverses some of the unintended consequences of the earlier Court of Appeal decision in *Superstrike v Rrodriques*.[631] A landlord is required to protect a deposit only once; there is no need to comply again with the formalities each time a tenancy is renewed.

RENT CONTROL

A system of rent control goes back to 1916 and was operating side by side with security of tenure. The present Act that deals with rent control is the Rent Act, 1977, under which the aim is to keep the rent below market levels. However, under the Housing Act, 1988, the philosophy is to prohibit landlords charging excessive rents while not against the recovery of market rents and, unlike the 1977 Act, a landlord can charge a premium on the grant or assignment of an assured tenancy. The position under the different regimes concerning rent control is set out separately below

Fixed-Term Assured Tenancies

Where the term is fixed in an assured tenancy, there is no rent control during the term under the Housing Act, 1988. Whatever rent the parties have decided as to the rent being charged will be effective, and the rent may be increased according to any clause to review the rent or by any subsequent agreement by them.

Periodic Assured Tenancy

Under the 1988 Act a periodic assured tenancy continues until it ends under an appropriate ground that becomes available to the landlord; he is not allowed to terminate the tenancy by a notice to quit. When a fixed term tenancy ends, a statutorily assured tenancy arises under the security mechanism under the Act and, likewise, continues until a ground for possession becomes available. In these two situations, the Act provides how the rent can be increased.[632]

---

[631] [2013] EWCA Civ 669.
[632] Housing Act, 1988, s 13. Any rent review clause under the original assured tenancy is excluded from the new tenancy as it is replaced by the statutory rent review procedure (*London District Properties (Management) Ltd v Goolamy* [2009] EWHC 1367, [2010] 1 WLR 307).

The rent can be increased only if the landlord serves a notice in the prescribed form proposing a new rent to take effect on a new period of the tenancy as indicated in the notice. The new rent cannot take effect within the first year of the tenancy. This does not apply to a statutory periodic tenancy. Once the rent has been increased, following the procedure above, another increase cannot take effect within a year. Having regard to these rules, the increased rent cannot apply within certain minimum periods from the date the notice was served.

Assuming the tenant does not refer the landlord's notice to a rent assessment committee, the increased rent will take effect on the date set out in the notice. Any reference to the committee must be done before the commencement of the new period as proposed in the landlord's notice. The alternative to this procedure is for the parties to agree a new rent.

Where the matter is referred to the committee, they will determine the new rent which the dwelling "might reasonably be expected to be let in the open market by a willing landlord under an assured tenancy".[633] Any assessment over £100,000 a year (previously £25,000) will have the effect of taking the tenancy outside its assured status.[634] In assessing the rent, the committee has to ignore matters such as any improvement carried out by the tenant or any adverse effect on the rent caused by a breach of a covenant to repair by the tenant.[635] Any new rent assessed will take effect in accordance with the date in the landlord's notice, though the parties can agree otherwise. However, the committee may decide on a later date on account of any hardship on the part of the tenant.

Assured Shorthold Tenancy (AST)

In the case of periodic assured shorthold tenancies, the procedure set out in relation to increasing the rent of an assured tenancy can apply.[636] Before the commencement of the 1996 Act, all shorthold tenancies created were for fixed terms and, accordingly outside these provisions. However, if any fixed term tenancy becomes a statutory

---

[633] *Ibid*, s14.1.
[634] *R v Rent Assessment Panel, ex p Cadogan Estates Ltd* [1998] QB 398.
[635] Housing Act, 1988, s 14(2). In this regard, the default must be by the present tenant (*N & D (London) Ltd v Gadsdon* [1992] 1 EGLR 112).
[636] Housing Act, 1988, s 14(9), inserted by the 1996 Act, s 104, Sch 8.

periodic tenancy on expiry of the fixed term, the provisions will apply. There is no minimum period of six months as in relation to an assured shorthold created after the commencement of the 1996 Act. This means that the provisions that relate to periodic assured tenancy and statutory periodic assured tenancy are of wider application.

Further Procedure. There is a further procedure under the 1988 Act that is applicable only to AST. This procedure enables a rent initially agreed by the parties to be submitted to the committee under section 22.[637] It differs from the procedure discussed above which merely is a review of the rent that has been in operation for a certain period. A tenant of an AST may apply by notice using the prescribed form for the committee to make a determination of the rent which "the landlord might reasonably be expected to obtain under the assured shorthold tenancy" under section 22(1). This policy is not available for a statutory periodic tenancy, and can be invoked only once. Where an AST was created on or after 28 February, 1997, the procedure can be invoked by the tenant only within six months from its creation.[638]

When to Make a Determination. Section 22(3) prevents the committee from making a determination unless:

(a) there is sufficient evidence of similar dwellings in the locality regarding assured tenancies, whether or not AST; and

(b) the rent agreed by the parties is significantly higher than what the landlord might reasonably be expected to obtain.

Under this procedure, the committee has no power to increase the rent. The tenant is unlikely to succeed in the absence of sufficient comparables, nor where the rent is not significantly excessive. It is unlikely tenants of AST will avail themselves of this procedure to get the rent reduced in the light of a lack of security of tenure in respect of AST.

---

[637] Housing Act, 1988.
[638] Housing ACT, 1988, s 22(2)(aa), inserted by the 1996 Act, s 100.

SECURITY OF TENURE

The stringent system of security of tenure that existed in the past has been relaxed to a large extent. Under the present regime, an assured tenancy may be terminated only in accordance with the provisions of the Housing Act, 1988, as amended by the Housing Act, 1996. The parties cannot contract out of the statutory provisions relating to security of tenure.[639] But where the tenancy has ceased to be an assured tenancy, e.g., the tenant no longer occupies as his only or principal home, the landlord is entitled to claim possession by any of the grounds allowed under the general law.

Periodic Assured Tenancy

Section 5 of the Housing Act, 1988, provides that in respect of a periodic tenancy any notice to quit served by the landlord on the tenant shall be of no effect.[640] But a notice to quit may be served by the tenant to terminate such a tenancy. As discussed later, a court order on a ground for possession can terminate the tenancy.

Fixed-term Assured Tenancy

This type of tenancy may be brought to an end by an act of the tenant, e.g., surrender, under section 5(2) of the Act. Where there is a break clause in the tenancy permitting a premature release from the tenancy, the tenancy can be terminated by the tenant. While the tenant can terminate a tenancy in these situations, the landlord needs a court order, based on a ground for possession, to do so. Also, where a fixed term tenancy contains a power to terminate the tenancy in certain circumstances, the landlord may exercise that power.[641] Unless the tenancy is terminated by the tenant or by a court order, the tenant will continue to occupy the premises, after the fixed term, as a statutory periodic tenant, under section 5(2) of the Act.

---

[639] As in the Rent Act 1977. In *Bankway Properties Ltd v Pensfold-Dunsford* [2001] 1 WLR 1369, there was a clause for a five-fold increase in the rent designed to enable the landlord to obtain possession, but it was held to be unenforceable as it was an attempt to evade the mandatory scheme for security of tenure.
[640] See *Love v Herrity* [1991] 2 EGLR 44.
[641] See *Aylward v Fawaz* (1996) 29 HLR 408.

The right of the landlord to determine the tenancy under section 5 does not include *forfeiture* as an available method of terminating an assured tenancy.[642] Neither does section 146 of the LPA, 1925, relevant. However, where the landlord would have had grounds for forfeiture of the lease, he may be able to rely on some of the statutory grounds for possession[643] and such grounds must be permitted by the tenancy terms for termination.[644]

Ending of Statutory Periodic Tenancy. Any such tenancy arising after a fixed-term tenancy can be ended only by the tenant or by an order of the court based on a ground for possession as applicable to a periodic assured tenancy.

Terms of the Statutory Periodic Tenancy. The period for this tenancy is based on how rent was last payable, e.g., monthly. Rent and other terms are the same as under the expired fixed term under section 5(3). The implied terms, such as for assignment and sub-letting, and the procedure in respect of increasing the rent are the same as already discussed.[645]

Variation of the Terms. Other than the payment of rent, either of the parties may request a variation of the terms of the tenancy. In the event there is any reluctance to accept the new terms suggested, the other party may refer the notice to the rent assessment committee for determination of those terms or some other terms which might reasonably be expected in respect of an assured periodic tenancy under section 6 of the Act.

GROUNDS FOR POSSESSION

The grounds for determining an assured tenancy are specified in Schedule 2 to the Housing Act, 1988. An order of the court to determine such a tenancy can be made only if the judge is satisfied as to the relevance of one of the grounds.[646]

---

[642] *Artesian Residential Investments Ltd v Beck* [2000] QB 541.
[643] These are the mandatory grounds 2 and 8 and the discretionary grounds other than 9 and 16.
[644] Housing Act, 1988, s 7(6).
[645] See section 15 of the Act in respect of assignment and other matters.
[646] See *Baygreen Properties Ltd v Gil* [2002] 3 EGLR 42 as to consent orders.

Statutory Grounds for Possession.

Once a statutory ground has been established for possession by the landlord, that is the end of the matter and an order for possession is then mandatory under Sch 2, Part I, of the Act. In other cases, an order for possession will only be made if the judge considers it reasonable in the circumstances in accordance with Sch 2, Part II. Here the judge has a wide discretion enabling him to consider all relevant circumstances at the date of the hearing. The three categories of grounds for possession are (a), (b) and (c) set out below.

(a) <u>Mandatory Grounds</u>. There are 8 mandatory grounds.

(b) <u>Discretionary Grounds</u>. In addition to the mandatory grounds, there are 10 discretionary grounds.

(c) <u>Special Mandatory Ground</u>. This special mandatory ground applies only to AST, and is based on the landlord serving a valid section 21 notice on the tenant.

Where a fixed-term tenancy has expired, any possession order made by the court in respect of it will also terminate any statutory periodic tenancy which has arisen by virtue of section 7(7). In order to invoke the Act in claiming possession, the landlord is required to serve a notice in the prescribed form under section 8 of the Act. The grounds relied on must be specified. Although there is no need to set out verbatim the words used, the substance must be fully set out.[647] Once notice is served, the landlord must commence court proceedings in accordance with the time limits under section 8. The time limits vary, depending on the ground for possession.[648]

Mandatory Grounds for Possession

These grounds once proved must result in an order for possession. Before discussing Grounds 1 to 8, the other mandatory ground

---

[647] *Mountain v Hastings* (1993) 25 HLR 427, in respect of ground 8.
[648] Section 151 of the 1996 Act has amended the time limits, the main effect is to enable speedy proceedings in respect of ground 14.

relating only to an AST is discussed first. This ground is not among the consecutively numbered grounds 1 to 17 set out later.

Assured Shorthold Tenancy (AST). The mandatory ground for AST is under section 21 of the Housing Act 1988 and it is confined only to an AST. Where the AST has ended and the tenant is occupying under a statutory periodic tenancy, the court must make an order for possession, assuming that the two months' notice in writing has been properly served[649] on the tenant for possession. It used to be the practice of some landlords to serve a notice at the same time when the tenancy is created or later to expire the fixed-term tenancy ends. For example, the notice may be served at least two months before expiry of the term. An order for possession cannot take effect before expiry of the fixed-term tenancy.[650] As will be seen later, for all new ASTs granted after 1 October 2015, a section 21 notice cannot be served on a tenant within 4 months of the commencement of the tenancy. In the event a statutory periodic tenancy has arisen, following expiry of the fixed-term, before the notice is served, the date in the notice cannot be earlier than the earliest date upon which the tenancy could have been terminated[651] by notice to quit. Some details relating to the service of section 21 notice is set out later.

With regard to an AST created since 28 February, 1997, it should be noted that a court order for possession may not be made to take effect earlier than six months after the commencement of the tenancy.

In *McDonald v McDonald*[652] Article 8(2) of the ECHR 1950 was considered in this case. Receivers under instruction of the mortgagee had to serve a section 21 notice for possession to the tenant occupying under an AST. One of the issues was whether Article 8 concerning the private right of the tenant applied. The tenant's appeal against a decision to uphold a possession order was dismissed. There was no

---

[649] Housing Act, 1988, s 21(1) as amended s 98 of the 1996 Act. The period of the notice could be longer for quarterly and longer periods of the tenancy (as explained later).
[650] See *Lower Street Properties Ltd v Jones* (1996) 28 HLR 877. Proceedings cannot be commenced before expiry of the notice.
[651] But for section 5(1), which prevents termination by a landlord' notice to quit.
[652] [2014] EWCA Civ 1049, [2014] BPIR 1270 Arden LJ, CA (Civ Div). In relation to a public landlord, a tenant may rely on Article 8 (private family life) to the extent that the Article imposes a procedural obligation to provide the tenant with an opportunity for a court to consider the proportionality test (*Manchester City Council v Pinnock* [2011] 2 AC 104).

clear and constant jurisprudence of the ECHR that the proportionality test implied into art. 8 applied where there was a private landlord. There was a small group of cases where the EctHR had applied the test. But in no case the landlord had an unconditional right under the tenancy agreement to return of the property on a date which had passed.[653] But there is other authority to the effect that the proportionality test did not apply in the instant case as it would interfere with arrangements made between private parties. Even if the test had applied, the court would still have made the possession order. There was some £200,000 owing to the mortgagee which could not be recovered without making a possession order. In any event the instant court was bound by *Poplar Housing and Regeneration Community Association Ltd v Donoghue*[654] to hold that section 21 was compatible with the Convention, precluding it from holding that the proportionality test applied. The mortgage conditions had to be interpreted purposively to enable the receivers to realise the charged property in an orderly and efficient way. And this required possession to be taken to sell the property.

1. <u>Landlord Occupied or Intends to Occupy.</u> This ground applies where the landlord has served a written notice before the beginning of the tenancy that this ground may be used to recover possession. Either the landlord or another joint landlord occupied the dwelling as his only or principal home in the past before the commencement of the tenancy or, in the absence of such condition, the landlord or a joint landlord requires possession of the dwelling as his, his spouse's or his civil partner's only or principal home. The intention to occupy the dwelling does not have to be proved in the first case. This ground is not available if the dwelling was acquired for gain or profit whilst it was occupied. With regard to the written notice that must have been served, the court may dispense with the requirement if in the interest of justice it is just and equitable to do so.[655] Section 12 of the Act provides for the payment of compensation if it becomes known later that possession was obtained by reason of misrepresentation or the concealment of a material fact.

---

[653] *Brezec v Croatia (7177/10)* [2014] Hlr 3, *Zrilic v Croatia (46726/11)*, *Buckland v United Kingdom ((40060/08)* (2013) 56 EHRR 16, [2013] CLY 1560.
[654] [2001] EWCA 595, [2002] QB 48.
[655] *Mustafa v Ruddock* (1998) 30 HLR 495.

2. <u>Mortgagee's Powers of Sale.</u> This ground is available where the dwelling is mortgaged, and the landlord defaults whereby the mortgagee's power of sale arises. The mortgage must have been created before the creation of the tenancy. Again, written notice must have been given before the commencement of the tenancy, but as in Ground 1 the court can dispense with this requirement. In the event the mortgage was created during the period of the tenancy, any sale by the mortgagee will be subject to the tenancy.[656] This means that the ground is not applicable. Where the tenancy is not binding on the mortgagee, the latter can obtain possession under the general law instead of under the 1988 Act.[657] But this is not available to the landlord.

3. <u>Out of Season Holiday Lettings.</u> This ground is to enable a landlord who usually let out property on holiday lets during the summer to regain possession when a property is let out of season. The ground applies where a fixed-term tenancy does not exceed eight months. Again, written notice must be given to the tenant before commencement of the tenancy that possession might be required again for holiday lettings. Therefore, an out of season letting cannot be an assured tenancy. Also, a letting for holiday is also excluded from being an assured tenancy.[658]

4. <u>Vacation Lettings of Student Accommodation.</u> This ground is similar to ground 3 and is based on the same principle. Lettings to students are precluded from being assured tenancies under Schedule 1 to the Housing Act. However, the letting of student accommodation during the vacation period is capable of being an assured tenancy. To recover such accommodation let during the vacation, certain conditions must be satisfied:

(a) the letting must be for a fixed term not exceeding 12 months;

(b) the dwelling must have been subject to an excluded student letting during the 12-month period prior to the commencement of the letting; and

---

[656] *Barclays Bank plc v Zaroovabi* [1997] Ch 321.
[657] *Britannia Building Society v Earl* [1990] 1 WLR 422.
[658] Housing Act, 1988, Sch 1, Pt I, para 9.

(c) written notice must have been given prior to the beginning of the tenancy that possession might be required under ground 4.

5. <u>Minister of Religion.</u> This ground is to enable the owner of a dwelling which is normally used to accommodate a minister of religion to make it available for such a purpose. In this regard, this ground allows the landlord to gain possession of the dwelling, both when it is occupied by a minister of religion and when it is being occupied by another tenant. The requirement to satisfy is that written notice must have been given to the tenant prior to the commencement of the tenancy that possession might be recovered under this ground.

6. <u>Intention to Demolish or Reconstruct.</u> This ground is similar to what is under section 30(1)(f) of the Landlord and Tenant Act, 1954, in respect of business tenancies. A landlord who intends to demolish or reconstruct the whole or a substantial part of the dwelling may invoke this ground to recover possession. It is available only to the original landlord or a successor who acquired the reversion without any consideration. Once the ground has been established, the landlord will be liable to pay for reasonable removal expenses and, as under ground 1, will be liable for compensation where recovery of possession was based on misrepresentation or concealment.

7. <u>Death of Periodic Tenant</u>. If a tenant without a spouse or civil partner dies, the tenancy will devolve according to his will or rules of intestacy. In such a situation, ground 7 will apply. The landlord must commence proceedings to recover possession within a year of the death if he wants to evict anyone in the dwelling. This ground does not apply to a fixed-term assured tenancy, which will devolve under the deceased's will or the rules of intestacy, and will continue as an assured tenancy if the beneficiary satisfies the conditions necessary for such a tenancy. On expiry of the fixed-term tenancy, a statutory periodic tenancy will arise and, as such, it will be subject to Ground 7 on the tenant's death. If the beneficiary does not satisfy the said conditions, the tenancy will end on expiry of the fixed term.

8. <u>Two Months' Unpaid Rent</u>. This ground is commonly invoked for the recovery of possession if at least two months rent is in arrears.[659]

---

[659] There are two further discretionary grounds that deal with rent arrears. See grounds 10 and 11.

Ground 8 is one of two exceptional mandatory grounds (the other is Ground 2) under which possession can be obtained during a fixed-term tenancy. To invoke Ground 8, the rent must be lawfully due; if it is in excess of what was determined by the rent assessment committee it is not lawfully due.[660] The arrears must exist both at the date of service of notice of proceedings under section 8[661] and at the date of the hearing. As this is a mandatory ground, the court cannot suspend or postpone the order.

It may be possible for the tenant to argue that rent is not lawfully due if the landlord has failed to provide the tenant a name and address for serving notices. In this regard, section 48 of the Landlord and Tenant Act, 1987, provides that rent is not to be treated as due in the absence of providing such details. This argument will provide some time to the tenant and, possibly, the opportunity to pay at least some of the rent to prevent the mandatory possession order from being issued.

In *Masih v Yousaf*[662] the notice seeking possession was held to be valid where it had referenced the relevant mandatory Ground 8 of the Housing Act 1988, Sch. 2, and had referred to at least two months' rent being owed, even though it had not mirrored the statutory language. That was sufficient to give the tenant the information required to enable her to consider what action she should take. At the hearing the landlord was granted possession of his property.

Discretionary Grounds for Possession

Under the following grounds, the court has a discretion whether to make an order for possession. This discretion is exercised under section 7(4) for making an order when it is reasonable to so. Where appropriate, the court may adjourn the proceedings or stay or suspend the execution of the order, if any, or allow some time to the tenant as it thinks fit. Conditions may be imposed, including the payment of rent, and if such conditions are complied with, any order made for possession may be discharged.

---

[660] The rent is after any equitable set off: *Baygreen Properties Ltd v Gil* [2002] EWCA Civ 1340, [2002] 3 EGLR 42.
[661] *Mountain v Hastings* (1993) 25 HLR 427; *Marath v MacGillivray* (1996) 28 HLR 484.
[662] [2014] EWCA Civ 234.

9. <u>Alternative Accommodation.</u> This ground applies when suitable alternative accommodation is made available to the tenant. In this case, the landlord may require the dwelling subject to the tenancy for some purpose and is prepared to make suitable alternative accommodation to the tenant when the order for possession takes effect. The assessment of suitability can take into account any adaptations or alterations that are, at the time, proposed to be made.[663] The alternative accommodation will also be an assured tenancy or equivalent security of tenure.[664] The premises must be reasonably suitable with regard to the means of the tenant and his family requirements in relation to place of work, extent and character.[665] But the accommodation does not need to be pleasant and commodious as the existing one.[666] The rent could be higher than what the tenant pays for the present accommodation assuming he has the means to pay.[667]

Where the tenant has sub-let most of the premises subject to his tenancy and occupies only a small part, it is possible for the landlord to seek possession of the whole premises by providing a new tenancy to the tenant in respect of the part that is actually occupied by him at present.[668] In this situation it is unlikely that the tenant can argue that the part occupied by him is not suitable to his needs. If an order for possession is granted, the tenant will be granted a new tenancy in respect of the part occupied by the tenant and the landlord will become the direct landlord of the sub-tenants.

Where a landlord is able to invoke Ground 9 successfully, he will be required to compensate the tenant for any moving expenses as required by section 11 of the 1988 Act.

10. <u>Some Rent Unpaid.</u> This ground applies where some rent is in arrears at the date on commencement of proceedings for possession and also at the date on serving of the notice.[669] In this regard, there is a difference with respect to Ground 8. The rent need not be unpaid by the date of the possession hearing and, in terms of amount, may be

---

[663] *Boreh v Ealing LBC* [2008] ECWA Civ 1176.
[664] Housing Act, 1988, Sch 2, Pt III, para 2.
[665] See *Siddique v Rashid* [1980] 1 WLR 1018.
[666] *Hill v Richard* [1983] 1 WLR 478.
[667] *Cresswell v Hodgson* [1951] 2 KB 92.
[668] *Mykolyshyn v Noah* [1970] 1 WLR 1271; cf *Yoland Ltd v Reddington* (1982) 263 EG 157.
[669] See *Baygreen Properties Ltd v Gill* [2002] 3 EGLR 42 CA. The rent due is after deduction for any equitable set-off.

less then two months rent in arrears. In view of the courts' discretion, it is unlikely an order will be made for immediate possession for a single breach in this regard. Any order made can be suspended or postponed and may be subject to conditions.

11. Persistent Delay in Paying Rent. This is the third ground that relates to rent arrears. It differs from the other two (Grounds 8 and 10) in that it is concerned with persistent delay in paying rent which is lawfully due. An order may be made for possession even where at the date possession proceedings are commenced there are no arrears of rent. Any order made for possession may be subject to conditions.

12. Other Breaches. This ground is concerned with breaches other than for non-payment of rent. It affords the landlord a ground for possession where the breach is not serious or capable of being remedied. In most cases no order will be made but if made can be suspended. In considering the seriousness of any breach, an important factor is whether the breach is remediable and whether it is continuing. This ground cannot be relied upon if the landlord has waived the breach.

13. Deterioration of the Dwelling-house. The landlord may be able to obtain possession under this ground where the dwelling or any part of it has deteriorated on account of the act, neglect or default of the tenant or other person residing in the dwelling. If the deterioration is caused by any lodger or sub-tenant, the onus is on the tenant to remove them. This ground puts a responsibility on the tenant to look after the premises.

14. Nuisance or Annoyance or Conviction for Illegal or Immoral User. This ground applies where the tenant or anyone connected with the tenant has caused a nuisance to neighbours. Possession can be obtained if:

(a) any such person is guilty of nuisance or annoyance to people residing, visiting or otherwise engaged in a lawful activity in the locality; or

(b) has been convicted of using the dwelling or allowing it to be used for immoral or illegal purposes or of an arrestable offence committed in, or in the locality of, the dwelling-house.

Before a judge decides to postpone a possession order there has to be cogent evidence that the course of conduct which gave rise to the conviction will not be repeated.[670]

The degree of control by the tenant over the person who has caused the problem will be taken into account in considering whether to make an order for possession.[671] The court will also consider the actual or likely effect which the nuisance or annoyance has had or could have on people in the locality.[672]

The fact that the tenant is unable to control the person misbehaving does not rule out the possibility of a possession order, nor does the fact that an anti-social behaviour order has been made against him.[673]

14A. <u>Domestic Violence.</u> This was introduced by section 149 of the 1996 Act and for use to help social landlords to recover possession of family housing from the remaining occupant after his family have left in consequence of domestic violence. The reason for the family (other spouse or civil partner and children) leaving must be attributable to the violence, which is the dominant, principal or real cause.[674] In order to rely on this ground, the landlord must register as a social landlord or a charitable housing trust. The court must be satisfied that the spouse or partner is unlikely to return.

In *Metropolitan Housing Trust Ltd v Hadjazi*[675] the fact that the violent partner had moved put before committing the acts of violence did not prevent the application of the ground for possession.

15. <u>Condition of Furniture.</u> Where deterioration of furniture provided under the tenancy is subject to ill-treatment by the tenant or other residents, Ground 15 can be used to obtain possession. If the

---

[670] *Knowsley Housing Trust v Prescott* [2009] L & TR 24 QBD.
[671] *West Kensington Housing Association Ltd v Davies* (1999) 31 HLR 415.
[672] *London Quadrant Housing Trust v Root* [2005] L & TR 23 (tenant's partner repairing and scrapping cars and threatened neighbours).
[673] *Knowsley Housing Trust v Mc Mullen* [2006] 20 EG 293 (CS).
[674] *Camden LBC v Mallett* (2001) 33 HLR 204 (CA).
[675] [2010] EWCA Civ 750.

deterioration is caused by a lodger or sub-tenant, the ground can be invoked only if the tenant has failed to take reasonable steps to remove him.

16. Tenant Ceasing to be in Landlord's Employment. This ground applies where an employee of a landlord failed to vacate premises which were rented to him as part of his employment, which has ceased. The landlord does not have to prove that the premises are required for another employee.

17. Tenancy Granted by Reason by False Statement. Section 102 of the Housing Act, 1996, introduced this ground because of the increasing proportion of housing for the less privileged being provided under assured tenancies by charitable bodies and registered social landlords. It is a ground for possession when the landlord was induced to grant the tenancy by a false statement. It must be proved that the statement was made knowingly or recklessly by the tenant or any joint tenant or other person acting on the tenant's instigation.[676]

SERVING OF SECTION 21 NOTICE RELATING TO AST

There has been changes in law relating to the section 21 notice and related matters, following the enactment of the Deregulation Act, 2015, under which the Assured Shorthold Tenancy Notices and Prescribed Requirements (England) Regulations, 2015,[677] were made. As the Act came into force on 1 October, 2015, and does not apply to ASTs created before this date, the pre-2015 Act position relating to the section 21 notice is discussed first.

Position Before 1 October 2015

The few paragraphs below apply to the section 21 notice in respect of ASTs granted before 1 October 2015. For these tenancies, the old law will continue to apply until 1 October 2018.[678]

---

[676] *Merton LBC v Richards* [2005] EWCA Civ 639, [2005] HLR 44 (secure tenancy under the Housing Act, 1985).
[677] 2015 No 1646, as amended by the Assured Shorthold Tenancy Notices and Prescribed Requirements (England) (Amendment) Regulations, 2015, No 1725, due to a few anomalies in the prescribed section 21 Form 6A.
[678] See Deregulation Act, 2015, section 41(1)(2) & (3).

The Housing Act, 1988, refers to "the last day" of the tenancy, but a notice which refers to "the end" of it is perfectly valid.

In *Spencer v Taylor*[679] the Court of Appeal held that, following the expiry of a fixed-term AST, a landlord can serve a notice pursuant to section 21(1) of Housing Act, 1988, rather than pursuant to section 21(4). In any event, a notice served under the latter is valid if it specifies an incorrect date for possession but also includes a saving provision from which the correct date can be calculated.

Part 1 of the Housing Act, 1988. In general, an assured tenancy created on or after 28 February, 1997, is an AST by virtue of section 19A. Where a fixed-term tenancy is granted, a periodic tenancy automatically follows under the same terms and for such period as the rent was last payable under the fixed term tenancy in the light of section 5(2) and (3).

Section 21 provides for the recovery of possession against an assured shorthold tenant, under both a fixed term and periodic tenancies. In this regard, there are two notices under section 21(1) and (4):

(1) <u>Subsection (1) Regarding Fixed Term AST</u>. Where a notice is served under subsection (1) on or after the coming to an end of a fixed term AST, the court shall order possession if the AST "has come to an end and no further assured tenancy (whether shorthold or not) is for the time being in existence, other than an assured shorthold periodic tenancy (whether statutory or not)" and notice has been served by the landlord giving the tenant "not less than two months notice in writing stating that he requires possession of the dwelling-house". As can be seen here, there is no requirement for a date to be specified in the notice. By virtue of subsection (2), a notice under subsection (1) "may be given before or on the day on which the tenancy comes to an end".[680]

(2) <u>Subsection (4) Regarding a Periodic AST</u>. Where a notice is served under this subsection, "a court shall make an order for

---

[679] [2013] EWCA Civ 1600.

[680] For a new AST, a section 21 notice cannot be served within 4 months of the creation of the AST, having regard to the Deregulation Act, 2015, section 36, which has inserted subsection (4B) to the Housing Act, 1988.

possession of a dwelling-house let on an assured shorthold tenancy which is a periodic tenancy if the court is satisfied –

> (a) that the landlord or, in the case of joint landlords, at least one of them has given to the tenant a notice in writing stating that, after a date specified in the notice, being the last day of a period of the tenancy and not earlier than two months after the date the notice was given, possession of the dwelling-house is required by virtue of this section; and
>
> (b) that the date specified in the notice under paragraph (a) above is not earlier than the earliest day on which, apart from section 5(1) above, the tenancy could be brought to an end by a notice to quit given by the landlord on the same date as the notice under paragraph (a) above."

A relevant case on section 21 is *Lower Street Properties Ltd v Jones*[681] in which a notice was served under subsection (4) without specifying a date but did specify that possession was required at the end of the period of the tenancy ending after the expiry of two months from the date of the service of the notice. This notice was held to be valid as the tenant was able to ascertain the date referred to having regard to the wording as set out in the notice.[682] However, in *Fernandez v McDonald*,[683] the landlord served a section 21(4) notice specifying the wrong date and without including a saving provision. Therefore, the notice was held to be invalid.

New Statutory Provisions with Effect from 1 October 2015

The matters covered here relate to compliance with certain prescribed legal requirements: a requirement of the landlord to provide the "How to Rent" booklet, time limits, the prescribed Form 6A for the section 21 notice, the notice period under section 21(4), the time limit for the start of court proceedings, preventing retaliatory eviction, and repayment of rent paid in advance. Some of the matters discussed were already provided by previous legislation. The new provisions

---

[681] (1996) 28 H.L.R. 877, CA
[682] This was followed in *Notting Hill Housing Trust v Roomus* [2006] EWCA Civ 407; [2006] 1 WLR 1375; [2007] HLR 2.
[683] [2003] EWCA Civ 1219; [2003] 1 WLR 1027; [2004] HLR 13

apply to all ASTs in England granted on or after 1 October 2015, but from 1 October 2018 they will apply to all ASTs in existence at that time.

A. Compliance with Certain Prescribed Legal Requirements. A section 21 notice will not be effective if the landlord contravenes any prescribed legal requirement[684] which relates to any of the following:

(a) the condition of the dwelling-house or the common parts;

(b) the health and safety of occupiers of dwelling-houses; and

(c) the energy performance of dwelling-houses.

To serve a valid section 21 notice, the landlord or his agent must ensure that there is no complaint by the tenant as to the condition of the dwelling-house.[685] A section 21 notice cannot be served in the absence of an Energy Performance Certificate (EPC) or there is no landlord's gas safety certificate[686] available for the property and already served on the tenant. Any failure to comply with these requirements will render the section 21 notice invalid. Usually compliance with these requirements is done early, even before the grant of a tenancy. If copies of these documents were already given to the tenant, it is advisable to attach another set of copies with a section 21 notice to avoid any dispute.

B. Requirement of Landlord to Provide the "How to Let" Booklet. This is a booklet from the Department of Communities and Local Government setting out a checklist for renting in England and is available on the Web.[687] The landlord must serve an up-to-date copy on the tenant when the tenancy was granted and to avoid any dispute a copy should be attached to the section 21 notice.

---

[684] Housing Act, 1988, s 21A, inserted by the Deregulation Act, 2015, s 38.
[685] Deregulation Act, 2015, s 33.
[686] The Gas Safety (Installation and Use) Regulations 1998 (No 2451) requires that a copy of the gas certificate is provided to tenants within 28 days of issue, but meeting this deadline is not a condition of serving a section 21 notice.
[687] https://www.gov.uk/government/publications/how-to-rent

This requirement does not apply in respect of social housing or in the event the landlord has already provided the tenant with a still valid version of the booklet under a previous tenancy.

C. Prescribed Form 6A for the Section 21 Notice. This form must be used in respect of any grant of an AST on or after 1 October 2015 in England.[688] It is for new tenancies only. But there is no need to use it if the "new" tenancy is a statutory periodic tenancy which arises following the expiry of a fixed-term AST that was granted before 1 October 2015. However, from 1 October 2018, the prescribed Form 6A will apply to all ASTs in existence at that time.

Although the old regime regarding the section 21 notice applies to ASTs granted before 1 October 2015, the new Form 6A, which has already been amended,[689] still states that it can be used for all ASTs. This means that the landlord has the option of using it for an AST granted before 1 October. However, to be on the safe side, it is advisable to use the old section 21 notice with a view to avoiding any argument that the notice is defective. An example will make this clear. If a periodic AST was created before 1 October 2015, and the new Form 6A is used to terminate the tenancy, it will be necessary to include an expiry date. It is possible that this date may not be correct and, therefore, the notice will be ineffective. Compare this with the old section 21 notice that should be used for a periodic AST. The old section 21 notice does not include an actual expiry date but rather a "saving clause" is used, from which the tenant can determine the expiry date.

D. Notice Period Under Section 21(4). The notice period for all fixed-term ASTs and periodic ASTs granted on or after 1 October 2015 does not have to expire "on the last day of the period of the tenancy". This "last day" scenario has resulted in a great deal of problems for landlords and many section 21 notices were invalidated. This requirement has been removed in respect of all new ASTs granted on or after 1 October, 2015.

The law now requires a notice to be given for two months before possession can be obtained. However, where there is a periodic tenancy, where the period is greater than a week to week or month to

---

[688] Housing Act, 1988, s 21(8), as inserted by the Deregulation Act, 2015, s 37, and SI No 1725 of 2015 (under which the prescribed Form 6A was made).
[689] See SI No 1725 of 2015, which has amended SI 1646 of 2015.

month basis, the period of the notice will be more than two months. For example, where rent is payable on a quarterly, half yearly or yearly basis, the periods will be 3 months, 6 months and 6 months (which is the maximum period). Therefore, for periodic tenancies, it is crucial to check the period to ensure the correct length of notice is served to determine the tenancy.

E. Time-limits for Serving Section 21 Notice. A section 21 notice under subsections (1) and (4) cannot be served on a tenant within 4 months of the start of the tenancy, if the tenancy was granted on or after 1 October 2015.[690] In the case of a replacement tenancy created in favour of the same parties and the same property, a section 21 notice cannot be served within 4 months of when the original tenancy began.[691]

F. Time-limit for Commencement of Court Proceedings. Once a section 21 notice has been served in respect of a fixed-term AST or a periodic AST (such as a week to week or month to month tenancy), proceedings for possession must be commenced within 6 months of the date of the notice.[692] The numbering of the paragraphs is referred to as sections in Form 6A. The section 21 notice, according to section 3, states that a notice is valid for 6 months from the date of issue, except where there is a periodic tenancy under which more than two months' notice is required. A quarterly tenancy requires 3 months notice and a half yearly or yearly tenancy requires 6 months' notice, in which case the notice is valid for 4 months from the date set out in section 2 of the prescribed form itself, i.e. the section 21 notice.

G. Preventing Retaliatory Evictions. Within 6 months of the service or suspension of any relevant improvement notice by the local authority on the landlord, the landlord cannot serve a section 21 notice on the tenant.[693] The same applies if the tenant has made a complaint to the landlord regarding the condition of the property, and he has failed to respond to the complaint within 14 days of receipt or failed to provide an adequate response.[694] In the latter case, the tenant

---

[690] Housing Act, 1988, s 21(4B), inserted by the Deregulation Act, s 36(1) & (2).
[691] *Ibid.*
[692] Housing Act, 1988, s 21(4D), inserted by the Deregulation Act, 2015, s 36.
[693] Deregulation Act, 2015, s 33 (1) & (2).
[694] *Ibid.*

can complain to the local authority, who is required to carry out an inspection of the property. If the local authority serves an improvement notice on the landlord or carries out emergency work in response to the tenant's complaint, any section 21 notice served on the tenant will be deemed to be ineffective, proceedings in the court will be struck out and a further section 21 notice cannot be issued until after 6 months.[695]

The provision in the above paragraph does not apply if the landlord is a private registered provider of social housing. The same applies:

(a) if the eviction notice is served by a local authority on account of the tenant's breach of the tenancy terms;

(b) where the property is in the market for sale; or

(c) the property is subject to a mortgage which was granted before the start of the tenancy.

H. Repayment of Rent. Where a tenant is entitled to a repayment of rent paid in advance and a section 21 notice determines the tenancy before the end of a period of the tenancy, the landlord is required to return a pro-rata rent.[696] This covers the number of whole days the tenant was not in occupation of the dwelling. A formula is set out in section 21C(2) in the Housing Act, 1988, for calculating the repayment rent.

SUCCESSION TO AN ASSURED TENANCY

The right to succession applies where an assured tenant has died. Section 17 of the Housing Act, 1988, is the legislation under which a succession to an assured periodic tenancy or a statutory periodic tenancy is possible. As originally drafted, section 17 did not provide for a civil partner to succeed to a tenancy of a deceased person.[697] The House of Lords first held that as the specific legislation was gender specific, in respect of a relationship between a man and a woman that it could not include a same-sex relationship. However, their Lordships

---

[695] See the Deregulation Act, 2015, s 33 (2) & (6).
[696] Housing Act, 1988, s 21C, inserted by the Deregulation Act, 2015, s 40.
[697] See *Fitzpatrick v Sterling Housing Association* [2001] 1 AC27. Also, the Rent Act, 1977, allowed succession which was construed to include same-sex partner.

reviewed their decision in *Ghaidan v Godin-Mendoza*,[698] in the light of the Human Rights Act, 1998, and the Convention Rights, and held that the Rent Act provision could be construed so as to extend succession rights to same-sex partners to eliminate its discriminating effect. The decision in *Ghaidan v Godin-Mendoza* has since been applied to a similar situation under section 17 of the 1988 Act,[699] and now statutory force has been provided to the decision in this case.[700]

Only one person can be a successor to a tenancy. Any failure to reach an agreement where more than one person satisfies the requirement, the matter will be decided by the county court under section 17(5) of the 1988 Act. The tenant's will or intestacy rules are excluded where succession rights are established. Although of minimal value, these rights would appear to apply to a shorthold periodic tenancy.[701]

A succession right to a tenancy applies only once. This is because section 17 applies where the deceased tenant was not himself a successor. Therefore, on the passing of the successor, the landlord can obtain possession of the premises.

The rights to succession are inapplicable where the deceased tenant was holding under a fixed-term assured tenancy, nor does Ground 7 for possession apply. The tenancy will continue to be assured where a beneficiary who acquires the tenancy on the death of a tenant satisfies the assured tenancy requirements. If such requirements are not satisfied, e.g., where he cannot prove that he occupies as his only or principal home, the tenancy will be terminated on expiry of the term under the general law. In the absence of any person qualifying to be a successor on the death of an assured periodic tenant, the tenancy will devolve on the deceased's estate. However, the landlord can obtain possession under a mandatory ground.

In *Amicus Horizon Ltd v Mabbott's Estate*[702] the tenancy was in the sole name of the deceased tenant, who with her partner had no committed husband and wife relationship; the relationship was not

---

[698] [2004] 2 AC 577.
[699] *Nutting v Southern Housing Group Ltd* 2 [2005] PC & R 14.
[700] Section 81 the Civil Partnership Act, 2004, Sch 8 wef 5 December, 2005 (SI 2005 No 3175)
[701] See *Lower Street Properties Ltd v Jones* (1996) 28 HLR 877.
[702] *Sub nom, Amicus Horizon Ltd v Brand* [2012] EWCA Civ 895, [2013] 3 FCR 47, Ward LJ, CA (Civ Div).

akin to a marriage. Both of them had been careful to claim benefits separately; that was not a public affirmation of a husband and wife relationship. The judge's decision was one for him to reach, and it was correct. Therefore, the appeal in respect of a succession claim was dismissed.

SUB-TENANTS

Sub-tenants are afforded the same rights as tenants under the 1988 Act. In this regard, a sub-tenant can invoke any provision in his favour against his landlord (the head tenant). The sub-tenant's position is as follows:

(a) When the tenancy, under which he holds, is terminated, the sub-tenant will retain security of tenure if he falls within section 18 of the Housing Act, 1988.

(b) Section 18 protects only a lawful sub-tenant, e.g., where the sub-tenancy was not created in breach of a covenant against sub-letting.

(c) He must qualify as an assured tenant against his immediate landlord.

(d) He can have an assured tenancy, regardless of whether his landlord has an assured tenancy.

End

CHAPTER 13

PUBLIC SECTOR HOUSING – SECURE TENANCY

INTRODUCTION

Prior to the enactment of the Housing Act, 1980, residential tenants in the public sector were not accorded any statutory protection. It was thought that public bodies, not being profit-making organisations providing housing for the less privileged, could be relied upon in acting in a fair manner in the exercise of their powers. Rather belatedly, public sector tenants may now enjoy what is known as a "secure tenancy". Subject to many variations and modern improvements, this type of tenancy is based on the Rent Act protected tenancy. The relevant statutory provisions are contained in Part IV of the Housing Act, 1985.[703]

Part I of the 1980 Act provided for:

(a) a statutory security of tenure similar to, although not identical with, what is available to private sector tenants; and

(b) a statutory right of a tenant to buy his home from his public sector landlord

These provisions in (a) and (b) above are now in Part IV and Part V of the Housing Act, 1985. Security of tenure as provided for in section 79 of the 1985 Act is in relation to what is known as a "secure tenancy". This is a tenancy:

(i) which relates to a dwelling house let as a separate dwelling,

(ii) in respect of which the landlord is within a list of "public sector" bodies such as local authorities, new town corporations, and housing action trusts,

(iii) in respect of which the tenant (excluding a corporate

---

[703] See also Pt V and the Leasehold Reform, Housing and Urban Development Act, 1993, Pt II concerning the right to buy.

tenant) who occupies the dwelling as his only or principal home[704] or, where the tenancy is a joint tenancy, each of the joint tenants (excluding a corporate tenant) or at least one of them occupies the house as his only or principal home;[705] and

(iv) which is not within any of the exceptions contained in the Local Government and Housing Act, 1989.

Unlike the private sector, there is no rent control in respect of housing in the public sector analogous to the system of rent officers and rent assessment committees.

SECURITY OF TENURE

Tenants in the public sector enjoy security of tenure similar to assured tenancies of private tenants.[706] As in the private sector, the landlord cannot recover possession without a court order based on one of the grounds under section 82 of the Housing Act, 1985.[707] While a periodic tenant can serve a notice to quit, the landlord cannot[708] (unless a ground for possession is available), and this applies to a fixed-term tenancy after expiration of the term when it automatically becomes a periodic tenancy. In the event a fixed-term tenancy is forfeited, on termination a periodic tenancy arises and such a tenancy can only be terminated under a ground for possession.[709] Here forfeiture is not necessarily a ground for possession.

A secure tenancy is the most common form of tenancy provided for residential purposes by local authorities and other public sector

---

[704] The requirement of the only or principal home does not have to be fulfilled all the time: *Islington LBC v Boyle* [2011] EWCA Civ 1450. It is sufficient if fulfilled on expiry of a notice to quit served by the landlord.

[705] Sections 80-81 of the Housing Act, 1985, an occupier may pass in or out of a secure tenancy, depending on a change of landlord or a change of the tenant's circumstances; *Kay v Lambeth LBC* [2004] EWCA Civ 926, [2005] QB 352

[706] In respect of sub-tenants, see *Basingstoke & Deane BC v Paice* [1995] 2 EGLR 9.

[707] As amended by section 14 the Anti Social Behaviour Act, 2003. Grounds for Possession of Dwelling-Houses let under Secure Tenancies are set out under Sch 2 to the 1985 Act.
Part I.

[708] *Hammersmith & Fulham LBC v Monk* [1992] 1 AC 478.

[709] Housing Act, 1985, ss 82(3), 86(1)(b).

providers. Secure tenants have strong rights, and can only be evicted in certain situations. A secure tenancy can only be terminated if one or more grounds set out in Schedule 2 to the Housing Act, 1985, can be satisfied and a court order is made for possession. Many of the grounds under which possession may be obtained are similar to those in the private sector.

Grounds for Possession Under Schedule 2 to the 1985 Act. There is a list of grounds for possession. If possession is ordered by the court, it will have the effect of terminating the tenancy when the order is executed.[710] Some of the important grounds for possession are:

(a) Breach of covenant or for non payment of rent. In *John Boyd v Incommunities Ltd*[711] the Court of Appeal dismissed an appeal against the High Court decision in which possession was granted to a social housing landlord for arrears of rent and anti-social behaviour. The Court of Appeal confirmed that proper weight had been given to the hearsay evidence which supported the finding of anti-social behaviour.

(b) Nuisance to others committed by the tenant or other people in the premises. In *Kensington & Chelsea Royal London Borough v Hislop*[712] it was held that because of continuing nuisance to neighbours the tenant's purchase would make housing management difficult. A case in which a possession order under this ground was refused is *North Devon Homes Ltd v Brazier*.[713]

(c) Neglect of the premises, furniture or the common parts.

(d) False statement made knowingly or recklessly to obtain the tenancy.

(e) Domestic violence (added by the 1996 Act).

---

[710] *Ibid*, s 82(2). In *Knowsley Housing Trust v White* [2008] UKHL 70, [2009] 1 AC 636 in which the HL declined to reconsider the earlier cases regarding tolerated trespassers in respect of secure tenancies, and confirmed by the SC in *Austin v Southwark LBC* [2010] UKSC 28, [2010] 3 WLR 144.
[711] [2013] EWCA Civ 756.
[712] [2004] HLR 26.
[713] [2003] 2 EGLR 14.

In addition to the above, there are a few special grounds, such as to make the premises suitable for a disabled person, who no longer resides in the premises. To obtain possession in respect of most of the grounds, the court will have to be satisfied that not only in relation to the particular ground invoked but also that it is reasonable to make the order for possession. However, the question of reasonableness does not apply to the following grounds:

(a) the premises are overcrowded;

(b) there is an intention to demolish the premises;

(c) there is a proposal for disposal under a scheme for redevelopment; and

(d) conflict with the purposes of a charity landlord.

But in any of these cases, the court must be satisfied that suitable alternative accommodation is made available to the tenant, including a tenant who has to vacate the premises that were designed for a disabled person who no longer resides in the premises, mentioned above.[714]

A court order can be rescinded or revoked before its execution with the result that the secure tenancy is revived. Where the order has not been rescinded but the landlord agrees to accept rent, the tenant will be regarded as a "tolerated trespasser".[715] A new tenancy agreement can be created between the parties, though very rarely.[716]

Where a tenancy of land is held by more than one person, those persons hold the tenancy jointly. In *Hammersmith and Fulham LBC v. Monk*[717] ("*Monk*"), the House of Lords unanimously held that, where such a tenancy is a periodic tenancy, which can be brought to an end by a notice to quit, the common law rule is that, in the absence of a

---

[714] Housing Act 1985, s 84(2), Sch 2 as amended by the Housing & Planning Act, 1986, s 9(1).
[715] *Lambeth LBC v Henry* [2000] 1 EGLR 33; *Pemberton v Southark LBC* [2000] 1 WLR 1672; *Lambeth LBC v O'Kane* [2006] HLR 2; *Newham LBC v Hawkins* [2005] 2 EGLR 51.
[716] *Newham LBC v Hawkins* [2005] 2 EGLR 51.
[717] [1992] AC 478.

contractual term to the contrary, the tenancy will be validly determined by service on the landlord of a notice to quit by only one of the joint tenants.

In *Sims v Dacorum Borough Council*[718] the Supreme Court unanimously dismissed the appeal against a judgement of the Court of Appeal, which had upheld an order for possession made against the *Sims* in circumstances where his wife, as joint tenant of a secure weekly tenancy, had unilaterally terminated the tenancy, following the House of Lords' decision in *Hammersmith & Fulham LBC v Monk*. Mr Sims had argued that the ruling in *Monk* should be revisited as it was incompatible with his rights under Article 8 of the European Convention on Human Rights ("ECHR") (respect for his home) and/or Article 1 (peaceful enjoyment of possessions). Sims failed to persuade their lordships in this regard. They decided that the rule in *Monk* was not incompatible with Article 1 nor had there been a violation of Article 8. Being a public sector tenant, Sims had been entitled to, and did, raise a proportionality argument in the County Court, which had been decided in the landlord's favour.

Compensation Right. A tenant of a local authority under a secure tenancy[719] may claim compensation when the tenancy ends for certain improvements begun on or after 1 February 1994.[720]

Protection of Other Joint Tenant. When one of two joint tenants under a secure tenancy gave notice to quit, the other joint tenant who remained in possession, albeit as a trespasser, was protected from eviction.[721] The word "home" cannot be defined by domestic law. The respondent's link with the premises are sufficient and continuous, so they must be regarded as his home. The fact that the tenancy has come to an end does not mean that the premises cease to be his home.[722]

---

[718] [2014] UKSC 63; [2014] All ER (D) 126 (Nov).
[719] As the landlord must be a local authority, but this may not include all secure tenants.
[720] Commencement date of section 122 of the Leasehold, Housing and Urban Development Act, 1993 (Commencement and Transitional Provisions No 3) Order 1993 (SI 1993/2762), art 4).
[721] *Harrow LBC v Qazi* [2004] 1 AC 983 HL.
[722] *Ibid*, per Lord Hope of Craighead at pp 61, 62 & 68.

Damages for Wrongful Eviction. In *Loveridge v London Borough of Lambeth*[723] the Supreme Court unanimously allowed an appeal challenging the Court of Appeal's decision to set aside the damages awarded to the appellant under section 28 of the Housing Act 1988 following his unlawful eviction by Lambeth LBC. As the appellant was a secured tenant of a one-bedroom flat owned by Lambeth LBC, his eviction was wrongful when Lambeth LBC thought he had died as the reason for his absence. On his return from a long holiday to Ghana, he found all his possessions had been removed and a new tenant was occupying the flat.

DEMOTED TENANCIES

The concept of "demoted tenancy" was introduced by the Anti-social Behaviour Act, 2003, in respect of a tenancy in the public sector. Where a person residing in or visiting the dwelling has engaged in or threatened to engage in certain forms of anti-social behaviour, or the premises are used for unlawful purposes, the court may make a "demotion order" on an application by the landlord. Such an order will be made by the county court if it is reasonable to make it in the circumstances.[724]

The court must be satisfied that it is reasonable to make the order.[725] The requirement of reasonableness is to the same effect as proportionality for the purposes of the ECHR, art 8.[726]

Any demotion order granted by the court will have the effect of terminating the secure tenancy, which will be replaced by a demoted tenancy. This tenancy will be a demoted assured shorthold tenancy under section 20B of the 1985 Act. This tenancy will last for at least a year, and during the demotion period the landlord, without establishing any grounds, can obtain an order for possession.

The provisions relating to demotion tenancies are intended to ensure that landlords do not seek an immediate order for possession in all cases of anti-social behaviour. The idea is designed as a warning and last chance to the tenant. It operates as an incentive for good behaviour. On account of his actions, the tenant has lost security, and this may have serious consequences for him.

---

[723] [2015] UKSC 65.
[724] Housing Act, 1996, s 82A, inserted by the Anti-social Behaviour Act, s 14.
[725] Sousing Act, 1985, s 82A(4); Housing Act, 1988, s 6A(4).
[726] *Manchester City Council v Pinnock* [2009] 32 EG 68 (CS) CA (Civ Div).

OTHER MATTERS

Two other matters for consideration are "introductory tenancies" and "succession".

Introductory Tenancies. This type of tenancies was introduced by the Housing Act, 1996, which a local authority may elect to implement. A tenancy is given as an introduction for a year (a trial period), which otherwise would have qualified as an assured tenancy. The Housing Act, 2004, amends the 1996 Act[727] by permitting the extension of the trial period by six months. Without advancing any ground, the landlord may during the trial period apply to the court for an order to terminate the tenancy. The court has no discretion to refuse the order,[728] but the landlord's reason must be provided whereupon the tenant may ask the landlord to review its decision. If the tenancy is not terminated during the trial period, the tenancy will become a secure tenancy after the trial period.

Succession. A succession on death to a secure tenancy is also permitted as in the case in the private sector and again only once. The tenancy must remain a secure tenancy when the right to succeed is to be exercised; if it is no longer a secure tenancy the right is lost.[729] The qualification to succession is that the successor must have occupied the dwelling-house as his only or principal home[730] as at the date on the death of the tenant. The successor must either be the tenant's spouse or civil partner or a family member.[731] As regards a family member, he must have resided in the premises for at least 12 months ending with the death,[732] though not necessarily in the same

---

[727] Sections 125A and 125B in the 1996 Act were inserted by section 196 of the 2004 Act to enable introductory tenancies to be created on or after 6 June 2005: SI 2005 No 1451.
[728] *Manchester City Council v Cochrane* [1999] 1 WLR 809.
[729] *Solihul Metropolitan Borough Council v Hickin* [2010] 31 EG 62 (CS) CA (Civ Div).
[730] See *Peabody Donation Fund Governors v Grant* (1982) 264 EG 925.
[731] The definition of family is exhaustive, but should not be interpreted more widely than the Human Rights Act, 1998; foster children are excluded and in compliance with the ECHR: *Sheffield BC v Wall* [2010] EWCA Civ 922.
[732] Section 87 of the Housing Act, 1985, as amended by the Civil Partnership Act, 2004, s 81, Sch 8.

premises.[733] A minor may be a successor.[734] In the event there are more claimants and no agreement is reached, the landlord is entitled to select the successor.

Family in relation to succession includes persons who live together as husband and wife and same-sex partners who live as civil partners. In the case of a couple, to be "living together as man and wife", they need to show that they have a settled intention to be regarded as such.[735] Only the following relatives are members of the tenant's family who qualify to succeed to a tenancy: parents, grandparents, children, brothers, sisters, uncles, aunts, nephews and nieces. Relations by marriage count as blood relations, blood relationships as relationships of the whole blood, and children include illegitimate and step children.[736]

<u>Suitable Alternative Accommodation</u>. The offer of such accommodation to a secure tenant must be judged in two ways:

(a) in respect of security of tenure; and

(b) with regard to being reasonably suitable to the tenant's needs[737] and that of his family. It may be that the loss of right to buy is relevant to assessing suitability of alternative accommodation.[738]

NO RENT CONTROL

There is no system of rent control for a secure tenancy as under the machinery provided by rent officers and rent assessment committees applicable in relation to private sector tenancies.

RIGHT TO BUY A PUBLIC SECTOR HOME

The right to buy by local authority tenants was conferred by the Housing Act, 1980, and is now to be found in Part V of the Housing

---

[733] *Waltham Forest LBC v Thomas* [1992] 2 AC 198.
[734] *Kingston Upon Thames BC v* [1999] 1 FLR 593, but the legal estate must be held in trust for the minor.
[735] *Westminster City Council v Peart* (1992) 24 HLR389.
[736] *Wandsworth LBC v Michalak* [2003] 1 WLR 617 CA (Civ Div).
[737] *Enfield LBC v French* (1984) 49 P&CR 223.
[738] *Manchester City Council v Benjamin* [2008] EWCA Civ 189.

Act, 1985.[739] Section 16 of the Housing Act, 1996, has extended the right to include some tenants of housing associations and registered social landlords. Under this right, secure tenants are entitled to buy their homes from a local authority landlord at a price substantially below the market value of the property.

This right to buy applies to public sector tenants, but the premises need not necessarily be the same as occupied by the tenant or from the tenant's actual landlord. This right arises if the tenant has been a tenant for at least five years. What can be bought are:

(a) the dwelling-house which is a house, of which the landlord is the freeholder, and the tenant will have the right to acquire the freehold;

(b) the dwelling-house which is a house, of which the landlord does not own the freehold, the tenant will be entitled to be granted a long lease; and

(c) where the dwelling-house is a flat, the tenant is entitled to be granted a long lease, regardless of whether the landlord is the freeholder.

In the case of the grant of a long lease, it will be for 125 years at a rent not exceeding £10 per annum. Schedule 6 to the 1985 Act provides for detailed provisions that govern both the grant of the lease and the conveyance of the freehold, as appropriate.

<u>Exclusions or Exceptions.</u> There are certain exceptions to the right to buy, such as where the landlord is:

(a) a charitable housing trust or housing association;

(b) a housing association that has never received a grant of public funds; and

(c) not the owner of the freehold or an interest sufficient to grant a lease (50 years for a flat or 21 years for a house).

---

[739] As further amended by the Leasehold Reform, Housing and Urban Development Act, 1993, and the Housing Act, 2004.

Other cases of exclusions are:

(a) where the dwelling is one of a group let to a physically disabled person or a person suffering from a mental disorder or the elderly;

(b) where the dwelling is due to be demolished within two years; and

(c) where the dwelling forms part of a building held also for other purposes and was let on account of the tenant's employment by the landlord.

Also, the landlord may apply to the court for the suspension of the right to buy on account of the anti-social behaviour of the tenant, under section 121A of the 1985 Act.

Discount on the Market Value

If all relevant conditions are satisfied, the tenant is entitled to buy at a discount on the market value reflecting the period he has been a public sector tenant.

Persons Who Can Exercise the Right

The right to buy can be exercised only by:

(a) a secure tenant or any person closely connected to him, such as a family member;

(b) in certain circumstances an assured tenant of a housing association or a registered social landlord if the landlord's interest has been transferred under section 17 of the Housing Act, 1996; and

(c) with the agreement of the landlord under section 123 in respect of a family who falls short of the residence requirement.

Family members who share the right to buy will be treated as joint tenants regarding the right to buy under section 123(3).[740]

---

[740] *Harrow LBC v Tonge* (1992) 25 HLR 99, [1993] 1 EGLR 49. Here the daughter of the deceased tenant was entitled to require the landlord to complete the sale as a

A person who is occupying as a licensee and who has acquired statutory protection under the 1985 Act, under section 79(3), is not eligible to buy. Where there is a joint tenancy, the right to buy belongs to all the joint tenants or to any of them as may be agreed by them so long as at least one of them occupies the dwelling as his only or principal home.[741]

Qualifying Period. Any secure tenant who wishes to exercise the right to buy must have been occupying the premises under a tenancy:

(a) for at least two years created before 18 January, 2005; or

(b) for at least five years if it was created on or after 18 January, 2005.[742]

An important point regarding the qualified period is that the amount of the discount is dependent upon it. The length of time is the period during which the tenant or his spouse or civil partner, if living together, has held the tenancy. This period does not necessarily have to be continuous, nor does it need to be a period immediately before the tenant's exercise of the right to buy. Further, there is no need for the tenant to have the same landlord or one particular dwelling-house. If there are joint tenants, only one of them need to satisfy the qualifying period.

Disqualified Secure Tenants

Section 121 of the Housing Act, 1985, prevents the exercise of the right to buy in these situations:

(a) where there is a court order requiring the tenant to deliver up possession of the dwelling-house to the landlord; and

(b) where a person or one of the persons in whom the right to buy belongs is an undischarged bankrupt or a petition is pending for

---

notice to buy was served before the death. The daughter could not succeed to the tenancy as her mother was a successor. A second successor is disallowed.
[741] Section 118(2), Housing Act, 1985.
[742] Section 119(1) of the 1985 Act as amended by section 180(1) of the Housing Act, 2004.

bankruptcy or has made a composition or an arrangement with his creditors while the terms are still unfilled.

Another disqualification relates to a case where the tenant is subject to a demotion order as provided for in section 82(A). Further, a tenant is required to satisfy the qualification to exercise the right to buy throughout the process. If he loses the right to buy before the contract has been concluded, he cannot proceed further.

Landlord's Disposal of Interest

A tenant will cease to be a secure tenant and will become an assured tenant where after 15 January, 1989, his public sector landlord has sold its interest in the dwelling-house to a private sector landlord, such as a registered social landlord. The effect of this is to prevent the tenant from exercising his right to buy. However, in such a case, section 171B of the 1985 Act preserves the right of the tenant, subject to certain modifications, as long as he continues to occupy the dwelling as his only or principal home.

Terms of the Purchase

The incentive to buy is the discount in the purchase price. The value of the dwelling-house is the price obtainable in the market by a willing seller. In accordance with section 127 of the 1985 Act, certain assumptions are made to ascertain the value. They are to disregard:

(a) improvements, if any, carried out by the tenant;

(b) any failure of the tenant to keep the dwelling-house in good internal repair;[743]

(c) service charges or improvement contributions. These will be assumed not less than the amounts as provided in the landlord's notice under section 125.[744]

The following assumptions in respect of the conveyance of the freehold to be made:

---

[743] Section 127(1)(b) of the Housing Act, 1985.
[744] Section 127(1)(c).

(a) the landlord as vendor was selling for an estate in fee simple (freehold) with vacant possession;

(b) that neither the tenant nor a family member residing with wanted to buy; and

(c) that the dwelling-house was to be conveyed with the same rights and obligations as it would be in pursuance of Part V of the 1985 Act.[745]

Where a lease is to be granted, the assumptions are:

(a) that the landlord as vendor was granting a lease with vacant possession for a fixed-term of 125 years, or, if the landlord's term is less than 125 years, for a fixed-term less than five days of the landlord's unexpired term;

(c) that the ground rent reserved in the lease would not exceed £10 per annum; and

(d) that the grant of the lease was to be made with the same rights and obligations as it would be in pursuance of Part V of the 1985 Act.[746]

Provision is made under section 128 for any dispute as to the value of the dwelling-house to be referred to the district valuer for determination.

<u>The Discount from the Market Value</u>. The discount available to the tenant will vary according to the circumstances of the case to include:

(a) the qualifying period[747] in respect of the time that the tenant has been a public sector tenant as mentioned above;

---

[745] Section 127(2).
[746] Section 127(3).
[747] Two years if the tenancy was created before 18 January, 2005, or five years if after that date.

(b) if the tenant is acquiring a house, the discount will be 35% after living in the house for five years plus 1% for each complete year after the 5 years but subject to a maximum of 70%; and

(c) if the tenant is acquiring a flat, the discount will be 50% after 5 years as a tenant plus 2% for each complete year after the first 5 years, and subject to a maximum of 70%.[748]

Based on the latest figures from the Department for Communities and Local Government,[749] the revised discounts are up to £102,700 in London and £77,000 elsewhere. These are great incentives for sitting tenants to purchase their homes in the public sector. Such an advantage is not available in the private sector where prices for both flats and houses have risen a great deal over the last two years or so, especially in London.

Where joint tenants are seeking to exercise the right to buy, under section 129(3) the discount will take into account the tenant who satisfies the longest period. The full discount will not be granted to a tenant who previously exercised the right to buy successfully.[750] Therefore, a tenant will not benefit to the full extent a second time round.

Removal or Suspension of the Right

Where a tenant has failed to pay any sum due to the landlord or rent for a period of four weeks or more, the duty to sell will be suspended[751] and only on the tenant paying the arrears will the suspension be removed. There is no duty on the part of the landlord to complete where:

(a) there is a demolition notice in force in respect of the premises; or

---

[748] Section 129(2) of the Housing Act, 1985. Section 131 enables regulations to be made regarding the maximum discount, which will vary according to the regions. The maximum discounts now in London range from £75,000 to £102,700 and elsewhere it is £77,000 (since 21 July 2014). There will be annual increases according to the CPI on 6 July each year from 2015.
Read more: http://www.dailymail.co.uk/news/article-2077627/Council-tenants-offered-discounts-50-000-homes-shake-Right-Buy-scheme.html#ixzz3MBKyQcsU.
[749] July 2014.
[750] Section 130 of the Housing Act, 1985.
[751] Section 138(2).

(b) where the tenant has ceased to be a secure tenant.

Suspension of the duty to complete can also apply when proceedings are pending.[752] Relevant proceedings in this regard include possession proceedings and proceedings for a demotion order, as dealt with earlier. Under section 121A(1)(2), an application can be made to the court to suspend the right to buy for a specific period in respect of anti-social behaviour.[753]

<u>Withdrawal by the Tenant</u>. The tenant is entitled to withdraw from the right to buy process up to and before completion by serving a notice in writing in this regard to the landlord. On a failure of the tenant to complete, the landlord can serve a notice on him to complete within a specific period not less than 56 days.[754] A second notice may be served as appropriate and, if the tenant does not respond within the specific time, the right to buy will be deemed to have been withdrawn by the tenant. Considering that the tenant is most likely to have a substantial discount from the market value of the premises, it is most unlikely that the tenant will not proceed to completion.

Possession, Homelessness and Proportionality Test

The case, *Ackereman-Livingstone v Aster Communities Ltd*,[755] was concerned with the Equalities Act, 2010, sections 136 and 15; Housing Act, 1996, section 193(2); ECHR 1950, art. 8; CPR 1998, Pt 24, r 55.8. The appellant (AL) was homeless and was temporarily rehoused by the local housing authority in a flat owned by the respondent housing association (X). AL was asked to choose more permanent accommodation, but he declined. Therefore, AL had become intentionally homeless, and the duty of the local housing authority under section 193(2) of the 1996 Act had ended.

AL claimed that possession proceedings amounted to discrimination. AL appealed against a decision that he did not have a seriously arguable case and that X had breached the 2010 Act, section

---

[752] Section 138 as amended by the Housing Act, 2004, s193.
[753] As set out in the Housing Act 1996, s 153A or 153B.
[754] Section 140.
[755] (Formerly *Flourish Homes Ltd) sub nom. Aster Communities Ltd (Formerly Florish Homes Ltd) v Ackerman-Livingston* [2014] EWCA Civ 1081, [2014] 1 WLR 3980, Arden LJ, CA (Civ Div).

15. It was held that the judge was correct by considering the defence of discrimination in the same way as one based on art. 8. The same proportionality exercise was involved.[756] In both types of cases the social landlord was pursuing proceedings to recover property that might be used to provide accommodation for other homeless people.

Regarding disability discrimination, a tenant who lost his property would still be entitled to a more limited housing duty by the local housing authority if he had a "priority need". Therefore on the facts, AL's circumstances were not sufficient to outweigh X's interests. Further, the potential prejudice to AL of a possession order was mitigated by the fact that the housing authority continued to owe him more limited duties under the 1996 Act. The judge was right to dismiss the trial summarily.

In *Southend-on-Sea Borough Council v Armour*,[757] the Court of Appeal upheld a decision of the county court dismissing a claim for possession against an introductory tenant on the basis that evicting him would be a disproportionate interference with his right to respect for his home under Art. 8 of the European Convention on Human Rights. The county court had been entitled to take into account the fact that, by the time of the trial, there had been no complaints about the tenant's behaviour for nearly a year.

The case, *Swan Housing Association Ltd v Gill*,[758] concerns housing discrimination. The appellant housing association's application for an anti-social behaviour injunction pursuant to section 153A of the Housing Act, 1996, was dismissed because the district judge found that the appellant had failed in its duty under section 149 of the Equality Act, 2010. However, the Court of Appeal allowed the appellant's appeal and granted the injunction. It held that the judge had erred in law, including in his findings that the respondent had a disability even though that had not been pleaded, alleged or proven on the evidence and that the appellant had been in breach of its duty not to discriminate. In circumstances where the respondent did not have a relevant protected characteristic, it could not be said that the appellant had failed to have due regard to the need to eliminate conduct prohibited by the 2010 Act.

End

---

[756] See *Manchester City Council v Pinnock* [2010] UKSC 45, [2011] 2 AC 104; *Hounlow LBC v Powell* [2011] UKSC 8, [2011] 2 AC 186.
[757] [2014] EWCA Civ 231.
[758] [2013] EWCA Civ 1566.

CHAPTER 14

LONG RESIDENTIAL LEASES ON HOUSES

INTRODUCTION

Until 1954 long residential leases at a rent less than two-thirds of the then rateable value enjoyed neither security of tenure nor rent protection. In fact, the tenant did not require protection in respect of rent, and on expiration it was fair to assume that a new lease would be negotiated in consideration of a new ground rent and a premium, unless the landlord wanted to resume possession. If the parties could not agree to a new tenancy, the landlord was entitled to possession. Such a situation was regarded as anomalous when at the same time a weekly tenant, who had incurred practically no capital expenditure was given some protection and yet a long residential lessee/tenant could face eviction on expiry of his term.

In an attempt to give some protection to tenants of long residential leases, the Leasehold Property (Temporary Provisions) Act, 1951, granted security of tenure to these tenants. The provisions in this Act were replaced by Part 1 of the Landlord and Tenant Act, 1954,[759] in respect of houses. In addition to the rights conferred on tenants under the 1954 Act, these tenants have been granted more substantial rights under the Leasehold Reform Act, 1967, in terms of enfranchisement or extension of their leases for another 50 years. However, some of these tenants, although they satisfy the 1954 Act, may not qualify under the 1967 Act to claim the additional benefits.

The importance of Part I of the 1954 Act has to a certain extent been diminished by the 1967 Act. But Part I of the 1954 Act was still applicable side by side with the 1967 Act. This was particularly the case where the additional requirement of the 1967 Act could not be complied with or, where it did, the tenant did not wish for some reason to exercise his rights under it.

As will be seen below many Acts of Parliament were passed since the 1954 Act conferring some protection with the later Acts providing greater protection ranging from security of tenure to extension of the long leases, the right to buy the landlord interests (enfranchisement)

---

[759] Again, Part I of the 1954 Act was replaced by the Local Government and Housing Act, 1989.

and the right to manage properties as well as the right of enfranchisement of flats or the extension of long leases of flats. The relevant Acts are:

(a) The Landlord and Tenant Act 1954, Part I.

(b) The Leasehold Reform Act 1967.

(c) The Housing Act, 1985 (public sector secure tenancies).

(d) The Landlord and Tenant Act, 1987.

(e) The Housing Act, 1988 (assured tenancies and AST).

(f) The Local Government and Housing Act, 1989 (replacing Part I of the 1954 Act).

(g) The Leasehold Reform, Housing and Urban Development Act, 1993.

(h) The Housing Act, 1996.

(i) The Commonhold and Leasehold Reform Act, 2002.

The 1967 and 1993 Acts were modified by the 2002 Act. The most significant change is in respect of the abolition concerning the original residency requirement as of 26 July 2002. Other provisions in sections 121 to 124 in the 2002 Act have replaced the "nominee purchaser" in the 1993 Act with a right to enfranchise company.

In view of various statutes now governing residential properties of various types, the law has become very complicated. This chapter deals with long residential leases in respect of houses in particular. The first relevant Act in this area was the 1954 Act, Part I, which has been replaced by the 1989 Act. An intervening Act is the Leasehold Reform Act, 1967, providing for the right to buy the freehold interest or to extend the lease in respect of a house subject to a long lease. The Acts that deal with assured tenancies and assured shorthold tenancies (AST) are the Housing Act, 1988, and the Housing Act, 1996, and are already discussed in Chapter 12. The Act that deals with housing in the public sector is the Housing Act, 1985, and is covered in Chapter

13. Similar rights as in the 1967 Act in respect of houses were enacted in 1993 in respect of flats. In addition, there is the new concept in England and Wales enacted under the 2002 Act (below) which provides for the creation and management of developments[760] known as commonhold.

While this chapter deals mainly with long residential leases in respect of houses, other aspects discussed in later chapters are:

(a) Chapter 15 on collective enfranchisement of flats or a 90-year extension of existing leases on an individual basis.

(b) Chapter 16 on commonhold land.

The Leasehold Reform Act, 1967, was regarded by some as an Act with confiscatory provisions. However, a human rights' challenge failed in the seminal decision of *James v United Kingdom* (A/98).[761] Following this case is the Landlord and Tenant Act, 1987, which allows leaseholders of flats to acquire the freehold reversion to their flats where there is a management failure by the landlord. But the most significant development was in the Leasehold Reform, Housing and Urban Development Act, 1993, which extended enfranchisement rights to lessees of flats or rights to extend their leases by 90 years.[762]

LONG LEASES OF RESIDENTIAL PROPERTIES

The Landlord and Tenant Act, 1954, Part I, was the first Act to provide some protection to long leaseholders of houses. Although Part I has been replaced by the Local Government and Housing Act, 1989, a brief account is set out here as a background to the later Acts.

Long Leases Under Part I of the Landlord and Tenant Act 1954

Part I of the 1954 Act provided security of tenure to long leaseholders who had no protection whatsoever and would have had to deliver up possession to their landlords at the end of their leases. The Act in effect allowed them to remain in possession as statutory tenants under

---

[760] This concept has been established already in many countries. See *Strata Titles* by N. Khublall (Dr), published by Butterworth in 1995 in Singapore.
[761] (1986) 8 EHRR 123.
[762] See Chapter 15.

the Rent Act. Such a protection prevented landlords from recovering possession. Instead, a tenant was allowed to continue in possession, but had to pay a substantially higher rent, not a ground rent. However, a landlord could not demand a market rack rent, as the tenant was given the same protection regarding rent as any other tenant under the Rent Acts.

Part I of the 1954 Act is replaced by a new regime under the Local Government and Housing Act, 1989.[763] Under the regime of the latter Act, on termination of his long lease, the tenant is entitled to an "assured tenancy". The same applies even after the passing of the Housing Act, 1996, as he will continue to benefit from the entitlement of a full assured tenancy, instead of an assured shorthold tenancy (AST),[764] which hardly offers any protection of any value. The regime under the Leasehold Reform Act, 1967, which confers more attractive rights[765] to a tenant of a long lease of a house is discussed later.

The Regime Under the Local Government and Housing Act, 1989.

The 1989 Act which has replaced Part I of the 1954 Act applies only to houses, as indeed the Leasehold Reform Act, 1967. Long leaseholders of flats were excluded; it was not until 1993 they have been conferred with certain rights under the Leasehold Reform, Housing and Urban Development Act, 1993.[766] Again, the rights under this Act are discussed in Chapter 15.

The relevant provisions under the 1989 Act are in respect of what leases are covered by this Act and the right to security of tenure in respect of any qualifying tenancy.

<u>Qualifying Tenancy.</u> Protection under the 1989 Act is given to:

(a) a tenant who holds under a long lease at a low rent; and

(b) who satisfies the "qualifying condition".[767]

---

[763] Section 186 and Sch 10.
[764] Housing Act, 1988, Sch 2A, para 6, which was introduced by the 1996 Act, Sch 7.
[765] These relate to enfranchisement or an extended lease, both of which apply only to houses as opposed to flats.
[766] In respect of collective enfranchisement or a 90-year extension of leases on an individual basis.
[767] Housing Act, 1988, Sch 10, para 1.

The qualifying condition requires the tenant to show, in the event the tenancy was not at a low rent, it would qualify as an assured tenancy under the Housing Act, 1988. In considering the fulfilment of the qualifying condition, one has to ignore the very long lease created at a low rent in preference to the protection afforded by the 1988 Act. This means that:

(a) The premises must have been let as a separate dwelling. This is discussed in Chapter 12 under assured tenancy.

(b) The tenant is an individual, rather than a company.

(c) The premises must be within the limits as to rent or rateable value, defined in the 1988 Act, Schedule 1, para. 2A.[768]

(d) The tenant must have been occupying the premises wholly or in part as his only or principal home.

(e) The tenancy does not fall within any of the exclusions, such as a business tenancy, an agricultural holding, a holiday letting, a local authority or Crown tenancy, and without a resident landlord.

It is the date on termination of the long lease at common law when the qualifying condition must be satisfied. Paragraph 1(7) of Schedule 10 to the Act states that the original nature of the property and its original purpose for which it was let is deemed to be the same as the nature of the property and the purpose for which let at the time when the question arises. This is the end of the long lease when eligibility is being considered.

<u>Position on Expiry of the Long Lease</u>. On the termination of a long lease by effluxion of time, the landlord will be entitled to possession at common law. By reason of the 1989 Act, he shall be entitled to possession:

---

[768] In respect of tenancies granted since 1 April, 1990, the requirement is that the premium paid for the tenancy is below a limit based on a mathematical formula (Sch 10, para 1(2A) of the 1989 Act). As regards tenancies created before 1 April, 1990, the rateable value on 31 March, 1990, must be within the limits set out in para 2A of Schedule 1 to the 1988 Act (£1,500 in Greater London and £750 elsewhere).

(a) Only if he can prove that he is entitled to possession under certain grounds.[769]

(b) These grounds are broadly similar to those under the Housing Act, 1988.[770]

However, the tenant of the expired long lease will be entitled to an assured tenancy if the landlord is unable to substantiate any of the statutory grounds for possession.[771] Thereafter, as in the case of other assured tenancies, on proof of a suitable ground, possession by the landlord may be obtained under the 1988 Act.

<u>Machinery for Security of Tenure</u>. The 1989 Act artificially prolongs a long leasehold tenancy until it is terminated by notice based on a rather complicated procedure of:

(a) notice;

(b) counter-notice; and

(c) application to the court, if necessary.

In the course of this procedure, the tenant remains in possession of the premises; they are capable of being treated "as property" to be vested in the tenant's trustee in bankruptcy.[772] If the landlord decides to gain possession, he must serve:

(a) an appropriate notice on the tenant at least six months but not more than 12 months in advance; and

(b) stating the ground under which he is entitled to possession as required under Schedule 10, para. 4 of the 1989 Act.

---

[769] The 1989 Act, Sch 10, para 5.
[770] Such as for breach of covenants, nuisance or annoyance, requirement of the premises for the landlord's own occupation or that of his family, or for redevelopment.
[771] Sch 10, paras 4 & 9, of the 1989 Act.
[772] *De Rothschild v Bell* [2000] QB 33 (1954 Act, Part I).

The tenant is entitled to serve a counter-notice electing to remain in possession. Alternatively, he may simply continue in occupation in fulfilling the "qualifying condition". This being the case, if the landlord insists in gaining possession, he must make an application for a court order for possession.[773] Resulting from this application can be:

(a) if the landlord is successful, the tenant has to deliver up possession;

(b) in the event the application is unsuccessful, or if the landlord does not wish to retake possession without making such an application, the tenant will remain in possession;

(c) if (b) applies, the landlord may terminate the long tenancy by a notice proposing an assured monthly periodic tenancy under para. 4 of Schedule 10 to the 1989 Act;

(d) the notice under (c) has to state the date upon which the long tenancy will be terminated;

(e) except where a notice is served after the landlord's unsuccessful application to the court, the tenant must also be given at least six months but not more than a year's notice in advance; and

(f) the notice in (e) must also propose the terms of the new assured tenancy.

In the event the proposed terms in the notice in (f) are not accepted, the said terms must be settled by an application to the rent assessment committee in accordance with para. 10 of Schedule 10. In this case, the committee will assess the open market rent. If other terms are disputed, the committee will consider the terms which might reasonably be expected to be found in an assured monthly periodic tenancy of the dwelling-house, as opposed to an assured shorthold tenancy (AST).

---

[773] Sch 10, para 13.of the 1989 Act.

In view of the higher rent to be paid on termination of a long lease, in most cases, such tenants may opt for the greater rights conferred by the Leasehold Reform Act, 1967.

ENFRANCHISEMENT OR EXTENSION OF LEASE UNDER THE 1967 ACT

The Leasehold Reform Act, 1967, was enacted after many years of debates and attempted legislation to confer on an occupier of a house held under a ground lease to either buy the freehold interest or to extend the lease for another 50 years beyond the original term. This Act is applicable only to houses (not to flats).[774] The rights under the 1967 Act can be exercised during the currency of a lease or after the original term of the lease has expired. If the tenancy has been terminated the rights are extinguished. Once the landlord serves a notice to terminate the tenancy by either:

(a) proposing an assured tenancy, or

(b) seeking possession from the tenant,

the procedure under the Acts is set in motion.

Tenant's Notice in Pursuance of his Rights under the 1967 Act

Where it is intended to acquire the freehold interest in a house[775] or to extend the lease under the 1967 Act,[776] the tenant must serve the appropriate notice within two months of receiving the landlord's notice (as in the above paragraph).

With regard to a flat, where the tenant together with other tenants wishes to jointly acquire the building under the 1993 Act, that tenant together with the other tenants, must serve the relevant notice within four months of receiving the landlord's notice. Once such a notice is served on the landlord, the earlier notice of the landlord will no longer be effective. This right of enfranchisement or to extend the lease on

---

[774] The Leasehold Reform, Housing and Urban Development Act, 1993, applies to flats.
[775] The meaning of a house is given in section 2 of the Act
[776] Tenants of flats may have the right of collective enfranchisement or to extend their leases individually under the 1993 Act. This is discussed in Chapter 15.

an individual basis will apply only if the tenant or tenants fulfil the relevant qualifying criteria.

Qualifying Criteria under the 1967 Act. To enable a tenant to acquire the right to enfranchise or to be granted an extended lease under the 1967 Act, the following conditions must be satisfied:

(a) the relevant property must be a house[777] (flats are excluded from the 1967 Act);

(b) the tenancy must be a long tenancy; and

(c) for at least the last two years,[778] the tenant must have been a tenant of the house.[779]

The consequence of reducing the residence requirement enables non-resident tenants, such as companies, to acquire the freehold.[780] Where there are two or more long tenancies in respect of the same house, such as a long tenancy and a long sub-tenancy, the right is given to the sub-tenant as well.

The right of the tenant can be exercised by a family member of a deceased tenant provided he was resident in the house and it was his only or main residence.[781] Also, the right can be exercised by the

---

[777] The requirement under section 1 of the 1967 Act for the lease at a low rent has been amended two times. The first was the 1993 Act with effect from 1 November, 1993, to include houses with higher rents and rateable values, and the second was by the 2002 Act which under section 141 has abolished "low rents" with effect from 26 July 2002. Finally low rent test has been abolished altogether for tenancies granted after the commencement of section 300 of the Housing and Regeneration Act, 2008, on 7 September, 2009.

[778] Originally it was for 5 years or 5 out of the last 10 years. Now the residence test has been largely abolished (now only 2 years or two in the last 10 years), and now only leases granted for at least 35 years can be enfranchised. The residence requirement is retained to prevent a non-resident landlord of the house, who has sub-let the house in parts under long leases of flats to which the 1993 Act applies from profiting at the expense of the freeholder by acquiring the freehold. See *Earl Cadogan v Search Guarantees plc* [2004] 1WLR 2768.

[779] A case on the failure to satisfy the two-year period is *Free Grammar School of John Lyon v Helman* [2014] EWCA Civ 17 in which the Court of Appeal held that the receivers under a charge could not make a claim under the 1967 Act.

[780] *Hereford Ltd v Barnet LBC* [2005] 2 EGLR 72.

[781] Section 7(1) of the 1967 Act.

personal representatives of a deceased tenant if immediately before his death he was entitled to acquire the freehold or to extend the lease. A tenant who qualifies to acquire the freehold or to extend the lease may assign the right with the tenancy. However, under section 5(2) of the Act, the right to assign applies only with the benefit of the notice and in respect of the whole premises.

Meaning of "House". The requirement of what is a house has been controversial in the recent past. The basic definition in section 2(1) of the 1967 Act provides:

> "For the purposes of this Part of the Act, 'house' includes any building designed or adopted for living in and reasonably so called, notwithstanding that the building is not structurally detached, or was not or is not solely designed or adapted for living in, or is divided horizontally into flats or maisonettes."

The decision in *Boss Holdings Ltd v Grosvenor West End Properties Ltd*[782] was concentrated on the purpose for which the building was originally designed. However, the House of Lords left open questions over the extent of subsequent adaptation for commercial purposes that might result in a building ceasing to be a house. These questions have subsequently been considered in the conjoined appeals in *Day v Hosebay Ltd* and *Howard de Walden Estates Ltd v Lexgorge Ltd*.[783] In these appeals the Supreme Court (formerly the House of Lords) decided, contrary to some indications in *Boss* that properties which are now used entirely for commercial purposes were no longer "a house reasonably so called", whatever their original design or present appearance.

In *Housebay Ltd v Day*[784] an enfranchisement claim failed as the building in question was not a house at the relevant date within the meaning of section 2 of the 1967 Act.[785] In another case, *Henley v Cohen*,[786] the claimants failed to show that the judge was wrong in fact or in law in holding (a) that the premises were, at the relevant date, a house reasonably so-called, or (b) that, even if the judge were,

---

[782] [2008] UKHL 5; [2008] 1 WLR 289.
[783] [2012] UKSC 41.
[784] [2012] UKSC 41; [2012] 1 WLR 2884.
[785] See also *Cadogan v Magnohard* [2013] 1 WLR 24.
[786] [2013] EWCA Civ 480.

the claimants were not entitled to enfranchise, having regard to their conduct. This was in relation to their deliberate breach of clause 5 in order to carry out works in adapting the first floor for living in and thus bringing about the very state of affairs necessary for exercising a right to enfranchise pursuant to the 1967 Act.

Notice by Landlord Seeking Possession. Instead of proposing a new assured tenancy, the landlord may seek to obtain possession under certain limited grounds, such as for redevelopment,[787] or because the house is required for occupation as a residence by the landlord or an adult member of his family.[788] However, a possession order by the county court will only be made if the landlord can substantiate one or more of the few grounds at his disposal. The notice must be in the prescribed form[789] and it must state the date on which the tenancy is to end, which can be the end of the term or a later date. Such a notice must be served not earlier than 12 months or less than six months before the specified date. The said notice must:

(a) invite the tenant who is served with the notice to inform the landlord whether he is willing to vacate the premises;

(b) inform the tenant that in the event of his unwillingness to deliver possession that the landlord intends to apply to the court for an order and specify all the grounds on which the landlord intends to rely;

(c) make known the tenant's available rights to enfranchise or to extend his lease, and make the tenant aware of the consequences of the notice; and

(d) provide the names and addresses of persons known to have any superior interest in the property.

Tenant's Reply to the Notice. In response to the landlord's notice, the tenant has three options:

(a) he may decide to give up possession as at the date specified in the notice;

---

[787] Section 17 of the 1967 Act and ss 22 & 23 of the 1993 Act.
[788] Section 18 of the 1967 Act.
[789] Regulation 1997, SI 1997/3008; applies to Wales as well.

(b) he may decide to remain in possession in which case he should inform the landlord in writing as to his intention within two months of receiving the landlord's notice; and

(c) assuming the tenant qualifies to do so, he may seek to exercise his right of enfranchisement or to extend the lease.

If the tenant chooses (b) above and fulfils the qualifying condition, the landlord may apply for a court order to obtain possession within two months of the tenant's reply. In the absence of such a reply, the landlord has four months from the date of his notice to the tenant to apply for a court order. On a failure to make an application within these time limits, the landlord's notice will become ineffective.[790] Where the tenant fails to reply to the landlord's notice during the two month-period and does not satisfy the qualifying condition, the tenancy will terminate in accordance with the date specified in the landlord's notice.

Grounds for Possession

These grounds are set out in paragraph 5 of Schedule 10.[791] Except two of the grounds, all are covered by Schedule 2 to the Housing Act, 1988. With the exception of one ground for redevelopment, which is mandatory, all the others are discretionary. The mandatory ground is Ground 6 from Schedule 2 (omitting para. (c)). It entitles the landlord to recover possession for demolition and reconstruction of the whole or a substantial part of the property or carry out substantial works to it, which cannot reasonably be done without the tenant giving up possession. However, this ground may not be used where the tenancy is a former 1954 Act tenancy.

The discretionary grounds set out in Schedule 2 to the 1988 Act are:

(1) that suitable alternative accommodation will be made available to the tenant when the order becomes effective;

---

[790] Para. 15(2) of Sch.10 to the Local Government and Housing Act, 1989.
[791] Local Government and Housing Act, 1989.

(2) that rent arrears are outstanding both on the date when possession proceedings are commenced and on the date the landlord's notice to resume possession was served;

(3) the tenant has persistently delayed in paying rent which has become lawfully due whether or not any rent is in arrears on the date when proceedings for possession are commenced (Ground 11);

(4) an obligation, other than non-payment of rent, in the tenancy is broken or not performed (Ground 12);

(5) the condition of the dwelling or common parts has deteriorated on account of the tenant's neglect or default by the tenant or any person residing in the dwelling and, where the deterioration is caused by the tenant's lodger or sub-tenant, the tenant has failed to take steps as he ought reasonably to have taken to remove that lodger or sub-tenant (Ground 13);

(6) that the tenant or a person residing in or visiting the dwelling has been guilty of conduct causing or likely to cause annoyance to a person residing in or visiting the locality or has been convicted of using the dwelling for immoral or illegal purposes or an arrestable offence has been committed in or in the locality of the dwelling (Ground 14);

(7) in the case of a social landlord, the dwelling is occupied by a couple and one partner has left on account of violence or threats of violence to that partner or a member of his family residing with the partner (Ground 14A);

(8) that the condition of any furniture provided for use in accordance with the tenancy has deteriorated on account of ill-treatment by the tenant, person lodging with the tenant or a sub-tenant (Ground 15); and

(9) that the tenant or a person acting on the tenant's instigation induced the landlord to grant the tenancy by knowingly or recklessly making a false statement (Ground 17).

There are another two grounds within Schedule 10.[792] One is for redevelopment and the other is that the dwelling is required as a residence of the landlord or a member of his family.

Redevelopment by a Public Body. Under this ground the landlord requires possession after termination of the tenancy for redevelopment. The landlord proposes to demolish or reconstruct the whole or a substantial part of the premises (para. 5(1)(b)), and the landlord is a body with public function to which section 28 of the 1967 Act applies (para. 5(4)).[793]

Where reliance is placed on para. 5(1)(b), the court must not only be satisfied that para. 5(1)(b) has been established but also the following:

(a) that possession will be required on the date of termination; and

(b) that the landlord has made such preparation to proceed with the redevelopment as reasonable in the circumstances, or making reasonable preparation in respect of obtaining the requisite permissions and consents, such as planning permission and the consent of mortgagees or superior landlords.[794]

Landlord's Occupation.*Under this ground the premises are reasonably required by the landlord for his own residence or a member of his family[795] and where the landlord is not the immediate landlord, he will become such on the date of the termination.[796] This ground may not be used if the landlord's interest was purchased or created after 18 February 1966. If greater hardship will be caused to the tenant in making the order, the court will refuse to make the order.

---

[792] Local Government and Housing Act, 1989.
[793] Such bodies include local authorities, county, borough and district councils, housing action trusts, police authorities, health authorities, development corporations, colleges and universities.
[794] Para 13(7) of Sch. 10 to the Local Government and Housing Act, 1989.
[795] Family includes any son or daughter over 18 years of age or his spouse's father or mother.
[796] Para 5(1)(c) of Sch 10 to the Local Government and Housing Act, 1989.

Grounds 9 to 15 of Schedule 2 to the 1988 Act and the above Ground.*

Under these grounds, the court must be satisfied:

(a) that the landlord has established the ground; and

(b) that it is reasonable that possession should be granted to the landlord.

If the tenant does not satisfy the qualifying condition as at the date of the hearing for possession, irrespective of whether he has informed the landlord that he intends to remain in possession, a possession order will be made for the tenant to vacate the premises on the date of termination. Where no order is made, the landlord's notice will lapse and the tenancy will continue. In this situation, the landlord may serve a notice to the tenant proposing an assured tenancy within one month of the possession application being disposed of. Also, the landlord may withdraw his notice for possession at any time. If an application has already been made to the court, the court may make an order for the landlord to reimburse the tenant's costs.

TENANT EXERCISING RIGHT UNDER THE 1967 ACT

As mentioned earlier, the Leasehold Reform Act, 1967, confers a right on the tenant of a long lease in respect of a house (not a flat) to either acquire the freehold interest or to extend his lease by another 50 years. Contracting out of the Act is prohibited.[797] This Act originally did not apply where the rateable value was above certain limits or since the abolition of domestic rating (in 1990) if the premium paid for the long lease was above a specified sum.[798] However, those who were so excluded have now been conferred with the right to acquire the freehold by the 1993 Act,[799] but the price to be paid by such tenants is more favourable to the landlord than the original position in respect of houses under the 1967 Act.

---

[797] Section 23 of the Leasehold Reform Act, 1967. See *Rennie v Proma Ltd* [1990] 1 EGLR 119.
[798] Section 1(1) of the 1967 Act as amended.
[799] Leasehold Reform, Housing and Urban Development Act, 1993, s 63, has added s 1A(1) to the 1967 Act.

Enfranchisement Procedure

To exercise his right to acquire the landlord's superior interest or to extend his lease, the tenant is required to use the prescribed statutory form, stating whether he wants to acquire such interest or to extend his lease, not both in the alternative. A notice which is given in the alternative is invalid.[800] An inaccuracy in the required particulars does not invalidate the notice. However, a complete failure to provide one of the required particulars will probably do so.[801] As many notices usually contain errors and missing information, the preparation of the notice is not something for the novice.

In general, the courts are increasingly reluctant to declare statutory notices to be invalid as can be seen in the following cases:

(a) In *7 Strathray Gardens Ltd v Pointstar Shipping & Finance Ltd*[802] it was held that a failure to include prescribed information in a collective enfranchisement counter-notice not to be fatal as the omitted information was directory rather than mandatory.

(b) In *Tudor v M25 Group Ltd*[803] it was held that where there is a failure of a notice to comply with a statutory requirement, the court must consider whether Parliament intended the failure to render the whole process a nullity.

(c) It was held in *9 Cornwall Crescent London Ltd v Royal Borough of Kensington and Chelsea*[804] that there was no requirement for an enfranchisement counter-notice to propose either a realistic or bona fide and genuine purchase price.

---

[800] *Byrnlea v Property Investments Ltd v Ramsay* [1969] 2 QB 253. Certain omissions does not invalidate the notice on construction under *Mannai Investment Co Ltd v Eagle Star Life Assurance Co Ltd* [1997] AC 749. Other omissions could render the notice invalid. As regards irregularities on a tenant's notice, see *Earl Cadogan v Strauss* [2004] 2 P & CR 16.

[801] See the contrasting decisions in *Speedwell Estates Ltd v Dalziel* [2001] EWCA Civ 1277; [2002] HLR 43 and *Earl Cadogan v Strauss* [2004] EWCA Civ 211; [2004] HLR 33.

[802] [2004] EWCA Civ 1669.

[803] [2004] 1 WLR 2319 (CA).

[804] [2005] EWCA Civ 324. Cf the requirement of the initial notice to do so by *Cadogan v Morris* [1999] 1 EGLR 59.

(d) In *Long Acre Securities Ltd v Karet*[805] a building under Part I of the Landlord and Tenant Act, 1987, concerning right of first refusal, was held to be either a single building or a multi building estate.

The serving of a notice by the tenant will create rights and obligations as in a contract between a landlord and a tenant. Such a notice is registrable as a land charge in the case of unregistered land and as a notice in the case of registered land. The landlord is obliged to make the grant and the tenant is obliged to take the freehold or an extended lease, as the case may be. However, under section 18 of the Act, the landlord may reject the right of the tenant on the ground that he requires possession if the house is reasonably required as the only or main residence for himself or an adult member of his family and, if he is successful, compensation may be payable to the tenant.

Enfranchisement of Freehold. Where a tenant is entitled to claim the freehold, the conveyance of it will need to be free of incumbrances in accordance with section 8(1) of the Act. If there is any intervening interest, the owner of that interest will have to be paid a share from the purchase money, in accordance with the value of that interest.

The effect of the tenant acquiring the freehold free of incumbrances is to bring to an end the relationship of landlord and tenant and all covenants and conditions in the lease. However, under section 19 of the 1967 Act the former landlord, in exceptional cases, was able to retain certain management powers for the general benefit of the neighbourhood. For example, it applied to substantial residential estates held from a landlord if it was certified by the Secretary of State for the Environment that the landlord should retain control in the interest of maintaining control in respect of adequate standards of appearance and amenity and to regulate development in the area. An application for the Secretary's certificate had to be made before 1 January 1970.[806] Once such a certificate was granted, the landlord could apply for approval to the High Court in respect of a scheme containing the relevant powers.

---

[805] [2005] Ch 61 (Ch).

[806] Where the right to acquire houses only because of the increases in rateable value limits by the Housing Act, 1974, s 118, the date was 31 July 1976. In respect of houses brought within the 1967 Act by virtue of the 1993 Act, the application had to be made within two years of the 1993 Act coming into force.

Extended Lease. Instead of opting to acquire the freehold, a tenant may apply for a new tenancy for a term expiring 50 years after the end of the existing term.[807] The terms under an extended lease have been improved for the benefit of the tenant by reason of reforms introduced under the Commonhold and Leasehold Reform Act, 2002. Hitherto such terms under an extended lease were weak. There were no further rights, such as a further extension or enfranchisement, to a tenant of an extended lease in respect of a house under the 1967 Act. Further, the tenant with an extended lease had no security of tenure at the end of the extended lease. However, since 2002 the restriction preventing enfranchisement has been removed by the 2002 Act,[808] though the restriction as to no further extended lease remains. Also, the tenant of an extended lease is afforded some security of tenure on termination of the extended lease.[809]

Registration of New Lease. It is a requirement of the Land Registry that on completion of the acquisition of a new lease granted in substitution for an existing lease pursuant to section 14 of the Leasehold Reform Act, 1967, that an application is made for registration of the lease. If necessary, also an application should be lodged to give effect on the register to the deemed surrender of the existing lease which will have taken place by operation of law.

Landlord's Application Under Section 17 for Possession. In spite of the grant of a new lease incorporating the 50-year extension, the landlord can apply for possession under section 17 of the 1967 Act if he can substantiate that he requires possession for reconstruction.[810] This right can be invoked during the 12-month period before

---

[807] Section 14(1) of the 1967 Act. However, a tenant is not given this option under the 1993 Act under which he is given enfranchisement rights.
[808] Section 143(1)(a) of the 2002 Act has deleted s 16(1)(a) and amended s 16(4) of the 1967 Act.
[809] Section 143(2) of the 2002 Act has inserted s 16(1B) into the 1967 Act, which is: "Schedule 10 to the Local Government and Housing Act 1989 applies to every tenancy extended under section 14 above (whether or not it is for the purposes of that Schedule a long tenancy at a low rent as respects which the qualifying condition is fulfilled)."
[810] The landlord has to show to the satisfaction of the court that he requires possession to demolish or reconstruct the whole or a substantial part of the house and premises.

commencement of the last 50 years in the new extended lease by applying to the court for an order for termination of the lease. The tenant will be paid compensation by the landlord if an order for possession is made.

TERMS OF ACQUISITION AND BASIS OF VALUATION

As regards the extended lease, the rent will remain the same until the old term expires and, thereafter, a "modern ground rent" (MGR) will take effect. There will be a review after the first 25 years. The MGR is to represent the open market rent for the land without the building. The reason for this is that in equity the land belongs to the landlord and the building belongs to the tenant.

Assessment of the MGR. Where evidence of lettings of similar sites on building leases at full rental value are available (unlikely) a straight forward comparison can be made. Such evidence is unlikely to be available since a premium is paid in most cases with a corresponding reduction in the ground rent. There is more likely to be evidence of sale prices of unencumbered freehold sites, and a MGR may be assessed by comparison and analysis of these capital values. Once the capital value of a site is determined the annual equivalent is taken as a percentage thereof (e.g., 5 % to 6 %) and the resultant figure is the rent under section 15 of the 1967 Act. Another method is to take, say, 30 to 40%[811] of the capital value (depending on the location and market condition) of the standing house) to represent the capital value of the site from which 5 % to 6 % is taken as the rent under section 15.

Option to Acquire the Freehold. In the case of the option to acquire the freehold, there are three bases of valuation to determine the enfranchisement price:

(a) The first which is contained in section 9(1) of the 1967 Act applies to houses with a rateable value on 31 March, 1990, which is less than £1,000 in Greater London and £500 elsewhere. The recent decision of the Lands Tribunal in *Re Clarise Properties Ltd*[812] provides essential

---

[811] See *Graingers v Gunter Estate Trustees* (1977) 246 EG 55. There is no hard and fast rule but 40% is usually adopted for London.
[812] [2012] UKUT 4 (LC).

direction on the correct approach to a section 9(1) valuation, in its move away from a two-stage valuation in favour of a three-stage approach including the so-called "Haresign" addition.[813] Such a valuation requires expert valuation evidence.

(b) The second method under section 9(1A) was introduced by the Housing Act, 1974; it applies where the rateable value exceeds those figures under (a) above but does not exceed £1,500 in Greater London and £750 elsewhere. This applies to houses built after the abolition of domestic rating. Here there is no assumption of a 50-year extension of the lease. Most importantly for the benefit of the landlord, the price will reflect the special interest bid of the tenant, which relates to the marriage value.

(c) The third method under section 9(1C) applies to houses of high value brought within the scope of the 1967 Act by the 1993 Act and also to the houses brought in by the Housing Act, 1996, where the "low rent" test is not satisfied. Under section 9(1C) the valuation basis is the same as under section 9(1A) save that there is no reflection of the tenant's security of tenure at the end of the lease and compensation may be payable to the landlord under section 9A by reason of loss or damage attributable to the enfranchisement.

Determination of Enfranchisement Price Under Section 9(1)

Section 9(1) of the 1967 Act is concerned with low value houses. The enfranchisement price for a house with a rateable value not exceeding £1,000 in Greater London and £500 elsewhere is the open market price on a sale by a willing seller on these assumptions:

(1) That the tenant and members of his family living in the house are not buying, nor seeking to buy. The exclusion of purchasers with a special interest means that the price does not include any "marriage value";

(2) That the sale is for an estate in fee simple, subject to the long tenancy and to an extended lease, if none has in fact yet been claimed;

---

[813] *Haresign v St John's College (Oxford)* (1980) 255 EG 711.

(3) That there is a statutory right to enfranchise;

(4) That the purchaser is exonerated from any charge or liability of incumbrances on the interest of the tenant, or any interest directly or indirectly derived out of the tenancy;

(5) That the sale is on the terms to be included in the conveyance.

Properties with ground rents for many years were valued in the past in perpetuity. For a reasonably short reversion, the Court of Appeal adopted a valuation which capitalised the current ground rent on the 7% table, and added the capitalisation of the MGR (under the assumed extended tenancy), and derived from the capital value of the site on the 6% table.[814] The former practice of assuming the MGR to be 6% of the capital value, but capitalising it on the 8% table ("the adverse differential") was disapproved, unless

> "there be factors operating in the market to produce a genuine difference between the letting value of the site as represented by the ground rent and the price which an investor-purchaser would pay for the encumbered freehold."

The landlord must lead evidence of that.[815]

Valuation. In order to determine the price, a valuation would comprise the value of the present ground rent for the unexpired term of the original lease plus the value of the MGR for 50 years in accordance with assumption (b) above. Allowing for a rent review in the 25th year of this period, reverting thereafter to the full freehold value in possession.

The price, therefore, will reflect the value of the house, as distinct from the site, only to the extent of the value of a right to the house after a number of years. The number of years is made up of the

---

[814] *Official Custodian for Charities v Goldridge* (1973) 26 P&CR 191 (CA). Capitalisation on the 7% table was ordered on the acquisition of a London house let by a lease with 69 years to run: *Eyre Estate Trusteesv Shack* [1995] 1 EGLR 213 LVT. A challenge to this approach by way of an application for judicial review failed in *R (on the application of Welcome Trust Ltd) v Upper Tribunal (Administrative Appeals Chamber)* [2013] EWHC 2803 (Admin).
[815] *Wilkes v Larcroft Properties Ltd* [1983] 2 EGLR 94 (CA) (Civ Div).

unexpired term of the original tenancy plus the 50-year notional extension. This 50-year extension does not apply under the other two bases.

When the existing tenancy is approaching the expiry date the price will be greater as was the case with many Victorian building leases when the 1967 Act was passed. This is because the insignificant ground rent is valued for a very short period, the substantially greater MGR was valued for 50 years, deferred for the said short period, and the landlord's reversion is valued on the basis of the full market value deferred for the short period plus the 50 years. These three components make up the price to be paid.

Determination of Enfranchisement Price Under Section 9(1A)

It was obvious that with regard the first method under section 9(1) of fixing the price, the tenant stands to gain substantially at the expense of the landlord, even for low value houses. Therefore, a different method for calculating the price was applied to houses of higher values that were brought within the scope of the 1967 Act by the Housing Act, 1974. Thus, houses that had a rateable value on 31 March, 1990, between £1,000 and £1,500, in Greater London, and £500 and £750 elsewhere, the price is based upon certain assumptions resulting in the tenant having to pay more or less the market value

The price to enfranchise houses with rateable value exceeding £1,000 in Greater London and £500 elsewhere is the open market value on a sale by a willing seller. The assumptions under section 9(1A) set out below apply. The basis of the assumptions is that if the notice to enfranchise was given on or before the original term date, the tenancy will end on that date. If the notice was given later, the assumptions (1), (3) and (5) below apply as if the tenancy had ended then.[816]

(1) That the sale is for an estate in fee simple, subject to the long tenancy, and on the assumption that when it ends the tenant will have a statutory tenancy. But if there is no more than a remote possibility of the tenant exercising the right to claim a tenancy under the Local Government and Housing Act, 1989,[817] only a small deduction from

---

[816] Section 9(1AA) of the 1967 Act
[817] Formerly Part I of the Landlord and Tenant Act, 1954.

the vacant possession price will be made on that account.[818] If the lease becomes terminable after the death of an identified person, it is appropriate to judge its length by reference to life expectancy tables.[819]

Notwithstanding the presumption that the sale is subject to the tenancy, if the contractual term has expired, and at the relevant date the tenant only remains in possession by reason of the statutory tenancy, the valuation is as on a sale with vacant possession.

(2) That there is no statutory right to enfranchise or to claim an extended lease, and if an extended lease has been granted that tenancy ends on the original term date.[820]

(3) That the tenant has no liability for repairs, maintenance or redecoration, either under a long tenancy or any statutory tenancy.

(4) Where the current or a previous tenant effected improvements at his own expense, that the price is to be diminished by the amount attributable to the improvements,[821] but in valuing the house in its unimproved state, the potential for improvement is to be taken into account.[822]

(5) That the sale is subject to existing rentcharges charged on the tenancy, but only of an amount not exceeding the rent the tenant pays, and on the basis that the tenant is exonerated from any other liability from incumbrances charged on the tenancy until the end of the term.

(6) The sale is on the terms to be included in the conveyance.

---

[818] *Vignaud v Keepers & Governors of the Free Grammer of the School of John Lyon* [1996] 2 EGLR 79 (LT).
[819] *Bistern Estates Trust's Appeal* [2000] 2 EGLR 91 (LT).
[820] The right to enfranchise only subsists until the original term date: 1967 Act, s1(1), (2). The exclusion of an extended lease did not apply if the price was agreed or determined before 7 January, 1987, the tenant's notice to enfranchise was served before 7 November, 1986, or a notice claiming an extended lease was served before 5 March, 1986 (Housing Act, 1986, s 23(2)).
[821] If successive tenants have done work on the building, each can be considered separately and the increase attributable to each can reduce the price: *Shalson v Keepers and Governors of the Free Grammer School of John Lyon* [2004] 1 AC 802 (HL).
[822] *Fattal v Keepers and Governors of the Free Grammer School of John Lyon* [2005] 1 WLR 803 (CA).

It is obvious that this basis differs from that applicable to lower value houses in three main ways:

(a) There is no assumption that the tenant is not in the market to buy so as to exclude any higher bid. Therefore, the tenant is likely to make an enhanced bid, unlike the case under section 9(1) basis. This is likely to produce a marriage value which is to be shared equally between the landlord and the tenant.[823] Nothing further is to be added to the price payable to reflect the prospect of future transactions ("hope")

(b) Secondly, it is now to be assumed that if the tenant were to remain in possession at the end of the lease, it would be under an assured tenancy[824] at a market rent, so that would cause no diminution in the value of the premises.[825]

(c) Thirdly, the effect of the tenant's improvements is to be ignored.

Therefore, by reflecting the above assumptions the price will be calculated by taking into account:

(a) the capitalised value of the rent for the unexpired term of the existing tenancy;

(b) the market value of the landlord's reversion (both site and building) deferred for the period of the unexpired term; and

(c) an addition to reflect the higher bid a sitting tenant would make (i.e, part of the marriage value). However, this will not apply where the existing term exceeds 80 years at the date of the tenant's claim.

In the first method, the assumption of the a 50-year notional extension will have the effect of substantially reducing the market value of the reversion as it has to be deferred for a period of 50 years plus the period of the unexpired term of the existing tenancy and, therefore, a much lower price to pay for the house. In the case of a

---

[823] Section 9(1D) of the 1967 Act.
[824] Under the Housing Act, 1988. Earlier, the tenant would have had security of tenure under Part I of the Landlord and Tenant Act 1954.
[825] *Eyre Estate Trustees v Shack* [1995] 1 EGLR 213 LVT.

high rateable value property, the 50-year extension prior to enfranchising[826] under the 1967 Act could reduce the price substantially. This 50-year extension is now disallowed under the Housing and Planning Act, 1986, and the position is that it is assumed in calculating the price that there can be no notional extended lease. For this reason, a tenant of a high rateable value property is not allowed to extend the lease for 50 years prior to enfranchising, and where a lease has been extended it will terminate on the original date.[827]

In implementing the provision in section 9(1A), the Lands Tribunal valued the remainder of the ground rent and added a price for the reversion, discounted at a deferment rate. This rate is to take into account that the landlord will obtain the value of the reversion now rather than at the end of the lease. The value of the reversion is thus discounted to achieve this. The Court of Appeal accepted the deferment rates which the Lands Tribunal set for properties in the prime central London area at 4.75 % for houses and 5% for flats.[828]

> "It was entirely appropriate for the Tribunal to offer guidance ... and, unless and until the legislature intervenes, to expect leasehold valuation tribunals to follow generally that lead.[829]

However, as the Tribunal did not receive detailed evidence relating to properties outside that area, the Court of Appeal accepted that it was open to the parties to call further evidence to determine appropriate rates for those properties.[830]

In cases involving leases for unexpired terms of below 20 years, it is appropriate to apply *Sportelli*[831] formula as a starting point and then ask the question whether the position in the property market cycle at the valuation date should lead to a change in one or more of the components in the formula.

---

[826] *Mosley v Hickman* (1986) P &CR 248.
[827] Section 23 of the Housing and Planning Act, 1986, amending s 9 of the 1967 Act, but not retrospectively. There was a further amendment by the Commonhold and Leasehold Reform Act, 2002, ss 143(4), 180; Sch 14.
[828] *Earl Cadogan v Sportelli* [2008] 1 EGLR 137 CA.
[829] *Ibid* at p 99 per Carnwath LJ.
[830] *Ibid* at p 102.
[831] *Earl Cadogan and Cadogan Estates Limited v Sportelli* [2007] 1 EGLR153.

Determination of enfranchisement Price Under Section 9(1C)

The price for houses enfranchised only because the jurisdiction was extended is assessed on the same basis as for higher value houses, but with some variations. This applies where the right to enfranchise was extended under section 9(1C) by removal of the rateable value limit. It also applies under section 1(B) to a tenancy terminable on the death or marriage of someone other than the tenant granted before 18 April, 1980. Further, it applies if an extended lease has been granted and notice to enfranchise was given after the original term date.

There are two ways in which the price payable for a higher value house may be varied:

(1) Half the marriage value, resulting from the merger of the freehold and leasehold interests, is treated as belonging to the tenant. Hope value, deriving from the possibility of the landlord's later selling the freehold or a leasehold extension, and thereby increasing the landlord's share, is to be ignored.[832] But if the lease term has at least 80 years to run, the marriage value is deemed to be nil.

(2) A reasonable sum is added to the price to compensate the landlord for any loss or damage by diminution of the value of his other property, including loss of development value.[833]

As can be seen above, the basis of valuation under section 9(1C) is similar to that in section 9(1A) but subject to certain modifications for the benefit of the landlord.[834] In this regard, for example, there is no assumption that the tenant has a statutory right to remain in possession at the end of the contractual tenancy. The obvious effect of this is to increase the value of the landlord's reversion. Further, the landlord is entitled to be compensated if the enfranchisement will diminish the value of another property of the landlord.[835]

This third method under section 9(1C) is also used to calculate the value of a house brought within the scope of the 1967 Act by the 1996

---

[832] *Earl Cadogan v Pitts* [2010] AC 226 (HL).
[833] Sections 9(1C)(b) and 9A.
[834] Section 9(1C) of the 1967 Act
[835] Section 9A of the 1967 Act. Compensation payable in cases where right to enfranchisement arises by virtue of section 1A or 1B.

Act where the "low rent" test is not satisfied.[836] Both methods under section 9(1A) and section 9(1C) are sometimes referred to as a valuation for high value houses.[837]

No Hope Value Under Section 9(1)

In *Pitts v Earl Cadogan*[838] the House of Lords decided that there can be no "hope value" in valuations under section 9(1) valuation and also section 9(1A). A section 9(1C) valuation is the same as a section 9(1A) valuation save that no account is to be taken of the tenant's security of tenure at the end of the lease, and compensation may be payable to the landlord under s 9A. Compensation under section 9A is for loss or damage suffered by the landlord.

Adjustment of Rateable Value.

The rateable value in relation to the third valuation basis under section 9(1C) is to be adjusted if appropriate for the effect of improvements.[839] No date is given as at which the rateable value is to be ascertained for this purpose. The Act refers to the premises of which the rateable value "is…". The use of the present tense makes the likely date on which the notice to enfranchise was served.[840] But arguably it could be the date of hearing to determine the rent. However, the procedure for adjustment for the effect of improvements results in a certificate of the amount (if any) by which the rateable value would have been less on 1 April, 1973, which suggests that might be the relevant date.

The rights of enfranchisement of houses has been extended generally without limits by the Housing Act, 1974 and the 1993 Act. Where appropriate the rateable value can be adjusted to eliminate the

---

[836] Section 9(1C) of the 1967 Act.
[837] The Leasehold Advisory Service (http://www.lease-advice.org/) refers to two methods because there is not much difference between the second and third methods. Under section 9(1A) and section 9(1C) the house will be valued according to the special valuation basis, i.e., the value of the house plus a share of the marriage value, where there is no unexpired term exceeding 80 years.
[838] [2008] UKHL 71; [2010] 1 AC 226.
[839] Section 9(1B). But it cannot be adjusted if the tenant neither agrees a notional value nor applies to have one fixed: *Effra Investments Ltd v Stergios* (1982) 264 EG 449 LVT.
[840] This is supported by *Chada v Norton Estate Trustees* [1985] 2 EGLR 229 LVT.

effect of the tenant's improvements on the rateable value. This can be done by obtaining a certificate from the valuation officer.[841] For example, if the rateable value for a house in London is, say, £1,560 and £60 of that amount is attributable to the tenant's improvements, the rateable value will be adjusted to £1,500, which is within the upper limit.

Higher Value Houses with no Rateable Value

Higher value houses are those which either had a rateable value on March 31, 1999, of £1,000 in Greater London and £500 elsewhere, or, if they did not then have a rateable value, when the formula (see below) is applied the figure for R exceeds £16,333.[842] The third method under section 9(1C) applies to houses which only qualified for enfranchisement because the rateable value limit was removed.[843]

The formula to be applied in cases where there was no rateable value on 31 March, 1990, is:[844] $R = P \times I / 1 - (1 + I) - T$, where

P is the premium payable as a condition on the grant of the tenancy (including any payment of money's worth). Where there was no premium, P is zero.

I is 0.06;[845]

T is the term of the lease in years (disregarding a right of extension or premature determination).

R must not be greater than £25,000.

Improved Ground Rents.

These are assessed differently. The price to be paid for a "minor superior tenancy" is calculated according to a formula which obviates the need for any valuation. This applies on enfranchisement by a

---

[841] Section 1(4A) of the 1967 Act.
[842] The 1967 Act, s 9(1A)(i),(ii). The Secretary of State may vary the figure of £16,333 by order: Leasehold Reform Act 1967 s1(7).
[843] Section 1A(1) of the 1967 Act.
[844] Ss 1(1)(a), 9(1A)(ii) of the 1967 Act.
[845] The Secretary of State may by order vary the value of I: the 1967 Act s1(7).

subtenant to any tenancy with an expectation of possession not exceeding one month and a profit rent of £5 or less (Schedule 1 para. 7A(2) (there must be an apportionment between the value of the premises being enfranchised and other property, if necessary (Schedule 1 para. 7A(4)). The formula under Schedule 1 para. 7A(1), (5) is:

Price = Profit rent (R)/ Yield from 2.5% Consolidated Stock (Y) - (R// Yield from 2.5% Consolidated Stock (Y) - (R/(1+Y)^n

Where n = the remaining period in years for which the minor superior tenancy would have run if not extinguished by enfranchisement, counting any fraction as a full year.

To calculate the yield, the price of the 2.5% Consolidated Stock is taken to be the middle market price of the close of business on the last day of trading in the week before the tenant gives his notice to enfranchise.[846]

Lack of Agreement. In default of agreement between the parties, the price is determined by the Property Chamber of the First Tier Tribunal (formerly the LVT). There is a right of appeal to the Upper Chamber (Lands Chamber).[847] This is a rehearing and the appeal is determined on the evidence given to the Upper Tribunal and not on the evidence given below.[848]

Where a subtenant enfranchises, a price is calculated for each superior interest.

Lease Extension Instead of Enfranchisement

The 1967 Act confers a right on the tenant to extend his lease by another 50 years as an alternative to enfranchisement. Such a lease will be on the same terms as under the existing lease but with a 50-year extension added to the unexpired term at the same rent for the term of the existing lease followed by a "modern ground rent" (MGR)

---

[846] Sch. 1 para 7A(6), Leasehold Reform Act, 1967.
[847] Housing Act, 1980, Sch 22 para 2; Transfer of Tribunal Functions (Lands Tribunal and Miscellaneous Amendments) Order 2009 (SI 2009/1307).
[848] *Re London and Winchester Properties Ltd's Appeal* (1983) 45 P&CR 429 LT.

throughout the extended period. There is no price to pay for the 50-year extension, apart from paying an improved ground rent.

Dispute Relating to Valuation

The valuations produced by the parties are a fertile ground for disagreement. Major disputes usually relate to the capitalisation (yield) and deferment rates. The guidance given in the *Sportelli* case[849] should be considered. Also of concern sometimes in relation to section 9(1) valuation is whether the house should be valued on the basis of a cleared site or a standing house basis. The Lands Tribunal's decision in *Clarise Properties Ltd, Re*[850] provides some direction as to the correct approach to a section 9(1) valuation by moving away from a two-stage to a three-stage process, including the *Heresign* addition.[851]

Yields and Discount Rates. The Lands Tribunal tended to adopt rates between 6 and 8%, though since 1980 most leasehold valuation decisions have adopted 7%. In some decisions, higher rates have been used where the unexpired term is relatively long or where it is supported by market evidence.[852] In what is known as the *Sportelli* rate,[853] 4.75% was used but was adjusted to 5% for greater risk relating to site value. The case *Earl Cadogan v Grandeded*[854] was the final part of the *Sportelli* litigation, a House of Lords appeal in respect of collective enfranchisement. In a group of cases known as "nailrile"[855] the Lands Tribunal gave significant directions on yields and valuation of head leasehold interests and it believed a 44-year lease should be discounted by 7.5% with regard to the 1993 Act.

---

[849] Earl Cadogan v *Sportelli* [2008] 1 EGLR 132 (CA).
[850] [2012] UKUT 4 (LC).
[851] *Haresign v St John's College (Oxford)* (1980) 255 EG 711.
[852] See *Leeds v J&L Estates Ltd* (1974) 236 EG 819.
[853] See *Earl Cadogan and Cadogan Estates Limited v Sportelli* [2007] 1 E.G.L.R. 153, where a deferment rate of 4.75% for houses and 5% for flats was upheld by the Court of Appeal in 2007.
[854] [2008] UKHL 71 (the final part of the *Sportelli* litigation) in which the House of Lords decided in a collective enfranchisement the landlord was entitled to hope value for non-participating lessees. In a group of cases known as "nailrile" the Lands Tribunal gave significant directions on yields and valuation of head leasehold interests.
[855] *Nailrile Limited v Cadogan* [2009] 2 EGLR 151.

As valuation is not an exact science and rates keep changing according to market evidence, it is prudent to research this area for the most up-to-date information on rates, among other things. Yields vary according to the type of case and the state of the local property market. For freeholds, the rate may range from 5% or less where there is likely to be vacant possession in the near future and where the security is good to much higher figures, such as 15% where the property is old and dilapidated or where it is occupied by an unsatisfactory tenant. A low rate is indicative of a large increase in capital value when vacant possession is obtained.

Right to Buy Leases

The basis to calculate the price payable on enfranchising a house let under any of the following leases is always that applicable to higher value houses:[856]

(1) a lease granted on the exercise of the right to buy, including a right to buy a shared ownership lease;

(2) a lease of which the term is treated as a single term beginning at the start of the term of a lease in the first category;[857]

(3) a sublease directly or indirectly derived out of a lease in either of the first two categories; and

(4) a lease granted in substitution for one in any of the previous three categories.

Minor Superior Tenancies

The price to be paid for a "minor superior tenancy" is calculated according to a formula which obviates the need for a valuation. It applies on enfranchisement by a subtenant to any tenancy with an expectation.

---

[856] Housing Act, 1985, s175(1), (2).
[857] Section 3(3) of the 1967 Act.

SUMMARY OF THE MAIN AMENDMENTS TO THE 1967 ACT

The 1967 Act has been amended on many occasions, while some are of a technical nature many are more substantial. In 1969 section 82 of the Housing Act, 1969, made certain technical changes to valuation.

Substantial amendments were provided in the Housing Act, 1974, which extended eligible houses via an increase in rateable value limits for enfranchisement but at the same time allowing the landlord a more generous enfranchisement price. Also, provision has been made for an estate management scheme (EMS) to be approved in respect of rights retained over properties which have been enfranchised. Further, amendment was made to discount the value of any improvement attributable to the tenant or any previous tenant.

The Leasehold Reform Act, 1979, was passed to prevent landlords from artificially increasing the enfranchisement price by a device that had been upheld by the House of Lords in the case, *Jones v Wrotham Park Settled Estates*.[858] This amendment was followed by the Housing Act, 1980, by reducing the qualification period from 5 years to 3 years. Excluded from enfranchisement are certain types of shared ownership leases in respect of which tenants purchased part of an interest in the house, paying a rent with the right to purchase further interests in the property.

The Housing and Planning Act, 1986, made certain changes of a technical nature whereby lessees were prevented from taking advantage of the 1967 Act which allowed them to purchase more cheaply by combining an application to extend the lease with a claim to acquire the freehold. Further, the statutory basis for excluding shared ownership leases was reformulated.

The Leasehold Reform, Housing and Urban Development Act, 1993, made substantial changes to the 1967 Act. The most notable change is the removal of the higher rateable value limits by bringing otherwise all eligible houses within the scope of the 1967 Act. A new basis of valuation was introduced for houses that qualify for enfranchisement, including the landlord's right to receive additional compensation for any consequential loss, such as development value following enfranchisement. Qualifying leases were extended on account of changes to the low rent test condition and changes to the

---

[858] [1979] 38 P&CR 77.

definition of a long lease which comes to an end on death or marriage. However, leases made by charitable housing trusts and houses transferred to the public sector no longer benefit from enfranchisement. The estate management scheme (EMS) was extended to landlords in respect of other houses which have become eligible for enfranchisement under these amendments.

The 1993 Act introduced the collective right of enfranchisement to lessees of flats as well as an individual right to a lessee to require a new lease with a 90-year extension.

Further amendments to the 1967 Act were made by the Housing Act, 1996. The main change was in relation to the low rent test: leases which failed this test became eligible for enfranchisement if such leases were originally granted for terms exceeding 35 years. Also, where a lease failed the low rent test because it did not have a rateable value at the date on which the test is applicable now qualifies. The EMS was extended to houses which became enfranchisable. The low rent test was not abolished in respect of shared ownership leases granted by the public sector.

Many changes to the 1967 Act were made by Part 2 of the Commonhold and Leasehold Reform Act, 2002.[859] Some of the changes included virtually the repeal of the residence qualifying provision. A notable change was to enable leaseholders who are entitled to an extended lease, the right to enfranchise and the right to an assured tenancy on termination of an extended lease. Prior to these amendments, a lessee with an extended lease had no right to either enfranchise or to remain in the house as a statutory tenant once the extended period had started.

Recent amendments in Part 3 of the Housing and Regeneration Act, 2008, repeal the remaining aspects of the low rent test, though this test remains as a qualifying condition for extended lease claims. Schedule 4A to the 1967 Act has been amended to enable all landlords in the private and public sectors to grant shared ownership leases, but such leases will not qualify for enfranchisement unless the lessee has acquired 100 % of the equity.

The requirement under section 1 of the 1967 Act for the lease at a low rent has been amended two times. The first was under the 1993 Act with effect from 1 November, 1993, to include houses with higher

---

[859] In addition, major changes were made in respect of enfranchisement rights to flat leases, and radical new management provisions for leaseholds, such as new service charge consulation provisions.

rents and rateable values, and the second was by the 2002 Act which under section 141 has abolished "low rents" with effect from 26 July 2002.[860]

APPENDIX TO CHAPTER 14

Included in this appendix is the basis for deciding whether the enfranchisement price will be based on the site value for low value houses under section 9(1) or an enhanced value for high value houses under section 9(1A), or section 9(1C). Examples to demonstrate these methods of valuation are given later in this appendix.

DETERMINATION OF THE VALUATION BASIS

Most houses which now qualify under the legislation will be valued according to the special valuation basis (under section 9(1A) or section 9(1C). This basis includes a marriage value element to reflect the bid of the tenant, whereas it is not taken into account under section 9(1). A house that falls under the original valuation basis (site value) will have to satisfy certain qualifications as to rent and values plus a further value limit. These are set out under A and B below.

A. <u>Low Rent Test</u>.[861] In this regard, leases granted are considered before 1 April 1990 and those on or after 1990.

(a) For leases granted prior to 1990 the yearly ground rent payable on the date the lessee has served his notice and for the previous two years must be less than two-thirds of the rateable value (RV) of the house as at the latest of these dates:

(i) 23 March 1965; or

(ii) the first day the house was entered in the valuation list; or

(iii) the day of commencement of the lease.

---

[860] The low rent test has been abolished altogether for tenancies granted after the commencement of section 300 of the 2008 Act on 7 September, 2009.
[861] Although the original low rent test has been abolished in respect of eligibility to acquire the freehold, it is still relevant in setting the means of valuation.

However, where the lease was granted between 1 September, 1939, and 31 March, 1963, the rent must be less than two-thirds of the rental value.

(b) In the case of a lease granted on or after 1 April 1990, the rent on the day the lessee's notice is served on the landlord must be less than £1,000 pa in Greater London or £250 pa elsewhere.

B. <u>Value Limits</u>. These limits are based on when the lease was granted ((a), (b) or (c)).

(a) The lease was granted on or before 18 February 1966:

(i) In this case if the house first appeared in rating list before 1 April 1973, its RV on 23 March 1965, or on the day it appeared in the list, but if later it must not have been greater that £400 in Greater London or £200 elsewhere; or

(ii) If the house first entered the list on or after 1 April 1973 its RV on the first day it appeared must not have been greater than £1,500 in Greater London or £750 elsewhere.

(b) The lease was granted after 18 February 1966 but before 1 April 1990.

(i) if the appearance of the house in the list was before 1 April 1973, its RV on 23 March 1965, or if later the first day it appeared on the list, must not have been more than £400 in Greater London or £200 elsewhere; or

(ii) if the house first appeared in the list on or after 1 April 1973 its rateable value on the first day it appeared on the list must not have been greater than £1,000 in Greater London or £500 elsewhere.

(c) For a lease granted on or after 1 April 1990 the lessee must calculate the value of R, having regard to the formula:

$R = P \times I / 1 - (1 + I) - T$, where

P is the purchase price (premium) paid on the grant of the lease (if none, P = 0)

I is 0.06

T represents the number of years granted by the lease
R must be £25,000 or less.

Further Value Limits

Subject to satisfying the above qualifications, the house must also meet the further limits set out below to be valued by the original valuation basis within section 9(1):

(a) If the house had a rateable value on 31 March 1990, the RV must have been less than £1,000 in Greater London or £500 elsewhere.

(b) In the **absence** of a RV for the house on 31 March 1990, the value must not be greater than £16,333 with regard to the value of R in the above formula.

Which method applies depends[862] on the rateable value of the property. Under section 9(1) of the 1967 Act, one basis applies to lower value houses and another applies to higher value houses.[863] The other two methods are to value high value houses.

THE METHODS OF VALUATION

The Leasehold Reform Act, 1967, section 9, provides two distinct bases for the valuation of houses, but as discussed above three bases were set out under subsections (1), (1A) and (1C) of section 9. Those under subsections (1A) and (1C) are similar and are know as the basis for high value houses. These bases are as follows:

---

[862] Except in the case of some leases granted to a tenant under a secure tenancy who exercises his right to buy.
[863] Section 9(1A) of the 1967 Act. Also, there is section 9(1C) under which there is a slight difference from section 9(1A).

(a) Under section 9(1), the house will be valued according to what had been originally enacted, i.e., the value of the site.[864] This is the low rent test basis.

(b) Under section 9(1A) and 9(1C), there is a special value basis to value the house. This basis will take into account a share of the marriage value. The marriage value is the difference between the vacant possession value and the aggregate of both the existing lease of the house and the value of the landlord's freehold interest subject to the lease.

The method of valuation by the landlord or the leaseholder is determined by the qualification criteria. Assuming the lease satisfies the low rent test and the house is within the value limits, the valuation will be under section 9(1) and the original valuation basis will apply. All other cases, including those where the original lease had been extended under section 14 of the Act, will be valued according to the special valuation basis.

Special Valuation Basis. This basis of valuation generally produces a higher figure and, therefore, the enfranchisement price payable by the lessee would be higher than that under the section 9(1), the original valuation basis.

Open Market Value. In each case the, the requirement is to determine the open market value of the freehold interest. It is as if the house is being sold in the open market by a willing seller to a willing purchaser, disregarding a forced sale. The objective is to adequately compensate the landlord for his freehold interest by assessing a fair price, as far as practicable, on the basis of open market values. In the event the parties are unable to agree a price by negotiation, it can be referred to a First-tier Tribunal (Property Chamber) for determination. The tribunal will arrive at its determination independently without favouring any party.

Commencement of Enfranchisement Procedure. It starts with the serving of a formal notice of claim by the lessee. The lessee will have to pay all the reasonable costs incurred by the freeholder. The lessee

---

[864] As according to the White Paper, preceding the Act, in equity the house belongs to the tenant and the land belongs to the landlord.

can be advised by a valuation surveyor regarding all relevant costs and the market value of the freehold interest

The Original Valuation Basis under Section 9(1)

The reason for the site value basis under section 9(1) of the 1967 Act was that the freeholder owned the land but in equity the leaseholder owned the house. Under this basis, at the end of the lease only the bare land should revert to the freeholder, who could grant another lease at a "modern ground rent" (MGR). However, the reality is different, but the principle remains, i.e., to assess the present value of the land only in terms of a MGR the freeholder could receive in the market based on current rates.

Instead of opting to acquire the freehold interest, the 1967 Act provided that the leaseholder could extend his lease by another 50 years from the date of expiry of the present lease. The rent for the new lease in respect of the land only would be assessed to commence on the first day of the lease extension as a proportion of the value of the land. Thus the rent would reflect the site value only and is known as the MGR, which is far higher than the present ground rent.

In assessing the market value of the freehold interest to be paid by the lessee, it must be assumed that the lessee has extended his lease by the 50-year extension. This being the position, the valuation of freeholder's interest is made up of three components:

(a) the right to receive the rent reserved in the existing lease (including any higher rent on a review);

(b) the right to receive the MGR (during the notional lease extension for 50 years); and

(c) the right to the house with vacant possession after the end of the existing lease plus the 50-year extension.

The valuation reflecting the above three components can best be explained by an example.

Example

X decides to acquire the freehold interest under the 1967 Act procedure. It is assumed that X's lease has another 30 years to run at a ground rent of £6.50 pa and the present freehold vacant possession value is £200,000.

(i) <u>Assessing the Value of the Existing Term</u>: this is done by applying a multiplier (known as years purchase (YP) by valuers) to the ground rent (GR). The YP can be obtained from valuation tables.[865]

Ground rent	£6.50 pa
YP for 30 years @ 6.5% =	13.06
Capital value for the term	£ 90

This sum of £90 represents the value of the term being the loss of the rental income for the remaining 30 years. The 6.5% is assumed to be the yield in an investment of this type. The YP is a figure which can be extracted from the single rate valuation tables.

(ii) <u>Assessing the Value of the MGR for the 50-Year Notional Extension</u>. This is done as at the date of the claim, rather than being projected into the future. As there is hardly any evidence of sales of individual plots, a proportion of the value of the house on a freehold basis with vacant possession is taken. Reflecting his local knowledge, the valuer will assume a proportion of, say, 30% to 50% for the site. Once the site value is arrived at, the valuer will convert it into the MGR by "decapitalisation" using a yield rate possibly the same as for the ground rent (6.5%). Having done this, the valuer assesses the future income of the MGR for 50 years as at the date of the claim but as the MGR does not start until 30 years's time the capital value of the MGR has to be discounted (deferred) for this period by applying a present value factor obtained from the valuation tables. This resultant figure will represent the value for the first reversion.

The freehold vacant possession value of the house	= £200,000
Assume for the site 35% of this value	= £ 70,000

---

[865] *Parry's Valuation and Investment Tables*, Feb 2013, Routledge, Abingdon Oxon, by Alick Davidson (Author).

MGR pa is taken at 5.5%
of the site value of £70,000 = £ 3,850
YP for 50 years @ 5.5%   16.93
                                 £65,180
PV of £1 in 30 years @ 5.5%   0.2006
Capital value of 1st reversion £ 13,075

(iii) <u>Assessing the Value of the Freehold Value Deferred for 30 Plus 50 Years</u>. The next step is to assess the value of the freehold interest as at present but deferred for 80 years (i.e., 30 plus 50 years), bearing in mind that the freeholder is not entitled to this component of the total value until 80 years' time. Therefore, the present value (PV) factor (from the valuation tables) will be applied to discount this component, which is the value of the freehold interest (the house and land) in its present state. This is the second reversion and is calculated below.

Freehold value of house if vacant £200,000
PV of £1 in 80 years @ 5.5%   0.0138
Capital value 2nd of the reversion £ 2,760

Total Price

The full purchase price for the freehold is the sum of the three components, the value of the existing term, the present value of the MGR for 50 years (the first reversion) and the present value of the freehold house (the second reversion).

Therefore, the total price for the freehold is £90 + £13,075 + £2,760 = £15,925

The Special Valuation Basis (Market Value) under Section 9(1A) and 9(1C)

The second basis to arrive at the market value of the house is based on the reality that the freeholder is entitled to possession of the house (not a cleared site) at the end of the existing lease. Also recognised in this basis is the lessee's special interest in the purchase and it is in relation to the marriage value to be added to the open market value of the landlord's interest when the existing lease expires. As already mentioned, the marriage value is the difference between the value of the freehold house with vacant possession and the aggregate of the two interests valued separately.

Example of Marriage Value. The value of the lessee's interest in the house with a 70-year lease unexpired may be worth, say, £150,000 while the landlord's interest is, say, £10,000. If the lessee were to purchase the landlord's interest for this sum, the freehold value of the house with vacant possession might be worth, say, £175,000. Thus, by paying £10,000, the lessee would have a house which has increased by £25,000, resulting in a "profit" of £15,000, which in this example is the marriage value. It is this marriage value which will be shared equally between the parties, meaning that the lessee would have to pay £17,500 (10,000 + 7,500) instead of only £10,000.

The requirement to pay a proportion of the marriage value as required by the 1967 Act does not apply if the existing lease is more than 80 years unexpired. Thus while a lease granted for 99 years 20 years ago will necessitate the payment of a proportion of the marriage value, if the acquisition of the freehold interest had been done, say, 2 years ago there would not have been any such requirement as the existing lease would have had more than 80 years to run.

Example of the Special Valuation Basis. In this example, the house to be acquired by the leaseholder has an unexpired term of 70 years at a rent of £60 per annum. The capital value of the leasehold interest in the house might be worth, say, £200,000 whereas the same house in its present condition might have a freehold value of £220,000

(i) Valuation of the Unexpired Term. This is done as previously by applying a years purchase to the stream of income, which is the ground rent for 70 years, having regard to what an investor in real property would be prepared to pay for it.

Ground rent	£ 60 pa
YP for 70 years @ 7%	14.16[866]
Capital value of the term	£ 850

---

[866] Extracted from the *Parry's Valuation Tables*.

The 7% yield rate would reflect the nature of the risk. A valuer will normally assume a yield after consideration of other transactions, such as freehold investments in auction sales. Accurate evidence is not always available, and sometimes this could lead to disagreement between the parties, particularly their valuers. However, as present ground rents are generally low, their capitalised values do not vary much by the multiplier (YP based on slightly different yield rates).

(ii) <u>Valuation of the Reversion.</u> Unlike the position under section 9(1), in this special valuation there is no assumption that there is a notional 50-year lease extension. Thus, after the expiry of the present term, the valuation will reflect the full freehold reversion with vacant possession. Therefore, the valuer is required to estimate the full value of the reversion deferred for the term of the existing lease. As time passes the value of the existing lease diminishes while the value of the freehold increases. What has to be established now as at the date of the claim is the value of the leasehold interest in the house and the potential freehold value subject to the lease. The valuer will necessarily have to carry out research into local sales of comparable houses.

For the purpose of this example, it is estimated that the freehold value with vacant possession (VP) will increase by 10%. Therefore, the value will be £200,000 + 10% = £220,000. The law provides that after expiry of a long residential lease the lessee is entitled to remain in possession under an assured tenancy paying the market rent. The effect of such an assured tenancy in some cases is to reduce the value of the freehold interest, though this is not assumed to be the case for this example.

The £220,000 as arrived at above has to be discounted for 70 to reflect the present value. The present value multiplier extracted from the valuation tables is taken at the same 7% rate used in the valuation of the ground rent for the term.

Capital value of the freehold with VP £220,000
PV of £1 for 70 years @ 7%   0.0088
Capital value of the reversion   £1,936

(iii) <u>The Total Investment Value of the Freehold</u>. This is the aggregate of the values for the term and the value of the reversion, i.e., £850 +

£1,936 = £2,786, say £2,800. This is the price the freehold is likely to achieve in an open market sale.

(iv) <u>Assessment of the Marriage Value</u>. The marriage value is the increase in value arising by the merger of two interests in the hands of the lessee following his enfranchisement claim or any lease extension. This potential "profit" only arises on account of the enfranchisement claim as the freeholder is compelled to sell his freehold interest to the lessee. As the existing lease does not exceed 80 years, the legislation requires the parties to share the marriage value equally as shown below..

Freehold value with VP	£220,000
Less	
(1) Present leasehold value £200,000	
(2) Present freehold value £ 2,800	£202,800
Marriage value	£ 17,200

Half of the marriage value is £8,600.

(v) <u>Enfranchisement Price</u>. Sharing marriage value at 50:50 between the parties, the enfranchisement price is made up of £2,800 + £8,600. Therefore, it is £11,400.

v) <u>Exclusion of leaseholder's improvements.</u> Like the other method of valuation under section 9(1) above, any additional value in the property arising from improvements by the lessee at his own expense is to be disregarded. The same applies if the improvements were carried out by his predecessor.

End

CHAPTER 15

RIGHTS CONFERRED ON LONG LEASEHOLDERS OF FLATS

INTRODUCTION

This chapter covers a number of matters in relation to flats. These are the right of first refusal (RFR) whereby the landlord is required to make an offer of his interest to his leaseholders before putting it in the market.[867] The other important matters discussed are:

(a) collective enfranchisement of the landlord's interest in a building or block of flats; and

(b) the right of long leaseholders of flats to extend their leases.

The RFR and those under (a) and (b) above are conferred on tenants of flats by statutes of recent origin. These statutes are:

(a) The Landlord and Tenant Act 1987, Part I, as amended by the Housing Act, 1996, in respect of the RFR; and

(b) The Leasehold Reform, Housing and Urban Development Act, 1993, in respect of collective enfranchisement and lease extension.

The benefit of collective enfranchisement in respect of flats may not be as beneficial to the tenants as the right to extend their leases because of the price to pay on enfranchisement. Compared with the enfranchisement of low value houses under the Leasehold Reform Act, 1967, under which the price to pay could be low,[868] the price on collective enfranchisement of flats could be on the high side. This is because there is no reflection of a notional extension of the lease by 50 years[869] and the need to take into account a proportion of the

---

[867] The Landlord and Tenant Act, 1987, Part I, confers this right.
[868] In respect of houses with low rateable values. (see Chapter 14).
[869] Whereas for houses the notional extension of the lease has the effect of reducing the value of the landlord's reversion, in the case of a flat the value of the landlord's reversion is deferred for only the unexpired term of the existing lease. Compared

marriage value in the price. For this reason many leaseholders of flats may prefer individually to extend their leases by 90 years on payment of a premium to the landlord.

RIGHT TO MANAGE A BUILDING

Qualifying long leaseholders (tenants) of flats are entitled to establish and join a "Right to Manage Company" (RTM company) through which they may take over the management of their building.[870] Before a building can be considered for such management, it must be, *inter alia*, "a self-contained building" or "a self-contained part of a building, as required by section 72 of the Commonhold and Leasehold Reform Act 2002. Other requirements under this section are that the building must contain two or more flats held by qualifying tenants, and the total number of flats held by such tenants is not less than two-thirds of the total number of flats contained in the premises.

In order to qualify for the RTM you have to be, *inter alia*, a leaseholder under a long lease as defined under sections 76 and 77 of 2002 Act. Such a lease is for a term certain exceeding 21 years and a shared ownership lease where the total share held by the tenant is 100%. In *Corscombe Close Block 8 RTM Co Ltd v Roseleb Ltd* [871] Roseleb owned the freehold to a block of 15 flats. Four of the flats had been let on 125 year leases to a housing association. In turn the flats were let under shared ownership leases. None of the shared ownership tenants had acquired a 100% share. The claimant company wanted to take over the management of the block and served notice to that effect. *Roseleb* said that the notice was not valid because it had been served on the four shared ownership leaseholders instead of on the housing association. A tribunal (LVT) held that the notices were invalid, but the Upper Tribunal reversed that decision. A tenant holds a long lease if he satisfies any of the conditions in sections 76 and 77, regardless of the share held. Therefore, section 76(2)(e) in respect of the 100% share ownership would appear to irrelevant.

---

with a house, the total period of deferment is made up of the unexpired term of the lease plus the 50-year notional extension. In addition, the price of the flat includes a proportion of the marriage value element on account of the merger of two separate interests, except where the unexpired term of the existing lease is 80 years or more.

[870] Commonhold and Leasehold Reform Act 2002

[871] [2013] UKUT 81 (LC).

Starting the Process Regarding RTM. The process starts with the RTM company invoking section 78 of the 2002 Act by serving a "notice of invitation to participate" on qualifying leaseholders informing them of their right to join the company. If there is sufficient participation as required by the Act, the RTM company, after at least 14 days of serving the notice, may serve a notice of claim on the landlord, informing him that it intends to acquire the right to manage, pursuant to section 79. In this regard, there can be only one notice of claim in force at any time according to section 81, but such a notice may be withdrawn at any time under section 86. The Upper Chamber (Lands Chamber) has held that a failure by a RTM company to serve a notice of invitation to participate on all qualifying leaseholders does not necessarily have the effect of invalidating the process; the issue is whether there has been substantial compliance and the prejudice caused to the tenant.[872] Further, the Tribunal held that where the RTM company has served an invalid notice, it is not required to withdraw that notice before serving a fresh notice of claim.

A few cases in which the notices of claim by the RTM companies were invalid are:

(a) *Assethold Ltd v 13-24 Romside Place RTM Co Ltd* [873] as the landlord was incorrectly named; and

(b) *Assethold Ltd v 7 Sunny Gardens RTM Company Ltd*[874] as the notice was not served on the deceased's personal representatives in accordance with s.78 of the 2002 Act. The RTM company had failed to adduce any evidence that the defect in compliance with the statutory procedure had not caused prejudice so its claim was dismissed.

A landlord who wishes to oppose the claim must serve a counter-notice as required by section 84. Once this counter-notice is served, the relevant tribunal has jurisdiction to determine whether the RTM company has the right to manage. With effect from 1 July 2013 in England, the appropriate tribunal is the First-Tier Tribunal (Property Chamber), replacing the LVT, which is retained in Wales.

---

[872] *Avon Freeholds Ltd v Regent Court RTM Co Ltd* [2013] UKUT 213.
[873] [2013] UKUT 603 (LC).
[874] [2013] UKUT 509 (LC).

In *Triplerose Ltd v 90 Broomfield Road RTM Co Ltd*[875] the Court of Appeal has unanimously held that a RTM company can only acquire the management of one building and not, for example, all residential buildings on an estate. In the above case, the RTM company had sought to acquire the right to manage more than one block of flats on an estate.

RIGHT OF FIRST REFUSAL (RFR)

The right of first refusal (RFR) is conferred under Part I of the Landlord and Tenant Act 1987 as amended by the Housing Act, 1996. This is a right given to tenants of flats in a building where a landlord is proposing to sell his interest in the building. This is different from enfranchisement.[876] He is required by law to make an offer first to the tenants before putting it for sale in the open market. In this regard, he is required to serve formal notices on the tenants stating what is his intention regarding the building and must provide a period of time for them to consider his offer. During this period, he cannot sell to any other person, nor offer the interest at a price to anyone less than what he proposed to the tenants or sell on different terms. There is a criminal sanction for a breach of these legal obligations by the landlord.

Despite the above requirements, if the landlord, nevertheless, sells without providing the RFR to the tenants, the tenants can serve a notice on the new owner demanding:

(a) details of the transaction and the price paid; and

(b) that the new owner to sell to the tenants at the price he paid for the landlord's interest.

Principles of RFR

The important principles that relate to RFR are set out below.

---

[875] [2015] EWCA Civ 282.
[876] Given by the Leasehold Reform Act, 1967, to tenants to acquire the freehold of houses (discussed in Chapter 14), and the right under the 1993 Act given to tenants of flats to acquire the superior interest (discussed later in this chapter). As an alternative, tenants of flats are given the right to extend their leases by 90 years.

(a) This right of RFR is not a means of forcing the landlord to sell his interest to the tenants but rather to enable the tenants to buy it, in preference to others, if the landlord is interested in selling it. There is a right to force a sale to the tenants contained in the Leasehold Reform, Housing and Urban Development Act, 1993, but this is not the position relating to the RFR.

(b) The tenants are able to purchase that interest before it is offered for sale in the open market or by auction.

(c) The right is invoked automatically if a landlord decides to sell thereby enabling the tenants to react to the landlord's offer. This offer can be withdrawn at any time before any binding contract is concluded.

(d) The right is available both to leaseholders of flats and regulated tenants occupying flats under the fair rent system.

(e) The price for the interest in respect of all the flats in the building is set by the landlord, or by auction. No other body or person can set the price. However, there is an important restriction preventing the landlord selling to another party on different terms or at a lower price than that originally offered to the tenants within 12 months of his notice, unless the landlord again makes an offer to the existing tenants on the new terms and/or at the lower price.

(f) Under certain circumstances, the price set may be lower than that which could be achieved through a collective enfranchisement (discussed later). Also, the price could also be higher.

(g) The procedure to follow regarding the making of the offer is set out in the 1987 Act. As already mentioned, there is a criminal sanction if the landlord does not comply with the statutory requirements. The same applies where the building is being sold by a receiver, a trustee in bankruptcy or an executor or personal representatives following a grant of probate or letters of administration.

(h) The RFR is not available to tenants of certain bodies, such as local authorities and housing associations. The same applies, in some cases, where there is a resident landlord in the building.

Qualifying Building, Landlord and Tenants

RFR applies only where the building, the landlord and the tenants meet certain requirements.

<u>The Building</u>. For the building to qualify there are three requirements:

(a) it must contain at least two flats;[877]

(b) non-residential use of the building must not exceed 50%;[878] and

(c) qualifying tenants must hold over 50% of the flats in the building.[879]

A building is generally understood to mean a separate building or, in some cases, a part of a building which may be divided vertically from another part. In this regard, in the absence of a definition as to the meaning of a building, a common sense approach should apply. Therefore, a floor containing flats above a shop are not a separate building. However, a semi-detached house converted into flats is a separate building. Also, the building must contain at least two flats.

The building will be excluded where the use comprises more than 50% of non-residential use. In this regard, any common parts of the residential building, such as staircases and landings, are excluded.

<u>The Landlord</u>. The RFR is excluded in respect of a landlord in the following list:

---

[877] A flat is defined by section 60(1) as a separate set of premises, whether or not on the same floor forming part of the building, and is divided horizontally from some other part of the building, and is constructed or adapted for use for the purpose of a dwelling.

[878] Any part or parts of the premises is or occupied or intended to be occupied otherwise than for residential purposes and the internal area of that part or parts together exceeds 50% of the internal area of the premises, but disregarding the internal area of the common parts (section 1(3)).

[879] Section 1(2) of the 1987 Act.

(a) most housing authorities, such as local authorities, new towns and development corporations;

(b) registered social landlords and unregistered fully mutual housing associations;

(c) charitable housing trusts; and

(d) where a resident landlord lives in the building, provided:

- (i) the building is not a purpose-built block of flats, but for example is a house which has been converted into flats since its original construction; and
- (ii) the landlord actually lives in the building which has his only or principal residence and has done so for more than a year.

The right only applies where an immediate landlord decides to sell. Such a landlord is the person to whom tenants pay their rent, and he will be entitled to possession of a flat when the lease expires.

<u>Qualifying Tenants</u>. Qualifying tenants comprise leaseholders and most tenants holding under fixed or periodic tenancies. Those tenants specifically excluded are shorthold and assured tenants, business and agricultural tenants and those whose tenancies are based on their employment, including sub-tenants. Also, a tenant who has interests in three or more flats in a building is excluded. In other words, such a tenant does not have the right of first refusal.[880]

Disposals

A sale by the landlord is a sale of the freehold or a headlease in respect of all the flats. Alternatively, the landlord could propose to create a new headlease, which is a new interest in the building. In either case, if the conditions relating to the building, the landlord and tenants are satisfied, the RFR exists and the disposal must first be offered to the tenants.

---

[880] As seen from this paragraph, the 1987 Act adopts a negative definition of a qualifying tenant.

Under section 4(3) a disposal is defined to mean a disposal whether by creation or the transfer of an estate or interest and includes the surrender of a tenancy[881] and the grant of an option or a right of pre-emption. A disposal will not include an interest passing on devolution under a will or intestacy,[882] but the RFR applies to a contract to create an estate or interest in land.[883]

While most disposals will trigger the RFR, note the landlord is exempt from the following:[884]

(a) the grant of single tenancies, as the RFR applies to the whole building;

(b) the grant of an interest relating to a mortgage as security for a loan;

(c) a disposal to a receiver or trustee in bankruptcy;

(d) a disposal by way to an associated company of the landlord;

(e) disposals resulting from collective enfranchisement under 1993 Act;

(f) disposals as invoked by compulsory purchase orders;

(g) disposals by charities to other charities;

(h) certain disposals arising from matrimonial and family proceedings;

(i) a disposal by two or more persons within the same family to a different combination of the same family or a transfer by family members to reduce the number; and

(j) any disposal to the Crown or to a government department.

---

[881] *Kensington Heights Commercial Co Ltd v Camden Hill Developments Ltd* [2007] EWCA Civ 245.
[882] Section 4(3)(b).
[883] Section 4A, inserted by the Housing Act, 1996.
[884] Section 4(2).

Relevant Disposal

To determine whether a disposal triggers the RFR, it is necessary to consider whether it affects the relevant premises which are "to be ascertained in an objective way disregarding the disposal concerned."[885] The airspace immediately above a block of flats to which access was occasionally required for maintenance was held to be included.[886] A disposal also includes an agreement to surrender.[887] Also included is a contract to assign rights relating to an estate or interest in land. However, this does not include a contract for a disposal within the category of exempt disposals and, therefore, are not relevant disposals as listed above.

Landlord's Notice of the Offer

The notice is required to be served in respect of a separate building and this can sometimes cause confusion where there are several blocks in an estate. In such a case, the landlord should treat the blocks as separate buildings and serve notices in respect of each building. If all the conditions are satisfied, a landlord proposing to dispose of his interest must serve a formal notice on the qualifying tenants making the offer of first refusal. Any breach of this requirement will attract on conviction a fine of level five, currently £5,000.[888]

There are five different forms of notice, depending on the particular circumstances of the disposal:

(a) section 5A regarding a simple sale by contract;

(b) section 5B in respect of an auction sale;

(c) section 5C concerning a grant of an option or right of pre-emption;

(d) section 5D as regards a sale not pursuant to a contract; and

---

[885] *Dartmouth Court Blackheath v Berisworth Ltd* [2008] 09 EG 200 at [46] per Warren J.
[886] *Ibid.*
[887] *Kensington Heights Commercial Property Ltd v Campden Hill Developments Ltd* [2007] Ch 318 (giving a right to the grant of a new lease: Landlord and Tenant Act, 1987, s 52C).
[888] See sections 5, 6-10 & 10A.

(e) section 5E concerning a sale not based on a monetary consideration.

<u>Service of the Notice</u>. The landlord's notice has to be served on the qualifying tenants, and this requirement is satisfied if notices are served on at least 90% of them. Where there are less than ten such tenants the notice should be served on all. In the event where there is a right to manage (RTM) the premises, a copy of the notice must also be served on the RTM company, if one exists.[889]

<u>The procedures</u>. As regards the section 5A notice, where the landlord intends to sell in the open market, and the qualifying tenants are expecting the offer, they can inform the landlord of their nominated person if they have accepted. On a failure by the qualifying tenants to notify the landlord of their nominated person within the required period, the landlord is free to dispose of the interest in the open market, though not on different terms or at a price which is lower than what was proposed to them. The details regarding notices concerning disposals under the other sections (referred to above) can be found in the Act.[890]

<u>New Landlord to Inform the Tenants</u>. Where a building has been sold to a person who has become a new landlord, the tenants may know nothing about a sale until they receive a communication from the new landlord. This could be much later than when the sale took place. A "new" landlord of a property containing at least one dwelling is required to inform the tenants of his name and address[891] by notice (Section 3 Notice) which must be served by the date when rent is due, according to the lease. Where the next date is within two months of the date of his acquiring the property, the date is the end of the two months. Any failure to serve this notice will render the new landlord liable to criminal prosecution and on conviction is liable to a level 4 fine up to £2,500.

---

[889] Commonhold and Leasehold Reform Act, 2002, Sch 7, para 7.
[890] Leasehold Advisory Service – Right of Refusal (information booklet available on the Internet): www.lease-advice.org/publications/documents/document.asp?item=16
[891] Section 3, Landlord and Tenant Act 1985 - a section 3 notice.

Where the RFR should apply, the new landlord must also serve a notice,[892] advising each tenant of his rights. This notice must be served, irrespective of whether the original landlord had served any notice relating to an offer on the qualifying tenants prior to the disposal. The notice must provide:

(a) that the sale to the new landlord was one to which Part I of the 1987 Act applies;

(b) that all qualifying tenants have the right to:

    (i) obtain information about the disposal; and
    (ii) acquire the new landlord's interest in the building; and

(c) the time limits in which these rights may be exercised.

Regardless of whether the disposal to the new landlord complies with the statutory requirements of the RFR, this section 3A notice must be served. This applies notwithstanding that the tenants would not, in this case, be entitled to the rights set out in the notice. It is a procedure which must be followed, on pain of a criminal sanction of up to a level 4 fine (£2,500). The object of the notice is simply to alert qualifying tenants to the possibility of a breach of their rights and are given the necessary information to take action.

<u>The Tenants' Right to Require Information.</u> If the tenants become aware that the transfer was not in accordance with the RFR, a majority of the qualifying tenants (more than 50%) may seek information by notice from the new landlord.[893] This notice must be served within four months of the date of receipt by the tenants of the section 3A notice or by other documents indicating that the disposal has taken place, and alerting the tenants to the existence of their rights and by which time such rights must be exercised. The new landlord must respond to the notice within one month.

---

[892] Notice under section 3A of the Landlord and Tenant Act 1985 (a S3A notice).
[893] Under section 11A of the 1987 Act.

The Tenants' Right to Acquire the Landlord's Interest

Qualifying tenants who can show a breach regarding the RFR can require the new landlord to sell his newly acquired interest to them, on the same terms as he acquired it from the former landlord.

Acquisition Procedures. The procedure that applies for acquiring the interest will depend on the disposal that has taken place. The rights are under:

(a) Section 12A: the right to take the benefit of a contract where completion has not taken place;

(b) Section 12B: the right to compel resale where completion has taken place and the building has been transferred to the new landlord; and

(c) Section 12C: the right to compel the grant of a new tenancy where the former landlord has surrendered his tenancy (concerning a headlease of all the flats) to the new landlord.

Rights Against Subsequent Purchasers

Where the qualifying tenants have been denied the RFR they can pursue their rights of remedy even after the new landlord sells his interest to another. In a situation where the original purchaser has already disposed of his interest but receives a request for information in a notice under section 11A from the qualifying tenants, he must:

(a) send a copy of both the notice and his response to the notice to the new purchaser; and

(b) advise the qualifying tenants of the name and address of the new purchaser.

Similar action must be taken by him where the qualifying tenants have served a notice under sections 12A, 12B or 12C (mentioned above) by passing it on to the subsequent purchaser. Also, he must notify the tenants of the name and address of the new purchaser. Where the notice is forwarded to the subsequent purchaser, the subsequent purchaser becomes bound by the requirements of the notice. Where the qualifying tenants had not served a notice under sections 12A, 12B or 12C prior to the subsequent transfer, they may still serve notice on the subsequent purchaser, nevertheless.

Disputes

Disputes relating to the RFR generally can be taken to the county court for resolution.[894] However, matters arising in respect of notices served under sections 12A, 12B and 12C, other than their validity, may be taken to the leasehold valuation tribunal (LVC).

RIGHTS GIVEN TO LEASEHOLDERS OF FLATS UNDER THE 1993 ACT

The cost of investing in a flat in the market involves a large capital outlay, yet as time passes, being a wasting asset, the value decreases and becomes unsaleable until the value becomes nil on expiry of the lease. This has been a source of some dissatisfaction to tenants in addition to the question of insufficient control with regard to the level of service charges, management and maintenance. The rights conferred by the Leasehold Reform Act, 1967, to long leasehold tenants of houses were not extended to their counterparts in respect of long leaseholders of flats.

However, in 1993 the Leasehold Reform, Housing and Urban Development Act was passed to remedy the plight of such tenants. The 1993 Act was amended by the Commonhold and Leasehold Reform Act, 2002. These Acts conferred on tenants of flats, who satisfy certain conditions, the right to compel the sale of the freehold of the building or part of the building. In the event of the presence of an intervening interest, such as a headlease, this must generally be acquired as part of the purchase by the tenants. As an alternative to enfranchisement, to acquire the superior interests, leaseholders of flats instead can seek individually to extend their lease terms.

A leasehold valuation tribunal (LVT) has been given jurisdiction to determine any question concerning the terms of interest which a

---

[894] Section 52 of the 1987 Act.

nominee purchaser acquires following notice to exercise the right of collective enfranchisement.[895]

Collective Enfranchisement

"Collective enfranchisement" simply means that lessees of flats have the right to acquire the freehold of the building or block containing their flats. The use of the word "collective" in the term is important in that those lessees who participate are acting as a group to acquire the freehold of the whole building containing their flats.

Premises, Resident Landlord, Qualifying Tenants and Participating Tenants

These terms are explained below.

The Premises. Those premises that qualify will have to satisfy these requirements:

(a) the premises must consist of a self-contained building or part of a building;[896]

(b) at least two or more flats are within the premises and are held by qualifying tenants; and

(c) the total number of flats held by such tenants is at least two-thirds of the total number of flats which are contained in the premises.[897]

The definition of premises encompasses all properties, ranging from a converted house into two or more flats to and including a multi-storey block containing a large number of flats. A flat is defined as a separate set of premises:

---

[895] Section 21(2)(3) of the Leasehold Reform, Housing and Urban Development Act, 1993.
[896] *41-60 Albert Palace Mansions (Freehold) Ltd v Craftrule Ltd* [2011] EWCA Civ 185, [2011] NPC 23 (self-contained part can be part of the building that could itself be subdivided into smaller self-contained units).
[897] Section 3 of the 1993 Act as amended by the Housing Act, 1996, s 107, to include premises owned by multiple freeholders.

(a) which forms part of a building;

(b) which is constructed or adapted for use as a dwelling; and

(c) either the whole or a material part of the dwelling lies above or below some other part of the building.

The definition above includes not only purpose-built but also converted flats, and a proportion of the building could include non-residential use as well. This falls into mixed-use premises where, for example, a building could have shops or offices at ground level with flats on the upper floors. Where this is the case, the non-residential proportion must not exceed 25%, otherwise there is no right to collective enfranchisement.[898]

Disputes Concerning the Vertical Division of a Building. Disputes have surfaced with respect to the vertical division of a building or the degree of ease with which electrical and plumbing and other services can be separated. As to vertical division, flying freeholds are excluded. It is likely that any more than *de minimis* overlap between premises will prevent the potential for enfranchisement in view of a few court cases.[899] In relation to the provision of services, HHJ Marshall, QC, provided some helpful guidance in *Oakwood Court (Holland Park) Ltd v Daemon Properties Ltd* [900] The Queens Counsel (female) propounded a commonsense five-point approach. However, this will often be an elementary issue, which may require expert and legal advice.

Resident Landlord.[901] Where the landlord resides in the building by occupying one of the flats, collective enfranchisement may be excluded. This will only apply to a limited number of cases. To be excluded from enfranchisement the following conditions must be satisfied:

---

[898] Section 4(1) of the 1993 Act, as amended by the s 115 of the 2002 Act; *Indiana Investment Ltd v Taylor* [2004] 3 EGLR 63.
[899] See *Maleness v Howard de Walden Estates Ltd* (No 2) [2003] EWHC 3106 (H); [2004] 1 WLR 862.
[900] [2007] 1 EGLR 121.
[901] Defined in section 10 of the 1993 Act, as amended (and narrowed) by the 2002 Act, s 118.

(a) there must not be more than four flats in the premises;[902]

(b) the premises must not be a purpose built block of flats or a part of such a block;

(c) the same person must have owned the freehold of the premises before the conversion into two or more flats or other units; and

(d) the freeholder or an adult member of his family must have occupied a flat or other unit within the premises as his only or principal home during the previous twelve months.

The list above effectively means that the only premises that would be excluded would be a converted house or building into four or less flats by a freeholder who continues to occupy one of the flats.

Qualifying Tenants. A tenant generally qualifies if he is a tenant of a long lease, which was granted initially for a term of at least 21 years. Now, however, such a tenant[903] is any tenant of the flat[904] under a long lease still defined as a long lease of a term exceeding 21 years but there is no restriction as to the level of rent and without any resident condition. As most leases of flats were initially for 99 years or longer, the majority of the tenants of such leases will qualify as tenants for the purposes of the Act. In the event there are joint names on a tenancy the joint names will constitute the qualifying tenant of the flat.

In certain cases a tenant will fail to qualify; the main situation is where a lessee who would otherwise be a qualifying tenant owns three or more flats within the same building. The reason for this exclusion is to ensure that the right to collective enfranchisement is extended to owner-occupiers rather than property speculators or investors.

Participating Tenants. To proceed with a claim for collective enfranchisement a number of qualifying tenants are required to be involved in the process. These tenants are called the "participating

---

[902] Section 4(4) of the 1993 Act.

[903] Section 5 of the 1993 Act. Business tenants are excluded: s 5(2)(a). The 1993 Act does not apply in respect of tenants holding directly of the Crown

[904] *Slamon v Planchon* [2005] Ch 142 (meaning of resident landlord exemption). Also, note a qualifying person is any person who is a tenant of the flat.

tenants". In this regard, at least half of the tenants in a building need to participate to enable a valid claim to proceed. Once the process is completed, the "participating tenants" will become the freeholder of the entire block and they will, in effect, become the "landlord" of the tenants that are not participating in the acquisition.

Where the nominee purchaser in a collective enfranchisement had served an initial notice, but had failed to register the same, the notice could not be amended to include in the claim leases which were granted after the notice.

Formal Procedure

The procedure for collective enfranchisement commences by serving the initial notice on the landlord. On behalf of the participating tenants a company is usually formed and is designated as the Nominated Purchaser to acquire the freehold ultimately. This is the beginning of the statutory procedure. The contents of the notice are prescribed in detail and must be accompanied by a plan. Without a plan the notice is invalid.[905]

Where the nominee purchaser in a collective enfranchisement had served an initial notice, but had failed to register the same, the notice could not be amended to include in the claim leases which were granted after the notice.[906]

<u>Contents of the Notice from the Company</u>.[907] This notice must contain:

(a) information to the landlord such as the names of the qualifying tenants; and
(b) the purchase price.

No inaccuracy or misdescription will invalidate a notice, but this cannot save an invalid notice.[908] Once the initial notice is served, there should follow a period of preparation to ensure the participating

---

[905] *Mutual Place Property Management Ltd v Blaquiere* [1996] 2 EGLR 78 CC (Central London).
[906] *Regent Wealth Ltd v Wiggins* [2014] EWCA Civ 1078.
[907] This is the right to enfranchise (RTE) company incorporated for the purpose.
[908] *Sinclair Garden Investments (Kensington) Ltd v Poets Chase Freehold Ltd* [2007] 3 EGLR 29 Ch D.

tenants are fully aware of the implications so they can complete their action. At this stage they will need to understand the legal definitions of various terms in respect of the premises that qualify for collective enfranchisement.

Whilst the initial notice is in force, i.e., until a binding contract or vesting order is made, the freeholder may not make any disposal severing his interest in the specified premises or in any property specified in the notice.[909] Neither may any relevant landlord grant any further intermediate lease out of his interest. Equally, any contract to dispose of the whole or any part of the specified premises is suspended during the currency of the said notice.[910]

Counter-Notice. The landlord will respond by a counter-notice, the purpose of which is meant[911] to define the basic issues before commencement of proceedings. The counter-notice must state:

(a) whether he accepts the qualifying tenants right to enfranchise;

(b) whether he accepts the price proposed; and

(c) if he accepts the tenants rights but rejects the proposed price, the counter-notice must include a counter-offer.

The counter-notice should be given to avoid being compelled to do so pursuant to section 25 or 49.[912] The validity of a negative counter-notice challenging the initial notice rather than the right remains an open question.[913] Faced with such a challenge, if appropriate, it would be wise to make an application under section 22 of the Leasehold Reform, Housing and Urban Development Act, 1993.

---

[909] See *Earl Cadogan v Panagopoulos* [2010] EHWC 422 (Ch); [2010] 3 WLR 1125.
[910] Section 19(2) - (5).
[911] *Bishopsgate Foundation v Curtis* [2004] 3 EGLR 57.
[912] Albeit it has been suggested that the decision in *Willingale v Globalgrange Ltd* (2001) 33 HLR 17 in which the Court of Appeal held that 'may' meant 'must' might be vulnerable to challenge under the Human Rights Act 1998.
[913] See *Sinclair Gardens Investments (Kensington) Ltd v Poets Chase Freehold Co Ltd* [2007] EWHC 1776 (Ch); [2008] 1 WLR 768.

The price in the counter-notice need not be realistic.[914] The landlord should state what he wishes to retain but must not be too wide to effectively negate the rights to be granted over the property which he retains.[915]

Resolution by Court. If the landlord denies the tenants right, it will be a matter for the court to resolve.[916] The landlord may oppose the claim by an application to the court that he intends to redevelop the whole or a substantial part of the premises. This ground is only available if two-thirds of all the long leases of the flats within the premises are due to expire within five years from the date of the initial notice.[917]

A local valuation Tribunal (LVT) has jurisdiction to determine any question concerning the terms of the interest which a nominee purchaser acquires following notice exercising the right to collective enfranchisement. However, any dispute arising from the landlord's denial of the right to enfranchise is determined by the county court.[918] But one which is on the details of the claim, even if it concerns the extent of the land affected and, therefore, whether particular land can be acquired, is a matter for the LVT.[919]

The case, *Westbrook Dolphin Square Ltd v Friends Life Ltd*,[920] involves a long-running battle for control of Pimlico's Dolphin Square. The US private equity firm, Westbrook Partners, won a landmark enfranchisement case for them to purchase the freehold. The lengthy judgment contains detailed analyses of some very difficult legal and valuation concepts. Westbrook, being the claimant and nominee for the tenants claiming the freehold, defeated the defendant freeholder, Friends Life, on all seven grounds advanced at the trial. Barring any appeal by the defendant, the way is now clear for Westbrook to proceed with the purchase of the freehold at a price to be agreed or, failing that, determined by the Property Chamber of the First Tier Tribunal. The price is likely be the largest premium ever paid under the 1993 Act. Even if there is no further adjudication on

---

[914] *9 Cornwall Crescent London Ltd v Kensington & Chelsea LBC* [2006] 1 WLR 1186.
[915] *Ulterra Ltd v Glenbarr (RTE) Co Ltd* [2008] 4 EG 174 (LT).
[916] Section 22 of the 1993 Act.
[917] Section 23 of the 1993 Act.
[918] Sections 22, 90 of the 1993 Act.
[919] *Stephenson v Leatherbound Ltd* [2005] 3 EGLR 79 (LT).
[920] [2014] EWHC 2433 (Ch).

any other matter (unlikely), the valuation aspects of the claim are most likely to be pursued to the Upper Tribunal and perhaps further to the Court of Appeal.

<u>Withdrawal or Deemed Withdrawal</u>. Once there has been a withdrawal or deemed withdrawal, a further notice may not be served for a period of 12 months from the date of the withdrawal.

<u>Running of Time</u>. The time limit that appears to be the most problematic relates to the time limit of two months within which to act as shown in three cases, *Penman v Upavon Enterprises Ltd,* [921] *Sinclair Gardens Investments Kensington Ltd v Eardley Crescent No 75 Ltd* and *Goldeagle Properties Ltd v Thornbury Court Ltd.*[922] In *Penman* the tenant's application to the LVT was for the determination of both the price and terms of the transfer. There was an issue over the inclusion of an indemnity, but the LVT determined only the price. Within two months of the LVT's decision becoming final, the tenant applied to the court for a vesting order, whilst the issue regarding the indemnity remained unresolved. Rightly, the Court of Appeal held that the application was premature as the LVT still had jurisdiction to determine the further issue in respect of the conveyance which had been put before it but not decided.

In *Sinclair Gardens*, HHJ Huskinson went further holding that the LVT could determine terms that were in dispute at a later hearing even if the original application had determined the purchase price and costs as being in dispute. In *Goldeagle Properties Ltd,* the issue again was concerned with when the terms of the transfer had been agreed. However, the terms of the transfer had not been put before the LVT. The landlord insisted that time ran from the date the decision of the LVT became final. But the Court of Appeal held that section 24 did not prevent the LVT from dealing with un-agreed points in stages. "Once an application is made to the LVT within time, the LVT remain seized of all matters in dispute." per Jacob LJ. Ultimately, they accepted the views of Arden LJ in *Penman* that the controlling provision was the opening words of section 24(3) that time begins to run when all the terms have either been agreed or determined.

---

[921] [2001] EWCA Civ 956; [2002] L & TR 10.
[922] [2008] EWCA Civ 864; [2009] HLR 13.

Successful Enfranchisement

In the event the enfranchisement is successful, the company acting for the tenants will have to attend to these matters:

(a) to grant a leaseback for 99 years at a peppercorn rent to the former landlord in respect of any flat subject to secure tenancies;

(b) at the request of the former landlord to grant such a leaseback in respect of non-residential units or flats with no qualifying tenants.[923] This applies also to a flat occupied by a resident landlord where the right to enfranchise is not excluded because there are more than four units.

After enfranchisement, the company on behalf of the tenants will be managing the premises and, where it is necessary to maintain standards of appearance and amenity, the former landlord may be authorised to retain some control in respect of the enfranchised building. This is done via a management scheme,[924] but the former landlord must apply to a LVT within a certain time.

PRICE ON ENFRANCHISEMENT

Unlike the position under the Leasehold Reform Act, 1967,[925] the tenants must pay the total market price for the landlord's interest and all other superior interests.[926] Separate prices must be specified for each of the property interests which are the subject-matter of the acquisition. Although expert evidence is not absolutely required for this at this stage, the price must be realistic and are proposed in good faith.[927]

---

[923] Section 36, Sch 9 of the 1993 Act.
[924] Section 69 of the 1993 Act. As in the case under section 19 of the Leasehold Reform Act.
[925] In respect of houses with low rateable values, as originally enacted, though this is no longer the case.
[926] The freehold of the specified premises (separating the price if there is more than one freeholder), the price of the freehold of the appurtenant property, and the price for any leasehold interests to be acquired (as above).
[927] *Viscount Chelsea v Morris* (1999) 31 HLR 732; and *9 Cornwall Crescent London Ltd v Kensington and Chelsea RLBC* [2005] EWCA Civ 324; [2006] 1

Prior to the amendments made by the 2002 Act, the date for fixing the valuation was when the interest to be acquired was agreed or otherwise determined by the LVT. It is now the date when the notice to enfranchise was given to the landlord. Under section 32 and Schedule 6, the price reflects three components:

(a) the value of the freeholder's interest which is made up of:

    (i) the capitalised value of the rents under the existing tenancies; and
    (ii) the capital value of the landlord's reversion deferred for the number of years of the unexpired terms of the tenancies referred to in (i);

(b) the freeholder's share of the marriage value;[928] and

(c) any compensation payable to the freeholder on account of losses attributable to the enfranchisement.[929]

<u>Value of the Freeholder's Interest</u>. This is the open market value assuming that neither the nominee company acting on behalf of the tenants nor any tenant of the premises is seeking to buy. Other relevant assumptions are:

(a) that the landlord is selling his fee simple estate subject to the existing leases and any other intermediate interests;

(b) the right to enfranchise or to extend the lease is to be ignored;

(c) that any increase in value attributable to improvements carried out at the tenant's expense to be disregarded; and

(d) that the landlord is selling with and subject to the rights and burdens with and to which the conveyance to the nominee purchaser is to be made.[930]

WLR 1186 (albeit concerned with section 42 notices and counter-notices respectively).
[928] Sch 6, para 4.
[929] Sch 6, para 2 of the 1993 Act.

Valuation Aspects. Differences in the acquisition price are usually referred to the LVT. This leads the parties into the realms of valuation expertise, in relation to *Sportelli* [2006 -2010], marriage value and hope value. Matters usually disagreed upon are the capitalisation rate and deferment rates in valuing the freeholder's interest and the relativity to be applied to agreed virtual freehold values for the flats to arrive at a value for the tenants' current interest and marriage value. Some valuers in the recent past were of the view that the default capitalisation rate is 7%. However, the rate is best determined by reference to market transaction evidence if available. If not, resort can be made to the other non-binding decisions of the LVT. In relation to the deferment rate, the question is whether the binding guidance in *Sportelli* [2006-20010] which determined rates of 4.75% for houses and 5% for flats in prime central London properties should be disapplied or not in the particular circumstances of the case in question.

Notable cases in the recent past regarding rates include *Hildron Finance Ltd v Greenhill Hamstead Ltd*[931] refusing to disapply *Sportelli* to blocks of flats in Hampstead, and *Kelton Court Zuckerman v Calthorpe Estates Trustees* [932] determining a rate of 6% in a number of new leases in a block in Birmingham. The decision in *Daejan Investments Ltd v Benson*[933] materially reduces the management risk for which allowance was made in *Kelton Court Zuckerman*.

The Upper Tribunal has now determined that where the unexpired term is below 20 years, the *Sportelli* starting rate of 5% should be adjusted to 5.25% for terms of 17.3 to 17.8 and 5% for terms of 15.6 to 16.1 years to reflect pessimism over real growth rates. But the decision did consider terms of below 10 years. For these, different considerations may arise.

In relation to relativity, evidence of sales will be preferred, if possible, over the industry graphs.[934] If graphs are to be used, the

---

[930] Sch 6, para 3. The nominee purchaser is usually a right to enfranchise company (RTE).
[931] [2008] 1 EGLR 179 (refusing to disapply *Sportelli* to blocks of flats in Hampstead.
[932] [2009] UKUT 235 (LC).
[933] [2013] UKSC 54. See also *Alexander Voyvoda, Grosvenor West End Properties & 32 Grosvenor Square Ltd* [2013] UKUT 334.
[934] See *Nailrile Ltd v Earl Cadogan* [2009] 2 EGLR 151.

valuer should use a range of such graphs with reference to the location and type of property, suitably adjusted.

Marriage Value. This arises when the two or more separate interests are merged. The capital value of the merged interests is usually higher than the aggregate value of each interest valued separately. The proportion of the marriage value that forms part of the price is 50%, except where the tenant's lease has an unexpired term of at least 80 years, in which case there is no element for marriage value.

Compensation. It is reasonable for the freeholder to receive compensation for any loss attributable to the enfranchisement that has an adverse effect on his other properties. This could be a reduction in the value, or loss of development value, of another of the landlord's property.[935]

Intermediate Interests. Where one or more intermediate interests are to be acquired in respect of the enfranchisement, a separate price is to be paid for each such interest.[936] An owner of such an interest is also entitled to a share of the marriage value and compensation, if relevant.[937]

RIGHT TO EXTEND A LEASE UNDER THE 1993 ACT

Another right conferred by the 1993 Act is for a leaseholder of a flat to require the landlord to grant a new lease on the payment of a premium. In this regard, the 2002 Act has made significant amendments to the 1993 Act, thereby enhancing the rights of leaseholders. These amendments relate to:

(a) the need of both the "low rent" and residence condition, which used to apply to the right to a new lease, have been removed; and

(b) the only requirement now is that the tenant must be a qualified tenant under a long lease of the flat for the last two years before he can exercise the right to be granted a new lease.[938]

---

[935] Sch 6, para 5.
[936] Sch 6, para 7.
[937] Sch 6, paras 8 & 9
[938] Section 39 of the 1993 Act as amended by ss 130 & 131 of the 2002 Act

A qualifying tenant and a long lease are defined in the same way as for the right to collective enfranchisement. This has significantly extended the scope of the 1993 Act,[939] having regard to the needs of many tenants who do not wish to enfranchise but rather to renew their leases by a 90-year extension.

Right to a New Lease

Because of the complexity of collective enfranchisement[940] under the Leasehold Reform, Housing and Urban Development Act, 1993, and the large upfront purchase price to be paid, it has been relatively seldom used. It appears leaseholders of flats are more interested in acquiring new leases. Unlike collective enfranchisement, each tenant can act on his own. It was thought that the right of a lease extension could be used by those tenants who were disqualified for collective enfranchisement. However, it turned out that the lease extension became a general right. The right to a new lease is conferred by section 56 of the Act. Subsection (1) states:

> "Where a qualifying tenant of a flat has under this Chapter a right to acquire a new lease of the flat and gives notice of his claim in accordance with section 42, then except as provided by this Chapter the landlord shall be bound to grant to the tenant, and the tenant shall be bound to accept—
>
> (a) in substitution for the existing lease, and
>
> (b) on payment of the premium payable under Schedule 13 in respect of the grant, a new lease of the flat at a peppercorn rent for a term expiring 90 years after the term date of the existing lease."

This right is similar to its counterpart in the Leasehold Reform Act, 1967, in respect of a lease extension of a house. A few important changes were made by the Commonhold and Leasehold Reform Act,

---

[939] *Maurice v Hollow-ware Products Ltd* [2005] 26 EG 132. Here in a block with 28 flats which were sub-let, each tenant was entitled to a new lease.
[940] Collective enfranchisement makes a fundamental shift in the relationship between leaseholders and freeholders.

2002.[941] By reason of these changes, the only condition is that the leaseholder must have been a qualifying tenant under a long lease of a flat for at least two years before exercising the right to the new lease.[942] The previous tests regarding low rent and residence were abolished.

Statutory Procedure

To initiate the process for the granting of a new lease, a tenant is required to serve a notice on the landlord who will in turn serve a counter-notice on the tenant.[943] If the landlord does not respond to the notice, the tenant may apply to the court for a determination of the terms of the new lease in accordance with the tenant's notice.[944] The court will only make an order on being satisfied that the tenant is entitled to a new lease and the tenant's notice procedure was complied with.

The tenant is entitled to assign his rights with the lease, but this right of assignment cannot be exercised during any claim for the enfranchisement of the whole block of flats.[945] The landlord can refuse a new lease where the existing lease does not have more than five years to run from the date of the tenant's notice. In this regard, the landlord can apply under section 47 to the court on the ground that he intends to redevelop the premises.

<u>Consideration for the New Lease</u>. Where the parties are in agreement, a qualified tenant is entitled under section 56 to be granted a new lease at a premium with a peppercorn rent for a new term expiring 90 years after the unexpired term of the existing tenancy. For example, if the existing unexpired term is 10 years, the new lease will be for 100 years. The other terms of the new lease will be the same as in the

---

[941] Sections 130 and 131 of the Commonhold and Law Reform Act, 2002, amended section 39 of the 1993 Act.
[942] Section 39(2) of the 1993 Act.
[943] Sections 42 & 45 of the 1993 Act. See *Cadogan v Morris* (1998) 27 P & CR 336 in respect of unrealistic price proposal by the tenant and invalidity of the notice; *9 Cornwall Crescent London Ltd v Kensington and Chelsea Council* [2005] 4 All ER 1207 regarding no such rule as landlord's counter-notice; *Lay v Ackerman* [2004] HLR 40 in which misdescription of landlord did not invalidate the notice.
[944] Section 49(1) of the 1993 Act.
[945] Section 54 of the 1993 Act.

existing lease, but excluding any term for renewal or option to purchase.[946]

Premium as Consideration for the New Lease. The premium to be paid by the tenant for the grant of the new lease shall reflect the aggregate of:

(a) the diminution of the landlord's interest in the value of the flat assuming the tenant had no enfranchisement or extension rights, but without disregarding his right to the existing tenancy and extended tenancy;

(b) a proportion (50%) of the marriage value; and

(c) any entitlement to compensation in respect of any loss or damage to the landlord's other property resulting from the grant of the new lease.[947]

Landlord's Right to Terminate New Lease Subsequently. This is where the landlord intends to redevelop the premises in which the flat is contained. In this case, the landlord will have to make an application under section 61 to the court for possession. Such an application may be made during the 12 months ending with the original term date or at any time during the period of five years ending with the new term date. If possession is granted to the landlord for redevelopment, the tenant will be entitled to compensation. It will be based on the open market value or the tenant's interest in the new lease in accordance with Schedule 14 to the Act.[948]

SERVICE CHARGES

The Landlord and Tenant Act 1985 provides the basic rules relating to service charges. It defines what is considered to be a service charge and the requirements for reasonableness and prior consultation with leaseholders. Under section 18(1) of the Act a service charge is defined as:

---

[946] Section 57(4) of the 1993 Act.
[947] Sch. 13 of the 1993 Act as amended by the Housing Act, 1996, s 110, and the 2002 Act, ss 134-36
[948] Leasehold Reform, Housing and Urban Development Act 1993

"an amount payable by a tenant of a dwelling as part of or in addition to the rent

(1) which is payable, directly or indirectly, for services, repairs, maintenance, improvements or insurance or for the landlord's costs of management; and
(2) the whole or part of which varies or may vary according to the relevant costs."

The above definition does not overrule the lease as the item or service charge must still be included in the lease in order to be chargeable. Section 42 of the Landlord and Tenant Act, 1987, requires that where leaseholders are required under the terms of their leases to contribute towards the same costs, the monies must be held in one or more accounts under a trust.

The number of court cases on service charges is overwhelming:

(a) In *Friends Life Management Services Ltd v A & a Express Building Ltd*,[949] the court set out how the service charge for the last accounting period of a commercial lease should be calculated.

(b) The case, *Ground Rents (Regisport) Ltd v Dowlen*,[950] involves the issue under section 20B of the Landlord and Tenant Act 1985 in which the landlord must demand service charges within 18 months of incurring the costs (or serve notice stating that he has incurred the costs and that the leaseholders will be required to make a contribution at a later date).

(c) In *OM Property Management Ltd v Burr*,[951] the Court of Appeal had held that cost were incurred when the underlying liability crystalised, whether on payment or presentation of the invoice.

(d) *Barrett v Robinson*,[952] is a very important case on costs from the

---

[949] [2014] EWHC 1463 (Ch), [2014] 2 EGLR 53 ChD.
[950] [2014] UKUT 144 (LC).
[951] [2013] 1 WLR 3071.
[952] [2014] UKUT 322 (LC).

Upper Chamber (Lands). As most residential leases permit landlords to recover all their costs, in this case the landlord was able to recover all his legal costs.

(e) In *Windermere Marina Village v Wild and Others*,[953] the Upper Tribunal (Lands Chamber) considered whether section 27A(6) of the Landlord and Tenant Act 1985 renders void an agreement in a lease of a dwelling that the apportionment of service charge will be determined by a third party whose decision shall be final and binding. The agreement was held to be void.

(f) With regard to the true construction of a housing authority lease, the Court of Appeal held in *Morris v Blackpool Borough Council and Another*[954] that the local authority was entitled to charge certain management charges as part of the service charge recoverable under the lease.

(g) In the Court of Appeal *Phillips v Francis*[955] was concerned with: (1) the correct interpretation of service charge provisions in long leases of holiday homes and whether they permitted double recovery and (2) the interpretation of the consultation provisions contained in the Landlord & Tenant Act 1985 and subordinate legislation in relation to "qualifying works".

(h) In *Chaplair Ltd v Kumari*[956] the Court of Appeal held that a court can award costs on proceedings before the First-tier Tribunal (Property Chamber) or the Leasehold Valuation Tribunal (LVT) where there is provision for the tenant to pay the landlord's costs under the terms of the lease. The LVT had limited powers to award costs, *inter alia*, where the tenant had acted frivolously, vexatiously, abusively, disruptively or otherwise unreasonably in connection with the proceedings.[957] As an order for costs is always discretionary,

---

[953] [2014] UKUT 163 (LC).
[954] [2014] EWCA Civ 1384.
[955] [2014] EWCA Civ 1395 (CA); [2015] 1 WLR 741; [2015] HLR 3; [2015] 1 P & CR 9; [2015] L & TR 4 (Chancery Division: [2012] EWHC 3650 (Ch); [2013] 1 WLR 2343; [2013] L & TR 19).

[956] [2015] EWCA Civ 798.
[957] Commonhold and Leasehold Reform Act 2002, sch. 12, para. 10. The First-Tier Tribunal (Property Chamber), which has now replaced the LVT, has similar limited

where a lease allows costs to be recovered under a service charge, a tribunal can order that any costs incurred by the landlord in proceedings are not to be included in the service charge payable by the tenant.[958]

(i) In *Christoforou v Standard Apartments*[959] it was held that a landlord's contractual entitlement to costs against a tenant is an administrative charge which is caught by paragraph 10(4) of Schedule 12 to the Commonhold and Leasehold Reform Act, 2002, which after 1 July 2013 no longer applies in England or by any rule in the Tribunal Procedure (First-tier Tribunal) (Property Chamber) Rules 2013.

(j) With regard to terrorism insurance, the Upper Tribunal's decision in *Qdime Ltd v Bath Building (Swindon) Management Co Ltd & Ors*[960] found that the cost is a recoverable head of expenditure and was therefore payable by the leaseholders. Having regard to the landlord's discretion to insure, the Upper Tribunal had regard to the RICS Code, which provides at paragraph 15.12 (Second Edition) that "...serious consideration should be given to the taking out of terrorism insurance". Thus, the Tribunal found that the exercise of the discretion accords with the RICS Code.

(k) The decision of the Supreme Court in *Arnold v Britton*[961] has highlighted an important gap on how the law governs the assessment and recovery of residential service charges as well as providing lawyers with invaluable guidance on how the concept of "commercial common sense" fits into the task of interpreting contracts. Consideration was given to sections 18 and 19 of the Landlord and Tenant Act, 1985, which provides that service charges are variable according to the relevant costs of providing the services and are only payable if they are "reasonable".

---

powers in respect of costs: Tribunal Procedure (First-Tier Tribunal) (Property Chamber) Rules 2013/1169, r.13.
[958] Landlord and Tenant Act 1985, s20C.
[959] [2013] UKUT 586 (LC).
[960] [2014] UKUT 261 (LC).
[961] [2015] UKSC 36; [2015] 2 WLR 1593.

(l) In this case, *Arnold v Britton*,[962] the claimant was the lessor under a number of leases with the defendant lessees of chalets on a leisure park. The service charges are to be increased by compound interest of 10% per annum. Because of the phenomenal increase which will accrue over a number of years the defendants challenged the rate of increase and the claimant sought declaratory relief. The Court of Appeal held that the parties had known from the outset where they had stood and, therefore, the court could not, by a process of interpretation, mend a bad bargain suffered by the defendants. It would be wrong to rewrite the bargain.

(m) *Brickfield Properties Ltd v Botten*[963] addresses a simple but important point. The Upper Tribunal confirmed that, where a lease is varied pursuant to section 38 of the Landlord and Tenant Act, 1987, the effective date of variation can pre-date the decision ordering variation (i.e., it can have retrospective effect). The decision has implications for both landlords and tenants when such matters arise in the future. Tenants will not be able to benefit from an unintended windfall where they fail to respond to requests by a landlord to vary leases which do not allow them to recover 100% of their expenditure. It will also be the case that landlords will be unable to benefit from a discrepancy allowing them to recover more than 100% expenditure.

(n) *Johnson v County Bideford*[964] supports the contention that any invalidity in a service charge demand arising by virtue of a failure to comply with section 47 of the Landlord and Tenant Act, 1987, is capable of being corrected with retrospective effect so that demands were valid demands for the purposes of section 20B(1) of the 1985 Act.

<u>Leaseholders' Entitlement to a Summary of the Service Charge Account</u>. This right is conferred by section 21 of the 1985 Act. The landlord must provide a summary to show:

(a) how costs relate to the service charge demand, or if they will be inserted in a later demand;

---

[962] [2013] EWCA Civ 902.
[963] [2013] UKUT 133 (LC).
[964] [2012] UKUT 457 (LC).

(b) any items for which the landlord did not receive a demand for payment during the accounting period;

(c) any items for which a demand was received but for which no payment was made during the accounting period;

(d) any items for which a demand was received and payment was made during the accounting period; and

(e) whether any of the costs are associated to works for which an improvement grant has been paid or to be paid.

Reasonable Administrative Charges. Rights in respect of these charges were introduced by the Commonhold and Leasehold Reform Act, 2002. Such charges are defined as:

"an amount payable by a tenant as part of or in addition to rent which is payable directly or indirectly for:

(a) the grant of approvals under the lease or applications for such approvals;

(b) for or in connection with the provision of information or documents by or on behalf of the landlord or other party to the lease apart from the landlord and tenant;

(c) costs arising from non-payment of any money due to the landlord; and

(d) costs incurred in connection with a breach (or alleged) breach of the lease."

The Leasehold Advisory Service. A booklet issued by the Department for Communities and Local Government provides information relating to:

(a) service charges;
(b) administrative charges;
(c) insurance and ground rent;
(d) estate management scheme charges

(e) recognised tenants' associations; and
(f) forfeiture and possession

Service charges are one of the main areas for dispute between landlords and leaseholders. The above booklet sets out an account relating to:

(a) recover of service charges;

(b) the rights of the parties to challenge or substantiate the charges before the LVT;

(c) the obligations of the landlord to consult the leaseholders before carrying out qualifying works or entering into long-term agreements;

(d) the statutory controls on demands; and

(e) accounting for the charges.

Application to the LVT. An application to the LVT is to determine whether a charge is reasonable. However, if the charges have been previously agreed by the parties or finally determined by a tribunal or court or by post-dispute arbitration, there can be no application to the LVT.

RICS Code on Service Charges Relating to Commercial Property

What is set out here applies to a commercial property. The third edition of the RICS Code of Practice on service charges became operative on 4 February 2014. This Code sets out the best practice regarding service charges and can be found on the internet.[965] The aims of the Code are to ensure the following:

(a) fairness;
(b) transparency;
(c) good communication;
(d) timeliness;
(e) fast, effective resolution of disputes;

---

[965] http://www.rics.org/uk/knowledge/professional-guidance/codes-of-practice/service-charges-in-commercialproperty

(f) professional standard of service charge management; and
(g) providing of appropriate services at a cost representing value, though not necessarily the cheapest price.

Any failure by RICS members to adopt this Code may be evidence of negligence.

Reserve Fund

Long leases of residential properties may require leaseholders to contribute to a fund maintained by the landlord to meet recurring expenditure (though not every year), such as for the replacement of lifts or boilers for heating. This applies to commercial leases as well. The main problem relating to advance payment of any kind is who is entitled to any unused sum when the lease is ended, such as by a break clause. If the leaseholder is entitled to a refund what sum is he entitled to receive? It has been held that if this matter is not dealt with in the lease terms, the leaseholder may be entitled to a refund of a proportion of the monies.[966]

CONCLUSION

Enfranchisement of flats is a highly technical and specialist area of property law. Even the entitlement to the right poses numerous complex issues under both the 1967 and the 1993 Acts. Once there is no hindrance to entitlement, it is important to comply with the statutory requirements regarding the notice to the landlord to avoid any potential challenges. The time limits should be complied with. The next hurdle is associated with the complexities in determining the purchase price, having regard to the different bases applicable. At this stage, it will be difficult to avoid the need for an expert valuer.

In view of the amendments to the 1993 Act in respect of the granting of a new lease, the tenant is likely to be placed in a better position compared with the collective right to enfranchise in respect of the whole block. Tenants can act individually to request a new lease from the landlord. However, to be absolutely sure whether it is better to act collectively to acquire the freehold or to apply for a new lease of 90 years plus the existing unexpired term on an individual

---

[966] See *Friends Life Management Services Ltd v A & A Express Building Ltd* [2014] EWHC 1463 (Ch).

basis, a comparison should be made reflecting the position in each case. This will necessarily involve a cost benefit analysis involving the services of a valuation surveyor, which could be expensive.

APPENDIX TO CHAPTER 15

This appendix provides valuation examples and other relevant information regarding a 90-year extension of a lease and the price to pay on a collective enfranchisement.

VALUATION FOR LEASEHOLD ENFRANCHISEMENT OF FLATS

Based on Part II of Schedule 6 to the Leasehold Reform, Housing and Urban Development Act, 1993, the price to be paid for the freehold shall include:

(a) the capitalised rental income (ground rents) in respect of the unexpired terms;

(b) the freehold reversionary value on expiry of the leases (the reversion);

(c) the marriage value;

(d) the value of other interests, such as Rent Act tenancies, commercial properties, garages; and

(e) compensation for injurious affection (other losses)

Marriage Value. The marriage value is the increase in value arising from merging the freehold and leasehold interests. This potential value is to be shared between parties on a 50:50 basis. The parties are the landlord and the RTE company, acting on behalf of the relevant lessees. The valuers acting on behalf of the parties will rely on local knowledge and experience in assessing the increase in the value of the flats. The increase will reflect the ability of the enfranchising lessees to grant themselves very long leases (999 year leases) at no premium.

Injurious Affection. This is to compensate the freeholder in respect of any diminution in value in respect of another property of the landlord arising from the forced sale. It could be attributable to the removal of right to develop an adjoining property of the freeholder.

Valuation to Enable RTE Company to Make Offer. Although there is no requirement for a formal valuation, it is prudent to obtain one to enable an offer price in the initial notice to be made to the freeholder. The offer need not be the same as in the valuation. The freeholder has the option of either accepting the offer or he may set out his asking price in the counter notice. This could lead to negotiation and a settlement of the enfranchisement price, failing which either party may apply to the First Tier Tribunal (Property Chamber) in accordance with specified time scales. Subject to submissions from both parties, the Tribunal will determine all outstanding matters relating to the price. These are:

(a) the value of the freehold interest;

(b) the value of any other interest or land appurtenant to the acquisition;

(c) the potential marriage value following the enfranchisement;

(d) the splitting the price between the freeholder and any intermediate landlords; and

(e) any compensation for injurious affection.

The role of the Tribunal is to decide on the basis of the evidence independently and will not necessarily decide on what the parties have proposed. The enfranchisement price will be based on the general open market values as required by law on the assumption of a willing vendor and willing purchaser basis. The objective is to adequately compensate the freeholder for being deprived of his property. The difficulty is to assess the "open market value" in the climate of an artificial situation imposed by the leaseholders' statutory rights.

Principles and Valuation Methods

The valuation is based on the application of conventional methods using factual data and assumed information with assistance from valuation tables. What are known are the unexpired term of the lease and the rent reserved. Using his experience, market analyses of recent transactions in the locality and an estimate of a yield rate, the valuer has to arrive at the market value of the flats, and the likely increase in that value following enfranchisement.

It should be appreciated that property valuation is not a precise science and, therefore, cannot produce a definite value, regardless of the skill and experience of the valuer. It is only an estimate based on market data, and it is inevitable that the party's respective valuations will be different, in many cases by a wide margin.

<u>Freehold Property</u>. A freehold property which is subject to long leases is normally valued on an investment basis, having regard to:

(a) the rental income (mainly from the rents reserved in the leases); and

(b) the freeholder's entitlement to possession on expiry of the term (the reversion).

Therefore, at any time the value of the freehold interest is based on the present value of a stream of income and the discounted value of the reversion using an appropriate yield rate. The value is comparable to an investment, i.e., what should be paid today to acquire the right to receive an income for a certain period, reflecting a particular yield rate and/or to be entitled to a capital repayment deferred for the said period of the income. An example is used to demonstrate the principles and valuation method

Example

Six flats in a small freehold block are leased individually to six lessees at a ground rent of £50 each for 99 years. The unexpired term is 70 years for each flat. The current value of each flat is £160,000

(i) <u>Valuation of the Term</u>

The total rental income: £50 x 6 flats = £300 pa for the block

This rental income (ground rent) is multiplied by the Years Purchase (YP) (a multiplier usually obtained from valuation tables). In order to decide on an appropriate YP, the valuer must use his skill and available market conditions in assuming a yield rate. A rate of 5% is chosen before extracting the YP from the valuation tables.[967]

Rental income	£ 300 pa
YP for 70 years @ 5%	19.34
Capital value or rental income	£5,802

(ii) <u>Valuation of the Reversion</u>

Current market value of a flat	£160,000
Six flats	6
Total value of lessees' interests	£ 960,000

A lease is a wasting asset which diminishes over time and eventually to zero on expiration of the lease. Therefore, this implies that a long lease is worth more that a short lease for the same property. As the enfranchising lessees have the opportunity to grant themselves lease extensions, they can create generally some improvement in the value of the individual flats. If the unexpired term of the current lease (before the extension) is very long, the improvement in value after the extension may not be much. The shorter the unexpired term, the greater the value of the improvement. The valuer will have to use his skill, experience and market research to estimate the improvement value.

In the valuation of a flat, the valuer must disregard any improvements carried out by the lessee. Where there are substantial improvements, the valuer is required to estimate the additional value to the flat attributable to the improvements. This estimated additional value will have to be discounted from the estimated present value of the flat. This procedure effectively means he has to value the flat without the improvements.

With regard to the reversion, the valuer must ascribe a value to each flat to represent what it could be sold for on expiry of the current

---

[967] *Parry's Valuation and Investment Tables* by Alick Davidson, Estate Gazette, 2013.

term. In this regard, it must be assumed the lessees will grant themselves very long leases, e.g., 999 years. Also, as most long leaseholders will enjoy statutory protection in the form of assured tenancies on the expiry of their leases the improved value is sometimes discounted by a small percentage to reflect that the freeholder will not obtain vacant possession of a flat on expiry but that the tenant will pay a periodic rent. However, for the purposes of this example, it is ignored.

It is assumed in this example that, after enfranchisement, the value in the market for each flat would be increased by 10 % from £160,000 to £176,000. This is the future value of each flat.

Improved value of each flat: £176,000 x 6 = £1,056,000 (future value)

To discount this future value to the present value, a multiplier, i.e., the present value (PV) of £1 for 70 years at 8% is taken from the tables to produce an investment value. The yield rate is assumed to be higher because of the nature of the risk, much higher than for the valuation of the ground rent. Deciding on the yield rate is the most controversial factor.

Improved value of 6 flats	£1,056,000
PV of £1 deferred 70 years @ 8%	0.0046
Discounted value of the flats	£ 4,858

(iii) The Freehold Investment Value

The investment value of the freehold (the freeholder's present interest) therefore is represented by the sum of the values of the unexpired terms and the reversion:

£5,802 + £4,858 = £10,660

This is price the interest is likely to command in an open market sale.

The Marriage Value

The marriage value after the enfranchisement is the increase in the value of the 6 flats. This increase arises from the lessees granting themselves much longer leases. This potential "profit" resulted from the freeholder's obligation to comply with the legislation to sell the freehold interest. The marriage value is to be shared on a 50:50 basis between the parties. However, where the unexpired term of the lease exceeds 80 years the marriage value is disregarded.

The calculation of the marriage value is done by using the figures already estimated above. Taking the figures from the previous example above:

From the improved value of the 6 flats, i.e., £1,056,000, is deducted the aggregate of the value of the lessees' present interest, £960,000, and the value of the freeholder's interest, £10,660.

Therefore, the marriage value is:

The improved value of the property		£1,056,000
Less		
(i) Value of lessees' interest	£960,000	
(ii) Value of the freehold	£ 10,660	£ 970,660
Mrriage value		£ 85,340
A 50:50 apportionment		£ 42,670

As can be seen in this example, the marriage value is considerably higher than the value of the freehold interest. It is based on the estimated increase in the value of the flats. The higher the increase, the higher is the marriage value. The value of the flats will depend on local market evidence and the skill and experience of the valuer. Most importantly, the longer the unexpired term of the existing leases, the lower the marriage value until it becomes zero.

Marriage Value of Participating Leaseholders

In the example above all the lessees participated in the enfranchisement. Where there are many flats and some of the lessees of flats do not participate, their flats are not included in the calculation. These lessees will not benefit from the purchase of the freehold interest and they will not be able to extend their leases without the payment of a premium to the new freeholder at a later date.

Enfranchisement Price

The enfranchisement price is the aggregate of the present value of the freeholder's interest and 50 % of the marriage value, assuming there is no compensation for injurious affection.

Value of the present freehold interest £10,660
Apportioned marriage value   £42,670
Enfranchisement price   £53,330

Therefore, the price to pay by each lessee is £8,888, say, £8,900.

The above example is only for demonstration of the valuation process. Obviously, there will be major differences between the parties, most likely in relation to:

(a) the yield rate; and

(b) the amount by which the value of each flat has increased.

    In addition to the payment for the enfranchisement by the lessees, they will also be liable for all costs incurred by the freeholder including their own costs.

VALUATION FOR 90-YEAR LEASE EXTENSION

Based on Part II of Schedule 13 to the Leasehold Reform, Housing and Urban Development Act, 1993, as amended, the premium to be paid for the new lease shall reflect:

(a) the diminution in the value of the landlord's interest in the flat (the difference between the value of his interest now subject to the present lease and the value of his interest following the grant of the new 90-year lease to run from the expiry of the present lease);

(b) the landlord's share of the marriage value; and

(c) compensation for any loss arising from the grant of the new 90-year lease.

Diminution in the Value of the Landlord's Interest

This diminution is made up of two components:

(a) the loss of the income from the ground rent during the remainder of the original term as the whole term of the new lease will be at peppercorn rent); and

(b) the loss due to the additional 90-year period wait for the reversion.

The Marriage Value

The marriage value is the likely increase in the value of the flat on account of the grant of the new lease. This increase in the value shall be shared equally (50:50) between the parties according to the Act.

The Compensation

The landlord will be compensated for any loss or damage arising from the grant of the new lease, such as any loss of potential development value.

General Market Values

The requirement under the legislation is that the value of the interest to be acquired should be based on general market values, assuming a willing vendor and a willing purchaser. The landlord should be adequately compensated for the diminution in the value of his property.

Principles and Methods of Valuation

Valuation of property is not a precise science as it is based on a great deal of assumptions and the application of methodical calculations. Important assumptions regarding yield rates, having regard to analyses of recent market transactions of similar properties in the locality. As far as possible, an experienced valuer will monitor the local property market to produce acceptable figures.

However, it should be appreciated that a valuation cannot produce definitive values. At best it will be an estimate what a purchaser will be prepared to pay. Valuations under the 1993 Act procedures will in most cases result in a variation between the parties' respective figures. An experienced valuer will be able to anticipate the likely variations.

The usual method which is used to value a freehold property subject to a long lease is the investment method. This will reflect the rental income for the unexpired term and the value of the reversion at the end of the term. Therefore, the value of the freehold is the capitalized present rental income and the present value of the reversion.

In a valuation for a lease extension under the 1993 Act, what has to be estimated by calculation is the diminution in the freehold interest having regard to the lease extension at a peppercorn rent. Here the landlord loses the ground rent for the unexpired term of the existing lease and he has to wait for another 90 years to get possession of the flat (the reversion). This can be illustrated by an valuation example.

Valuation Example

X is the lessee of a flat with an unexpired term of 70 years, at a ground rent of £60 per annum and the present market value of the leasehold interest is £160,000.

(i) <u>Valuation of the Term</u>

This aspect of the valuation requires the valuer to apply the years purchase (YP) multiplier to the ground rent.[968] In order to extract the relevant YP from the valuation tables it is necessary to assume a yield rate which varies according to the type of property and the risk. The yield is taken as 5%.

Ground rent	£ 60 pa
YP for 70 years @ 5%	19.34
Capital value of the term	£1,160

From the calculation above, it is estimated that a property investor would be prepared to pay £1,160 to receive an income for 70 years at

---

[968] The years purchase (YP) can be calculated but most valuers extract the relevant YP from valuation tables. See *Parry's Valuation and Investment Tables* by Alick Davidson, Estate Gazette, 2013.

a yield of 5%. The yield is assumed in the light of analysed market data such as auction prices. The yield is the most important information in a valuation and there is likely to be a difference between the parties. The yield rate used is for demonstration purposes rather than reflecting market condition.

(ii) Valuation of the Present Reversion

The present value of the leasehold flat is £160,000. As leasehold is a wasting asset the value decreases over time eventually to zero on its expiration. The longer the lease the higher the value. Therefore, a lease extension can generally increase the value of the flat. The valuer is required to estimate the value of the leasehold flat on the basis of his market research in recent transactions in the locality.

In the event improvements were carried out to the flat, they will have to be disregarded in estimating the value of the flat. Substantial improvements could add significantly to the value of the flat. The additional value, not the cost, has to be taken into account and then deducted to arrive at the value without the improvements.

In the case of the reversion, a value must be determined as an indication what the flat could be sold for on expiry of the current term. As most long leaseholders are entitled to statutory protection (assured tenancy) on the expiration of their long leases, the improved value is sometimes discounted to reflect the likely possibility that the landlord will not obtain vacant possession. However, this is not envisaged in this example.

It is assumed that the grant of the new lease would increase the market value of the flat by, say, 10% to produce a valuation of £176,000, i.e., an additional £16,000.

As before, a multiplier is taken from the valuation tables to reflect the investment value of the reversion. Here, the valuation of the reversion is discounted by applying the present value of £1 for 70 years at the same rate of 5%. Based on *Sportelli* this 5% discounted rate was widely used. However, there have been many cases which have successfully challenged this case.

Improved Value of the flat	£176,000
PV of £1 for 70 years @ 5%	0.0328
Value of the reversion	£ 5,773

(iii) Diminution in the Landlord's Interest

The amount by which the landlord's interest has been reduced is made up of the value of the term and the reversion less the value of the reversion on expiry of the new lease (for 160 years). In most cases this is negligible on account of the reversion being too far into the future.

Value of the reversion after the grant of the 90-year extension
Present value of £1 deferred for 160 years (i.e., 70 + 90) is 0.0004071
Therefore, £176,000 x 0.0004071 = £72

The diminution in the landlord's interest is shown below:

The term (70 years)	£1,160
The reversion deferred 70 years	£5,773
Term and reversion	£6,933
Less reversion after new lease	£ 72
Diminution in the freehold value	£6,861

The Marriage Value

As mentioned above, the marriage value results from an increase in the leasehold value on account of the lease extension (from 70 years to 160 years). This increase has to be shared equally (50:50) between the parties. According to Schedule 13, the calculation is the difference between two aggregate amounts as set out under (a) and (b) below:

(a) The Present Interests
    (i) The value of the lessee's present interest in the flat
    (ii) Plus the landlord's present interest without the new lease
    (iii) Plus the value of any intermediate interest

(b) The New Interests
    (i) The value of the lessee's interest with the benefit of the new lease
    (ii) Plus the value of the landlord's interest subject to the new lease
    (iii) Plus the value of any intermediate interest

There is no marriage value where the unexpired lease exceeds 80 years. The figures from the example above are used to calculate the marriage value.

The present interest of the lessee	= £160,000
Plus landlord's present interest	= £ 6,933
	£166,933
The lessee's interest based on the new lease	= £176,000
Plus the landlord's new interest	= £ 72
	£176,072

Amount of marriage value: £176,072 less £166,933 = £9,139

The marriage value is divided equally between the parties. Therefore, the lessee is required to pay £4,570 (half of £9,139) plus the diminution in the landlord's interest, which is £6,861. The total of these two sums is £11,431.

Therefore, the premium for the extended lease is £11,431.

The above example is to demonstrate how the valuation is carried out, but it should not be used in any individual circumstance without professional advice as there could be significant variation in the yield rates. This is usually the avenue of major conflict between the parties. In addition, there is usually a major difference regarding the increase in the value of the flat.

End

CHAPTER 16

COMMONHOLD[969]

INTRODUCTION

The tenure under commonhold is not an entirely new concept. There are many countries where there is a workable system under which owners of flats and units in multi-storey buildings are reasonably satisfied in the method of ownership of their respective flats or units, the management of the buildings and the allocation of charges for services received. There are considerable variations in what have been introduced in different countries. In New South Wales, Australia, the idea of strata titles was introduced to make it convenient to legally subdivide buildings into various individual units for sale and purchase and to facilitate a better system of managing such buildings.[970]

The commonhold system of property ownership in England and Wales has been introduced by the Commonhold and Leasehold Reform Act 2002 (CLRA). It has been introduced with a view to remove some of the important disadvantages relating to a leasehold interest, one of which is that a lease is a depreciating asset until it becomes nil on expiry of the lease term. Other disadvantages are concerned with bad management by the landlord and high service charges.

As regards circumventing the concept of the wasting asset associated with a lease, the new system involves the indefinite freehold tenure of part (e.g., a flat) of a multi-occupancy building together with shared ownership and responsibility for the common parts and services. It is not a new concept as it has been used in a number of countries for most of the previous century. It exhibits important features of the "strata title" and "condominium" in use in Australia and the USA respectively. There is also the strata title

---

[969] Book on *Commonhold* by Guy Fetherstonhaugh, QC, Mark Sefton and Edward Peters, Oxford University Press, 2004. This book contains forms and precedents at pp 398 to 616 and the Act as well.
[970] See N Khublall (Dr), *Law of Real Property & Conveyancing*, 3rd Ed., 1996, FT Law & Tax, p 831.

concept which has been introduced in Singapore since the 1960s, which includes both freehold and leasehold land.[971]

The commonhold in England and Wales is an alternative to the leasehold system of land-holding. It is not a new type of legal estate under English law since 1925, but is accommodated under the existing law. A registered freehold proprietor can apply to the land registrar to register his freehold estate as commonhold land under the name of a company incorporated under the Companies Act, 1985. However, since 2002, only a very small number of commonholds has been registered, whilst a great deal of innumerable long leaseholds continue to be granted and registered at the land registry. Developers tend to favour the selling of flats in their developments by granting long leaseholds.

THE COMMONHOLD SYSTEM

The system is based on what is termed a "commonhold development". This is effectively a block of properties comprising purpose built or converted properties. Such properties could be a block of flats, or a building that contain units for various uses, ranging from residential flats to offices and shops within the development. A block or large building with many different units on the various floors will necessarily have common parts and will require services. These are owned and managed by what is known as a "commonhold association". This is similar to a nominee purchaser in a collective enfranchisement under the 1993 Act. Each owner of a unit in a block or building has two interests:

(a) one interest is in the unit (i.e., a flat) he owns; and

(b) a collective interest in the common parts by virtue of his membership of the commonhold ownership.

COMMONHOLD LAND

Any freehold land can be registered as commonhold land, except the following:

---

[971] See the book, *Strata Titles*, by Dr Nat Khublall, Butterworth, 1995, concerning the Singapore system.

(a) land which is not registered at the Land Registry;

(b) land registered with a leasehold title;

(c) commonhold land

(d) flying freehold (land above ground level (raised land) unless all the land between the ground and the raised land is subject to the same application); and

(e) contingent interests (where the interests are not absolute but subject to conditions).

The word "commonhold" is defined in section 1(1) of the 2002 Act in terms of what is required for its creation. Land is commonhold land if:

"(a) the freehold estate in the land is registered as a freehold estate in commonhold land,

(b) the land is specified in the memorandum of association of a commonhold association as the land in relation to which the association is to exercise functions, and

(c) a commonhold community statement (CCS) makes provision for rights and duties of the commonhold association (CA) and unit-holders (whether or not the statement has come into force)."

    The above definition requires the relevant land to be registered as a freehold estate in commonhold land. Reference is made to the land in the memorandum of association of the commonhold association and in the CCS mention is made about the rights and duties of the CA and the unit-holders. Only freehold land can be registered, and from (b) above it is the commonhold association which is registered as the proprietor of the land. According to (c), there are two entities, the commonhold association and the unit holders. While the association is the registered proprietor of the land, the unit-holders are the owners of units within the commonhold.

    Leaseholders of flats in a block cannot apply for registration under the Act. In order to do so they will have to acquire first the freehold estate from their landlord, possibly under the 1993 Act[972] in a collective enfranchisement, or they can try to persuade the freeholder to apply on their behalf. The consent of the registered proprietor of freehold land must first be sought before any application can be made to register the land as freehold estate in commonhold land.[973]

<u>Land Excluded</u>. Certain lands are excluded. Agricultural holdings within the meaning of the Agriculture Act, 1947, and farm business tenancies cannot become commonhold land, and the same applies to land with a contingent title, i.e., where the ownership is subject to change on the occurrence of a certain event.[974]

Commonhold Unit and Unit-Holder

To register land as commonhold land there must be a minimum of two commonhold units as required by section 11(2)(a). The system is designed to apply to a variety of situations, from blocks of flats or offices, other commercial developments with freestanding industrial units to parking spaces or gardens. The units referred to above do not necessarily need "to contain all or any part of a building".[975] Also, a commonhold unit may comprise two or more areas of land, not necessarily contiguous.[976] There is a requirement that each commonhold unit within the commonhold to be specified in the CCS and reference be made to a plan.[977]

Section 12 defines a unit-holder, being a person entitled to be registered as the proprietor of the freehold estate in a unit whether or not he is registered. This provision is designed to cater for any delay that normally occurs between the sale of a unit and registration of the new owner at the Land Registry. For all intents and purposes, it is the new owner who is regarded as the unit-holder.

---

[972] Leasehold Reform, Housing and Urban Development Act, 1993.
[973] Section 3 of the 2002 Act.
[974] Schedule 2, para 3 of the 2002 Act.
[975] Section 11(4) of the 2002 Act.
[976] Section 11(3)(d).
[977] Section 11(1) & (3).

CREATION OF A COMMONHOLD

In order to create a commonhold, the first task is to create a commonhold association and to prepare the CCS under the 2002 Act. The association is actually a private company, registered under the Companies Act, 1985.

Commonhold Association (CA)

A commonhold association is limited by guarantee. Its memorandum of association provides that:

(a) an object of the company is to exercise the functions of the CA in respect of designated commonhold land; and

(b) £1 is the amount required to be specified.[978]

A CA is created in like manner as any other company pursuant to section 10 of the Companies Act, 1985, and both the memorandum of association and articles of association must be submitted to the Registrar of Companies. Other particulars to be provided are the director(s), the secretary and the relevant fee for incorporation. As in the case of another company, the articles of association:

(a) provide the day to day rules for the internal running of the association; and

(b) set out the rules regarding membership, holding of meetings, voting, and the appointment, retirement and powers of directors.

The memorandum of association is a constitutional document setting out its objects, the name of the company, its registered office and that the liability of members is limited.

Control and Management. A principal aim of the 2002 Act is to keep control of the CA in the hands of the unit-holders, and for this reason membership is restricted to owners of units within the CA.

---

[978] Pursuant to s 2(4) of the Companies Act, 1985.

Joint Unit-holders. Where there are joint unit-holders, only the name of one joint owner of a unit can be entered in the register of members, and the name must be nominated by the joint owners. In the absence of such nomination, the first name will be entered. Any dispute among the joint owners can be resolved by an application to the court.[979]

Effect of the Transfer of a Unit. A unit-holder who has transferred his unit to another will cease to be a member of the CA, but he will continue to be liable for any liability incurred before the transfer.[980]

Liability to Corporation Tax. The CA is subject to corporation tax like any other corporation on its income. Since it is not registered as a charity, there is no exemption. Some Commonwealth jurisdictions confers a favourable tax treatment on "not-for-profit" companies.

Commonhold Community Statement (CCS)

Section 31(1) of the 2002 Act defines the CCS as a document which makes provision in respect of the specified land pertaining not only to the rights and duties of the CA, but also the rights and duties of the unit-holders. Under section 31(3) the CCS may:

(a) impose a duty on the CA;

(b) set out a provision for taking decisions in respect of the management of the commonhold or any other matter pertaining to the association; and

(c) impose a duty on a unit-holder.

With regard to (c) above, a unit-holder is required to:

(1) to pay money;

(2) to grant access;

---

[979] Sch 3, para 8 of the 2002 Act.
[980] Sch 3, para 12 of the 2002 Act.

(3) to give notice;

(4) to avoid entering certain transactions in respect of a commonhold unit for a specified purpose;

(5) to avoid entering works (including alterations) of a specified kind;

(6) to avoid causing nuisance or annoyance or a specified behaviour; and

(7) to indemnify the CA or a unit-holder in respect of costs arising from the breach of a statutory requirement.

Compared with a lease concerning leasehold land, the CCS in respect of commonhold land is the most essential document. It allocates rights and duties between the CA and the unit-holders, who are the individual members of the CA. Whereas there is no prescribed form for a lease, there is one for the CCS.[981] The standardisation of documents in time should make the transfer of a unit, unlike a lease, relatively simple and inexpensive.[982]

<u>Form and Contents</u>. The prescribed form of the CCS is required to contain all prescribed provisions as set out in regulation 15(2).[983] These pertain to various details and definitions; they are in respect of plans, limited use areas, percentage allocated to each commonhold unit, votes allocated to each member, procedure to be followed regarding non-payment of any assessment; insurance of the common parts, repair and maintenance, procedure for transferring a unit, procedure for letting and restriction relating to it, CA's right to divert rent from tenant or sub-tenant in respect of non-payment of any assessment, procedure regarding amendment to the CCS, procedure in respect of notices, procedure relating to dispute resolution, development rights and any further local rules.

---

[981] Section 31(2) of the 2002 Act.
[982] Simon Garner & Alexander Frith, *Landlord and Tenant*, Oxford University Press, 5th Edition, 2008, p 508. There is now a 7th Edition published on 7 February 2013.
[983] Sch 3 to the Commonhold Regulations: SI 2004/1829, amended by Commonhold (Amendment) Regulations 2009, *SI* 2009/ 2363.

The powers which are in the CCS are subject to the provisions in the Act, the memorandum and the articles of the CA.[984] By virtue of section 31(7), a duty conferred by a CCS on a CA or a unit-holder is not subject to any other formality.

Development Rights

The CCS may confer rights to permit a developer who has applied to develop land as commonhold to undertake development business or to facilitate his business.[985] If in the course of the transitional period the developer transfers his estate in the commonhold to another person, that person is to be treated as the developer in respect of the estate transferred under section 59(1) & (2). This means that a purchaser will succeed to the development rights. No person can be treated as the developer with development rights outside of the transitional period unless at one time he has been the registered proprietor of one or more units and continues to be the registered proprietor for at least one such unit.[986]

Developers are at liberty to dispose of newly built independent units (flats) or housing with common facilities on long leases if they so wish. Despite the advantages which can accrue to unit-holders under a commonhold, developers continue in most cases to grant long leases in respect of their developments. The main advantage of a commonhold is that there will be no depreciating asset as in the case of a leasehold title; the titles of unit-holders in a commonhold are freehold.

COMMONHOLD REGISTRATION

The commonhold is not a new estate in land, but is a mechanism whereby a set of independent rights and obligations are created over land. As already mentioned, it is not a new type of interest in land. A commonhold can only be created where land is already registered as freehold estate in the first place.

Once a CA is registered under the Companies Act, 1985, and a CCS is formulated, the relevant land may now be registered as commonhold land at the Land Registry. Such a registration is the

---

[984] Section 31(4) of the 2002 Act.
[985] Section 58(2) of the 2002 Act.
[986] Section 59(4) of the 2002 Act.

main aspect of the commonhold system. It is a voluntary system (or code) in the ownership of land.

Registered Freehold Owner

To enable land to be registered as commonhold land, to reiterate it must have already been registered as freehold land in the land register. Only the person who is the registered proprietor of freehold land can apply to register the said land as commonhold land by virtue of section 2(1)(a). A person who is not yet registered as the freehold owner may apply, but the Land Registrar will only act if he is satisfied that the applicant is entitled to be registered.[987] Also, the land can only be registered as commonhold land if no part of it is already registered as commonhold land. In a situation where part of the land is already registered as commonhold land, what should be done is to add land to an existing commonhold in accordance with the rules in section 41.

Application Procedure. A commonhold association already in existence can apply in the prescribed form.[988] The form must be sent with these documents:

(a) the CA's certificate of incorporation pursuant to the Companies Act, 1985, s13;

(b) both the memorandum of association and the articles of association of the CA;

(c) the CCS;

(d) a certificate of the directors of the CA stating that:

    (i) the documents in (b) and (c) above satisfy the regulations,
    (ii) the application satisfies Schedule 2, and
    (iii) the CA has not traded, and has not incurred any liability which has not been discharged;

---

[987] Section 2(1)(b) of the 2002 Act.
[988] Form CM1 in Sch 1 to the Commonhold (Land Registration) Rules 2004, SI 2004/1830.

(e) where consent is required from any registered proprietor of the land, the consent itself (Form CON 1), any order dispensing with the requirement for consent, or evidence of deemed consent; and

(f) where the commonhold is being registered with unit holders, a statement on Form COV that section 9 should apply.

It is likely that where a developer has built or is in the course of developing flats or other units he holds the freehold estate. The Act allows a developer in this situation to register a commonhold scheme prior to disposing of the units within the scheme. Where this is not the case, the Act envisages that existing freehold land may be converted to commonhold by following the application procedure set out above but before doing so must obtain the consent of any one having an interest in the land.

Without Unit-holders. This applies where land is being developed by a developer, who has registered a commonhold prior to selling of units. In this case the application is not accompanied with a statement under section 9(1(b), i.e., "under section 7(2)(a) the application is accompanied by a statement by the applicant requesting that this section should apply." In this case, the developer is registered as proprietor of the freehold estate in the commonhold land. But at this stage, the rights and duties in the CCS will not apply until a unit is sold and the purchaser is entitled to be registered with the freehold estate of one or more of the commonhold units.

With Unit-holders. This situation is where a development is being converted to a commonhold and people with interests in the land have given their consent. The application should be accompanied with a statement under section 9(1)(b) that section 9 should apply. In this regard the statement on Form Cov, which provides a list of the commonholod units and details of the initial unit-holders. In this situation there will be no transitional period, and the commonhold will be set up without delay, and on registration:

(a) the CA becomes registered as the proprietor of the freehold estate of the common parts under section 9(3)(a);

(b) the initial unit-holders (or joint unit-holders) specified in the CCS shall be entitled to be registered as the proprietors of the freehold estates regarding those units without the need for an application to be made;[989]

(c) the rights and duties as set out in the CCS shall come into force pursuant to section 9(3)(e); and

(d) where there is a lease of the whole or part of the commonhold land, it shall be extinguished.[990]

Documents of Title. Once the commonhold is registered, each unit-holder will receive official copies of both the unit title and a title of the common parts. The same applies when a unit-holder has disposed of his unit to another person.

CONVERSION OF A BLOCK OF FLATS

A block of flats is eminently suitable for conversion to a commonhold. In order for this to be done, the long leaseholders of the flats must first purchase the freehold reversion. This can be done either under private treaty with the freeholder or under their rights of collective enfranchisement. In this regard, it is necessary for all the long leaseholders and their mortgagees to consent to the conversion.

TRANSFERRING UNIT IN A COMMONHOLD

As in the case of a lease, the CCS which allocates rights and duties to the CA and the unit-holders may restrict the uses to which a unit can be put. Any sale or transfer of a unit for a legitimate use will be in order. As a commonhold unit is a valuable asset, it is important that a unit-holder is free to dispose of it as he sees fit. This is provided for in section 15(2) under which the CCS may not prevent or hinder a transfer of a unit. With regard to section 15(1) a transfer is defined as being a transfer of a unit-holder's freehold estate in a unit to another person:

---

[989] Section 9(3)(b) & (c).
[990] Section 9(3)(f).

(a) regardless of the payment of any consideration;

(b) irrespective of being subject to any reservation or other terms; and

(c) whether or not the transfer devolves by operation of law, such as by death or bankruptcy.

Once a transfer has taken place, the new unit-holder must notify the CA within 14 days using Form 10 or other appropriate form. On such a transfer, the new owner will take the place of the former unit-holder and he will be subject to the same rights and obligations as in the CCS. Any charge or interest created by the previous unit-holder will also affect the new unit-holder.

Before an actual transfer, a prospective purchaser of a unit can seek from the unit-holder a commonhold unit information certificate, which can be requested from the CA. The CA has a duty to provide it within 14 days in Form 9. This certificate should state the current debts owed to the CA and that the CA may require the new unit-holder to pay the said debts.

LETTING IN A COMMONHOLD

For the purpose of a successful function of the commonhold, the letting of a residential unit is restricted somewhat. This is to avoid the very problems associated with the granting of long leases from resurfacing, i.e., by carving out terms of years from the freehold estate. There is also the additional complexity in that the leases were created within the commonhold scheme.

In relation to a commonhold scheme, a unit is residential where the CCS states that it shall be used only:

(a) for residential purposes; or

(b) for residential and other incidental purposes.[991]

A term of years absolute granted in a residential commonhold unit, or a part of a residential commonhold unit, must satisfy these conditions:

---

[991] Section 17(5).

(a) no premium is allowed;

(b) the term cannot exceed seven years;[992]

(c) it must not contain an option or agreement to renew or extend the lease whereby the total term shall exceed seven years;[993] or

(d) must not contain a provision for the tenant to make payments to the CA in discharge of payments for which the unit-holder is liable.[994]

By virtue of section 17(3), any instrument or agreement which purports to create a lease, contrary to the above conditions shall be of no effect.[995] Where any lease fails because of section 17, a party to the instrument or agreement can apply to the court for the purpose of giving effect to the lease, for the return or payment of money, and for making such other provision as the court thinks fit.

There is no restriction in respect of the letting of a non-residential unit, but any such letting will have to reflect the provisions of the CCS in accordance with section 18.

Within 14 days of completing an assignment of a tenancy of a commonhold unit, the new tenant must notify the commonhold association.[996] The prescribed form of notice must be used.[997]

DISPOSAL OR CHARGING PART OF A COMMONHOLD UNIT

The 2002 Act preserves the right of a person to dispose of his unit, or subject to certain restrictions in respect of residential units, to grant a lease. In addition, under section 20(2), a unit-holder is entitled to create a charge of his unit. But the subdivision of a unit for the purpose of disposing any part is prohibited under section 21(1). But this is subject to a number of exceptions:

---

[992] Except if it is granted as a compensatory tenancy for a tenancy extinguished by virtue of s7(3)(d) or s 9(3)(f), such a tenancy may be granted for up to 21 years (reg 11, para (1)(b) & para (2).
[993] Reg 11, paras 11(1)(c), (d) & (e).
[994] Reg 11, para (1)(f).
[995] Section 17(3).
[996] Model CCS (Commonhold Regulation 2004 (SI 2004/1829) Sch 3), para 4.7.19).
[997] Form 16 (SI 2004/1829), Sch 4; or a form to the same effect.

(a) a unit-holder is permitted to create a lease in respect of only part of a residential unit if the conditions specified above are met;

(b) a unit-holder can create a lease in respect of any part of a non-residential unit under section 21(2)(a); and

(c) a unit-holder can transfer the freehold estate in part only of a commonhold if the CA consents in writing to the transfer.[998]

Any instrument or agreement that purports to create or transfer an interest contrary to section 21 shall be of no effect. Where land becomes commonhold land and before this event there was an interest in the land, that interest will be extinguished in accordance with section 21(4) and (5).

COMMON PARTS

The common parts in a commonhold may be small or large, depending on the nature of the development, and may include corridors, stairwells, gardens, parks, garages, swimming pools, gims and any other shared facilities. These are defined in section 25(1) to be excluded from any commonhold unit. Common parts are in the ownership of the CA.

Use of Common Parts.

The CCS may include a provision for restricting the classes of person who may make use of a specified part of the common parts or impose a restriction to which it may be put,[999] and will be known as a limited use area. This is particularly useful regarding gardens to which only certain unit-holders have access or parking spaces which are allocated to some unit-holders, but whose maintenance is that of the CA.

The CA is liable to maintain the common parts and provides for their insurance. No alteration is allowed unless it is approved by an ordinary resolution of members in a meeting. The CA is prevented or restricted from transferring its freehold estate or creating an interest in

---

[998] Section 21(2).
[999] Section 25(2).

any part of the common parts. This does not include a charge for the purposes of section 27.

A charge cannot be created in respect of the common parts. If a charge was already in existence, that charge will be extinguished when the CA is registered as proprietor of the common parts. The same applies when land is added under section 30 to the common parts. However, in accordance with section 29, the CA may raise funds against the security of the common parts under a mortgage. This must be approved by a resolution of the CA under section 29(1).

ALTERING THE SIZE OF A COMMONHOLD UNIT

There may be a good reason to alter the size of a unit. Any such alteration to increase or decrease the size has to be done with the consensus of the CA.

MANAGEMENT OF A COMMONHOLD

By virtue of section 35, the CA has a duty to manage the commonhold. This duty is exercised via the directors, who are empowered to permit or facilitate as far as possible:

(a) the exercise by each unit-holder, including a tenant of a unit, of his rights; and

(b) the enjoyment of each unit-holder, including a tenant, of the freehold estate in his unit.

This duty with regard to management is also about enforcing rights and obligations, in addition to what is set out above. In this regard, the directors are required to use their powers to prevent, remedy or curtail any want or failure of a unit-holder, or tenant, in complying with a requirement or duty imposed by the Act or the CCS.

<u>Directors</u>. Rules about the directors' appointment and powers are within the articles of association. Under Article 38 there must be a minimum of two directors, who do not need to be members of the CA according to Article 39. This being the case, the members of the CA can appoint a professional person to manage the CA. Where the tasks of management are extensive, such as in a large commonhold, it may

be beneficial to members to make such an appointment. Where there are less than six members in the CA, the number of directors can be just one.

<u>Voting</u>. Where appropriate, resolutions of the CA are required to be passed by a vote of members who must be given an opportunity to exercise their vote in accordance with the articles of association.[1000] Voting should be in person or by proxy.[1001] A unanimous resolution is passed if there is no vote against it.[1002]

Commonhold Assessment

There must be a commonhold assessment based on an annual estimate of the income required to be raised from unit-holders. This is to defray the estimated expenses of the CA. A notice of the proposed assessment is to be served on each unit-holder in Form 1, stating:

(a) the amount of the estimate;

(b) the percentage allocated to the unit-holder;

(c) details as to dates of the required payments; and

(d) inviting the unit-holder to make written representations to the CA within a month of receiving the notice.

In the event any representation is made, the directors are required to consider it before serving a further notice in Form 2 providing details about payments and dates when they are to be made. In cases of urgent works to be carried out, the directors may request payment of an emergency assessment on Form 3. In such a case, there cannot be representations from unit-holders. The request for the payment must provide the reasons why an emergency assessment is necessary.

<u>Reserve Fund</u>. In the course of the first year in which the commonhold is registered, the directors may commission a qualified person to consider whether it is appropriate to set up a "reserve fund"

[1000] Section 36(2).
[1001] Articles 27 to 36.
[1002] Section 36(4).

in respect of future expenses. If appropriate, a notice in this regard must be served on unit-holders in Form 4 inviting them to make representations. As an alternative to appointing a qualified person, the unit-holders may themselves request the directors to do so by an ordinary resolution. The directors must review the decision to set up such a fund at regular intervals. Also, they should ensure that unnecessary sums are not accumulated. A reserve study must be done every 10 years.

<u>Dispute Resolution</u>. In this regard, detailed provisions are set out in the CCS, and they must be used when disputes by a unit-holder or a tenant require a resolution. Disputes may arise:

(a) when a unit-holder or a tenant is seeking to enforce against the CA a duty to pay money or a right in an emergency;

(b) a dispute may be referred directly to the ombudsman if the CA is a member of an approved ombudsman scheme; or

(c) they may bring legal proceedings.

The procedures are standardised and can be initiated by serving a "complaint notice" in Form 17 in respect of a complaint against the CA. Form 19 is used in relation to a default notice by a CA against a unit-holder or tenant, while Form 21 is for a complaint between unit-holders or tenants. Once such a notice is served, the other side is required to reply on the prescribed form within 21 days. Where no resolution is reached by negotiation or by mediation, the matter may then be referred to the ombudsman, if relevant (see (b) above) or legal proceedings may be brought.[1003]

[1003] In certain countries, an elaborate machinery is set up for the resolution of such disputes. For example, In Singapore, judicial tribunals (known as strata title boards) are specifically convened; 2 members from a panel of about 20, sit together with the president or deputy president in each tribunal. The author of this book was a part-time member for 8 years in those tribunals. See *Strata Titles* by Nat Khublall, Butterworths, 1995.

TERMINATING A COMMONHOLD

The final topic in this chapter is on termination of a commonhold. Such a termination is either voluntary, where the CA passes a winding up resolution, or where a court order is made following a petition by a creditor to declare that the CA is insolvent. There is very little scope, if any, for a voluntary winding up in view of the recent introduction of this type of land holding. A winding up of this type may be attributable to:

(a) where the building has outlived its usefulness, due to its age or obsolescence;

(b) where it has been destroyed or damaged and the unit-holders are not interested in repairing or rebuilding it; or

(c) where a developer is interested in acquiring the entire land for redevelopment.

In the case of insolvency of the CA, other civil remedies could resolve the situation. For example, a charging of the common parts could be pursued before any need for the drastic step of making a petition to the court for a winding up of the CA.

Vountary Winding Up

In this regard a winding up resolution by the CA shall be effective only if:

(a) it is preceded by a declaration of solvency having regard to section 89 of the Insolvency Act 1986;

(b) the CA passes a termination statement resolution prior to the passing of the winding-up resolution; and

(c) each resolution is passed by at least 80% of the members voting in favour.[1004]

[1004] Section 41(1) of the 2002 Act.

Resolution by 100% of Members. Where a resolution is passed by 100% of the members in favour, the liquidator shall make an application to terminate the CA within six months of the passing of the termination.[1005] If he fails to do so within six months, then a unit-holder or other prescribed person may make the application under section 44(3). Such an application is to the Registrar that all the land in respect of which the particular CA exercises functions should cease to be commonhold land.[1006] The application for termination must be made on Form CM5; a termination statement should be attached to the form.

Agreement of 80% of Members. Where a resolution to terminate secures 80% of members voting in favour, the procedure is for the liquidator to apply to the court within the prescribed period for an order to determine:

(a) the terms and conditions under which the termination application may be made; and

(b) the terms of the termination statement which will accompany a termination application.[1007]

In this case, the liquidator is required to make the application within three months of the order pursuant to section 45(3). In the event the liquidator fails to act within three months, a unit-holder or other prescribed person may make the application for termination under section 45(4)..

Termination Statement

On termination of a commonhold following a termination application, the CA is entitled to be registered as proprietor of the freehold estate in each commonhold unit.[1008] There is a need for a termination statement which must specify:

[1005] Section 44(1) & (2).
[1006] Section 46(1).
[1007] Section 45(2).
[1008] Section 49(3).

(a) the proposals of the CA regarding the transfer of the commonhold land; and

(b) how the CA's assets to be distributed.

In this regard, the CCS itself may provide for such a termination statement regarding arrangements about unit-holders' rights in respect of land ceasing to be commonhold land. In such a case, the termination statement has to comply with the provision in the CCS.[1009]

Winding up by the Court

Where there is no resolution by the CA for a voluntary winding up, a petition under section 124 under the Insolvency Act, 1986, can be made to wind up the CA by the court. Under section 51, an application can be made for a succession order to enable the commonhold development to continue to exist after the CA has been wound up.

CONCLUSION

A commonhold is not a new estate in land, contrary to the belief of some people. It is a means by which an alternative to the long leasehold system of holding flats, can arise since 2002. Leaseholders of flats are sometimes at the mercy of their landlords regarding poor management and high service charges, not to mention the value of their flats depreciate over time. The commonhold does not only address these aspects but most importantly their units are not wasting units as in the case of leasehold flats, whose values diminish ultimately to zero by the end of the leasehold terms.

Although collective enfranchisement under the 1993 Act provides a right to eliminate the landlord and for the owners of flats to take control over the management of the building, very few enfranchisements have taken place. Leaseholders are more interested in extending their leases on an individual basis. At the same time, most of the flats developed and sold in recent years continue under the leasehold system rather than being brought under the commonhold

---

[1009] Section 47(2),(3) & (4).

system. Perhaps the reason for this is attributable to the need to establish a company under the Companies Act, 1985, and if the owner(s) of the company so inclined transfer the freehold title of land developed as flats into the name of the company which in turn will apply to the Land Registrar for registration of the land as commonhold land. This does not appear to be as complex as it may seem to some people. But yet it appears to deter developers from adopting the commonhold regime.

In the years since the 2002 Act became law, only a handful of commonholds have been registered whilst hundreds of thousands of long leases have been granted during the same period. In view of this state of affairs, perhaps there should be some incentive to developers to encourage them to adopt the new regime. An incentive can take many forms. One in particular can relate the cost of obtaining the grant of planning permission specifically for development in relation to commonholds. The pros and cons of the two systems should be considered and, where possible and desirable, the legal rules should be amended with a view to greater participation in commonholds.

End

CHAPTER 17

BUSINESS TENANCIES

INTRODUCTION

Until the intervention of Parliament in the previous century, the rights and obligations of the parties to a business tenancy were governed exclusively by the general law. The terms of the contractual tenancy had to be complied with until it came to an end either by effluxion of time or by notice from either party. However, the position now is that there are various statutes[1010] which confer rights, additional to what is in the lease or tenancy, and invariably in favour of the tenant.

An important statutory right conferred on business tenants is protection against eviction as it is necessary principally because a tenant with an established business is in a vulnerable position. Such a tenant stands to lose his goodwill and may suffer a great loss if he has to move elsewhere. In addition, he could lose out further, having adapted the premises at his own expense to suit his trade, by having to incur the adaptation costs again in moving to other premises. Another right conferred by Parliament is to prevent the landlord from forcing a sitting business tenant from paying a higher rent than he would obtain by letting to another tenant. Further, certain rights concerning improvements are given to business tenants. The various Acts and other provisions conferring rights on business tenants are set out below:

(a) Part I of the Landlord and Tenant Act, 1927 (matters relating to improvements);

(b) Part II of the Landlord and Tenant Act, 1954,[1011] (matters relating to security of tenure and control of rent);

[1010] Tenancies granted after 1995 are subject to the Landlord and Tenant (Covenants) Act, 1995, which prevents the original parties being bound by privity of contract in respect of an assignment.

[1011] As amended by the Part I of the Law of Property Act, 1969, and the Regulatory Reform (Business Tenancies) (England and Wales) Order 2003 (SI 2003/3096) operative from 1 June 2004. The reform under the 2003 Regulations amended a number of matters in the Act, though leaving undisturbed the fundamentals therein.

(c) Regulatory Reform (Business Tenancies) (England and Wales) Order 2003, SI 2003/3096 (amended a number of matters in the 1954 Act, though leaving undisturbed the fundamentals therein); and

(d) the Landlord and Tenant Act Part II (Notices) Regulations 2004, SI 2004/1005.

Important provisions in the 1927 Act relate to compensation for improvements carried out by the tenant. The 1927 Act had given a business tenant limited rights to a new lease, or compensation in lieu, provided the tenant could show that he and his predecessors in title were carrying on a trade or business at the premises for not less than five years and by reason whereof a goodwill had become attached to the premises so as to enable the landlord to re-let at a higher rent than would otherwise be the case.

The provision relating to security of tenure under Part I of the 1927 Act were considered inadequate, and, because of the complicated procedural requirements in making a valid claim, many such claims failed on technical grounds. For this reason, the relatively ineffectual provisions concerning security of tenure were replaced by provisions in Part II of the 1954 Act, which does not contain any requirement as to goodwill, and prohibits contracting out unless authorised by the court, though now can be excluded by agreement.[1012] The provisions regarding compensation for improvements continues in an amended form.

BUSINESS TENANCY

A business tenancy is the same as any other tenancy except that the tenant is given certain rights under the 1927 and 1954 Acts (as amended). For the protection under the 1954 Act, the business tenant as occupier of the subject premises must fall within the definition in section 23 of the Act. This section states:

[1012] Amended by the Regulatory Reform (Business Tenancies) (England and Wales) Order 2003, SI 2003/3096 (by s 22), which inserted a new provision into the 1954 Act, being s 38A, that allows the parties to enter into an agreement to exclude security of tenure.

"(1) Subject to the provision of this Act, this part of the Act applies to any tenancy where the property comprised in the tenancy is or includes premises which are occupied by the tenant and are so occupied for the purposes of the business carried on by him or for those and other purposes."

Only a tenancy of premises occupied for business purposes is covered by section 23, not a licence to occupy land, where there is no relationship of landlord and tenant. In *Cameron Ltd f Rolls-Royce plc*[1013] a licence to occupy commercial premises granted under an agreement for a lease, pending the grant of the lease itself, was not severable from the lease. The licence was granted in relation to the acquisition of a larger interest and, therefore, it was not capable of amounting to a protected lease under the 1954 Act.

SECURITY OF TENURE CONFERRED ON A BUSINESS TENANT

The security of tenure under Part II of the Landlord and Tenant Act, 1954, is achieved in two ways:

(a) by the automatic continuation of the tenancy at the date when it would otherwise naturally come to an end; and

(b) by a right conferred on the tenant to have a new tenancy in certain circumstances.

The conferment of a right to have a new tenancy goes far beyond the right of a protected residential tenant under the Rent Act, 1977.

Application of Part II of the 1954 Act

This part of the Act applies to "any tenancy where the property comprised in a tenancy is or includes premises which are occupied by the tenant and are so occupied for the purposes of a business carried on by him or for those and other purposes."[1014] Three points under this section 23(1) definition need further consideration as set out below.

[1013] [2008] L&TR 22.
[1014] Section 23(1) of the Landlord and Tenant Act 1954.

1. <u>Meaning of Business</u>. The term "business" is defined in subsection (2) of section 23 to include a trade, profession, occupation or employment and any activity carried on by a body of persons whether corporate or incorporate. This definition is extremely wide and will extend to non-profit making activities including a charity engaged in the management of a hospital[1015] and a sport club.[1016]

Section 23(1A)[1017] clarifies the position where premises are occupied by a company as opposed to an individual. There is also section 23A which provides for occupation or the carrying on of a business:

(a) by a company in which the tenant has a controlling interest; or

(b) where the tenant is a company, a person with a controlling interest in the company shall be treated as equivalent to occupation or the carrying on of a business by a tenant.

From the above, the statute appears to suggest that any activity of a company is for business purposes. An example in this regard is in relation to the case *Addiscombe Garden Estate v Crabbe*,[1018] where the trustees of a tennis club took a lease of tennis courts and a club house. The court held activity of the tennis club to be a business purpose. But the scope of the word "activity" is not to be regarded as infinite, as per the words of Megaw LJ:[1019]

> "Though [an] activity is something that is not strictly trade, a profession or an employment, nevertheless to be an 'activity' for this purpose it must be something that is correlative to the conceptions involved in these words."

In the case of mixed-use premises, such as business and residential uses, it should be noted that the statutory codes are regarded as mutually exclusive. For the purposes of the 1954 Act, Part II, the

---

[1015] See *Hills (Patents) Ltd v University College Hospital Board of Governors* [1956] 1 QB 90.
[1016] See *Addiscombe Garden Estate v Crabbe* [1958] 1 QB 513 (lawn tennis club).
[1017] Inserted by SI 2003/3096.
[1018] [1958] 1 QB 513 (lawn tennis club).
[1019] *Hillil Property v Narine Pharmacy* (1980) 39 P&CR 67 at p 74.

business use must be a significant purpose of the tenant's occupation of the premises.[1020]

2. <u>Meaning of Tenancy</u>. The word "tenancy" is widely defined in section 69 of the Act and includes any tenancy agreement such as a lease, under-lease, an agreement for a lease or an under-lease, a tenancy created by virtue of any statute including the 1954 Act itself, but not a mortgage or licence. The true intention of the parties will be considered rather than the name given to the document.[1021] A tenancy at will is excluded.[1022]

3. <u>Meaning of Occupation by a Business Tenant</u>. The premises must be occupied by a tenant for the purpose of a "business" as defined above. Personal occupation is not required; the occupation may be by a manager or agent, and the occupation does not have to be by an individual. In *Hills (Patents) Ltd v University College Hospital Board of Governors*[1023] the Board of Governors have been held to be the occupiers. Where there is a sub-lease in respect of part of the premises and the remainder is used for carrying on a business by sub-letting, the occupation is not for business purposes. However, a lodging house where rooms are occupied by licensees may be construed as business premises within the meaning of the Act.

Tenancies Excluded from Part II of the 1954 Act

The following tenancies are expressly excluded under section 43 from protection:

(a) Agricultural tenancies (protection was given by the Agricultural Holdings Act, 1986).[1024]

(b) Mining leases.

[1020] *Cheryl Investments Ltd v Saldanha and Royal Life Savings Society v Page* [1978] 1 WLR 1329 (two appeals heard together).
[1021] *Addiscombe Garden Estate v Crabbe* [1958] 1 QB 513 (lawn tennis club).
[1022] *Mansfield & Sons Ltd v Botchin* [1970] 2 QB 612.
[1023] [1956] 1 QB 90.
[1024] But changes have been made to relax security of control under the Agricultural Tenancies Act, 1995.

(c) Licensed Premises. This head includes tenancies of public-houses and the like (but not hotels, restaurants, inns and places where a bar is ancillary to the main purpose such as a theatre).

(d) Service tenancies in writing. These include tenancies granted to a person by reason of his holding an appointment, employment or office.

(e) Protected residential tenancies. These tenancies are protected under the Rent Act, 1977.[1025]

(f) Short tenancies. These include short lettings of up to six months (or by extension up to 12 months).

Contracting Out of the Act

Section 38A[1026] allows a landlord and tenant to enter into an agreement to exclude the provision relating to security of tenure. To ensure its validity, the landlord must serve on the tenant a notice in the prescribed form. The purpose of the notice is that the tenancy is to be excluded from the provisions in sections 24 to 28 in respect of security of tenure without any authorisation by the court. Before 1 June 2004, the parties were required to make a joint application to request the court under section 38(4) to authorise the agreement excluding security. Therefore, the position now is that the parties can agree to the exclusion of the above section without an application to the court provided the tenancy is for a fixed term of years certain.[1027] The agreement is void unless the landlord's notice served on the tenant is in the prescribed form, or substantially in the prescribed form,[1028] normally 14 days before they enter into such an agreement. Further, the tenant must sign a declaration acknowledging receipt of

---

[1025] There is some protection to an assured tenancy under the Housing Act 1988.
[1026] This section was inserted under the Regulatory Reform (Business Tenancies) (England and Wales) Order 2003, SI 2003/3096 in the place of the old section 38(4).
[1027] *Newham LBC v Thomas-Van Staden* [2008] EWCA Civ 1414, [2009] 1 EGLR 21.
[1028] *Chiltern Railway Co Ltd v Patel* [2008] EWCA 178, [2008] 2 P &CR 12.

the form and accepts the consequences.[1029] The court's jurisdiction is retained for sanctioning exclusion in cases where the old rules apply.

Section 38A also allows the parties to agree the date and the circumstances of surrendering the tenancy plus the terms of the surrender. An agreement by the parties is subject to the need for the service of notice and the signing of a tenant's declaration.

Problem with Contracting Out. In this regard, it is important not to allow the tenant to remain in possession at the end of the tenancy. However, any payment and acceptance of rent after the end of the fixed term could well result in the implied grant of a new periodic tenancy as was held at first instance in *Barclays Wealth Trustees (Jersey) Ltd v Erimus Housing Ltd*.[1030] But on appeal, based on the circumstances of this case, the decision was reversed. The Court of Appeal held that *Erimus Housing Ltd* did not become an annual tenant at the end of the fixed term tenancy when it held over. There was no negotiation for a new lease and, therefore, it was inappropriate to draw the inference that the parties had intended that *Erimus Housing Ltd* should become an annual tenant.[1031]

Agreement for a Further Lease. Under section 28 where there is an agreement between the parties that the current tenancy is to be superseded by a further tenancy, then the Act shall not continue to apply to the current tenancy.

Breach of Prohibition Against Business User. If the lease contains a covenant which prevents the tenant from using the premises for business purposes and they are nevertheless used in contravention of the covenant, the tenant will not be protected by the Act under section 23(4). However, if the tenant is allowed to use the premises for a certain specified business only, but uses the premises for a business other than the specified business it seems that the tenant will be protected.

[1029] Section 38A of the 1954 Act. The 14-day can be waived but the tenant's declaration has to take the form of a statutory declaration. Refer to SI 2003/3096 for the form of the notice.
[1030] [2013] EWHC 2699 ChD.
[1031] *Erimus Housing Ltd v Barclays Wealth Trustees (Jersey) Ltd* [2014] EWCA Civ 303.

Protection to the Tenant Under the Act

A business tenant is given security of tenure by the simple provision that the tenancy which falls within Part II of the Act "shall not come to an end unless terminated in accordance with the provisions of this Part of this Act."[1032] Thus, when his lease expires, a business tenant is not obliged to quit, but is entitled to continue in occupation under the same terms as before, save that the rent may be different.

However, a tenancy may be determined by a notice to quit given by the tenant or by surrender or forfeiture, but apart from cases such as these a tenancy can only be determined in accordance with the special machinery of the Act, i.e., by either the landlord or the tenant serving the appropriate notice to quit.

<u>Statutory Methods of Termination</u>. There are four ways under the 1954 Act to terminate a tenancy:

(a) the landlord can serve a section 25 notice to terminate the tenancy;

(b) the tenant making an application under section 26 to the court for a new tenancy which is successfully opposed by the landlord;[1033]

(c) the tenant giving notice to the landlord under section 27(2) to terminate the tenancy; and

(d) under section 28 both parties may agree to a new tenancy, which effectively terminates the existing tenancy.

TERMINATION OF TENANCY BY TENANT

Section 27 of the Landlord and Tenant Act 1954 provides the tenant, who does not wish to renew its tenancy, with a flexible right to end the tenancy on or after the contractual expiry. By virtue of section 24 of the 1954 Act, a business tenancy will continue until brought to an end in accordance with the Act. Where the tenancy is yet to expire and the contractual expiry date is over three months in the future the tenant under section 27(1) may serve not less than three months' notice on the landlord bringing the tenancy to an end on the contractual expiry date. Alternatively, Section 27(1A) provides that

---

[1032] Section 24(1) of the 1954 Act.
[1033] Section 24(1) of the 1954 Act.

the tenancy will come to an end on contractual expiry if the tenant has vacated on or before that date. The tenant cannot end the tenancy any earlier than the contractual expiry date of the existing tenancy without the landlord's approval. Serving notice is preferable as it prevents a continuation tenancy from arising.

Where a tenant intends to rely on section 27(1A), it should take great care to ensure it vacates fully and on time. However, if the tenancy has continued beyond the contractual expiry date, by virtue of section 24, under section 27(2) the tenant may serve not less than three months' notice to bring the tenancy to an end at any time. The tenant should also consider these points:

(a) once a notice to terminate has been served, it is irrevocable and the tenant has no right to remain after the termination date;

(b) if the tenant has previously served a section 26 request, it cannot later serve a section 27 notice; and

(c) once a section 27 notice is served, the tenant cannot subsequently serve a section 26 request as he has lost all statutory renewal rights.

Break Clause to Terminate Tenancy. On the creation of a tenancy, the parties are at liberty to incorporate a break clause whereby the tenant can be conferred with a right to terminate the tenancy before the expiry date of the lease. There are usually certain requirements which the tenant may have to satisfy in order to invoke the break clause.

A recent case on a break clause is *Friends Life Ltd v Siemens Hearing Instruments Ltd.*[1034] In this case the Court of Appeal held that a requirement that a break notice be "expressed to be given under section 24(2) of the Landlord and Tenant Act 1954" was a condition of exercise of the right to break the term of years. As such a right was in the nature of a unilateral contract, the Court had no power to hold that the requirement served no purpose and did not need to be complied with.

[1034] [2014] EWCA Civ 382.

LANDLORD'S NOTICE TO QUIT

A tenancy which is protected by the 1954 Act can only be terminated by the landlord serving a notice to quit in the prescribed form.[1035] The notice must comply with both the terms of the tenancy and the provisions of the Act. The minimum period of the notice to quit is six months, even in the case of a weekly tenancy, and in some cases it may be as much as twelve months.

With effect from 1 June 2004, notice should be given on Form 1 if the landlord does not oppose the grant of a new tenancy or Form 2 if opposed.[1036] Before this date there was no specified form for the notice.

Requirements of Section 25 Notice (by the Landlord)

The notice must comply with the following requirements:

(a) the notice must be served by the competent landlord, i.e., the person in whom the immediate reversion is vested and, if he himself holds a leasehold interest, the unexpired term must be at least 14 months;

(b) it must specify a date for the termination of the tenancy;

(c) it must require the tenant to reply within two months after receipt to notify the landlord in writing whether or not at the date of termination, the tenant is prepared to give up possession; and

(d) it must state whether the landlord will oppose an application to the court for the grant of a new tenancy and, if so, for what reasons (i.e., the grounds on which the landlord will rely).[1037]

It should be noted that the competent landlord is not necessarily the same person to whom the tenant pays the rent. An immediate landlord whose term is less than 14 months is entitled to be compensated, unless he has consented to the service of the notice.

[1035] Section 25 Notice.
[1036] Landlord and Tenant Act Part II (Notices) Regulations 2004, SI 2004/1005.
[1037] Section 25(6).

Counter-notice by the Tenant under Section 25(5). Prior to the reform of the 1954 Act, effected by the 2003 Regulations,[1038] the tenant was required to serve a counter-notice on the landlord, following the landlord's notice for termination of the tenancy, if he decided to challenge the notice to terminate the tenancy. After this, in the absence of any agreement by the landlord, the tenant would make an application to the court for the grant of a new tenancy not less than two months nor more than four months after receipt of the section 25 notice. By not strictly following the time limits, a tenant could lose all his rights.[1039] The position now is that no counter-notice is required,[1040] and the landlord can apply to the court for an order to terminate the tenancy provided that neither of them has made an application to the court for a new tenancy,[1041] and as long as the application is made before the date specified for termination in his section 25 notice.[1042] For the court to order a termination of the tenancy, the landlord must satisfy the court as to one or more grounds of opposition, failing which the court will order the grant of a new tenancy.[1043] Instead of the landlord making the application to the court, the tenant can do so for a new tenancy before the date specified for termination.[1044]

The Basic Features of the Act

The first basic feature of the Act is that the tenant is entitled to stay on after expiry of his lease and that if the landlord wants him to leave the landlord must serve at least six months' notice to quit which complies with the requirements of the Act. The second feature is that the tenant is entitled to apply for a new tenancy. The tenant may apply for a new tenancy for two reasons:

[1038] SI 2003/3096.
[1039] See *Beanby Estates Ltd v Egg Stores (Stamford Hill) Ltd* [2003] 1 WLR 2064 (s 25 notice sent by recorded delivery, deemed by s 23 of the 1927 Act to have been served on posting, no receipt, so application to court was out of time.
[1040] The original section 29(2) of the 1954 Act was replaced by SI 2003/3096, reg 5.
[1041] Section 29(2) & (3) of the 1954 Act as substituted by SI 2003/3096.
[1042] Section 29A, inserted by SI 2003/3096.
[1043] Section 29(2) substituted by SI 2003/3096.
[1044] Section 24(1). The time limit is set out in section 29A, inserted by SI 2003/3096.

(a) either because the landlord has served a notice on him to quit and he has replied within two months of the notice; or

(b) where the landlord has served no notice to quit, the tenant feels that the right to continue in possession under section 24 is not enough as he may prefer a definite term so that he can make proper plans, especially if he is running an expensive business. Therefore, the tenant can request a new tenancy.

TENANT'S REQUEST FOR A NEW TENANCY

The tenant may apply expressly to the landlord for a new tenancy under section 26 in the prescribed form[1045] and must satisfy the following requirements:

(a) it must state the commencement date of the new tenancy proposed by the tenant;

(b) the property to be comprised in the new tenancy must be specified;

(c) it must state the terms, including the rent, proposed in the new tenancy;

(d) the duration of the proposed tenancy must be specified, if not the term of the current tenancy will be implied; and

(e) the notice must be served on the competent landlord.

In *Lie v Mohile*[1046] the Court of Appeal decided that an application for a new tenancy made by one of two business partners was not a valid application where the existing lease was held by both of them. It was held that both joint tenants must join in any application for a new tenancy under the 1954 Act, unless there is an applicable statutory exception.

[1045] Wef 1 June 2004 the prescribed form is Form 3 of the 1954 Act, Pt II (Notices) Regulations 2004, SI 2004/1005. Before this date notice was given in Form 8 of the Landlord and Tenant Act 1954, Pt II (Notices) Regulations 1983, SI 1983/133.
[1046] [2014] EWCA Civ 728.

Section 23 of the Landlord and Tenant Act, 1927, sets out the rules governing the service of notices. A notice must be in writing and can be served personally or sent to the last known place of abode of the person to be served. Even if a notice is invalid on account of some deficiency, it may be deemed to be valid if accepted by the person receiving it, as acceptance waives his right to claim that the notice is invalid. Therefore, the notice should be read carefully to ensure its validity.[1047] The notice procedure must be complied with fully as a failure in a required step within the strict time limits could result in losing one's rights.[1048]

A notice sent by recorded delivery is deemed by section 23 of the 1927 Act to have been served on posting.

Landlord's Counter Notice Under Section 26(6). Where the tenant has made a request for a new tenancy, there is no need for the landlord to reply as in the case of a counter-notice by the tenant under section 25(5), but he may reply to the tenant's request within two months stating that he intends to oppose any application to the court for a new tenancy on any of the grounds under section 30, discussed later. Thus, a landlord will be limited to opposing any application subsequently made to the court on those grounds only, provided they are sufficiently and clearly specified in his counter-notice.

If the landlord does not serve a counter-notice within the time limit allowed, he will lose any right to oppose an application for a new tenancy.

Out of Court Negotiation. Once a request has been made by the tenant for a new tenancy and a counter notice has been served by the landlord opposing the grant, each party will know the other's intention. If the landlord's grounds cannot be contested, the tenant may decide to quit without making an application to the court. On the other hand, the landlord may not be in a position to substantiate his grounds for possession. In this situation, it is open to the parties to negotiate, if possible, to reach an out of court agreement as to the terms of the new tenancy. The 1954 Act encourages negotiation. The tenant is usually in a strong position and, in the absence of any

---

[1047] A case on this is *John Lyon v Mayhew* (1997) EGLR 88 (CA).
[1048] See *Beanby Estates ltd v Egg Stores (Stampford Hill) Ltd* [2003] EWHC 1252 (Ch); [2003] 1 WLR 2064.

agreement, the court has the power in the last resort to order a new tenancy or to settle any of the terms which are still in dispute.

Time Constraint for Negotiation. This is the period during which any negotiation by the parties must be completed. Under section 29(3) the tenant's application to the court must be made not later than four months nor earlier than two months of the original notice by the tenant for a new tenancy. Therefore, it is important that within four months, even if negotiations are still proceeding, the tenant should make an application to the court in order to preserve his rights.

Powers of the Court to Make an Order for a New Tenancy

The powers of the court to force the landlord to grant a new tenancy or to make an order to terminate the tenancy are contained within sections 29 to 31 of the 1954 Act, subject to amendments made in 2003.[1049] Section 29A has been added to amend the time limits for making an application to the court. Now any application made by the tenant or the landlord under section 24(1) or by the landlord under section 29(1) (or termination without renewal) must be made before the end of the statutory period. This period is that ending:

(a) where the landlord serves a section 25 notice on the date specified in the notice; and

(b) where the tenant has requested a new tenancy under section 26 immediately before the date specified in the request.

New Procedure for a New Tenancy

A tenant's claim for a new tenancy should comply with the procedure in Part 8 of the Civil Procedure Rules 1999 (the CPR). The claim is subject to certain modifications introduced by Pt 56 of the CPR. No claim can be made after 15 October, 2002, without reference to Pt 56.

Terms of the new Tenancy by Order of the Court

[1049] By the Regulatory Reform (Business Tenancies) (England and Wales) Order 2003, SI 2003/3096.

Where a tenant is successful in his application to the court for a new tenancy, the rent and other terms are determined as follows:

1. <u>Rent</u>. The rent is to be that which the premises "might reasonably be expected to be let on the open market by a willing lessor" but disregarding:

    (i) any effect on rent due to the premises being occupied by the tenant or his predecessors in title;
    (ii) any goodwill attached to the premises by reason of the carrying on of the business by the tenant and his predecessors in title;
    (iii) any improvements carried out by the tenant or his predecessor within 21 years prior to the application, other than in pursuance of an obligation under the tenancy; and
    (iv) the value of a licence (in the case of licensed premises) if the benefit of it can be regarded as belonging to the tenant.

2. <u>Term or Duration</u>. In the absence of any agreement, the duration of the new tenancy is to be whatever the court considers reasonable in all the circumstances not exceeding 15 years.[1050] The length of the old tenancy is likely to be taken into account, unless there is a good reason not to do so. When inflation is high, shorter leases, such as 3, 5 or 7 years, are common, unless the tenant argues for a longer lease and is willing to accept a rent review clause. Under section 62 of the Law of Property Act, 1969, the court is empowered to include a rent review clause.

3. <u>Premises Within the New Tenancy</u>. The premises under the old tenancy will normally be subject to the new tenancy. Under section 32 of the 1954 Act, the court may settle any dispute as to the extent of such premises. If the tenant agrees, he may be ordered to take a tenancy of only a part of the premises;[1051] any dispute as to "rights enjoyed by the holding" may be settled by the court.

4. <u>Other Terms of the Tenancy</u>. In the absence of agreement between the parties, all other terms may be settled by the court, being terms which are reasonable in all the circumstances.[1052] The court will

---

[1050] Section 33 of the 1954 Act, amended by SI 2003/3096.
[1051] Section 7 of the Law of Property Act, 1969.
[1052] Section 35 of the 1954 Act.

generally adopt the terms of the current or old tenancy but either party may show cause why a particular term should be excluded. In *O'May v City of London Real Property Co Ltd*[1053] by reason of the current tenancy the landlord was made responsible for repair and services, the tenant paying the fixed service charge. The House of Lords rejected the argument to make the tenant liable for repairs and the full cost of services, paying a corresponding lower rent as the effect would be to transfer the risk of indeterminate financial burdens.

If the landlord can show a sufficient reason to change the payment structure under the new lease, this will be ordered so as to require the tenant to pay for repairs and other items in addition to the rent.[1054]

Interim Continuance of Rent. There may be considerable delay between the serving of the section 25 or section 26 notice and the grant of a new tenancy. In such a situation, the landlord may apply within six months of the termination of the old tenancy to the court for the fixing of an interim rent. This applies where there will be a hearing by the court. The provisions in respect of an interim rent are contained in the new sections 24A to 24D of the 1954 Act.[1055] These provisions are somewhat complicated reflecting various circumstances. An application may be made for the interim rent to be decided by the court.

In fixing the interim rent the court must have regard to the current rent. The general formula is to assess a rent on a year to year basis for the whole property.[1056] Recent cases in this regard are *Neale v Witney Electric Theatre*[1057] and *Humber Oil Trustees Ltd v Associated British Ports*.[1058]

Tenant Not Obliged to Accept New Tenancy. The tenant is not obliged to accept the new tenancy ordered by the court. Under section 36(2), the tenant may apply, within 14 days, to the court to have it

---

[1053] [1983] 2 AC 726; see also *Carnplace Ltd v CBL (Property Investment) Co Ltd* [1984] 1 WLR 696 (in which guarantor term imposed).
[1054] *Edwards & Walkden (Norfolk) Ltd v City of London Corporation* [2012] EWHC 2527 (Ch).
[1055] Substituted in the place of the old section 24A by Article 14 of the Regulatory Reform (Business Tenancies) (England and Wales) Order 2003, SI 2003/3096.
[1056] Landlord and Tenant Act, 1954, s 24D(2).
[1057] [2011] EWCA 1032 (Civ).
[1058] [2012] EWHC 1336 (Ch).

revoked. The tenant may take this course if he considers the rent and other terms are unsuitable to him.

Continuous Possession Under Succeeding Tenancies. When a new tenancy ends, it is possible for the tenant to be granted another new tenancy, and so on. This could mean that the tenant and his successors in title could be in the premises for a very long period until the tenant decides to quit or the landlord can establish to the satisfaction of the court one or more of the grounds for possession specified in section 30.[1059]

Tenant Vacating Premises on Expiry of Fixed-Term Tenancy. The tenant is required under section 27(1) to give three months' notice to prevent a continuation tenancy arising under section 24 on expiry of the of the fixed term. However, the Court of Appeal in *Estelle v Pearl Assurance plc*[1060] confirmed the tenant could terminate the tenancy simply by vacating the premises even before the expiry of the contractual term. Although this decision has been criticised by some, it has been given statutory force by the new section 27(1A), which gives tenants the option of vacating the premises at the end of the term as an alternative to serving notice under section 27(1). Also, a tenant can terminate his contractual tenancy in any manner open to him at common law.[1061]

LANDLORD'S GROUNDS FOR POSSESSION

The court will order the grant of a new tenancy unless the landlord has established one or more of the statutory grounds in opposition to the tenant's application for a new tenancy. The landlord is confined to those grounds as are stated in the notice served on the tenant or his predecessor in title to determine the tenancy or in a counter-notice served on the tenant within two months of receiving the request for a new tenancy. The landlord's grounds in opposition are as follows:

Ground (a) Breach of Repairing Obligation. The tenant ought not to be granted a new tenancy in view of the state of the premises caused

---

[1059] The 1954 Act as amended by section 7 of the Law of Property Act, 1969.
[1060] [1997] 1 WLR 891.
[1061] *Bentley & Skinner (Bond Street Jewellrrs) Ltd v Searchamp Ltd* [2003 EWHC 1621 (Ch)

by the tenant's failure to honour his repairing obligations. The breaches must be serious, and the court will consider the severity of the breach, including the tenant's willingness to rectify the breach and his past conduct.[1062] When considering whether there had been a failure to comply with repairing obligations, the court is required to consider whether "in view of the state of repair of the holding", brought about by the tenant's failure to repair and maintain, the tenant "ought not to be granted" a new tenancy.[1063]

Ground (b) Tenant's Persistent Delay in Paying Rent. The tenant ought not to be granted a new tenancy by reason of his persistent delay in paying rent.[1064] This could cause problem in meeting the landlord's own obligations. The landlord will have to establish a history of non-payment, rather than occasional delays in paying rent. An outstanding arrear currently is not regarded as a persistent delay. But late payment tolerated by the landlord who had not insisted on strict performance of the lease terms was not a good ground for opposing renewal in a particular case.[1065] The factors which are taken into account are:

(i) whether persistent delay causes the landlord any inconvenience or expense;
(ii) whether the tenant is able to show a good cause for the delay and that it was exceptional;[1066] and
(iii) whether the tenant is in a position to ensure future payments such as by providing a deposit or offering to pay interest in any future arrears.[1067]

Ground (c) Other Substantial Breaches. The tenant ought not to be granted a new tenancy in view of other substantial breaches by him of his obligations under the current tenancy, or for some other reason concerned with his use or management of the premises. There must be

---

[1062] *Lyons v Central Commercial Properties Ltd* [1958] 2 All ER 767.
[1063] *Youssefi v Mussellwhite* [2014 EWCA Civ 885, [2014] 2 P&CR 14, More-Bick, LJ, CA (Civ Div)..
[1064] *Ibid* (a similar approach applies under section 30(1)(b) as for section 30(1)(a) in respect of what the court is required to consider).
[1065] *Hazel v Akhtar* [2002] 2 P & CR 17 CA (Civ Div).
[1066] *Hurstfell Ltd v Leicester Square Property Co Ltd* [1988] 2 EGLR 105; [1988] 37 EG 109.
[1067] *Rawashdeh v Land* (1988) 2 EGLR 109 (CA).

a substantial breach. This ground was used where a tenant breached a local authority enforcement notice.[1068]

In *Horne and Meridith Properties Ltd v Cox*[1069] the tenant was denied a new tenancy under ground (c). The Court of Appeal dismissed the appeal as substantial breaches were established under section 30(1)(c) of the 1954 Act. The judge in considering whether a new tenancy ought to be granted looked at the history of litigation between the parties, the purpose of which was to vindicate supposed rights under the tenancy, it would not be right for H to have to accept a warring tenant. The refusal of a new tenancy was the right thing to do given the totality of the tenant's behaviour.

Under section 30(1)(c), the approach to consider is broader than what to consider under grounds (a) and (b).[1070] The court is entitled to focus on not merely "other substantial breaches" but also or alternatively on "any other reason connected with the tenant's use or management of the holding".

Ground (d) Suitable Alternative Accommodation. The landlord has offered and is willing to provide suitable alternative accommodation for the tenant on reasonable terms. If the landlord is unable to provide the accommodation on termination of the tenancy specified in the section 25 notice or the tenant's request for a new tenancy but can satisfy the court that it will be available at a later date, he will still be successful under section 31(2).

Ground (e) More Valuable as a Whole. The tenancy was created by a sub-letting of part of the property and the landlord might reasonably expect to re-let the property as a whole more advantageously and, consequently, he requires possession for the purpose of re-letting or otherwise of disposing of the property as a whole. This ground arises very rarely.

Ground (f) Demolition or Reconstruction. On termination of the current tenancy, the landlord intends to demolish or reconstruct the premises or a substantial part, and that he could not reasonably do so without obtaining possession of the premises. The burden is on the

---

[1068] *Turner & Bell v Searles (Stanford-le-Hope) Ltd* (1977) 33 P & CR 208.
[1069] [2014] EWCA Civ 423, [2014] 2 P&CR 18, Lewison LJ, CA (Civ Div).
[1070] *Youssefi v Mussellwhite* [2014] EWCA Civ 885, [2014] 2 P&CR 14, More-Bick, LJ, CA (Civ Div).

landlord to show his intention at the time of the hearing.[1071] The question at the trial is rather whether the landlord has a real prospect of forming, and proving that it has formed, the necessary intention by the anticipated future trial date.[1072] The landlord cannot succeed on this ground if the tenant is willing to allow the landlord to carry out the intended work without unduly disrupting the tenant's business by incorporating such a right in the new tenancy or by accepting the new tenancy of only part of the premises.[1073] A tenant who is prepared to move temporarily to an alternative building while the works are being carried will not necessarily be saved by section 31A where the interference with the holding is to be substantial.[1074]

If planning permission is granted after the hearing at first instance for possession but there is an appeal, the Court of Appeal can take into account the planning permission.[1075]

Ground (g) Landlord's Intention to Occupy the Premises. On termination of the current tenancy the landlord intends to occupy the premises for the purpose of his own business or for his residence. This ground is not available to a landlord whose interest was purchased or created less than five years prior to the termination of the current tenancy.[1076] The landlord will have to establish a real intention which is a question of fact, though the landlord does not have to show that he himself will occupy the premises. It was shown in one case that trustees could occupy through the agent of a parish priest.[1077]

Where the landlord cannot establish one or more of the above grounds to the satisfaction of the court, a new tenancy will be ordered on terms decided, if necessary, by the court

Further Points Emerging from Cases Relating to Grounds (f) and (g)

[1071] *Betty's Café Ltd Phillips Furnishing Stores Ltd* [1959] AC 20.
[1072] *Somerfield Stores Ltd v Spring (Sutton Coalfield) Ltd (in administration) (No 2)* [2010] EWHC 2084 (Ch); [2010] 47 EG 142.
[1073] The 1954 Act, s 31A, added by the Law of Property Act, s 7. A relevant case is *Heath v Drown* [1973] 2 All ER 561; [1973] AC 496.
[1074] See *Redfern v Reeves* (1979) 37 PC&R 364 (CA); *Graysim Holdings Ltd v P&O Property Holdings Ltd* [1995] 3 WLR 854 (HL).
[1075] *Dogan v Semali Investments Ltd* [2005] 3 EGLR 51 CA (Civ Div).
[1076] Section 30(2) of the 1954 Act.
[1077] *Parkes v Westminster Roman Catholic Diocese Trustee* (1978) 36 P&CR 22.

Once the premises are demolished and reconstructed, the landlord can use them himself. The landlord must have a genuine intention and present financial ability to carry out the demolition and reconstruction. As regards intention to reconstruct, the landlord must be prepared to prove the following:

(a) that planning permission has been obtained;

(b) that the necessary licences and consents have been obtained;

(c) that plans and specifications have been obtained; and

(d) contracts for carrying out the work have been agreed or can be agreed very shortly.

The building need not be totally demolished and reconstructed; substantial demolition and reconstruction has been held sufficient.[1078] The date by which the landlord must have formed an intention to demolish and reconstruct the premises is not given in the Act, but it was held in *Bety's Café v Phillips furnishing Stores Ltd* [1079] by the House of Lords that the intention must be proved to be in existence at the date of the hearing of the tenant's application. The date for determining this intention was also held recently in *Hough v Greathall Ltd*[1080] to be the date of the hearing. It should be noted that where the landlord gets possession, having established this ground, but subsequently changes his mind, the tenant has no remedy.

The work may be carried out by an agent or contractor or by the order of a proposed new tenant under an agreement for a building lease, but in the last case it would seem that the landlord should retain some measure of control.[1081] The landlord cannot get rid of the business tenant in order to sell the property with vacant possession to a prospective developer since the present landlord will not have the necessary intention to demolish and reconstruct.

[1078] *Bewlay (Tobacconists) Ltd v British Bata Shoe Co* [1959] 1 WLR 45.
[1079] [1959] AC 20.
[1080] [2015] EWCA Civ 23 CA.
[1081] *Gilmore Caterers Ltd v St Bartholomew's Hospital* [1956] 1 QB 387.

Compensation Payable to the Tenant if Ordered to Leave

Where an order for possession is made against the tenant on one or more of the specified grounds, the tenant may be entitled to compensation under section 37,[1082] in certain circumstances, for the loss of his right to a new tenancy. If an order for possession is made on the basis of one or more of the last three grounds (e), (f) and (g) (given above), then the tenant is entitled to recover from the landlord a sum of money by way of compensation. Compensation is calculated in accordance section 37(1) of the 1954 Act.

A tenant need not apply to the court in seeking compensation for disturbance. Where the landlord states in his section 25 notice, or in his counter-notice in response to the tenant's request for a new tenancy, that he intends to oppose the request on grounds (e), (f) or (g), the tenant is entitled to claim compensation. This applies even if the tenant does not apply to the court or if he makes one but withdraws it later. Prior to the amendment of the Act in 1969, it was necessary to go to court.

The current compensation is the rateable value if the tenant has been in occupation for less than 14 years or twice the rateable value if he and his predecessors have been in occupation for 14 or more years multiplied by an appropriate factor depending whether the lease was for 14 years or more or less than 14 years.[1083] The appropriate multiplier is fixed by the Secretary of State.

The rateable value is that which appears in the valuation list as at the date when the landlord served his section 25 notice or when the tenant made a request for a new tenancy.

Long-standing business tenants attract higher compensation by virtue of section 37(3) and in which case the compensation is twice the rateable value multiplied by the appropriate factor if:

(a) the premises comprised in the tenancy have been occupied for the purposes of a business carried on by the occupier for those and other purposes during the whole of the 14 years immediately before the termination of the current tenancy; or

---

[1082] Landlord and Tenant Act, 1954
[1083] Section 37(2) & (3) of the 1954 Act.; Local Government and Housing Act 1989, Sch 7; Landlord and Tenant Act 1954 (Appropriate Multiplier) Order 1990, SI 1990/363.

(b) if during those 14 years there was a change in the occupier, and the person who was occupier immediately after the change was the successor to the business carried on by the person who was the occupier immediately before the change.

Where part of the premises has been occupied for 14 years or more and the rest for a period less than 14 years, the compensation is calculated separately for each part and added together (section 37(3A)). Some latitude is allowed for short periods out of occupation.[1084]

In *Baccltiocclti v Academic Agency Ltd*[1085] it was held that whenever business premises are empty for a short period, it should not be regarded that business occupancy does not exist, as long as during the relevant period there is no alternative occupier or non-business usage.

However, the 14-year period must be strictly observed for maximum compensation. In *Department of the Environment v Royal Insurance*,[1086] the 14-year period was strictly applied as 13 years and 363 days were held to be insufficient to qualify for the higher multiplier. Compensation will not be available where the tenant has been in occupation for less than five years: the length of occupation can, however, be aggregated with that of a predecessor carrying on the same business.

The parties can contract out of the compensation provisions in only narrow circumstances set out in section 38 of the 1954 Act. They can agree that compensation will not be paid after the right to that compensation has arisen, i.e., once the tenant has already given vacant possession.

Compensation Based on Misrepresentation

This compensation is awarded under section 37A of the 1954 Act.[1087] The tenant can apply to the landlord for compensation if the tenant has not applied for a new tenancy or has not been granted a new tenancy because the landlord has misrepresented facts to the tenant or

---

[1084] *Bacchiocchi v Academic Agency Ltd* [1998] 1 WLR 1313.
[1085] [1998] 3 EGLR 157.
[1086] [1887] 1EGLR 83.
[1087] Section 37A was inserted by the Regulatory Reform (Business Tenancies) (England and Wales) Order 2003, SI 2003/3096. Access to s 37A is via this Order, not the Act itself.

to the court or has concealed the material facts. Unlike the compensation mentioned above with reference to the rateable value of the premises and a multiplier, the compensation under this head is for the tenant's loss or damage sustained on account of the refusal of the grant of a new tenancy, including an element for leaving the premises.

A case in which a claim for compensation was rejected for misrepresentation is *Saturn Leisure Ltd v Havering LBC*.[1088] No new tenancy was granted to the company because of the grounds of intention to redevelop and persistent non-payment of rent. Compensation of £150,000 was accepted to quit the premises. Later, the company alleged that the council had misrepresented the facts in that it had a settled intention to pull down an ice rink, regardless of anything else. However, the High Court held that the council was transparent in that its plans were contingent.

The decision in *Inclusive Technology v Williamson*[1089] was for extra compensation on account of misrepresentation. A new lease was refused on redevelopment ground. However, the landlord decided not to redevelop on account of a change in market conditions and an increase in the projected costs, but did not inform the tenant of the change of its plans. The tenant continued to believe the landlord would be able to satisfy ground (f) which was not the case. He was entitled to extra compensation on account of the landlord's unfair dealing.

COMPENSATION FOR IMPROVEMENTS

Under the common law a right to compensation for improvements carried out by the tenant depended entirely upon the express agreement entered into by the parties, or in the case of agricultural holdings to local custom. In the absence of any agreement, the maxim *"quic quid plantatur solo solo cedit"* applies, and the benefit of all improvements the tenant has carried out will pass at the end of the lease together with the land to the landlord without compensation, however much the value of the premises may be increased. Because of this common law rule, therefore, business tenants would be reluctant to carry out any improvements without any assurance that they would be able to stay on for a period during which the cost would at least be notionally written off. The position now is that

---

[1088] [2014] All ER (D) 167 (Nov); [2014] EWHC 3717 (Ch).
[1089] [2009] EWCA Civ 718; [2009] 3 EGLR 49.

business and agricultural tenants have certain limited statutory rights to compensation for improvements if they should quit at the end of their tenancy.

The 1954 Act has now conferred a right on the tenant to apply for a new lease but this does not necessarily mean that the Landlord and Tenant Act, 1927, has been rendered obsolete. As already mentioned, there are certain cases under which the landlord can claim possession, and the tenant will not get a new tenancy. On the other hand, the tenant may simply wish to leave after the expiry of his current tenancy. In both cases the tenant is entitled to claim compensation under the 1927 Act.

Premises (or Holdings) Within the 1927 Act

The Act covers premises which are held under a lease and used wholly or partly for carrying on any trade, business or profession. It does not include:

(a) any agricultural holding within the meaning of the Agricultural Holdings Act, 1986, or a business farm tenancy under the Agricultural Tenancies Act, 1995;[1090]

(b) cases where the tenant carries on the business of sub-letting the premises as residential flats;[1091]

(c) cases where the holding is let to a tenant expressed to be a holding under an appointment, office or employment under the landlord; [1092]

(d) premises used to carry on a profession, where the profession is not regularly carried on within the premises;[1093] and

(d) mining leases.[1094]

In mixed-use premises, compensation will be paid only for improvements carried out in relation to the business purposes.[1095]

[1090] Section 17(1) of the Landlord and Tenant Act, 1927.
[1091] Section 17(3)(b).
[1092] Section 17(2).
[1093] Section 17(3)(a).
[1094] Section 17(1).

Improvements Within the Act. The tenant is entitled to claim compensation for improvements carried out by him or his predecessors in title provided the rental value of the premises under the lease has been increased in value by reason of the improvements in accordance with section 1. Improvements do not include trade fixtures or fixtures which belong to the tenant and removable by him. The following improvements do not attract the right to compensation:

(a) improvements carried out before 25 March, 1928;[1096]

(b) improvements began before 1 October, 1954, and were made pursuant to a statutory obligation; and

(c) improvements carried out pursuant to any contract for valuable consideration.[1097]

Avoiding the Effect of the 1927 Act. A landlord can avoid the application of the 1927 Act by:

(a) inserting a covenant in the lease obliging the tenant to carry out improvements to which the landlord agrees;

(b) inserting a covenant which obliges the tenant to reinstate the premises on expiry of the lease to the state in which they were at the commencement of the tenancy; and

(c) demolishing the premises or changing the use on termination of the tenancy.

Since the end of 1953 it is no longer possible to contract out of the 1927 Act.

Preliminary Procedure

In order to qualify for the right to claim compensation on quitting at the end of the tenancy, the tenant must comply with the condition laid

---

[1095] Section 17(4).
[1096] Section 2(1)(a) of the 1927 Act.
[1097] Section 2(1)(b).

down in the Act. Before making any improvements, he must prepare plans and specification relating to the intended improvements and together with a notice serve on the landlord. If the landlord raises no objection, the tenant may proceed with the work. On the other hand, the landlord may agree to carry out the proposed improvements himself in return for additional rent. In the event no agreement is reached between the parties, the landlord may, within three months of receiving the tenant' notice, serve on the tenant a notice of objection.

On receipt of the landlord's notice of objection to the proposed improvement, the tenant may apply to the court[1098] or, if so specified in the lease, to an arbitrator. Either the court or the arbitrator, after the hearing, may certify that the improvement is a "proper improvement". The court may make amendments to the proposal and impose conditions as it sees fit. The tenant may also apply to the court if the landlord undertakes to carry out the work but fails to do so. The appropriate court is the county court.

The Tenant's Claim for Compensation

The tenant must follow the correct procedure in making his claim for compensation. The claim must be made in the prescribed form in writing with the following particulars:

(a) a description of the holding and the business;

(b) the nature of the claim, the cost and other particulars of the improvement, the date when it was completed and the amount claimed; and

(c) the signature of the tenant or his agent.

Once the court is satisfied with the application, it must issue a certificate stating that:

(a) the improvement is of such a nature that will add to the letting value of the holding at the end of the tenancy;

[1098] The application is to the county court having regard to CPR Part 8 procedure. The new provisions contained in CPR Pt 56 and PD 56 set out the rules for contents and form of the application.

(b) the improvement is reasonable and suitable having regard to the character of the holding; and

(c) the improvement will not diminish the value of any other property of the landlord or superior landlord.

If necessary the court may modify the plans and specifications. However, the landlord may prevent a certificate being granted to the tenant if he offers to carry out the improvement himself.

Amount of compensation

Section 1(1) of the 1927 Act states that the amount of compensation shall not exceed the lower of the following two amounts:

(a) the net addition to the value of the holding as a whole attributable to the result of the improvement; or

(b) the reasonable cost of carrying out the improvement on expiry of the tenancy subject to a deduction for putting the works constituting the improvement into a reasonable state of repair, except where such cost is covered by the liability of the tenant under any covenant or agreement in respect of repair of the premises.

The "net addition" referred to in (a) above is an addition to the open market value. Section 1(2) of the 1927 Act, however, provides that if the improvement will be of less value to the landlord because of the purpose for which he intends to use the premises, this reduction in value should be taken into account in assessing the compensation to be paid to the tenant.[1099]

In particular, changes such as demolition, structural alteration or change of use of the premises by the landlord and the time between the termination of the tenancy and the change should be taken into account. For instance, if the landlord intends to demolish the premises as soon as he gets possession, no compensation will be paid to the tenant as the improvement is of no value to the landlord.

End

[1099] *National Electric Theatres v Hudgell* [1939]. Ch 553; [1939] 1 All E.R. 567.

CHAPTER 18

AGRICULTURAL HOLDINGS AND TENANCIES

INTRODUCTION

The relationship between the parties to an agricultural tenancy is governed by the general law and a number of statutes conferring rights to a tenant as in the case of other tenancies. However, in contrast to other special classes of tenancies, subject to statutory provisions, it is the land itself which is used in the case of an agricultural tenancy, and not the buildings which themselves form part of the land let. In view of the nature and subject-matter of agricultural tenancies, special rules were developed, especially with regard to the date of their commencement and termination and with regard to the party's rights and obligations during such a tenancy and on its termination.

Like most residential and business tenancies, agricultural tenancies are also subject to statutory provisions. The Landlord and Tenant Act (LTA), 1851, was concerned with the removal of fixtures and emblements and was the first important Act affecting agricultural tenancies. Next came the Agricultural Holdings Act (AHA), 1875, which gave tenants for the first time the right to claim compensation for improvements to agricultural holdings. This was followed by the AHA, 1923, which consolidated the earlier legislation and provided for the payment for unreasonable disturbance of the tenant. The Agriculture Act, 1947, provided for the establishment of the Agricultural Land Tribunals, among other important matters, such as a measure of security of tenure for the agricultural tenant.

The most important provisions in the earlier Acts were consolidated in the AHA, 1948. This Act, was amended from time to time. The post-1948 Acts are the Agriculture (Miscellaneous Provisions) Acts, 1954, 1963 and 1968 and the Agriculture Acts 1958 and 1970. The combined provisions of all these Acts were aimed at the following:

(a) providing security of a written agreement and security of tenure;

(b) ensuring efficient farm management throughout the tenancy;

(c) conferring rights to fair compensation on termination of the tenancy; and

(d) providing for the settlement of disputes by arbitration.

The principle on which the above Acts was based was that tenant farmers need security of tenure. This was intended to encourage them to improve their farms by spending on stock and other capital equipment. This principle is reflected in the AHA, 1986, which has replaced earlier legislation. However, it has been departed from by the introduction of the "farm business tenancy" code enacted in the Agricultural Tenancies Act, 1995. The aim of the 1995 Act was to:

(a) to encourage new lettings of farmland by removing security of tenure; and

(b) to encourage diversity in the use of land.

The main objective of the 1986 Act was to confer security usually for life. This was underpinned by the Agriculture (Miscellaneous Provisions) Act, 1976, which introduced the scheme of succession to tenancy by members of the tenant's family. Under the 1995 Act, no new 1986 Act tenancy could be created, except those arising on a statutory succession.

The 1986 Act applies to tenancies created before 1 September, 1995, while the 1995 Act applies to tenancies granted on or after 1 September, 1995.

AGRICULTURAL HOLDINGS

The two main aspects which are discussed under this main heading are what is meant by an agricultural holding and what is security of tenure

Definition of Agricultural Holding

The main concept in the 1986 Act is the "agricultural holding". It is defined as:

"the aggregate of land (whether agricultural land or not) comprised in a contract of tenancy which is a contract for an agricultural tenancy".[1100]

The contract refers to an agricultural tenancy, which is one where, having regard to the terms of the tenancy, the actual or contemplated use of the land at the date of the contract or later and any other relevant circumstances, substantially the whole of the land is let for use as agricultural use.[1101]

The term "agriculture" is widely defined in section 96(1) of the 1986 Act, and in this regard an agricultural holding can be of any size (there is no minimum size). Again, "agricultural land" is widely defined in that it means land which is not merely used for agriculture but is "so used for the purposes of a trade or business".[1102] So long as the use of the land is agricultural, the business need not.[1103] However, non-commercial agricultural use does not qualify. This is somewhat confusing in that even though the use is agricultural, it does not qualify if it is non-commercial.

Security of Tenure

As in the case of certain residential and business tenancies, security of tenure was also granted to tenants of agricultural tenancies under the 1986 Act, though not under the 1995 Act in respect of business farm tenants. Security of tenure confers a right to continue to occupy the land after the contractual tenancy has ended. What are discussed in this part of the chapter are yearly tenancy, notice to quit, the validity of the notice to quit and the notice procedure

Yearly and Other Tenancies. Security of tenure is conferred by the 1986 Act by restricting the circumstances in which the landlord can validly serve a notice for the tenant to quit. Tenancies less than a year, a yearly tenancy, one for a term of years and a licence to occupy land are considered. The machinery for security of tenure applies to all:

[1100] Agricultural Holding Act, 1986, s 1(1).
[1101] Section 1(2) of the 1986 Act; Subsection (3) deals with change of user.
[1102] Section 1(4). See the case *Brown v Tiernan* [1993] 1 EGLR 11.
[1103] *Rutherford v Maurer* [1962] 1 QB 16 (grazing horses of a riding school).

(a) A tenancy which is less than a year to year tenancy is deemed to be a yearly tenancy.[1104]

(b) A tenancy for a term certain of two years or more (unless a notice to quit has been served) thereafter continues as a yearly tenancy after the fixed term.[1105]

(c) A licence to occupy the land for any period takes effect as a tenancy from year to year.[1106]

(d) Most agricultural tenancies granted before 1 September, 1995, are deemed to be or have become yearly tenancies.

In all these cases, the right of the landlord is restricted under the 1986 Act. Only in certain circumstances he will be entitled to recover possession by serving a notice to quit on the tenant. However, a tenancy for a term greater than one year but less than two is not converted into a yearly tenancy as it will expire by effluxion of time without the security of tenure machinery being applied to it.[1107] Also, under section 2(3) of the Act, there is a specific exception in respect of a letting or licence in contemplation of the use of land either for grazing or mowing or both during a specified period of the year. As an example, a landowner with excess land to his needs may let the excess land to a neighbouring farmer for, say, grazing up to 364 days,[1108] without attracting the security of tenure provisions.

Also, these provisions do not apply to a sub-tenant against the head landlord. But in *Gilborne v Burton* [1109] a sub-tenant was treated as a tenant under an "artificial transaction" doctrine.[1110]

[1104] Section 2(1) of the 1986 Act. See *Calcott v J S Bloor (Measham) Ltd* [1998] 1 WLR 1490.

[1105] Section 3(1) of the 1986 Act. Though subject to an exception in s 5, the parties cannot contract out of this provision.

[1106] Section 2(2) of the 1986 Act. *Bahamas International Trust Co Ltd* [1974] 1 WLR 1514 (though exclusive occupation is necessary). See also *McCarthy v Bence* [1990] 1 EGLR 1 in which the effect of *Street v Mountford* [1985] AC 809 on section 2(2).

[1107] *Gladstone v Bower* [1960] 2 QB 384; *Keen v Holland* [1984] 1 WLR 251. No protection as a business tenancy applies: *EWP Ltd v Moore* [1992] QB 460.

[1108] *Reid v Dawson* [1955] 1QB 214; *Watts v Yeend* [1987] 1 WLR 323.

[1109] [1989] QB 390.

[1110] cf *Barrett v Morgan* [2000] AC 264. Here a notice to quit served by the landlord on the tenant effectively terminated the sub-tenancy also.

Notice to Quit. A yearly tenancy at common law may be terminated by serving at least six months' notice on the tenant expiring on the anniversary of the tenancy. In the case of an agricultural holding, the period of the notice is extended to12 months by virtue of section 25(1) of the 1986 Act. The parties cannot contract out of this provision.[1111] The period of the notice applies to both parties. The requirement at common law that the notice must terminate at the anniversary of the tenancy is retained. Therefore, in view of the extended period, it may be up to two years before a notice to quit can expire.

Validity of Notice to Quit. Only in two circumstances a valid notice to quit an agricultural holding can operate effectively. These are:

(a) when the landlord at the time of serving the notice can rely on any of the eight specified grounds;[1112] and

(b) when the local Agricultural Land Tribunal approves the operation of the notice following its service.[1113]

This approval or consent in (b) above may be given only under certain specified grounds, such as greater hardship would be caused if consent is withheld rather than giving it. Where this is the case, compensation is payable to the tenant, except in cases of default.

A notice may be served and operate under certain grounds without further consent where:

(a) bad husbandry can be proved;

(b) there is a failure by the tenant to pay rent or he fails to remedy a breach capable of being remedied;

[1111] Cf *Elsden v Pick* [1980] 1 WLR 898 (waiver).

[1112] Sch 3 to the 1986 Act, which does not detract from the ECHR in distinguishing between different grounds of termination, and in providing different routes in challenging a notice to quit for different grounds of termination: *Lancashire County Court v Taylor* [2005] 1 WLR 2668. The grounds other than (a) to (e) above are: (1) the compulsory retirement of a smallholder, (2) land required for use other than for agriculture, and (3) notice given by the Minister for the purpose of an amalgamation scheme.

[1113] Sections 26 & 27 of the 1986 Act.

(c) there is an irremediable breach of a covenant;

(d) the tenant's bankruptcy; and

(e) on the death of the tenant or sole surviving tenant.

Ground (e) above is the most important as it is the only ground which (where the tenant is an individual rather than a company) must become available at some time. The importance of this ground was reduced when the Agriculture (Miscellaneous Provisions) Act, 1976, gave the right of succession to the tenancy to certain members of the deceased's family. However, under section 34 of the 1986 Act, this right has now been largely confined to tenancies created before 12 July 1984.

Procedure to Follow in the Notice. The rules of the procedure relating to the notice must be complied with. A tenant who wishes to invoke the security of tenure provisions on receipt of a notice to quit must serve a counter-notice. The right of security of tenure cannot be ousted by contracting out of the Act.[1114] If the tenant is of the view that the notice is not based on one of the permitted grounds, all he has to do is to claim the protection of the relevant section under which the Tribunal's consent is required.[1115]

Where the landlord's notice relies on one or more of the permitted grounds, the tenant's counter-notice must claim arbitration as to whether those grounds are relevant.[1116] As there are stringent time limits applicable to the notices, the tenant may lose his right of protection in the event a notice is not properly served.[1117]

Rent Under the Tenancy

In the absence of any agreement between the parties, the rent payable for an agricultural holding is to be fixed by arbitration based on the rent which the holding might reasonably be expected to be let by a

---

[1114] *Johnson v Moreton* [1980] AC 37; *Featherstone v Staples* [1986] 1 WLR 861.
[1115] Section 34 of the 1986 Act. See *Crawford v Elliott* [1991] 1 EGLR 13.
[1116] Sections 83 & 84; Agriculture Holdings (Arbitration on Notices) Order 1987, SI 1987/710, Part III. However, a notice with false statements known to the landlord is of no effect: *Rous v Mitchell* [1991] 1 WLR 469.
[1117] *Magdalin College, Oxford v Heritage* 1974] 1 WLR 441.

prudent and willing landlord to an equally prudent and willing tenant reflecting the current level of rents for comparable lettings. Any scarcity element must be disregarded.[1118] Matters to be disregarded in fixing the rent are:

(a) the fact that the tenant is in occupation of the holding;

(b) any improvements carried out by the tenant; and

(c) any deterioration for which the tenant is responsible.

Rent Review. The rent may be reviewed either by agreement or arbitration at certain intervals of not less than three years.[1119]

FARM BUSINESS TENANCIES

Due to the steady decline of farming, new provisions were enacted to deregulate agricultural lettings in favour of more freedom to contract in the sector. By reforming the law along these lines, the Agriculture Tenancies Act, 1995, introduces the concept of the farm business tenancy. This applies to any agricultural tenancy granted on or after 1 September, 1995.

The objectives of this new Act are:

(a) to encourage new lettings, which were hindered by security of tenure;

(b) to regulate the form and duration of the notice to quit, rather than conferring security of tenure;

(c) to facilitate diversification in non-agricultural business use, such as the provision of golfing or equestrian facilities; and

(d) to enable a farm business tenant to obtain compensation for improvements on quitting. This is not wholly new as it featured in earlier legislation but the tenant may also be entitled to compensation

---

[1118] Section 12 of the 1986 Act.
[1119] See *Mann v Gardner* [1990] 61 P&CR 1.

under a new head, such as for a planning permission not yet implemented.

The lack of security of tenure in the 1995 Act is a significant departure from the previous legislation in the sector. However, some would argue that on account of the many loopholes in the previous legislation prior to 1995 many farmers did not enjoy security of tenure.

The Farm Business Tenancy

As defined in section 1 of the Agriculture Tenancies Act, 1995, a farm business tenancy is a tenancy which complies with the business conditions together with either:

(a) the agriculture conditions; or

(b) the notice conditions in the section, and is not excluded by section 2.

Any tenancy which began before 1 September, 1995, is excluded, and the same applies to any which, although commencing on or after that date, falls within the 1986 Act pursuant to the transitional provisions in section 4 of the 1995 Act. The creation of a genuine licence falls outside the ambit of the 1995 Act, while a sub-letting is included in accordance with section 38(1).

The "business conditions" referred to above are that:

(a) all or part of the land is farmed for the purpose of trade or business; and

(b) the land has been so farmed since the commencement of the tenancy.

By virtue of section 1(6) there is a rebuttable presumption that the second condition[1120] is established if the first has been complied with. The "agriculture conditions" are concerned with the character of the tenancy which is primarily or wholly agricultural, having regard to:

[1120] That is, the agriculture condition or the notice conditions.

(a) the term of the tenancy;

(b) the use of the land;

(c) the nature of any commercial activities carried on in respect of the land;[1121] and

(d) any other relevant circumstances.

The "notice conditions" are that on or before the "relevant day":[1122]

(a) the landlord and the tenant gave each other a written notice identifying the land to be comprised in the tenancy; and

(b) stating that the person giving the notice intends the tenancy to be and remain a farm business tenancy; and

(c) that, at the commencement of the tenancy, its character was primarily or wholly agricultural, having regard to the terms and any other relevant circumstances.

There are two types[1123] of farm business tenancy. They are:

(a) In the absence of the notice conditions being satisfied, the tenancy ceases to be a farm business tenancy where its character ceases to be primarily or wholly agricultural.

[1121] As in section 1(8) of the 1995 Act: "Any use of land in breach of the terms of the tenancy, any commercial activities carried on in breach of those terms, and any cessation of such activities in breach of those terms, shall be disregarded in determining whether at any time the tenancy meets the business conditions or the agriculture condition, unless the landlord or his predecessor in title has consented to the breach or the landlord has acquiesced in the breach."

[1122] In accordance with s 1(5) "In subsection (4) above 'the relevant day' means whichever is the earlier of the following—
(a) the day on which the parties enter into any instrument creating the tenancy, other than an agreement to enter into a tenancy on a future date, or
(b) the beginning of the tenancy."

[1123] Burn, E H and J Cartwright, *Modern Law of Real Property*, 17th Edition, 2006, Oxford University Press, p 389.

(b) On the other hand, where the notice conditions are satisfied, the tenancy will remain in the ambit of the 1995 Act even though diversification into a non-agricultural business prevents it from being primarily or wholly agricultural, provided that at least part continues to be farmed for the purpose of a trade or business.

Where (b) above applies, the non-agricultural business will not cause security of tenure under the Landlord and Tenant Act, 1954, Part II, to apply.[1124] To enable this to be the case, the landlord should ensure that the notice conditions are satisfied to prevent the unwitting application of the 1954 Act provisions. Such a transfer may take place, even if the notice conditions are complied with, if it can be proved that all farming activity has been ceased on the land.

Rent Under the Tenancy

The parties will agree the level of the initial rent in the tenancy. However, the 1995 Act provides a system for a subsequent rent review. This applies notwithstanding any agreement to the contrary, except where the document creating the tenancy expressly states:

(a) that the rent is not to be reviewed; or

(b) provides for review, so long as not upwards only, in a manner which does not involve the exercise of any judgment or discretion.[1125]

Where any review is index-linked, reflecting (b) above, the statutory rent review procedure does not apply.

Written Statutory Notice for Rent Review. Subject to the exceptions referred to above, either the landlord or the tenant may serve a notice on the other party requiring a rent to be payable from the review date shall be referred to arbitration. This review date for the payment of the rent must be no sooner than 12 months nor later than 24 months after the date on which the notice is given. Except where otherwise agreed in writing, the review date is to coincide with an anniversary of the commencement of the tenancy and must be later than the first

---

[1124] A farm business tenancy is excluded from the business tenancy code under s 43(1)(aa) of the 1954 Act inserted by the 1995 Act, s 40, Sch para 10(b).
[1125] Section 9 of the 1995 Act.

three years of the commencement of the tenancy or from a previous review either by arbitration or agreement.[1126]

Once the notice to review the rent has been served, the parties are at liberty to agree on the machinery for the rent review. They can choose an expert valuer as they see fit, but in default an arbitrator will be appointed.[1127] The appointed arbitrator may:

(a) increase or reduce the rent; or

(b) direct that the existing rent to continue unchanged.

The level of rent properly payable is the rent at which the holding might reasonably be expected to be let at in the open market by a willing landlord to a willing tenant, reflecting the terms of the tenancy and other relevant factors. Matters to be excluded in determining the rent are:

(a) any increase in the rental value attributable to the tenant's improvements which he was not obliged to carry out under the tenancy and for which he has received no consideration or compensation;

(b) any reduction in the rental value caused by any deterioration or damage or permitted by the tenant; and

(c) any effect on the rental value by reason of the fact that the tenant is a sitting tenant.[1128]

Termination of the Farm Business Tenancy

A termination of the tenancy will require a notice to quit although the 1995 Act provides no security of tenure to a farm business tenant. Such a notice is required by the common law which has somewhat been modified by statute. The position regarding termination is set out below.

[1126] Section 10. However, the parties may agree in writing to either a shorter or greater period of three years
[1127] Section 12. At any time ending six months of the review date, either party may apply to the President of the RICS for the appointment of an arbitrator..
[1128] Section 13 of the 1995 Act.

(a) Where there is a fixed term not exceeding two years, it will be terminated on expiry of the term, or, whatever its duration, it can be terminated by forfeiture which applies to any tenancy if certain conditions are satisfied.

(b) As regards periodic tenancies, other than from year to year, the 1995 Act does not regulate their termination.

(c) In the case of a fixed term exceeding two years, or a yearly tenancy, the 1995 Act provides a special code for the termination of a farm business tenancy. These two types of tenancies are discussed below.

<u>Fixed-term Exceeding Two Years</u>. In this case the tenancy does not terminate on expiry of the term but continues at the end of its term as a tenancy from year to year, unless either party serves a written notice under section 5(1) of the 1995 Act on the other at least 12 months but less than 24 months before the term date of his intention to terminate the tenancy. In the event the tenancy continues, the terms of the original fix-term tenancy will apply in so far as they are consistent with a yearly tenancy.

<u>Yearly Tenancies</u>. In this case, either as originally granted or resulting from the expiry of a fixed-term tenancy, as explained immediately above, a notice to quit will only be valid if it is in writing and it is to take effect:

(a) at the end of a year of the tenancy; and

(b) is served at least 12 months but less than 24 months before the date on which it is to take effect.[1129]

As regards a farm business tenancy granted for a fixed-term greater than two years which contains a provision (a "break clause") allowing the service of a notice to quit the whole or part of the holding during the fixed-term, the notice is valid only:

[1129] Section 6(1) of the 1995 Act. Under s 6(2) the notice may be served before the end of a fixed term to end the yearly tenancy on the first anniversary of the term date.

(a) if it is in writing; and

(b) if served at least 12 months but less than 24 months before the date on which it is to take effect.[1130]

The position is presumably that no yearly tenancy will arise under section 5(1) of the Act where a valid notice has been served.

The Parties' Agreement Regarding Notice to Quit

As seen above, a notice to quit a Farm Business Tenancy must be given at least 12 months - but less than 24 months - in advance. However, following the changes introduced by the Regulatory Reform (Agricultural Tenancies) (England and Wales) Order 2006,[1131] landlords and tenants can now agree on whatever maximum notice period they wish. The position now is that they could agree to set a five-year notice period, or they could agree that a notice to quit must still be given less than 24 months in advance. There has been no change to the minimum notice period, which is still 12 months.

The parties can still use a special break clause in a fixed-term tenancy, but it will require either at least 12-months' notice in advance or a mutually agreed surrender of tenancy. This means that a notice to quit can be served more than 24 months in advance of a break clause.

<u>Modification of the Common Law Rules</u>. The statutory modifications of the common law rules relating to termination of a tenancy will apply notwithstanding any agreement to the contrary.[1132] By complying with the statutory rules as to both form and duration in respect of a notice, the tenancy will end in the same manner as at common law, with no right of renewal conferred on the tenant. Unlike the position under the 1986 Act, there is no necessity for the landlord to establish a specified ground for possession. This is a departure from earlier legislation in respect of security of tenure and it involves a significant distinction between the 1986 and the 1995 Acts.

[1130] Section 7 of the 1995 Act.
[1131] SI 2006/2805, came into effect on 19 October 2006.
[1132] Sections 5(4), 6(1) & 7(1) of the 1995 Act.

Compensation for Improvements

The final matter for discussion is the right of compensation from the tenant's improvements on quitting the farm. At least this right mitigates the tenant's lack of security of tenure under the 1995 Act. He can use all or part of the compensation for relocation to another farm when the farm business tenancy ends. On termination of his tenancy whether by agreement or following a notice by either party to quit, the tenant is entitled to compensation from the landlord in respect of:

(a) any physical improvement made by the tenant on the holding, such as a building; and

(b) any "intangible advantage" to the landlord obtained in respect of the holding, such as an unimplemented planning permission[1133] obtained by the tenant. This is a new aspect of compensation, which is not covered in earlier legislation.

With regard to (a) and (b) above, the landlord must have given his written consent to the tenant to carry out the improvements or to apply for the planning permission.[1134] Generally the compensation is equal to (a) and/or (b) below:

(a) the amount by which the holding has increased in value at the end of the tenancy by reason of the improvements; and

(b) in the case of an unimplemented planning permission, the amount which is attributable to the fact that the relevant development is authorized by the planning permission.[1135]

The amounts in both (a) and (b) can be claimed, if relevant. They are not alternatives. The amount of compensation will be reduced if

---

[1133] Section 15 and 16 of the 1995 Act. There is no right to any compensation if the improvement is removed or the intangible advantage does not remain attached to the holding. Where a planning permission has been implemented by the tenant, he will benefit from the compensation arising from the improvement to the holding.

[1134] Section 17 and 18 of the 1995 Act. Any dispute is to be referred to arbitration under section 19.

[1135] Section 21(1) of the 1995 Act.

the parties have agreed in writing that the landlord should make a contribution towards the tenant's improvements under section 20(2) and where a grant has been received out of public funds under section 20(3). With effect from 19 October, 2006, the parties may agree in writing to an upper limit on the amount of compensation.[1136]

Summary of the 1995 Act Changes

Important changes resulting from the 1995 Act are:

(a) a tenant is given very little security of tenure;

(b) there no minimum tenancy term;

(c) even after diversification away from agriculture the tenancy will remain a farm business tenancy and will not be converted to a business tenancy;

(d) contractually agreed rent reviews will apply but subject to three-yearly reviews;

(e) there is a provision for compensation in respect of improvements, including for unimplemented planning permission;

(f) the tenant can remove his fixtures almost at will during the term; and

(g) disputes are to be resolved by arbitration.

Following the enactment of the Agriculture Tenancies Act, 1995, there has been a significant departure from the earlier legislation. There is hardly any security of tenure to a farm business tenant, while a tenant's family members can succeed to a tenancy granted before 1 September, 1995.

End

[1136] Section 20(4A) & (4B), as inserted in the 1995 Act by the Regulatory Reform (Agricultural Tenancies) (England and Wales) Order 2006

AUTHOR'S OTHER BOOKS AND A BRIEF BIOGRAPHY

1. Law of Compulsory Purchase and Compensation, Butterworths 1984, 338 pages.
2. Law of Real Property and Conveyancing in Singapore, Longman, 1986, 447 pages.
3. Singapore Property Tax, Longman – Law & Valuation, 1988, 299 pages.
4. Law of Real Property & Conveyancing, Longman, 2nd Edition, 1991, 722 pages.
5. Development Control and Planning Law (main author), Longman, 1991, 434 pages.
6. Taxation Relating to Investments in Real Property, Longman, 1993, 378 pages.
7. Compulsory Land Acquisition, Butterworths, 2nd edition, 1994, 388 pages.
8. Strata Titles, Butterworths, 1995, 604 pages.
9. Law of Real Property & Conveyancing, FT – Law & Tax, 3rd Edition, 1996, 1085 pages.
10. Peasant Farmer to Professor & Beyond, eBook, Amazon KDP, 2012, 438 pages.
11. Wills and Estate Administration, eBook, Amazon KDP, 2012, 265 pages.
12. Teaching and Learning in Higher Education, eBook, Amazon KDP, 2012, 643 pages.
13. Taxation of Real Property, eBook, Amazon KDP, 2012, about 500 pages
14. India: Wisdom & Achievements, eBook, Amazon KDP, 2014, over 400 pages.
15. Revived Expectations, eBook, Amazon KDP, 2014, 192 pages.
16. Landlord and Tenant Law, eBook, Amazon KDP, 2016, 413 pages.

The seven eBooks above are also available as print on demand books from Createspace some with effect from 2014.

Most of the above books from 1 to 9 were of seminal importance in uncharted areas. Six of those books together with five refereed papers were examined by a number of professors for the purpose of awarding a higher doctorate degree (DSc) in the United Kingdom. This degree in the UK is far higher than a PhD and is rarely awarded.

About the Author

The author, who is a barrister and a chartered surveyor, has acquired three degrees, including a UK higher doctorate degree (DSc). He has had a varied career over 50 years as a farmer, a clerk with the British Transport Commission, positions with the now defunct Greater London Council, Estates Officer for the New Towns Commission (UK) and as the Deputy Chief Valuation Officer of Guyana before entering into full-time university teaching in 1974 and attaining professorial status in 1988. He was also an active member of a judicial tribunal in Singapore for 8 years.

He left academia in 1996 to practise as a barrister in England and Wales. As can be seen from the list above, he has written nine textbooks in law and taxation, and seven eBooks. In addition, he has written 33 academic papers, some of which were published in refereed journals, and many were presented at various international conferences in countries such as Australia, the USA, Germany, Spain, Malaysia, Hong Kong, the Netherlands, the UK (University of Oxford) and Singapore. His expertise is in real property law, property taxation and valuation, compulsory acquisition and development control..

In his early days in Hong Kong he wrote six study manuals for students within a few years (something very unusual at the time among academic staff). Moving to the National University of Singapore in 1983, he wrote nine textbooks within 12 years. In addition to full-time teaching, he was involved in part-time academic work at the University of Guyana, Hong Kong University and Oxford Brookes University in the UK.

End

Printed in Great Britain
by Amazon